· DENNIS KING

GET
THE FACTS
ON ANYONE
THIRD EDITION

MACMILLAN • USA

ACKNOWLEDGMENTS

For their help on this third edition, I am especially indebted to Geraldine Pauling, Kalev Pehme, and my agent, Nancy Love.

Third Edition

Macmillan Reference USA
A Pearson Education Company
1633 Broadway
New York, NY 10019

An Arco Book

MACMILLAN is a registered trademark of Macmillan, Inc.
ARCO is a registered trademark of Prentice Hall, Inc.

Library of Congress: 99-60769
King, Dennis.
Get the facts on anyone/Dennis King.—3rd ed.
p. cm.
Includes bibliographical references.
ISBN 0-02-862821-7: $14.95
1. Public records—United States—States—Handbook, manuals, etc.
2. Biography—Research—Methodology—Handbooks, manuals, etc.
3. Investigations—Handbooks, manuals, etc. I. Title.
JK2445.P82K55 1995
353.0071'4—dc20 94-30034
CIP
ISBN: 0-02-862821-7

Manufactured in the United States of America.

10   9   8   7   6   5   4   3   2   1

CONTENTS

4 ▪ Finding "Missing" People 41

7 • Collecting the "Identifiers"   133

8 • Credit and Financial Information   153

INTRODUCTION

The purpose of this manual is to assist researchers in compiling accurate background or profile information on individuals, business entities, and nonprofit organizations. It can be used as a "where's what" guide for finding the answers to relatively simple questions, or as a manual for comprehensive (deep background) investigations.

The manual is organized in a cumulative manner, proceeding from nuts-and-bolts techniques (such as locating a person whose address is unknown) to the backgrounding of individuals and then to more complicated research tasks. You will find that methods mastered at one stage retain (indeed, increase) their usefulness at later stages.

County courthouse and state government records are a major focus of this book. It is not easy to generalize about these records because of the variations in filing systems, laws, and administrative policies affecting the public's right to know. Sometimes the descriptions are based on my own experience with New York City records. In other instances, I rely on what I believe to be the most common system. To avoid oversimplification, I make frequent use of the words *may, might, sometimes,* and *often.* I try to provide several alternative methods for gaining each type of information, leaving it to you to select the way that best fits your investigative requirements.

While attempting to meet the needs of researchers of all types, this book includes special tactics for journalists and public-interest researchers who lack the access to confidential government records enjoyed by law enforcement officers. The book also contains tips for those who want to avoid the kinds of trickery employed by collection agencies, skip tracers, and private investigators. Although I describe a few typical ruses (they are, for better or worse, part of the real world of investigating), I also try to show that a researcher who exercises his or her ingenuity can usually find an alternative path to the same information or an alternative body of equally useful information about the person or entity under investigation.

1.

Basic Concepts

1.1 The Paper Trail

We live in a record-keeping society. Millions of Americans work in white-collar jobs involving creation, storage, and dissemination of data for government, business, or private institutions. The computerization of this function since the late 1960s has produced vast changes in research techniques in every field. The great turn-of-the-century pioneer of investigative journalism, Lincoln Steffens, would be awestruck by the resources that have replaced the ledger books and filing cabinets of his day.

Years ago, the term "paper trail" was coined to refer to the vast wealth of records accumulated about an individual during his or her lifetime. Today, the trail of paper has largely become a trail of computer bytes, yet the underlying concept is more valid than ever: It is almost impossible for anyone in our society to avoid leaving a trail of personal information in the files of government and private institutions. These documents provide a record of virtually every major event in a person's life: birth, baptism, high school and college graduation, military service, marriage, births of children, purchase of a home, deaths of parents, movement from one job to another, major illnesses, retirement, death. Also on record will be divorces, personal bankruptcy filings, criminal convictions, judgments obtained against subject in civil cases (with any liens or wage garnishments resulting therefrom), and even a list of the subject's unpaid parking tickets.

By following the paper trail, you can study the influences before your subject's birth that helped to mold his or her life—the backgrounds of both parents, their marriage(s), the births of older siblings, and the family's genealogical records going back generations. You can also follow your subject beyond the grave—by going to the probate court to find out what happened to his or her estate.

Records compiled by utility companies, banks, and credit card vendors will also be part of your subject's paper trail. Usually kept for limited periods only, these records will include lists of every phone number dialed from the subject's home or office phone, every deposit made into (or every check drawn on) his or her bank account, and every credit card transaction. Although such information is supposed to be confidential, private investigators with the right connections routinely gain access to it.

The subject's paper trail may include dozens of news articles about his or her activities. A budding investigator should therefore learn how to access these articles through newspaper and periodical databases, clippings "morgues," and the microfilm collection at the local public library.

Corporations and nonprofit organizations also leave a paper trail. Like an individual, a corporation has its "birth certificate" (certificate of incorporation), its "marriage certificate" (merger papers), and its major and minor crises (lawsuits and bankruptcy proceedings). It may even have a "death certificate" (certificate of dissolution). National and local business periodicals often report on such events as assiduously as the tabloid press reports on the escapades of movie stars.

1.2 The People Trail

The aim of following the paper trail is not simply to accumulate as many documents as possible. Although documents are important in their own right, they are also useful because they lead you to human sources: first, the people with direct personal knowledge of your subject; and second, experts with background knowledge who can steer you to the direct sources and can also help you interpret what you find.

In backgrounding an individual, you might seek out his or her former neighbors, co-workers, or business associates. In backgrounding a corporation, you might contact its customers, suppliers, stockholders, or former employees. In backgrounding either individuals or corporations, you would want to talk to their adversaries in any lawsuits. You would also want to talk to someone with a rosier viewpoint: the individual's best friend or the corporation's public relations consultant.

Success in any investigation depends on the skillful interweaving of the paper trail and the people trail. The paper trail leads to people with special knowledge, who in turn steer you to new documentation, which then leads to people with even more (and hopefully deeper) knowledge. This spiral process, from documents to people and back again, gradually leads you to the heart of the investigation, possibly even to the "smoking gun."

1.3 Parallel Backgrounding

If your subject is closely linked to a particular business or organization, the latter will have its own paper/people trail. By following it, you may obtain information about the subject that is unavailable from his or her personal records. For instance, the personal records on Mr. Y may contain no negative information, but the city housing authority's files on his contracting firm may contain documents suggesting that this supposedly solid citizen is involved in rigging bids.

The same principle also works in reverse: If your main target is a business enterprise or nonprofit organization, you may gain startling insights by examining the personal backgrounds of its principals or officers. That seemingly innocuous annual report of your local community development corporation may appear in a different light after you learn that the city has padlocked two buildings owned by the executive director because of illegal gambling on the premises.

Parallel backgrounding also may involve looking into the affairs of one or more of Mr. Y's business associates, relatives, and the like, to gain information about or insight into Mr. Y himself. (A classic example of this was the media's focus in the early 1970s on Richard Nixon's close friend Bebe Rebozo.) Or, to gain insight into Corporation Z's business tactics, you might take a look at its chief rival (especially if the latter's business methods are better documented than Z's in lawsuits and government enforcement proceedings).

We are speaking of four basic types of parallel backgrounding: Personal/Personal; Personal/Corporate; Corporate/Personal; Corporate/Corporate. If you are beginning a complicated investigation, you might draw up a chart with each of these headings. As you accumulate names and other information, jot down possible leads under each heading. You probably won't have time to follow up more than a few, but the chart will help you to determine priorities.

1.4 Indirect Backgrounding

Essentially, *indirect backgrounding* is parallel backgrounding on a grand scale. You may find that your subject is linked in complex ways to various economic or political interests. The only way to understand the significance of the relationships involved—and to identify which, if any, of the individuals or organizations warrant parallel backgrounding—is to analyze this larger environment. This approach can sometimes lure you into unproductive areas, but it can also pay big dividends. In one case, background research on the economy of a West African nation to which a New York businessman had often traveled helped to identify possible Libyan connections of that businessman. In another case, inquiries into the history of the Teamsters Union and of certain Midwest organized crime families led to a major breakthrough in understanding neofascist leader Lyndon LaRouche's links to the underworld.

Indirect backgrounding, like direct backgrounding, involves both a paper trail (in this instance, books, newspaper and periodical articles, and various archival gleanings) and a people trail (chiefly, the "experts").

1.5 Operative Backgrounding

Operative backgrounding is the level at which you put everything together; it is *not* to be confused with or conflated into the indirect backgrounding technique just described. Operative backgrounding is the process of figuring out how things work in a particular area of money and power and then interpreting the facts in light of that understanding. To understand a city politician, you have to understand the world in which he or she moves—the relationships between the politicians and established wealth on the one hand, and between the politicians and organized crime on the other. You have to understand the mechanisms of legal and illegal graft through which transactions among these three forces are conducted. Likewise, to understand a local hoodlum, you have to know how organized crime works—its division into so-called crime families, the characteristic businesses these families get into (and why), how they "launder" their illegal income, and how they deal with both the politicians and the police. The principle also applies to my own specialty, the study of cults and extremist groups. Here you enter a world where greed and the desire for power and status are covered up by high-minded ideologies (or theologies) that must be decoded to discover the underlying interests and the real meaning of the incessant factionalism (often just an inverted form of capitalist competition taking place in a frog pond with status rather than cash as the payoff).

Because this book is not a political treatise, I have dealt with operative backgrounding only when necessary to explain specialized areas of research. But the best achievements in investigative journalism usually are a result of having gained deep insight on this level. Such insight is what guides the reporter almost uncannily to the right sources and enables him or her to synthesize the information that has been gathered. You will not always learn very much about how things work from academic social scientists, who all too often sanitize reality or disguise their lack of understanding by constructing a veil of ideological or pseudoscientific jargon words. For a healthily pragmatic view (including the necessary dose of cynicism about human nature), seek out veteran City Hall and crime reporters—especially those in retirement. Better yet, cultivate insiders in the worlds of business and politics. It is not easy to get CEOs in a particular line of business to open up, but you can always find someone on a lower echelon—or a retired or fired executive or an independent consultant—who knows as much if not more about the way the industry works and who is willing to talk frankly.

2.

Some Basic Research Tools and Resources

2.1 Directories, Manuals, and Internet Hot Pages

Following are descriptions of directories, manuals, Web sites, and other sources that will be extremely useful to you in mastering the art of investigative journalism or for learning other types of investigative work:

- **Telephone directories.** You should obtain the current white pages and yellow pages (the latter in both its consumer and business editions) for your entire metropolitan area. When the new editions are delivered, don't throw out the old ones. You will need them in tracing persons and businesses dropped from the current edition. And if friends or relatives of yours have a directory from, say, ten years ago, in the attic, ask them to give it to you—it will save you tedious trips to the public library to look at old directories on microfilm. This is especially important in California where almost half the public has obtained unlisted numbers in recent years—the old directories may reveal the addresses of those who never moved and at the least will lead you to their former neighbors.

  For nationwide listings, you should purchase a CD-ROM directory, such as Select Phone, as well as place several online people-finder and business-finder directories on your hot-page list (for more details on such directories, see section 4.2, "Important Search Tools").

  Many researchers swear by *The National Directory of Addresses and Telephone Numbers*, which contains 140,000 fax and phone numbers for the most essential business, nonprofit, and government entities in all 50 states. Another important resource is the *AT&T Toll-Free*

National 800 Directory (240,000 listings), which is available both in print and online. Add its online address (att.net/dir800) to your hot pages now.

- **State and local government directories.** Most states and large cities publish annual volumes that give the addresses and phone numbers—and sometimes the functions—of all state or local government agencies and legislative committees. These volumes also provide the names and phone numbers of legislators, legislative committee staffers, and key administrative officials. Most important, they contain lists of all professional and commercial licenses required by the state or city government and the agency responsible for each license. Some of these directories (or the equivalent information) are now available online at the given local or state government Web site. An index of such sites is at www.inil.com/users/dguss/wgator.htm (select "Government Directories" and "U.S. County Government Sites").

- **Directories and guides to the federal government.** The *United States Government Manual,* published by the Government Printing Office, outlines the organizational structure, functions, and key personnel of each federal department or agency (the online version is at www.access.gpo.gov/nara). The *Congressional Directory* describes the various congressional resources, including committee and subcommittee research staffs. You might also consult, at the public library, *Congressional Quarterly*'s CQ Staff Directories (especially the *Congressional Staff Directory* and the *Federal Staff Directory*), and Lesko's Info-Power III, which describes how to obtain free information from federal and state agencies on a wide variety of subjects. These directories can help you figure out which bureaucrat or congressional aide is most likely to have access to the information you need, and which department or agency is most likely to have public records (or records accessible under the Freedom of Information Act) relevant to your research.

- **Guidebooks to public records.** If you intend to do much investigating outside your own metro area, invest in *The Public Record Research System (PRRS),* which is available in bound volumes or loose-leaf binders, or on CD-ROM (see the bibliography in this book). Through this very detailed reference set (which is for investigators what the *Physicians Desk Reference* is for doctors), you can learn where to write for particular records, which offices will provide information over the phone (crucial for any reporter on deadline!), and the limitations of, and jurisdictional lines between, public records depositories of all types in every state and county. If the price for this set is too steep, you can either buy the loose-leaf binder that includes your state (all three binder volumes include the same introduction that explains the various record systems in detail), or you can pick out the volume(s) from the bound set (or subsidiary volumes) that deal with the types of records most relevant to your needs.

The Web site for BRB Publications, the publishers of the *PRRS,* includes further information on these products (go to www.brbpub. com). BRB has launched a separate Web site (www.publicrecordsources.com), which offers free searches of BRB's database of public record providers (this is an expanded version of the information contained in *Public Record Online).* You can search this database by information category to find local or national public records search firms, online information-broker gateways, and companies that maintain databases of various types of public records. This BRB service provides a detailed profile of each vendor and enables you to zero in on the vendors whose databases or other services are open to "casual" or "one-time" requesters rather than being restricted to private investigators and others who pay hefty subscriber fees. The site also includes links to the Public Record Retriever Network (firms that specialize in hands-on county courthouse searches) and to many government sites offering free public records. Add both of these BRB Web addresses to your hot pages *now.*

Another important print resource is privacy activist Robert Ellis Smith's *Compilation of State and Federal Privacy Laws,* which describes more than 600 state and federal laws affecting privacy. By telling you what's not available (and what perhaps shouldn't be, but is), this book can help you plan your public records search strategy.

In some localities, in-depth "where's what" directories to municipal, county, or state records have been compiled (either in published or unpublished form) by college journalism departments, daily newspapers, public-interest groups, or specialty publishers. Check with the librarian of your local daily newspaper—or with any nearby college journalism department—to see whether there is a manual for your city or state. If a local newspaper has produced a private manual for its staff reporters, request a courtesy copy. Note that the same kinds of public records are kept in every locality (albeit in different formats and under varying restrictions); thus, a manual for one locality will be useful in another.

Reyn Inc. offers a free online public records guide for southern New York and northern and central New Jersey that is more detailed than any other guide I've seen; it takes you room by room, terminal by terminal, through every county courthouse, hall of records, and other important public records site in the region. This resource (located at www.courtguide.com) will soon include public records guides to the Washington, D.C., area and other East Coast localities. Add it to your hot pages *now.*

▪ **Investigative how-to books.** Dozens of how-to manuals are listed in this book's bibliography. For starters, buy Steve Weinberg's *The Reporter's Handbook,* the official manual of Investigative Reporters and Editors (IRE); and Alan M. Schlein's *Find It Online*, which focuses on computerized investigating.

▪ **Offbeat snooping manuals.** You can learn all about the use of false ID, illegal electronic surveillance, computer hacking, money laundering, and similar arcane skills in scores of books offered by mail-order publishers. Many of these manuals are written by and for criminals and rarely differentiate between what is legal and what can land you behind bars. Yet they contain much valuable information for an investigator. You can peruse online catalogs of such books at www.loompanics.com and www.paladin-press.com.

▪ **Library reference works.** The current editions of most major reference works will be too expensive for you to purchase. Instead, you will have to consult them online (if you are a subscriber to DIALOG, CompuServe, or a similar online database vendor) or at the public library. (For very simple questions from these books, you can use your public library's telephone reference service; see section 3.1, "Getting Facts Fast.") The most essential single library reference book for an investigator is Gale's *Directories in Print*, which describes approximately 15,500 national, state, and local directories (including defunct and suspended directories, which are important in checking out a person's past) in dozens of subject categories. The richness of information in this "directory of directories" is extraordinary. If you consult it at the beginning of your investigation, you can work out an efficient plan of which other reference works to consult and in which order. Another essential work is *Encyclopedia of Associations*. Get to know both these books well!

Note that many libraries will throw out the old edition of a reference book or offer it for sale at a nominal price as soon as the new edition hits the shelf. If you become friendly with your local reference librarian (as every investigator should), you can learn when the old edition is about to be discarded. For instance, an old edition of the *Martindale-Hubbell Law Directory* volume that covers your state can be invaluable for quick reference regarding the professional backgrounds of local politicians and lobbyists—many, if not most, of whom will be lawyers. However, you should never allow yourself to rely on a back-edition directory when your research task requires the compiling of the most thorough and up-to-date information.

▪ **Periodicals.** For tips on the latest investigative techniques, subscribe to *The IRE Journal*, a bimonthly newsletter published by Investigative Reporters and Editors. You might want to order a full set of the back issues since 1978 (available at a very reasonable price). A cumulative index of *The IRE Journal* is now available online at www.ire.org. Another useful journal is the monthly *Link-Up*, which describes new products for users of online services, CD-ROM, and the Internet; you can subscribe at www.infotoday.com.

- **Investigative conference proceedings.** IRE holds annual national conferences, as well as regional and specialized conferences, with extraordinarily detailed panels on investigative techniques. Cassette tapes of every panel at every national conference and most regional conferences since 1989 are available from Sound Images Inc. in Englewood, Colorado (www.soundimages.net). Tip sheets summarizing the presentations at these and earlier conference panels can be accessed at www.ire.org.

  Note that private investigators and the information industry hold similar conferences and conventions; a listing of such events is included in *On the Record*, a quarterly newsletter from BRB Publications (available online at www.brbpub.com, where you can also order a free subscription). To see whether the panel presentations from one of these events (or from earlier events sponsored by the same organization) are available on cassette or in published form, contact the organization in question.

- **Catalogs from reference book publishers and database vendors.** Get on the mailing lists of these companies for catalogs, supplements, and press releases that can keep you up to date on their products. Or, periodically check their Web sites. The Web addresses for some of the most important publishers and vendors are listed in this book's bibliography. Add the Web site for Gale (www.gale.com) to your hot pages *now*.

- **Hot pages for investigative journalists.** The following Web addresses should be added to your hot pages now. Some are directories that provide links to other sites; others are important sources of information in their own right.

  www.ryerson.ca/~journal/megasources.html
  Outstanding; provides links to directories of experts, people finders, search indexes and various gateways. Emphasizes Canadian as well as U.S. resources.

  www.dir.yahoo.com/News_and_Media/Journalism/Web_Directories
  A guide to journalism-related Web directories.

  www.reporter.org/beat
  Web links organized according to the newsroom "beat" structure.

  ajr.newslink.org
  Links to a wide range of special resources and directories for journalists.

  www.ire.org
  How-to resources for journalists and an index of over 12,000 articles from every area of investigative journalism.

  www.nicar.org
  How-to resources pertaining to computer-assisted reporting.

www.rcfp.org

Describes legislation limiting the access of reporters and the general public to various kinds of information (in other words, tells what should be available but isn't).

www.spj.org

Advice and updates on how to use federal, state, and local freedom of information laws.

www.pir.org

The online version of NameBase, a giant index of names of individuals, corporations, and organizations cited in thousands of works of investigative journalism since the 1960s.

www.inil.com/users/dguss/wgator.htm

A superb directory of investigative resources on the Web; includes links to law enforcement wanted lists, sex offender registries, unclaimed property lists, bankruptcy records, missing persons lists, property records, and many other types of information.

While you are studying this book, take the time to explore each of these online resources. They will probably lead you to dozens of other fascinating Web sites that you will want to add to your hot pages. When you get to that stage, however, you must divide your hot pages into subdirectories or you'll lose track of them.

2.2 City Directories

Ever since the nineteenth century, specialized publishers have produced household-by-household and store-by-store marketing directories, commonly known as *city directories*. These books are used by telephone or door-to-door sales teams, direct mail firms, fundraising experts, pollsters, newspaper subscription departments, and essentially anyone who needs marketing information that will identify potential customers or supplement the demographic information found in U.S. Census reports. Such directories are also used by private investigators, skip tracers, police detectives, and newspaper reporters to locate individuals and compile background information on them. By using back as well as current editions of such directories, along with back and current editions of phone books, you can gather a remarkable amount of information about someone in a short time.

The city directory is compiled using door-to-door or telephone surveys. It may tell how many people live in a household, how long they have resided there, where the head of the household works (or at least what his or her occupation is), the name of each household resident, and the general income level of the neighborhood. By tracing a person's name through back issues of a city directory, you can get a bare-bones picture of his or her family through the years.

Usually revised each year, the city directories include alphabetical, street, and numerical listings. The street listings will help you find your subject's present and/or former neighbors and also will give you an overview of the neighborhood environment.

Most large cities are no longer covered by city directories because urban mobility and the socioeconomic disintegration of inner-city life have rendered them impractical. However, city directories are often still published for the suburban communities surrounding the core cities. In addition, many medium-sized and smaller nonsuburban cities are covered, as are many small towns and rural areas (the latter by rural route directories).

The current and back editions of a city directory may be found at the local public library or chamber of commerce. Among city directory publishers, the biggest name is R.L. Polk & Company, which covers 2,500 communities.

In cities no longer covered by a city directory, the public library will have copies up through the final edition. A researcher can thus trace a longtime city resident's life up to that point. Furthermore, many persons listed in now-defunct city directories in the 1940s and 1950s later moved to suburban communities that are still covered. You can thus sometimes compile an uninterrupted record of successive residences, household members, and neighbors. (Even if you lose the city directory trail, you can pick it up with back-edition crisscross and telephone directories; see section 2.3 following and section 4.3, "Searching the Phone Directories.")

2.3 Crisscross Directories

A crisscross directory is based not on survey information but on a rearrangement of the telephone white pages. Where the white pages lists phone numbers alphabetically by customer's name, the crisscross directory lists them in numerical order and also by street address (it is thus often called a "reverse directory"). When you have a number but no name, you can look in the numerical listings and get both the name and address. When you have an address but no name, you can look in the street listings and get both the name and phone number. Sometimes the street listings and the numerical listings are in one volume, and sometimes they are separate. A volume including street listings is sometimes called a "street directory" or a "household directory."

Crisscross directories cover the large cities abandoned by the city directories. Although they provide less information than city directories, crisscross directories should never be underestimated as a source of information (especially if you use back as well as current editions). For instance, COLE's directories for the five boroughs of New York City can tell you how many years your subject has been listed at his or her current address, whether the subject's new listing is altogether new to the directory or only new for the given address, the identities of two or more people with different last names who are sharing a phone number listed separately under each name, the identities of two or more people with different last names who have separate phone lines at the same street address, the names and phone numbers of the subject's neighbors, and the approximate income level ("wealth rating") of the block.

COLE is one of the largest publishers of crisscross directories. Available for over 150 communities, COLE directories are leased rather than sold. They are available in both print and on CD-ROM. Detailed information on the products of COLE and other crisscross and city directory publishers can be found at US WEST's Directory Source Catalog (www.uswest.com). Crisscross directories are usually available at the local public library or chamber of commerce, as are city directories.

Online Crisscross

The chief drawbacks of the print versions of crisscross directories—in addition to their price—are that each directory covers only a single city, and that the directories for other cities are rarely available in your local public library. However, comprehensive nationwide crisscross searching is now offered by Internet people-finder directories, such as Infoseek (infoseek.go.com), as well as by CD-ROM directories such as Select Phone (see section 4.2, "Important Search Tools"). Note that the online directories are not necessarily more up-to-date than the printed ones because the online information itself mostly comes from already printed telephone directories.

2.4 The Law Library

Whether you're investigating an individual, a corporation, a nonprofit organization, a trade union, or an electoral campaign committee, all are subject to specific legal statutes, government regulations, judicial decisions, and administrative rulings. Hence, a law library (or the legal databases LEXIS and WESTLAW) can provide important information about your subject. For instance, you can look up the laws and regulations relating to Mr. A's activities as a street peddler, Dr. B's activities as a podiatrist, and Ms. C's activities as a stockbroker.

To guide your search for such information, there are four essential sets of books: the city code, the state code (for example, *McKinney's Consolidated Laws of New York Annotated*), the *United States Code Annotated*, and the *Code of Federal Regulations*. The designation "annotated" means that a set provides, along with the text of each section of the law, a summary of the most important decisions interpreting it. Each annotated volume, unless it is from the latest annual edition, will include a "pocket part," an annual update inserted in a pocket at the rear of the volume. The pocket part gives all new developments since the date of publication of the volume on the shelf and should *always* be consulted. Note that the *Code of Federal Regulations* does not have pocket parts; you must consult the *Federal Register* for the latest developments.

The various codes are indexed according to topics/key words in an easy-to-search manner. With the index (often itself a multivolume work) as your guide, your use of the federal, state, and local codes is limited only by your ingenuity and your knowledge of the subject's activities. Mr. A is a restaurant owner? Look at the municipal laws relating to eating establishments, including the health, fire, and sidewalk codes; also look at the city and state laws pertaining to the registration of small businesses. Ms. B is a freelance writer? Look at the state and federal tax codes and regulations pertaining to self-employed individuals who file itemized deductions.

If a person is engaged in a licensed occupation, the state code may guide you to a surprising array of official records (see sections 10.11, "Permits and Licenses," and 10.12, "Professional Licensing").On the federal level, you may want to skip the *United States Code Annotated* and go straight to the *Code of Federal Regulations*, which includes a volume called the *CFR Index and Finding Aids*. Suppose that you are investigating Mr. W, a right-wing arms dealer suspected of supplying machine guns to the Ku Klux Klan. Look under "Arms and munitions" and note the relevant subtopics, cited by "title" and "part." Turn to Title 27, Part 178 ("Commerce in Firearms and Ammunition") and Part 179 ("Machine Guns, Destructive Devices, and Certain Other Firearms"). Here you will find descriptions of the various filing requirements with which Mr. W must comply. Your next step: Check with the Bureau of Alcohol, Tobacco, and Firearms to find out which of the government forms filed by Mr. W are available under the Freedom of Information Act.

The federal government makes available the *Code of Federal Regulations* and the *Federal Register* at www.access.gpo/gov/su_doc. The U.S. Code can be accessed at uscode.house.gov or at law.house.gov. For the U.S. Tax Code, go to www.fourmilab.ch/ustax/ustax.html. To search state legal codes, you might begin at www.findlaw.com. Directories of legal reference sites on the Web can be found at www.legal.gsa.gov and at dir.yahoo.com/Government/Law.

2.5 Freedom of Information Laws

For generations, bureaucrats routinely denied the public access to most records of the federal government's executive arm. Congress initiated a new "open government" approach in 1966 by passing the Freedom of Information Act (FOIA). This law, as amended over the years, applies to all departments and agencies of the executive branch, including the armed forces and the Central Intelligence Agency; but it excludes Congress, the federal court system, and the president's immediate staff. Essentially, the FOIA says that the bureaucrats and brass must provide copies, to anyone who requests them (even a mobster in prison), of any government document except those covered by nine exemptions. Exempt documents (or exempt portions of documents) include classified national security information; trade secrets and other confidential business information; information that, if released, would violate personal privacy; information about ongoing law-enforcement investigations; information that might jeopardize a law-enforcement informant; and certain internal bureaucratic memoranda.

The exemptions may seem to provide loopholes for the bureaucrats to weasel out of giving you just about anything. In fact, a vast amount of material is readily available to anyone who bothers to request it. America's corporations and their foreign competitors use the FOIA assiduously to gather government documents that will give them a business edge. Journalists use the FOIA in preparing scoops that blast the very agency releasing the information (if there hasn't been more of this, it's because most journalists are too lazy to master this tool). Public-interest foundations use the FOIA to gather large libraries of national security documents that illuminate every conspiracy and intrigue of the Cold War years. Former radicals have used it to gather their own files from the FBI, and then have turned around and sued the FBI. I have used it as a journalist to gain information from the FBI, the CIA, the Department of Energy, and the State Department. In most cases, I found that the particular department or agency's FOIA staff complied with the spirit, as well as the letter, of the law, even though the material released was potentially embarrassing to the government. My experiences may not have been typical—many journalists have complained of bureaucratic stonewalling.

How can you use the FOIA to background a local businessman or mobster? Because of the Privacy Act, you can't expect a government department or agency simply to send you everything they have on someone. However, documents pertaining to businesses, nonprofit organizations, government contracts, and so forth with which your subject is associated will be available. You thus can do parallel and indirect backgrounding (see sections 1.3, "Parallel Backgrounding," and 1.4, "Indirect Backgrounding") on a broad scale, gaining much information about your subject in the process.

Let's say that you need information about Arthur, a community development corporation director in Chicago who has wangled tens of millions of dollars from the federal government to finance development projects for the black community, but has only a collection of almost-bankrupt enterprises to show for it. Under the FOIA, you can obtain the relevant files of the succession of federal agencies that gave him the money. These files will include much of the correspondence and many of the intra-agency memos that led up to each grant. (If the FOIA officer is really conscientious, you may even receive a copy of the letter from a U.S. senator in Arthur's state supporting Arthur's request for yet more money.) You also can get the audits and the records of any resulting investigations. You can see who in the agency pushed for the investigations and who, higher up, apparently quashed them.

Furthermore, you can look at the records from the Department of Housing and Urban Development (HUD) on a housing project financed by

Arthur's organization. You can look at the files of the Federal Deposit Insurance Corporation (FDIC) for the community savings bank controlled by Arthur—files that may include devastating criticism of the bank management selected by Arthur and his cronies. You can get the FBI's file on Arthur's late bodyguard (a former Black Panther) who died in the mysterious crash of a plane owned by Arthur, as well as the Federal Aviation Administration (FAA) report on that crash, license information about the pilot who died along with the bodyguard, and perhaps even Drug Enforcement Administration (DEA) files regarding the mysterious airstrip from which they had taken off. And as you collect all these documents, you will automatically be gaining the names of potential sources—those people in government, formerly in government, or outside government who opposed giving money to Arthur or who tried to blow the whistle on him.

The main problem with the FOIA is the time it takes to get an answer. Although the government is supposed to reply to any request within ten days, that reply is simply an acknowledgment that the request has been received and that it will be processed in its turn. The staffing of FOIA units is often inadequate, resulting in backlogs and long waits. However, departments with a low volume of requests and little need to redact documents for national security reasons may meet your request with reasonable promptness.

Recent changes in the FOIA include a "compelling need" provision to speed up requests in some cases. But the FOIA is best used in investigations that are not run on a tight deadline. And even if you have as much time as you like to gather the story, you should make your FOIA requests as soon as possible—the documents you receive may open up an entirely new avenue of inquiry.

Before making an FOIA request, always make sure that it is really necessary. I once asked the Federal Election Commission for information, under the FOIA, that was already on the public record as a matter of law and thus routinely available for the asking. The press officer called me to suggest gently that I withdraw my request so that he could send me the information immediately. Not all government agencies will volunteer such advice.

You should also check to make sure that the FOIA documents you've requested have not already been released. Each department or agency covered by the FOIA keeps an index of released (or "preprocessed") documents. If what you want, or part of what you want, is on the index, you can order copies directly from the agency's library without much delay. (New changes in the FOIA now require each federal agency to put online by the year 2000 its index of released documents.) Also, many released documents may be available directly from journalists, authors, or scholars who have previously obtained them; others may be accessible through the nonprofit National Security Archive (www.seas.gwu.edu/nsarchive) or in the Declassified Documents Reference System (www.psmedia.com/ ddrs.htm; also available on microfiche at many research libraries). Note that if none of the information you seek has been released pursuant to the FOIA, the very same information (or information just as good for your purposes) may be immediately available, at the nearest federal depository library, in a government audit report, in or a published congressional hearing.

Even if none of this applies to your information needs, you can still take steps to avoid a formal FOIA request. First, you can make an informal request to the agency in question, giving the bureaucrats a chance to look good by releasing the information immediately and thus demonstrating that *their* agency has nothing to hide. (If they display resistance at first, you have something to "threaten" them with: The paperwork they'll be stuck with if you're forced to go ahead with your FOIA request.)

A variation on this approach is to contact the press office of the agency and ask for the documents in the same manner as if you were making a routine request for a copy of a press release. Press officers often see themselves as expediters rather than by-the-book prevaricators. In some instances, if you tell them you are on a tight deadline, they will get you the information directly. (This works best if you have a very simple request, such as for a single document you already know exists.)

You might also ask your congressperson or U.S. senator to obtain the information for you. He or she can go through the particular department or agency's congressional liaison office and sometimes get the records you need within days. If your senator or congressperson won't help you (or is newly elected and lacking in clout), try a member of Congress who has a special interest in the issue you are researching.

If none of these options work, you will have to file your FOIA request and go through the red tape. The following suggestions, however, will help you get the maximum information with the minimum wait:

- Do your homework. Each agency is required under the Privacy Act to publish an annual description of its records systems and the categories of individuals on whom records are kept. These notices can be found in the *Federal Register* (described earlier in this chapter); you might also obtain a copy from the given agency's FOIA unit or from the agency's Web site. The biennial *Privacy Act Issuances* is a compilation of these notices from every agency covered by the act. It is available online at www.access.gpo.gov/su_docs. Also useful in figuring out what's in an agency's files is the Office of Management and Budget's monthly agency-by-agency inventory of every red-tape form and procedure by which information is gathered from the public. A copy of the inventory for a given agency can be obtained from that agency. To learn about defunct forms and procedures, request back copies of the inventory.

- Phrase your request clearly and be as specific as possible. If your request is vague or overly broad, the bureaucrats may use this as an excuse to deny it altogether. If the topic you are interested in is, in fact, quite broad, break it down into manageable chunks (for example, instead of making a single request for all FBI files on the KKK, make separate requests for files on specific Klan groups or on specific dead Klan leaders or dead Klan victims). For information on how to prepare a request, see the Web site of the Reporters Committee for Freedom of the Press (www.rcfp.org) or the Society for Professional Journalists (www.spj.org).

- Specify that you want all electronic records (bureaucratic email, electronic surveillance tapes, databases, and so on) as well as all paper documents pertinent to your request. And insist that any such records be provided to you on diskette (or in the case of large databases, on magnetic tape), not just as printouts (see section 3.3, "Collecting and Filing Your Documentation").

- Touch base with the FOIA officer or records analyst assigned to handle your request. A discussion with this person will give you a better idea of what's available and will provide him or her with a clearer understanding of what you are looking for. The result may be a narrowing or rephrasing of your request in the interest of faster results. In general, if you indicate a willingness to be helpful (*without* making yourself a pest) the FOIA officer will be inclined to go the extra mile for you.

- When you make a request for especially sensitive information, have another researcher ask for the same information using a differently crafted request. If the requests are processed by two different FOIA officers, one may release things that the other withholds.

- Try more than one agency. Copies of memos from Agency X will often end up in the files of Agency Y as well. Agency X might regard the memos as too embarrassing to release; Agency Y may release them without hesitation.

- File your request with an agency's field offices and regional offices as well as with its Washington headquarters; in some agencies, these units make their own determinations about FOIA requests.

- Think creatively. James Bamford, author of *The Puzzle Palace*, wanted to know the number of employees at the top-secret National Security Agency (NSA), the electronic surveillance and code-breaking agency. The NSA stonewalled him on this and on everything else. He eventually obtained the number of employees by making an FOIA request to the U.S. National Credit Union Administration for its records on the Tower Federal Credit Union, which is located at the NSA. He also used a loophole in the FOIA to obtain copies of the NSA's internal newsletter.

- If an agency gives you part of what you want, but withholds more, file an immediate appeal and also let the bureaucrats know you'll take the matter to court if necessary. Get your congressperson to write a letter on your behalf. Alert the chairpersons of the House and Senate FOIA oversight committees (in the Senate, this is the Subcommittee on Technology and the Law; in the House, it's the Subcommittee on Government Information, Justice, and Agriculture). Almost always, the bureaucrats will release a few more items to avoid a hassle.

- Seek help from experts. The FOI Center at the University of Missouri (www.missouri.edu/~foiwww) has a helpful staff and vast files on FOI problems and procedures on the local, state, federal, and international levels.

Many states have Freedom of Information statutes, known as "sunshine laws." Usually these laws (which apply to city and county governments as well as to the state) have fewer teeth than the federal FOIA, but if you keep pushing, threaten to sue, and gather the support of one or more state legislators or city council members, you can generally get at least part of what you need. If your state or city has an ombudsman's office, enlist its help. Note that state and city agencies often keep duplicate files: When reporters in Springfield, Massachusetts, were stonewalled by the Springfield License Commission regarding certain mob-connected liquor licenses, they turned to the state Alcoholic Beverage Control Commission for the duplicates. In general, the tricks for using the federal FOIA will apply to state sunshine laws with only minor variations.

2.6 Computers and Databases

Overview

Millions of Web sites and commercial and government databases can now be accessed by any home computer user who has a modem. The range and depth of information available online is awesome. Sitting at your computer, you can search actors' résumés, federal court indexes, Ph.D. dissertation abstracts, state medical licensing records, and the Web pages of complete strangers who want to tell the entire world about their recent trip to Bermuda. You can retrieve the full text of thousands of magazines and newspapers, in some cases going back 10 years or more, and find every mention of a person's name therein. You can search the campaign finance filings of every candidate for federal office and many state and local candidates as well. And you can summon up on your computer screen the Securities and Exchange Commission (SEC) filings of thousands of publicly held corporations.

Much of the information useful to investigators can now be found for free on the Internet. First, the federal government and state and local governments are now putting public records on government Web sites as well as selling the data to online vendors. One result is that you can now search the Library of Congress and U.S. Copyright Office databases directly without going through a vendor (although you still might want to use a vendor because of its superior search software). Another result is that you can search the state corporations registries and the UCC filings of many states at direct public-access Web sites. Second, many commercially produced research tools that once were available only by subscription are now being made available for free because the publishers can make more money this way from Internet advertising (for instance, *Thomas Register of American Manufacturers* is now free on the Web). Third, nonprofit organizations and private enthusiasts have pulled together vast compendiums of information on thousands of topics (for instance, the many Web sites devoted to tracking the voting records of political candidates). Fourth, millions of businesses and individuals have launched their own Web sites, providing detailed information about products and personnel (at the business sites) and personal careers and hobbies (at the individual sites). The emergence of such Web sites has revolutionized the task of profiling a business or gathering background information on an individual.

As fascinating as it is, the Internet is still dwarfed by the huge commercial database services such as LEXIS-NEXIS (which specializes in legal and news resources) and DIALOG (which is used for business, scientific, and academic research). These services are licensed by publishers and other database producers to market their products online to subscribers and other customers (the "end users"). DIALOG offers over 450 academic, business, and newspaper/periodical databases with a heavy focus on abstracts and indexes, but with many full-text sources as well. (The total system, with 9 terabytes of information and 6 billion pages of text, is many times larger than the World Wide Web.) Services such as DIALOG and LEXIS-NEXIS used to be too expensive for a private individual working at his or her home computer; now, however, such services are beginning to offer access to non-subscribers on a pay-for-use basis. It is at last becoming feasible for casual users to search the giant NEXIS newspaper/periodicals library for citations going back decades. It is still prohibitively expensive to download more than a few articles at a time; but if a researcher can at least get the citations, he or she will then know where to look on the microfilm at the public library.

To rival the traditional database vendors, companies such as Northern Light Technologies (www.northernlight.com) are now offering the archives of thousands of publications on a pay-per-*document* basis (the searching is free). Northern Light currently offers 5,400 journals, magazines, newswires, and reference services.

Today, you can also search an increasing array of CD-ROM databases at your public library for free. These products include marketing and demographic databases, biographical who's-who compilations, periodical indexes/abstracts covering hundreds of scholarly journals or general-interest magazines, full-text newspaper and magazine archives, and "corporate intelligence" databases. In addition, your public library may offer online products of leading reference book publishers. The advantage of using these library resources is that you not only can search for free to find your articles, you can also obtain a printout of the text for free.

Investigative Databases and Information Brokers

Certain types of databases are of special interest to investigators:

- Residential marketing databases compiled from telephone directories, U.S. Postal Service change-of-address files, magazine subscription and direct-mail lists, and many other sources. The largest cover upwards of 100 million households.

- Credit-reporting agency databases—for instance, Experian's Updated Credit Profile database, which contains information on 170 million people. Credit-reporting agencies are barred from giving out credit information on individuals except according to strict privacy guidelines, but this does not apply to noncredit "header" information on credit reports (current and former addresses, date of birth, the first six digits—if not the entire—SSN, spouse's name, mother's maiden name, and so on).

- Local, state, and federal government public records databases. Those most widely used by investigators include court indexes at the state trial court level, federal district court indexes and dockets, asset/lien records (especially Uniform Commercial Code [UCC] filings), county property records, and (when available) Department of Motor Vehicles (DMV) records.

The key to entering this world of online snooping is the so-called information broker. A brief list of such firms is found at the back of this book. A comprehensive directory is available online at www.publicrecordsources. com. The *information broker* is essentially a vendor who leases or purchases government and other public-access data for value-added resale or who provides a gateway into a variety of database sites so that you can do your own searching.

Some information brokers provide data only to high-volume users who pay hefty monthly minimum fees; others also offer their services to non-subscribers on a per-request basis. They will conduct a search of their own databases and also of the larger investigative database net, and email the results to you. The cost for a single search will be quite reasonable; but if you need frequent searches of UCC filings and other public records, find an information broker who charges a modest user deposit but no monthly minimum charges—and then do your own searches using this broker's gateway.

If you are going to purchase data (or access to data) from information brokers on a regular basis, you should exercise the same caution as any consumer. Ask where the information comes from (that is, how reliable are the source databases), how often the provider updates its own database from the source database, how often the source database itself is updated, how long it takes for information to get into the source database (for example, certain county records systems may have a backlog so that information is not entered into the computer until months after the filing), how well indexed a database is (that is, how narrowly you can define your search), how the data was originally inputted (for example, by scanning or by an operator typing it in) and with what margin of error, how many databases a provider has access to, how much experience the provider has in searching the particular databases you are interested in, whether the provider can help you interpret data that is retrieved in a coded or abbreviated form, and under what circumstances (if any) the broker is required to inform the subject of your inquiry that information has been requested about him or her.

Limitations of Databases

Online searching is no substitute for leg work. Veteran journalists will tell you that databases usually don't provide more than a small fraction of the information needed in preparing a major investigative article. In addition, the information in public-record and credit-reporting agency databases invariably has a rather large percentage of errors. Indeed, millions of Americans have been denied credit over the years because database compilers confused their names with those of persons who had failed to pay a debt.

If you are researching an article for publication, any negative information gathered from public record databases should be backed up by other evidence. Even then, never assume that the information is true without contacting the person about whom the record was purportedly compiled to make sure that you have the right person and to get his or her side of the story.

3.

Some Basic Techniques and Procedures

3.1 Getting Facts Fast

In preparing a single investigative article, you might need to consult ready-reference sources on dozens of occasions. Typical facts to be quickly researched might include the gross annual sales of a local corporation, the population and ethnic ratios of a nearby town, the age and current job of a former local congressman, or the law school background of an obnoxious local defense attorney.

Usually, you can answer such questions most efficiently by going to one of the many Web reference directories that provide links to a vast array of reference sites devoted to specific topics. For instance, if you go to www.yahoo.com/Reference, you will find thousands of reference sites divided into forty categories. Other reference directories can be found at www.refdesk.com, www.libraryspot.com, www.qns.com/~casey, and scholes.alfred.edu/Ref.html. (Add each of these Web addresses to your hot page list *now*.) Note that each reference directory provides links to most of the other reference directories. There is much overlap in what they list, but each organizes the listings differently; you should not rely exclusively on one directory.

Unfortunately, the Internet cannot answer every ready-reference question. Certain facts that you need immediately may be available only in reference publications that either are not available online at all or are available only at the publisher's expensive subscription-only site. In such cases, you can turn to the free telephone reference service at your public library. There are hundreds of such services at public libraries across the country. They are staffed by professional librarians who have at their fingertips hundreds of reference directories and other basic reference works, both in print and on CD-ROM.

When you call this service at your local library, always keep your requests simple. If the librarian doesn't have on hand the book or CD-ROM with the answer, he or she can at least tell you its title and refer you to the reference service at another library that does have it.

I have found that the public library reference services vary in quality. In some cities, the line may be perpetually busy or the number of directories at hand may be relatively small. In other cities, the service is excellent. If you can't get through to your local reference number, simply call a library in another city. While researching an article on the Teamsters Union many years ago, I used the telephone reference services of fifteen libraries around the country during a single week. (Obviously, this was before Al Gore invented the Internet.)

3.2 Telephone Information "Pyramiding"

Public library reference librarians generally allot only a few minutes to any given caller. If you have a question that is too complicated for them—and you can't find the answer on the Internet—the federal, state, and local governments maintain a vast cohort of public information officers, press secretaries, and legislative committee staffers who routinely answer questions from the public or refer callers to the appropriate government expert. To find out who to call, look in the government directories described in section 2.1, "Directories, Manuals, and Internet Hot Pages." If you're stumped, call the legislative office (*not* the community office) of your elected representative at the relevant level of government for advice. The Federal Information Center (fic.info.gov) may also help you identify sources of information at federal offices, either within your region or in Washington. After you reach the best expert in a given agency, he or she may steer you to an official in another agency or to someone in the private sector for additional information.

You can also seek information from a wide variety of private nonprofit organizations, such as trade associations and public policy institutes. Look in the subject listings in the *Encyclopedia of Associations* or search in the organization subdirectories at www.yahoo.com.

Other good sources of information include newsletter editors (you can find the right newsletter by looking in the listings by subject in *Newsletters in Print*) and corporate public relations or communications directors. Newsletter editors often have the answer at their fingertips, and the corporate public relations people will usually know exactly who in their organization to steer you to. I received much help from both newsletter editors and corporate PR types in researching this book.

With this wide range of sources, it is possible to find an answer over the phone quickly and efficiently—even if your questions are quite arcane. You are passed on from general to specific experts, or from experts in one aspect of your question to experts in another aspect. I call this "information pyramiding." Once you get the hang of it, it rarely takes you more than three or four calls to zero in on the person who has the definitive answer to your question.

3.3 Collecting and Filing Your Documentation

Your Manual Files

You can master every technique for gaining information, but it won't do you much good if everything gets lost in a huge pile of unsorted documents on your desk. This doesn't matter much if you're doing a relatively simple investigation, but if you are preparing a major piece of investigative journalism or compiling a deep background report that involves parallel backgrounding, you will be rapidly accumulating court documents and other public records, handwritten notes, photocopied pages from books, and clippings from a variety of newspapers and magazines. It is essential that you devote a period of time at the end of each day to filing and cross-filing this material. If you don't file your information for more than a couple of days, the pile of material will get out of hand. Not only will you not be able to locate things, you will find it very difficult to plan out your future research efficiently. You may discover an important lead one day, set it aside thinking you'll follow it up next week, and then completely forget about it.

There are as many filing systems as there are journalists. Here's my system: First, at the beginning of your investigation, have on hand several dozen filing folders. Use legal-length folders; if you use letter-sized ones, you'll have to fold documents before inserting them, which makes the file harder to search. As the documents accumulate during your research into a local businessman's past, make a folder for each aspect or important event or stage of his life (for example, college years, first job, 1987 lawsuit, divorce proceedings, 1989 federal prosecution—you might want to construct a chronology). Also make a folder for each of the subject's associates, business entities, and so forth, as well as folders on appropriate background topics. Before you file a document, highlight the important parts with a yellow marker. You will find that many documents or interview notes relate to more than one topic; in such cases, make multiple photocopies of the document or of its most important portions and place each copy in the relevant folder with highlighting specific to that folder. If you don't have a photocopier handy, you can place the document (with a red "X" on the front page) in the file to which it has greatest relevance and then insert in the other folder(s) a yellow-pad sheet bearing the reminder "See—1987 lawsuit file." You will find that some documents are relevant to many or almost every folder; in such cases, make an "Urgent—Multiple Use" file, and keep such documents there (also place them in the relevant folders if possible) to be consulted frequently. (Note that when you get down to writing, it is always preferable to have a copy of a document or article in *every folder to which it is relevant*, even if the copying and filing seem tedious at the time.) When a folder begins to fill up, divide it into primary-relevance and secondary-relevance folders.

My filing system flows from my approach to the gathering of documents: Photocopy everything of possible relevance in a court file, newspaper clippings file, library reference volume, and so forth. This is especially important in the early stages of an investigation: You won't know what's most important until you fit it into the larger picture.

When you find a damning public document—for instance, a deed of sale showing that a local politician bought a parcel of land two weeks before a zoning change raised the land's value dramatically—always get a certified copy from the county or city clerk's office immediately. Such documents have a habit of disappearing from the public files within a few days of your call to the politician to question him or her about it.

Now a piece of advice for which you will thank me many times over: Be prepared to feed those hungry photocopiers at your courthouse or public library. If the copiers require the use of vending cards dispensed from a machine, always take with you crisp five and ten dollar bills. If the copiers take bills directly, you should likewise also be ready with a sufficient number of crisp bills of the appropriate denomination. If the copiers take only coins but there is a coin dispenser that takes bills, be sure to bring enough bills but also bring rolls of quarters because these dispensers break down almost as often as the copiers do. If the copiers take only coins and there are no dispensers, be sure that you bring several rolls of coins. In general, you should be prepared with dimes as well as quarters because some coin-operated copiers don't take quarters but almost all take dimes. If you forget my advice about coins, you may have to traipse from office to office within the courthouse to find someone with change. And don't rely on the bank around the corner: Many branches nowadays will provide rolls of coins only to depositors, and most branches close two hours earlier than the courthouse file room does.

If you're searching case files, you never know what you might find. Estimate the number of coin rolls you think you'll need—and then double it.

Hopefully, copiers will all take credit cards by the time the next edition of this book is published!

Your Electronic Files

If you have a choice of obtaining a document in (or converting it into) electronic form as well as obtaining and filing a paper copy, do both. A computerized document can be instantly retrieved, edited, sent to other computers by email, copied instantaneously (no more trips to the local photocopy shop!), and merged in whole or in part with any of your other documents. Most important, you can search computerized files using powerful search software to discover interconnections between individuals or business entities you might otherwise miss.

While conducting your research, always be alert to how you can maximize the use of your computer. You may have a collection of recent clippings on a particular person or topic from your local newspaper that you have not yet manually indexed. If the recent archives of this newspaper can be accessed for free at the paper's Web site, you should download the electronic version of these clippings (and other relevant articles), thus creating the beginnings of your own electronic clippings library. You might also search DIALOG for earlier articles from the newspaper in question and download those that are most essential. If you're engaged in parallel backgrounding a high-achieving individual, you might download the *Who's Who in America* sketches on the subject and his or her present and past professional colleagues, business partners, college classmates, and so on. Indeed, you might download the personal Web pages of each of these individuals (and the Web pages of their business entities, if there's a connection to your subject). For downloading Web pages, I suggest you try SurfSaver, an inexpensive program that enables you to store Web pages directly from your browser into searchable folders. SurfSaver will create an archive from the downloaded material; it supports full-text, proximity, and other types of searches. (For more information, go to www.surfsaver.com.)

Whenever you approach an attorney for access to the depositions or trial testimony in a civil case involving a subject (see sections 9.6, "Pretrial Discovery," and 9.7, "Dealing with a Subject's Opponents at Law"), ask for a copy of the diskette the court reporter provided to the attorney (or a copy of the file the attorney's office created by scanning the court reporter's paper transcript).

Information on the Internet regarding your subject's business entities will be an especially rich source for your electronic files. For instance, you can download for free the latest SEC filings (and also the Web pages) of every corporation with which your subject is associated as an officer, director, or insider owner.

More and more federal, state, and local government records are becoming available for free downloading at government Web sites. At these sites, you can now find audits, legislative reports, and state crime commission findings as well as corporate and UCC filings. In addition, much government data is readily available on diskette, magnetic tape, or CD-ROM; much more can be obtained through a Freedom of Information Act (FOIA) request (for instance, bureaucratic email, which the federal executive branch must now retain to be in compliance with the FOIA).

Note: Whenever you deal with government entities on any level—federal, state, or local—always determine whether the information you need is available electronically. Never be content with a computer printout or other paper document if an electronic version is easily available.

Much of your documentation on Mr. C, the infamous political fixer whose depredations on society began long before the era of electronic archives, will be available only on paper. But here you have the option of adding these documents to your computer files by using a scanner and Optical Character Recognition (OCR) software that converts the scanned text into searchable and editable electronic text. For decades, scanning has been a feasible way to create electronic versions of neatly typed legal documents. Advances in OCR technology since the early 1990s now make it possible to easily scan in the texts of books and magazine articles, newspaper clippings, faxes, and other materials—even with a handheld scanner—to create a workable OCR document. The latest software can stitch things together neatly and give you (if you're working with clean copy) a 95-percent or better accuracy rate. Top-of-the-line software programs such as Omnipage Pro can read originals of rather poor quality and correct many of the OCR translation errors. The new OCR software can even preserve the exact format of the scanned page, including the typefaces, thus giving you something very close to a photographic image.

Note that you must proofread any scanned document to guarantee complete accuracy. If you don't have time to proofread everything fully, you should at least scan the document. Even an imperfect copy can be archived and searched for key words as you attempt to trace all the interconnections of your subject's business life. You should always keep the paper original, however, to check against the OCR version when it comes time to verify your quotations and other facts with your fact-checking department and your editor.

Although scanning technology has improved drastically, you should have an original that is as clean as possible. I suggest that you photocopy any important document that you might want to scan later on. Place the visually inferior version (whether the photocopy or the original) in your working file, and the scanner-friendly version in a pre-scan file. You can then highlight, scrawl margin notes on, fold, crease, smear, and spill coffee on the working copy to your heart's content.

After you have created electronic documents by downloading online data, scanning, and so forth, you must be able to search the hundreds of files on your hard disk efficiently. One of the most popular search software programs used by journalists and writers is ZyLAB's ZyINDEX. This program will index the entire contents of your hard disk, a process that takes several hours. Thereafter, the software can look through all your files almost instantaneously and retrieve information according to highly sophisticated search options.

Anyone interested in developing their own investigative archives as described in this section should become familiar with the Web page of the National Institute for Computer-Assisted Reporting at www.nicar.org and should subscribe to *Uplink*, NICAR's excellent monthly newsletter. NICAR has collected a library of government databases, which it sells to reporters for a modest price. It also conducts classes and seminars on the technical problems involved in the use of such databases.

3.4 Eliciting Information from Ordinary People and Those in High Places

Skip tracers and private investigators use various ruses to trick people into providing information. For instance, they may call up a friend of a skipped debtor and say they represent the estate of a relative who has left the skip some money. The friend, wanting to be helpful to his or her pal, often will reveal the new address or phone number.

Many times, ruses aren't intended to elicit closely held information but simply to make a person feel comfortable about discussing something he or she has no strong reason *not* to discuss. The ruse allays his or her suspicions of a stranger asking questions about a third party. It also gets around his or her antipathy toward bill collectors.

Apart from ethical concerns, the use of a ruse makes it more difficult to go back to the same source later. The person you manipulated into revealing an unlisted telephone number may turn out later to be the key to far more important information, but the trick you used the first time may have destroyed the possibility of any trust.

Journalists can avoid ruses under most circumstances because they have a built-in reason for their snooping—they are working on a news story, and their questions are part of that story. Most people understand this and respond politely and without suspicion. If they know the journalist is on a deadline, they'll often drop a pressing task to answer his or her questions on the spot.

Another advantage journalists have is that their craft emphasizes tracking down opponents and enemies of their subject. Whereas a skip tracer might pump a friend of the subject for information using a ruse, the journalist will naturally gravitate to the subject's enemy and get the same information (and more) in an above-board fashion.

Whether you are a journalist or a skip tracer, your success in eliciting information depends on your mind-set. Remember always that the average person has a natural desire to be helpful if he or she is not too harried at the moment or is not feeling ill. Approach each contact as if you were lost on a country road and seeking directions to the nearest town. As the conversation develops, let the contact know that you are trying to do a job on a deadline with your editor pressuring you (anyone who works for a boss can identify with this). Behave as if there's no doubt in your mind that the contact will help you. The more you believe this, the more it will become true—unless you sabotage things by being rude, unctuous, overly aggressive, or otherwise disagreeable. If you haven't learned basic human communication skills, there are many good books and seminars on the subject.

If you need a source's help on anything more than a simple question or two, you should strive to make your investigation personally meaningful to him or her. This means stimulating the source's sympathy, curiosity, or self-interest, and appealing (when appropriate) to his or her moral or political convictions. For instance, if you are working on an exciting or colorful story, try to get the person interested in what you've found out. If you are working on a story about a crooked politician, appeal to the person's indignation and desire to do right. If you are working for a defense attorney, appeal to the potential witness's natural sympathy for a little guy caught in the coils of the legal system.

A corollary of the preceding suggestion is to never *assume* that a source will be hostile. Once, in investigating an anti-Semitic group, I came across a sales brochure of a related investment scam. In it was included a picture of a light-haired, crewcut board member with a German name. I put him at the *bottom* of my list of potential sources to call. When I finally did contact him, however, he turned out to be a liberal college professor, not a far-rightist or neo-Nazi. And he was eager to talk. The group, he said, had used his name and picture without his permission after he had turned down their request for investment cash. He had been trying for months to get law enforcement to investigate them.

If a contact refuses to talk or slams the phone down, try him or her again in a few days with a slightly different pitch. The person may just have been in a bad mood, or you may have used the wrong approach the first time (for example, calling him or her at work rather than at home, or vice versa). I've had people scream and curse at me on the phone one day and be perfect lambs when I called back 24 hours later. Also, when working on long-range projects, I've had sources adamantly refuse to talk at the outset but be eager to talk six months or a year later. If you can't wait six months to talk to Mr. X, try talking to a friend or acquaintance of his—not only to find out what the friend or acquaintance knows but also to elicit his or her help in getting Mr. X to open up. (In investigating a cult, this might mean approaching a longtime defector to help line up an interview with a recent and still very nervous defector.) Also try approaching Mr. X outside his normal routine (for example, at an out-of-town convention rather than at his office). If he is a yuppie investment banker, put on your jogging shoes and approach him during his evening run in the park (if you are a male reporter, do *not* attempt this with a female source). An additional tactic (if, say, you're trying to collect information to establish the innocence of a criminal defendant) is a heartfelt letter to your potential source appealing to his or her best instincts.

If a contact consents to talk but then gives only very limited and vaguely worded information (but you know that he or she knows much more than he or she is saying), don't give up. Thank the person politely and ask if you can call him or her again when and if your research generates further questions. Most people will say yes, if for no other reason than just to get you off the phone or out of their office. But this lays a basis for calling them back without seeming too pushy. I have found that cautious bureaucrats or frightened cult defectors sometimes will open up marvelously during a second or third conversation if you don't push too hard.

If you are investigating the sinister Mr. Z, one of your most important sources will of course be Mr. Z himself. You must get his side of the story at some point, but when to do so is a complicated question. On the one hand, interviewing him early in the investigation may save you a lot of unnecessary digging. First, you may find he is not quite the villain you thought he was. Second, you may find him willing to provide important information in order to placate you, justify himself, or shift the blame onto one of his associates. Third, he may not perceive his own behavior the way you do; what is sinister to you may seem admirable to him and not at all to be covered up. For instance, I once spent weeks digging into a Teamster official's relationship to an ultra-right organization before calling him. I might as well have called him the first day and saved myself all that digging: He was proud of the connection and discussed it freely, regarding it as proof of his patriotism.

Of course, tipping off your subject too soon may trigger action that closes off important avenues of information. In investigating an elected public official, I suggest that you contact him or her early in the investigation with relatively noncontroversial but necessary background questions, then come back later with your zingers. In general, the less controversial or potentially damaging your investigation of a person is likely to be, the earlier you should approach him or her.

Note: Any reporter writing about persons in politics, government, or business has had to deal with the problem of the "gatekeeper" (the secretary who answers the boss's line and screens his or her calls). You call and call. Each time, the gatekeeper answers and tells you that the boss is on the phone or out of the office. You leave messages, but never receive a call back. In such cases, try calling when the gatekeeper is not there, so that your call will go through to the boss's direct line. I suggest that you try after 6 P.M., when the gatekeeper will probably have left the office. Assuming that the boss is a workaholic who stays late into the evening, he or she will probably be easy to reach in this manner (a variation on this is to call in the morning about a half hour before the gatekeeper arrives).

Another key issue is how to treat your subject (or a hostile source who is defending your subject) after interviewing him or her. Some practitioners of killer journalism (who are using their journalism to act out their neuroses) will indulge in gratuitous sarcastic remarks and value judgments about these interviewees in their ensuing article or column. Or they will gossip about an interviewee in scornful language to third parties (who sometimes will inform the interviewee or the interviewee's friends about this display of animus).

Such behavior is self-defeating as well as immature. It makes it very difficult for you to call the subject(s) of the article afterward for his/her/their reactions (such reactions can often set the stage for a follow-up article far more revealing than the first article). It ignores the fact that today's hostile source (for example, George the closet-gay New Right fund-raiser) may become tomorrow's friendly source (George the AIDS activist who has denounced his former colleagues as bigots). It guarantees that when the hostile source decides to stop being a sacrificial lamb for his or her superiors (as did Watergate's John Dean), you will be the *last* journalist he or she might choose as a conduit.

A rule of thumb: Put no gratuitous insults in your articles—stick to the facts. No attacks on aspects of the subject's life that are not pertinent to the issue at hand (for example, no references to Councilwoman Smith's son's drug arrests in an article on her campaign finances *unless* her son worked on her campaign or the information is otherwise directly relevant). And no gossiping about the subject to third parties. In other words, drive the moneychangers out of the temple, but don't forget the Golden Rule.

A touch of Golden Rule-style tolerance is frequently essential in dealing with problems posed by putatively eccentric or disreputable sources. It would be nice if investigative journalism involved only interviews with priests, rabbis, and an occasional professor of business ethics at a local college. Unfortunately, in many investigations, the only people with inside knowledge are those regarded as either weird or sleazy—you have to take what you can get. In investigating far-right politics, I have had to deal with many such people. Although some journalists have been burned by such relationships, my experience with borderline sources is that they often provide information as reliable as—and certainly a lot more interesting than—the information provided by impeccably respectable people (who, by the way, have their own tricks for covering up the facts).

The basic rule in dealing with so-called eccentric sources is to afford them the same respect as anyone else and to never violate their trust on the grounds that they somehow don't deserve the same straight dealing as ordinary folks. This does not mean becoming their doormat. You may find that they have a narcissistic tendency to call you collect from Alaska at 2 A.M. with their latest brainstorm. An experienced journalist-therapist, however, knows how to put an end to these excesses with a bit of Pavlovian conditioning (if they call after midnight, slam the phone down and then be noticeably cool to them at the outset of the next conversation).

Special problems of a different nature will arise when you encounter a government "whistle blower" or other source with vast inside information regarding a major story. You should always ask, at the outset of your dealings with such a source, for all the documentation—every scrap of paper, no matter how seemingly trivial—he or she has collected or can collect. Ask your source to bring as much of this documentation as possible to your first meeting (and also to bring the in-house phone directory of his or her company or agency so that you can begin your search for additional sources). But be aware that even with a thick folder of documents, a single conversation may only scratch the surface of what the source knows. Indeed, even a half dozen conversations and entire boxes of documents may fail to uncover a key piece of information that the source has but that he or she doesn't know is important and that you don't know enough to ask about. As you follow up leads from the earlier conversations and the documents—and thus get a clearer picture—you will often have to mull things over with your original sources again and again. All the more reason to be absolutely honest in your dealings with them: Maintain confidences and be careful not to misrepresent or misquote what they tell you. If you disagree with their interpretation of something, let them know forthrightly—don't spring it as a surprise in one of your articles.

I also suggest that you read the complete draft of your article (or of each article in your series) to your chief whistle-blowing sources; not only will it increase their sense of commitment, but they will probably spot subtle errors of emphasis if not outright errors of fact. Most reporters don't do this because they feel it might undermine their "control" of the story. In my opinion, however, reading the draft to a trusted source is as natural—indeed, as obligatory—as submitting it to your fact-checking assistant or your editor.

3.5 Interviewing

The first thing to remember about interviewing is *do your homework*. If your subject is an expert in a given field, and you come to the interview totally ignorant, he or she will be annoyed and thus less inclined to cooperate. (Your display of knowledge, however, should be restricted during the interview to the posing of intelligent questions; you are there to ask questions and listen to the answers, not to spout off. If you and the source want to *exchange* ideas, do so after the interview is over.)

Being prepared also means drawing up a list of questions and arranging them in some order of priority. You should ask yourself what the person might know *beyond* the obvious. Time and again while interviewing people, I've failed to probe far enough, failed to get to the key question—and it was usually because I called them hastily without preparing beforehand. (If, after you hang up, you realize you've missed a key question, call the source back immediately; this may actually start a longer and far more illuminating conversation.)

Whether you interview someone on the telephone or in person, you should consider carefully the best time and place for the interview. For instance, a potential source might feel constrained if interviewed in his or her office—but if you go to his or her home, the interview might be hampered by the presence of a spouse who doesn't want your source to get involved in any controversy. In such a case, the interview might best be conducted over lunch or at a tavern after work.

In both telephone and face-to-face interviews, you have a choice of taping the conversation, taking notes, or both. Taping someone on the phone without their knowledge is illegal in many states (and because you can't use the illegal tape in court or to convince your editor, why do it?). However, if you ask a person's permission to tape them over the phone, you may screw up the interview. If they consent, they often will be extremely cautious in what they say (remember, they are talking to a stranger they cannot see). If they don't consent, they'll think you have the machine on anyway and thus will talk much less freely than if you'd never raised the idea. These problems will probably not arise in a phone interview with an expert providing noncontroversial background information, but even then make sure that he or she feels comfortable about being taped.

When you interview someone in person, there is more leeway for using a tape recorder. If you have established a rapport with them and don't intend to ask anything that might seriously compromise them (and if the conversation is *on* the record), I would say the tape recorder is appropriate—just don't place it in their direct line of vision while they are talking. Otherwise, simply take notes. And even *with* the tape recorder on, you should take notes: It will save you from later having to listen to and transcribe material of little or no importance. Also, taking notes ensures against such common mishaps as the recorder not working properly or background noise ruining parts of the recording.

Both cassettes and notes should be marked for identification immediately: On the cassette label, write the name of the person interviewed and the date and place of the interview (this and other identifying information should also be at the beginning of the tape itself, the first words you speak after turning it on). On the first page of handwritten notes or at the beginning of notes taken by computer, put the name, date, time, and either the place at which the interview was conducted or the telephone number you dialed to reach the subject (plus the number from which you called). In taking notes by hand, write on one side of the page only (for later ease in photocopying); also number each page (1 of 3, 2 of 3, and so on) and print "END OF INTERVIEW" right beneath the last line of notes on the last page. While the interview is still fresh in your mind, type up and add to the notes on your computer (or make additions to the notes you typed during the interview). This should be done after brief telephone conversations (if they elicited significant information) as well as after formal interviews.

Unless you are using shorthand, the notes you end up with will be a mixture of the following elements:

1. The subject's exact words (the exact quote) as written down in your notebook on the spot

2. The subject's remarks as paraphrased or summarized on the spot

3. The subject's remarks as paraphrased or summarized later from memory

The cardinal rule is to never confuse (1) with either (2) or (3). Direct quotes from your interviewee, whether entire sentences or isolated phrases, should always be clearly set off in your notes either by underlining or by quotation marks. Also, additions made while going over the notes should always be placed in brackets.

After you have keyed in and added to your interview notes on the computer, do *not* destroy the handwritten originals (you will need them in dealing with your editor and your newspaper's libel attorneys before publication—and possibly in a libel defense thereafter).

A fourth element in note taking is your own interpretive remarks. Although a few of these will doubtless be part of your original notes, you should in general write these down separately afterward. Avoid writing down any negative personal observations about the interviewee in any of these notes. You don't want Mr. J to find, during his subsequent libel suit, phrases such as "uptight bureaucratic creep" or "egg on his tie— disgusting!" scrawled in the margin of your subpoenaed notes.

Before any interview, you should get the correct spelling of the person's name and also any generational designation. In interviewing public officials or corporate officers, be sure that you get their correct title *and* the correct name of the agency or company. There is nothing more annoying than to read an article in a weekly free-distribution newspaper (or a private investigator's report) in which the chairman of the city planning commission is referred to as the "director" of the "department" of planning. In dealing with a high-level official, get this information from his or her private secretary or an aide rather than bothering him or her with it during the interview.

If you interview someone in his or her office, observe carefully your surroundings: A diploma on the wall or pictures of family members on the desk may provide important leads. Also note the names of the interviewee's private secretary, the receptionist, and others. These people may hate their boss and become important sources later on.

Some journalists say you should observe carefully the interviewee's facial expressions and body language. I suppose it's better to observe these things than to keep your eyes closed, but I wouldn't make too much of it. The nerdish accountant who keeps clearing his throat when questioned about the sloppy bookkeeping in the city agency for which he works may not be manifesting job-related guilt at all. It may simply be that he feels intimidated by members of the press or has a post-nasal drip. If lie detectors are notoriously unreliable, why should pop-psychology theories on blinking and leg-crossing be any better?

Journalists and their sources can choose from a variety of arrangements regarding how the information from a given interview will be used. Ideally, the entire interview should be "on the record" (in other words, you can quote the person by name on anything he or she says). If he or she declines this, however, you can put forward various alternatives. First, suggest that some of the interview be on the record and some not (often, to make your story, you will need only a single quote on the record). If your source still refuses to be named, ask if you can quote him or her on a "not for attribution" basis, for example, as "a former top aide of Senator Foghorn" (no name given, but many people will be able to guess). Only if this doesn't work will you offer to do the interview as "background" (you attribute it only to vague "official sources" or "well-informed sources") or reluctantly agree to do it "off the record" (you use the information only if you can verify it from other sources or from documents and never refer even in the vaguest of terms to the existence of your original source).

A somewhat arcane arrangement within the Washington Beltway is that the reporter will attribute a statement to a certain official but will paraphrase rather than directly quote the statement. The source can then say the remarks were misrepresented if he or she gets any heat from the interview. Obviously, this and most of the preceding arrangements make sense only with media-savvy government officials and prosecutors. With ordinary people, just stick to "on the record" and "background."

In preparing for any interview, the question arises: Should you be the first to raise the question of attribution? In dealing with most government officials (except whistle blowers) or most politicians, I would say this: Let sleeping dogs lie, and just assume that everything is on the record. If the official is stupid enough not to set ground rules, he or she must pay the price. But in dealing with ordinary people, it's not so simple. Often they will tell you something openly, and then say halfway through the conversation or at the end, "Don't quote me on this." If you quote them anyway, they'll feel aggrieved and won't cooperate in the future. It is thus usually best to establish ground rules for the interview if you anticipate further dealings with the interviewee. However, I have had people agree to go on the record and then change their mind and call me at home afterward, begging me not to use their names. If this happens, you have to weigh carefully whether you are willing to risk alienating them and cutting yourself off from further information they might provide, and whether using their names will really create a hardship for them (they may just be having an irrational panic attack). Be aware that journalists who lack a caring attitude toward their sources not only lose them, but they also experience difficulty later in gaining the trust of friends or associates of the original source who may possess far more important information.

An important distinction to keep in mind is that between an anonymous source and a confidential source. An *anonymous source* is a source whose identity you will not reveal in your article or in conversations with third parties but whose identity you might disclose in a libel suit or under other special circumstances. A *confidential source* is one whose identity you have agreed to keep secret at all costs, even if you are jailed for contempt of court as a result. This should be agreed on at the outset if the source is giving you sensitive information. Obviously, you would prefer the source to be anonymous rather than confidential (and on the record rather than anonymous). I have had sources who began as strictly confidential agree to go public later on, as we got to know each other better.

3.6 Getting a Signed Statement

If you are working for an attorney, or if you are a journalist working on especially sensitive material, you will want to get signed declarations from some of the sources you interview. Some interviewers may do this with their notebook computer and portable printer, but the method described here involves the good old yellow pad with ruled lines and a pen (never a pencil). Write at the top of the first page "Declaration of John R. Doe." Begin the text, "I, John R. Doe, was interviewed on [date] between [starting time] and [ending time] at [place of interview] by [name of interviewer] who is a reporter for [name of publication]" (or: "… who is an investigator for [name of attorney]"). Then write down the source's occupation, place of employment, and home address, followed by each relevant fact of which the source has direct personal knowledge; do not include any mere speculation, no matter how juicy. Read each sentence to the source before you write it down so that he or she can affirm its accuracy. Keep the statement as brief as possible, locking the source into an affirmation of the absolutely crucial facts only. If you need more than one page, number them "1 of 3," "2 of 3," and so on. When finished, ask the source to read over the entire declaration carefully. If the source wants to make changes at this point, he or she should initial each change.

When all changes have been made, the source should sign each page and then write in his or her own hand at the bottom of the last page that he or she has read the preceding [number of pages] pages and [number of lines] lines (count the lines on the last page) and knows the contents to be true. Finally, have the source sign this affirmation on the spot or take him or her to a notary, who will verify his or her identity, witness the signing, and stamp the signature page with a notary seal. If you do much interviewing for attorneys, you should become a notary yourself. However, if you're a journalist who happens to be a notary, do *not* notarize the statement yourself: It won't be as credible as a statement notarized by a third party if you're subsequently sued for libel.

In most instances, a simple declaration (signed but not notarized) is sufficient. The notarized statement, or *affidavit*, is chiefly useful when the source is telling you explosive and potential libelous things. It's a way of putting sources to the test—if they are lying or wildly exaggerating, they will most likely back off from giving an affidavit. Even when you fully trust the information, an affidavit may be useful because it takes the source's commitment to a higher level—he or she becomes less likely to back out later. In addition, an affidavit is sometimes useful when a source refuses to allow you to quote him or her by name in your article; having the statement to show to your newspaper's editor and attorneys will help to convince them the information is reliable in spite of the source's insistence on anonymity.

Note: When you get a signed statement, also get the name, address, and telephone number of at least one person who will know how to contact your source if the latter moves.

3.7 "Advertising" for Information

When a person is searching for a missing relative and the trail runs dry, he or she may try placing classified ads in selected publications, asking those with information to come forward. Families searching for an abducted child may pass out flyers that include the child's picture and a reward offer, or they may go to the media. The police often circulate wanted posters and seek the aid of the TV program "America's Most Wanted." Well, journalists can do this also: Jessica Mitford, in preparing an expose of the Famous Writers School (a correspondence school), placed a classified ad in *Saturday Review* (a magazine whose readers she felt were likely to have fallen victim to the school's scam) asking former students to contact her.

Journalists can also do another type of "advertising." It's called going with what you've got. You take the partial, imperfect story you've uncovered and publish it as a way of attracting sources who can tell you the rest of the story.

I first learned about this tactic while working for the Manhattan weekly *Our Town* in the late 1970s. Assigned to a story on local newsstand distribution companies and "swag" (stolen newspapers and magazines), I was able to write a story describing how the scam worked but with no hard facts on who was behind it. *Our Town* published the story; within hours, we were getting calls from anonymous persons in daily newspaper circulation departments—and also newsstand operators—offering us information about the role of a corrupt union official. A similar thing happened several months later when we did an article on right-winger Lyndon LaRouche: Within days, calls were coming in from defectors from LaRouche's organization who had a wealth of information, some of which was about LaRouche's hidden control of one of Manhattan's largest computer software companies. We published a piece on this, eliciting, again, a spate of calls, this time from former clients and employees of the firm in question. One morning, I came into the office and found on my desk a complete computer printout of the firm's general ledger, apparently dropped off by a disgruntled programmer.

This technique worked in these cases because the published articles were so easily available to people with the information we needed. The "swag" scam was centered in Manhattan, the LaRouche organization had its headquarters in Manhattan, and LaRouche's computer company did much of its business in Manhattan. People with knowledge of these topics could pick up *Our Town* for free in midtown banks and other busy locations, and all three articles were on the front page. The lesson is this: Use your news articles as the journalistic equivalent of a want ad to find the sources you need. If your article appears in a paper that reaches the right audience (and that audience, depending on the topic, could just as well be a specialized newsletter with only a few hundred subscribers), the results may surprise you.

If you specialize in a particular journalistic topic—or have developed a reputation for going after villainy across the spectrum—you can advertise on a much broader scale: Go on radio and TV talk shows, solicit speaking engagements, hold a press conference on your latest findings, do newspaper and magazine interviews, and get other reporters around the country to quote you as an expert. Over the long run, this can pay big dividends. Much of the information for my 1989 book on LaRouche came from sources who first heard me on talk shows, or who saw my name in an article by another journalist, or who came up to the podium after one of my speeches.

Another approach is to cultivate people in organizations concerned with your topic who will then refer potential sources to you. In the mid-1980s, I had over a dozen Jewish, civil rights, labor, and anti-cult organizations passing on my name to victims of the LaRouche group; this also produced major leads. In addition, if you let other journalists around the country know that you are focusing on a given topic, they will call you when they are working on a relevant piece, and, in return for your help, will share their findings with you and introduce you to their sources.

I believe in getting other journalists involved to the maximum extent. If the story is a big one, there's always room for several people to work on different aspects. What one turns up will help the others. The tracking of LaRouche in the early 1980s, for instance, was the work of a network of journalists across the country. Whenever an article about LaRouche by freelancer Russ Bellant appeared in a Detroit paper, it would attract to him local ex-LaRouchians who would never have known to contact me in New York or Chip Berlet in Chicago or Joel Bellman in Los Angeles (and vice versa). Unfortunately, reporters on major dailies are often too paranoid or competitive to practice this cooperative approach.

One of the best forms of advertising is simply to have a listed home phone number in the telephone directory. This may produce some annoying messages on your answering machine (and certainly you might want to have your *address* unlisted), but it is essential that a journalist (especially a freelancer without a fixed office) be easy to contact by nervous potential sources. Some journalists keep their home phone numbers unlisted but widely publicize their email addresses by placing them at the bottom of their columns. I find this acceptable if the journalist is a staffer who is easy to reach at the newspaper's office anyway.

The Internet helps you reach out boldly for sources (and for volunteer research helpers), both locally and nationally. For instance, if you are preparing an article about certain carcinogens dumped in a local lake, you might send a request for information to all members of email lists and UseNet newsgroups concerned with this particular health issue. An appeal for tips regarding a local political scandal might go to certain bulletin boards on your local Freenet; an email request for help on an article relating to a particular religious cult might be sent to all legitimate religious groups on the college campuses where the cult is recruiting. The latter request might also be sent to anti-cult email lists and to academic newsgroups or conference groups that focus on the sociology of alternative religions. To draw attention to your request and to stimulate curiosity, you might attach to your message the text of an article you've written on the cult in question.

4.

Finding "Missing" People

4.1 Overview

A major problem in many investigations is locating a seemingly hard-to-find source or witness. Usually, such people are not deliberately hiding out (or at least not hiding out from *you*). Many prove willing and even eager to talk when and if you find them at their residence or place of employment. But what if you have only an outdated address for them? or if all you know is that the person lived somewhere in the Boston area many years ago? or if his or her phone has been disconnected and there's no forwarding number? or if the new number is unpublished?

Difficulty in finding people stems partly from the high rate of mobility in the American work force. A 1984 University of Michigan study found that 30 percent of interviewees nationwide had lived at their most recent address for less than two years. An earlier survey estimated that 16.6 percent of all citizens of voting age had changed their place of residence within the previous year. The close-knit neighborhood in which folks sit on the front porch in the evening and everyone knows everyone else is largely a nostalgic memory.

This trend is paralleled by a growing desire for privacy, even a kind of secretiveness. By the late 1990s, over one-fifth of all Americans had an unlisted number (a number unpublished in the white pages and unavailable through Directory Assistance). The trend is far more pronounced west of the Mississippi (19 out of 20 of the cities with the highest percentages of unlisted numbers are in the west) and rises to a peak in California's metropolitan areas, where about 65 percent of all telephone line subscribers have unlisted numbers. In addition, the percentages nationwide choosing to list their name and telephone number without their address (or with only a partial address or a post office box number) or choosing to use an initial instead of a full first name or to use a fictitious cover name have risen significantly.

Such efforts to maintain privacy are relatively ineffectual in today's computerized society. Skip tracers, private investigators, and other professional finders—who for decades relied on marketing directories and pretext phone calls to track down people who had moved or didn't want to be found—today have at their command powerful electronic search techniques to supplement their traditional methods. So-called *information brokers* are providing professional finders with routine access to giant databases compiled by credit-reporting agencies, mailing list vendors, and state and local governments; these databases track the overwhelming majority of American households on multiple levels. In addition, time-honored tools such as the crisscross directory are being used far more effectively today in an electronic format.

But databases are only as good as the information fed into them, and this information is often inaccurate or out of date. Some people contrive to drop out of the electronic information net temporarily, or they build a parallel database trail under a different name and at a different address. Their motives run the gamut: an ex-husband who wants to evade child-support or alimony payments, a criminal suspect who has jumped bail, a deadbeat who owes thousands of dollars to department stores, a cult member who believes her parents are instruments of Satan plotting to have her tortured by deprogrammers.

People who don't want to be found use a variety of predictable tactics. For instance, they put their telephone or utilities in someone else's name, or they use a false Social Security Number (SSN) on job applications. But most such people are inconsistent in using these tactics. They may give a phony SSN at one job but forget and give their real SSN at the next. They may list their phone number in a girlfriend's name but list the utilities in their own name. Finding them just means searching systematically through the various records systems until you find a weak spot.

The problem is more difficult when your subject knows how to conceal his or her location and identity in a systematic manner and has the discipline to stick to it. Some of these people go to elaborate lengths to construct a false identity by obtaining a birth certificate and other ID in the name of a person who was born at about the same time as themselves but who died in childhood (this is called "paper tripping"). If the FBI can't always find such people, you probably can't either. But at least you can find most non-paper trippers with the techniques outlined in this chapter.

4.2 Important Search Tools

A variety of online, CD-ROM, microform, and print resources exists through which you can search for anyone anywhere in the United States or Canada. Using these resources, you eventually can either locate your subject directly or locate relatives, friends, former neighbors, or ex-spouses who can put you in touch with him or her.

Online People Finders

The leading online people finder services include, among others, www.four11.com, www.anywho.com, www.bigfoot.com, www.whowhere. lycos.com, and people.yahoo.com. To search several of them from a single gateway without having to fill out the search information over and over, try www.theultimates.com (go to the "Ultimate White Pages"). To find a comprehensive directory of people finders, go to the Webgator site (www.inil.com/ users/dguss/gator.htm) and select "Telephone and Email Directories" (for more specialized types of locator services, select "Locator Databases").

Note that most people finder services obtain their telephone listings data from a small group of companies that input or scan it from telephone print directories nationwide. A people finder service may add its own software and certain information from non-telephone company records (such as magazine subscription databases), but the information is never entirely up to date. Furthermore, you will not find the names and addresses of persons with unlisted phone numbers in these databases unless the information comes from a non-telephone company source.

Information you can find through a people finder search might include the name as listed in the phone directory (and an alternative name used by the subject in the value-added records), phone number, apartment number, street address (including zip code), the neighborhood's wealth ratings, and alternate contact information for the subject, such as a fax number, email address, and Web page address.

By using an online people finder, you can search by first name or middle name alone, as well as by surname alone. You can also search for name spelling variations and by partial spellings (enter "ill" and find *Hillary* and *Bill*). You can perform similar searches for a partial address (for instance, if you have a street name but not the city name, or if you have only part of the street name or need to search for variations of the street name). After you have located the person, the people finder will even provide a map of his or her block and the surrounding streets, with instructions on how to get there.

Finding Email Addresses

Most people-finder services search for email addresses as well as for phone numbers (indeed, email addresses are being listed in the print telephone directories in some localities). Probably the best online service for finding email addresses is www.bigfoot.com, which claims the largest and most accurate listings. If you want to search for your subject's email address by way of his or her hobbies or the languages he or she speaks, www.whowhere.com is a good choice. To conduct a search using multiple services, go to www.theultimates.com and click the "Ultimate Email Directory."

Internet Versions of Directory Assistance Databases

WhoWhere Inc.'s site at www.whowhere.lycos.com gives you access to the same continuously updated databases (including the daily additions, deletions, and "moves") that the regional Bell companies use in answering Directory Assistance requests. The service costs $9.95 per month for the first 22 requests and 45 cents for each request thereafter.

Unlike the online and CD-ROM finders based on print directories, this service tells you whether or not a person has an unpublished number. The ability to confirm that the subject indeed lives in (or at least has phone subscriber service in) a given area can be the first step in a successful trace.

CD-ROM Telephone Directories, Street Atlases, and Gazetteers

The nationwide CD-ROM telephone directories draw on the same telephone print-directory-based databases as do the online people finders. They are not very expensive, and it makes sense to purchase one if you plan to do sweep searches for people with the same last name. The most highly regarded of these products is Select Phone; for details, go to www.infousa.com.

Digital street atlases of the entire United States are also available on CD-ROM. They can provide you with a clear understanding of the streets surrounding a given address and can also help you find an address when you only have limited information (a street name but no city, or only a partial street name). The top products in this field are DeLorme's Street Atlas U.S.A., Microsoft's Streets, and Rand McNally's Streetfinder Deluxe.

From the U.S. Geological Survey, you can purchase *The Digital Gazetteer of the U.S.*, a CD-ROM version of the government's Geographic Names Information System (GNIS). This database, which is also searchable online at mapping.usgs.gov, includes about two million names of past and present places, features, and sites throughout the United States with exact location, alternative or former names, and variant spellings of the official name. The database includes towns, villages, rivers, creeks, mountains, TV towers, shopping centers, cemeteries, campus dormitories, churches—almost everything except streets, roads, and railroads. It is useful in finding or backgrounding someone if you have only a fragmentary address, or if the village in which your subject was born is now 20 feet under the waters of a reservoir, or if the rural church where he or she was christened has been destroyed to make way for a shopping mall or interstate highway. This resource is best used in tandem with one of the TIGER-based street atlases, which include most of what the GNIS excludes.

Out-of-Town Phone Directories on Microfiche

UMI's Phonefiche is an annual microfiche collection of white-page and yellow-page directories from across the country. It includes over 2,600 domestic directories covering nearly 50,000 communities (about 90 percent of the nation). Your local library will probably have purchased a selective Phonefiche package (for example, the directories for your own state plus those for the largest cities nationwide). Phonefiche includes a community cross-reference guide: You can look up any community in the United States, and the guide will tell you which multicommunity phone directory or directories cover that community or any portions thereof. Likewise, you can look up any phone directory by title—say, the Grand Traverse Bay Area directory in Michigan—and get a list of all the communities covered in whole or in part by it.

Advantages of Phonefiche: It does not have the errors of the online people finders, which use second-hand data; it allows you to see the full text, size, and placement of yellow-page classified ads (important if you are trying to trace a person by his or her business or probable type of employment); and, because there is no storage problem with microfiche, your public library is likely to keep the back editions, thus allowing you to easily find a person's previous addresses.

Social Security Death Index and State Death Indexes

If you are searching for someone who has been missing for many years, or for an adoptee's birth mother, first check to see whether the person is still alive. The Social Security Death Index (SSDI), based on the Social Security Administration's death benefits masterfile, includes records of 60 million deaths of SSN holders, mostly since 1962 (the year in which reporting of this information became mandatory). The SSDI provides the deceased's birth and death dates, SSN, the zip code in which the deceased resided at time of death, the state and year in which the deceased's SSN was originally issued, and the zip code to which the last benefit was mailed (this is usually the zip code in which a spouse, grown child, or other close relative lived at the time). The SSDI is searchable for free at www.ancestry.com and www.familytreemaker.com. Family Treemaker also includes the SSDI in its Ultimate Family Tree CD-ROM package.

Death indexes from several states covering recent decades are available online at www.ancestry.com. The states include Connecticut, Kentucky, Michigan, North Carolina, Ohio, and Vermont. Here you may find names of people who died without SSNs and, in some cases, people who died before the SSA began to systematically compile such information. In some other states, recent death indexes may be available at the vital statistic bureau office (see section 10.1, "Vital Records").

When the Subject Can't Be Found Using Any of the Preceding Methods

In most cases in which you can't find someone, the problem is that the person you are seeking has had an unlisted phone number for many years and has kept a fairly low profile in other respects. But such individuals almost invariably have generated public-access records of some sort (something as simple as a water connect or a pet license), as well as having provided their address in loan or credit card applications (the address then ends up in the "above the line" or "header" information in credit reporting agency databases).

Later chapters of this book give instructions for how to search public-access records in your own locality, but if you don't know which locality a person is in, or if the locality is far from where you live, you may need to contact a public records retriever or online records vendor (go to www.publicrecordsearch.com for a comprehensive directory of such services). An online vendor can provide you with a gateway to a wide range of investigative databases. You can then do your own searching (subject, of course, to federal privacy restrictions and the varying privacy laws of the state in which your computer is located and the state in which the records are located).

4.3 Searching the Phone Directories

For finding local telephone numbers, the print directory is often more convenient than an online or CD-ROM search. It also may produce more accurate results because the online and CD-ROM directories take their data from second-hand sources (companies that scan in or directly input the data from print directories, sometimes generating errors that are not in the source book). In addition, back-edition print directories (usually on microfilm) are absolutely essential in tracing a person's past whereabouts and finding his or her relatives, former neighbors, and childhood friends as well as in finding his or her unlisted phone number.

For out-of-town listings, you will probably use online or CD-ROM directories, but you should never rely exclusively on a single service or product: Each database is different, not only in the accuracy and up-to-dateness of its listings taken from phone directories but also in its value-added information (apartment numbers, personal name variations, length of residence at the given address, and so on). When you use an electronic directory, don't be content to search by a single first and last name combination; search for all variations. If necessary, get an alphabetical listing of all persons within your search area who have the same last name as the person for whom you are searching.

Residential Listings

- Never assume that you have the correct spelling of a name; always check variant spellings. At the beginning of a list of same-spelling surnames, the hardcopy white pages often provides "see also" references to the variant spellings. For instance, in the Manhattan white-page directory, we look for Larry Kahn. At the beginning of the "Kahn" listings, we find the notice, "KAHN SEE ALSO CAHN, CONN." Your directory may not always include such notices, however. And a notice, if given, may not include all variants (the *New Dictionary of American Family Names* is useful in these cases).

- Familiarize yourself with the alphabetization and listing system of the particular directory you are using. For instance, in the Manhattan white pages, we find that initials precede first names (that is, "Jones, S.R." comes before "Jones, Samuel"); some abbreviations are listed alphabetically as if they were spelled out (that is, "St. Michel, Jacques" is listed as if it were spelled "Saint Michel, Jacques"); and names with prefixes are usually treated as a single word regardless of whether the person spells it with or without spaces (for example, "De La Cruz" and "DelaCruz" are listed in alphabetical order according to first name, with "DelaCruz, Amanda" coming before "De La Cruz, Anna").

- If you don't find the subject under his or her surname, look under the spouse's birth name and under linked names (for example, Mary Brown-Smith, Mary Smith-Brown, John Brown-Smith, John Smith-Brown, John & Mary Brown-Smith, and so forth). For more tips regarding such name variations, see section 7.1, "What's in a Name?".

- If you cannot find subject's first name in the listings under his or her surname, then check subject's middle name and nickname, if known. If you know only the initial for the subject's middle name, call all listed first names in the same-surname list that start with that letter (if you were searching for William D. King, a freelance writer, this is how you would find him—listed under Dennis King). Also check other variations; John Morris Jones could be listed as J. Morris Jones, J.M. Jones, J. Jones, or M. Jones. Note that if the subject is a woman, she may be listed under the male version of her name (for example, Stephen instead of Stephanie) or a similar-sounding male name (for example, Melvin instead of Melanie) to avoid sexually harassing phone calls from strangers. (Using an initial for the first name cannot provide this protection because telephone harassers usually assume that such a listing is for a woman.) Note that an online people finder that merges telephone directory information with data from other sources may provide one or more of a telephone subscriber's name variations, including the one for which you have been searching.

- If the same-surname list in the white pages is a long one, study the entire list carefully—it is easy to miss the crucial name. For instance, Zebulon Smith's name may not be under "Smith, Zebulon"—it may be back at the beginning of the list under "Smith, *Albert* Zebulon" or "Smith, Albert Z." Also, the subject's first name may be listed following the first name of his or her spouse in a joint listing: for example, "Smith, Zelda & Henry" (if you don't know Henry's wife is named Zelda, you will miss Henry altogether unless you search all the Smiths to the very end).

▪ Never assume that a number is unlisted, even if you think the person has some reason to need an unlisted number. On more than one occasion, I have been contacted by ace investigative reporters who complained about how many calls they had to make to get my number. When I asked them why they didn't just look in the Manhattan phone book (in which I am the only Dennis King listed) they told me that they just "assumed" I would have an unlisted number because I write about cults.

Business Listings

Always check under the subject's name in the business as well as the residential white pages. Millions of Americans, especially freelancers and self-employed professionals, have business listings under their own names. These names are usually listed in the same format as they are in the residential directory—with surname first—although alphabetized in sequence with corporate names and other nonpersonal names.

If you don't find your subject listed by surname in the business white pages, search for the names of any corporate or other business entities that seem to include the subject's name or his or her spouse's name in whole or in part. If subject John R. Simpson is operating a small home business, he might call it Simpson Enterprises, John R. Simpson Enterprises, Robert (his middle name) Simpson Enterprises, or JRS Enterprises, among other permutations. Note that the white pages are often inconsistent in handling the article "the"; if subject Simpson runs a literary agency out of his apartment, he might call it The Simpson Agency but the phone directory might list it as "Simpson Agency, the" (or vice versa). In addition, you should watch out for possessives: Simpson's Design Shop may be listed as "Simpson Design Shop" (or vice versa). Also watch for inadvertent transposition of names in home business listings; for example, John Simpson Co. becomes "Simpson John Co."

If you have a good idea what kind of business your subject might be engaging in, you could conduct your search in part using the yellow pages. For conducting your business-listing search with maximum efficiency, however, use the online yellow pages or Select Phone.

Subject's Previous Telephone Number

If your subject has recently moved but you don't know his or her new address, always call his or her old telephone number. Often, there will be a recording that tells you the new number. Or the old number may have been taken over by another member of the subject's previous household (for example, a roommate) who stayed when the subject moved out, and this person may know the new number. Or the old number may now be listed in the name of a friend, relative, or sublessee of the subject who moved in when your subject moved out, and this person likewise may know how to contact your subject.

The new holder of the phone number may stay in touch with the subject for years, so if the last listing for your subject in the local phone directory was 5 or 10 years ago, you should still call that number. At the least, you may get a stranger who was reassigned that telephone number and who may have received other calls from people trying to reach the subject. If this new holder of the number is a gossipy type, he or she may have picked up some interesting information.

Sweep Searches

Unless you have information to the contrary, begin your search with the localities closest to the subject's last known address: The overwhelming majority of people who move their residence remain within the same metropolitan area or state. This means checking all communities and area codes in the greater metropolitan area in which you think the subject is located, including "exurbia" as well as suburbia. People nowadays commute longer and longer distances—especially those who can "telecommute" part of the time. In searching for the residential address of someone believed to be working in the New York City area, I would check eastern Pennsylvania as well as New Jersey, Connecticut, and downstate New York. To find the residence of someone who is said to be working in the Washington, D.C., area, I would check West Virginia, Delaware, and eastern Pennsylvania as well as Virginia, Maryland, and Washington itself. If you are using a CD-ROM directory, make sure that you have the latest update and always supplement your CD-ROM search with online people-finder searches.

Directory Assistance can be useful in such a search because it uses phone company databases updated on a daily basis. However, Directory Assistance has a high rate of errors for a variety of reasons. If the operator tells you there is no listing under a certain name, always call back and try another operator (or, if your first request was processed by computer only, get a human operator and try again).

A request to Directory Assistance works best if you have the exact name under which the subject is likely to be listed or if the surname is an uncommon one. Note that you don't have to worry too much about correct spelling as long as you have the correct pronunciation; Directory Assistance automatically searches all variant spellings. Another virtue of Directory Assistance is that it will tell you whether a number is unlisted; thus you will at least know that the subject (or someone with the same name as the subject) is a phone company subscriber within the area code or the larger region that was searched.

To obtain a person's address as well as his or her number from Directory Assistance, you have to speak with a human operator. If a computer-generated voice answers your call, simply mumble the name you want searched in an unintelligible manner. The computer will automatically shift you to a human operator. However, this person will shift you back to the automatic voice response system the instant you give him or her the name you want searched. You should thus request the address as well as the number *before* you provide the operator with the name you want searched.

If you have to search a long list of same-surname individuals, a CD-ROM database may be your best approach. But whether you use an electronic directory, a collection of print directories, or Directory Assistance, always search the *entire locality*. Too often in past years I failed to find someone because I looked only in the New York City borough directories and the Nassau and Suffolk County directories—and was too lazy to reach up to the higher shelf for the Westchester and New Jersey directories. This mistake can also be made with a CD-ROM if, in searching for a person with an extremely common surname, you search community by community and fail to cover the entire metro area; or if, in using Directory Assistance, you fail to search all the area codes within the given search area.

Calling Lists

With the help of Select Phone, you can compile a same-surname calling list for any city, state, or region (or any zip code) you think is worth searching. And you can establish priorities based on various permutations of the subject's name or the spouse's name. If you are searching for George Morgan, you can isolate all the Morgans that include "George" or "G." as a first name or middle name or as part of a joint name. Even if you don't find *your* George Morgan, you may find an unrelated person with the same name who has received numerous phone calls in the past for your subject and may know how to reach him or her. (This other George Morgan may also recall news articles about the subject because his own friends and co-workers may have asked him, "Was that *you?*")

If you strike out with the Georges and Gs, don't give up. Try the various permutations for George's wife's first and middle names and also her maiden name. If this doesn't work, go to the full list of Morgans in localities in which relatives of George are most likely to be found, such as George's home city or state, other cities or states where he has lived for substantial periods (he may have moved there precisely because a relative was already there), and the area in which he lived most recently before dropping below the horizon.

Using this last method, you may find not only relatives of George but George himself: The number you call may be his own home with the phone listed under a middle name or nickname—or the name of another family member—that you didn't know about. If not, you may hit on a relative or ex-wife who will give you George's address and phone number on the spot.

If you're still stumped, try all the people with the same surname as George's wife before her marriage to him; you may find one of her parents or siblings, or her previous husband or previous in-laws.

4.4 You Have a Number and a Name, but Not the Street Address

Your subject may have chosen to list his or her phone number in the white pages without an address or with only a partial address (street but no number) or with a post office box number in lieu of a street address. In such cases, you can often find the subject's address through an online people finder that includes value-added information from non-phone directory sources. If this doesn't work, there are several alternatives you can try: If you reverse the number in the crisscross directory, you may find that another member of the household has a listing for the same number with the full address included. Or, returning to the white pages, you may find a single listing (with the address included) for a person having a different phone number from, but the same unusual surname as, your subject. Noticing that the first three digits of this person's number signifies a telephone exchange within the same exchange zone or central office service area as your subject's, you hypothesize that this person is either the subject's spouse or one of the subject's teenage children. So you call the *subject's* number and ask for the person listed at the other number; if the latter comes to the phone, you have just found your subject's street address (*unless* the other person is a relative who happens to be visiting your subject at the moment you call).

Sometimes a person who withholds his or her street address from the residential listings will provide that same address for a home business listing (see section 4.3). Although the white pages will not tell you whether or not the business telephone is actually located in the subject's home, you can look in the crisscross directory to see whether the business address is in fact in an exclusively residential neighborhood.

The street address (or the *full* street address) can also be obtained sometimes by looking in a back edition of the phone directory. Generally, if the number listed in the old directory corresponds to the number in the new one, the address in the old directory will be the same as that deleted from the new directory (unless the person moved within the same telephone exchange and asked to keep the previous number).

Note that you can determine the exchange zone or central office service area of your subject's phone service using the first three digits of his or her phone number. Your telephone directory may provide listings of these exchange numbers (not to be confused with the area code number) which you can use to match them to the appropriate city neighborhood or suburban community. If this information is not included in your directory, you can obtain it from the phone company or your local public service commission.

This information can help narrow your search: If you want to contact George Smith, and you believe he lives in a certain town in Nassau County on Long Island, and then if you find a "Smith, G." listed without an address, but with an exchange number corresponding to an eastern Suffolk County exchange zone, you can assign this listing a low priority.

Under some circumstances, the exchange number will not actually correspond to the exchange zone normally designated by that number. This might be the case if a residential or business customer has a "foreign exchange" line that provides him or her with service from a central office other than the one that usually serves the given address; or if a customer pays a premium to obtain a customized number corresponding to letters that spell out a message.

4.5 You Have a Number, but No Name or Address

If a phone number is listed in the telephone book, it is easy to reverse it and find out the name and address provided for listing purposes by the subscriber. In the past, this was done with the local crisscross directory; today, it can be done on a nationwide basis (any listed number from almost any community in the United States or Canada) using online people finders and CD-ROM products such as Select Phone.

Unlisted numbers are occasionally found in the online or CD-ROM directories if the database includes information from back-issue phone books. In most cases, the inclusion of such a number will occur because the phone subscriber changed the status of his or her number from listed to unlisted *without* requesting a new number.

If you don't find the number in the electronic directories, check back issues of the local crisscross directory. By going back several years, you may spot the number. If you do, there are two possibilities. First, the status of the number (as just mentioned) may have been changed from listed to unlisted by a subscriber to whom the number has been continuously assigned. Second, the original assignee of the number (listed) may have moved to another address, with the number then being reassigned to the current assignee (unlisted). You can tentatively determine which is the case by looking in the local telephone directory for the year *following* the one in which the number last appeared in the crisscross directory to see whether the person previously listed as having the number in question is now listed at a new local address with a new number.

If the unlisted number is from a community still covered (or until recently still covered) by a city directory, the latter can be helpful if it includes numerical telephone listings along with its street listings. If the local city directory no longer includes unlisted numbers, consult the most recent back edition that did include them.

Note: If you're a reporter who's just met a rather seedy source, a woman who's just met a guy in a bar, or anyone else dealing with a stranger, always reverse the telephone number they give you. Doing so may help you determine whether the person has provided you with his or her real name.

(Of course, you may find that the number is just an answering service, a fact that may or may not have any sinister import; or you may find that the number is listed in the name of another member of the subject's household.) Note that scam artists and other dubious folk frequently give out their real telephone number along with a phony name, figuring that most people don't know anything about reverse directories and would be too lazy to use them even if they did know.

4.6 Subject Has an Unpublished Number

Private investigators often have informants inside the phone company who will provide them with unlisted numbers. The publisher of a weekly I once worked for often obtained unlisted numbers through the Republican Party's county chairman, who probably got them in turn from some patronage hack in the criminal justice system. However, there are other ways to get an unlisted number—some of them almost ridiculously simple.

Finding Subject's Unlisted Home Phone Number

- Check the online "people finders" or information broker databases, which may include unlisted numbers obtained from old telephone books or from nontelephone company sources such as the "above-the-line" or "header" information in credit-reporting agency databases (see section 2.6, "Computers and Databases"). Even if such a search doesn't turn up the unlisted number, it may at least give you the subject's home address. Then you can use the street directory to find the numbers for the subject's closest neighbors and induce one of them to give you the unlisted number on a pretext.

- If Directory Assistance tells you the number is unlisted, always look in the phone book. The subject may have obtained his or her unlisted number very recently. If the subject has remained at the same address, you may find that the previously listed number is, in fact, the very number that is now unlisted (it costs less to unlist the old listed number than to get a new unlisted number). If the subject obtained his or her unlisted number on the occasion of a move to a new address, this number will, in most cases, be a new one; however, if you call the old number you may get a recording that provides the new one for the subject's friends and business associates. If the recording merely says the old number has been disconnected, try again in a few days—the new number may not be revealed on the recording simply because the telephone at the subject's new residence has not yet been installed.

- If there is no listing for the subject in the current phone directory, search the back editions at the public library. The subject's unpublished number for the past 10 years may have originally been his or her published number.

- Call the listed numbers of all persons with the same surname in the white pages. If the subject has several relatives nearby (especially in a smaller population center), this trick often produces quick results. You just assume that you have the right number and say, "I'd like to speak to Marvin Klenetsky." They say, "Oh, you have the wrong Klenetsky; he's at..." and they give you the number automatically. Unlisted numbers are not exactly a deep secret; often the relative doesn't even know that the number he or she is giving out is unlisted.

- The unlisted number may be found in a city directory. Unlike crisscross directories (which are based on the telephone white pages), city directories compile their information on each household using the survey method. The survey taker asks the member of the household contacted to provide, among other things, the household's phone number. Only a very small percentage refuse to give out the number, even if it is unlisted in the white pages. (If they do refuse, the city directory will at least tell you the address of the family and possibly the place of employment of the head of household.) In most large cities, city directories have been discontinued for many years. However, if you know that your subject has lived in the same home for decades but has never been in the phone book, you might want to check the final edition of the city directory on microform at your public library. The subject's current unlisted number—its unlisted status maintained all these years—may be in that final 1962 edition. Of course, a person who has lived in one spot so long will probably be very well known to his or her neighbors. You thus might find it easier to call longtime neighbors listed in the current street directory to obtain the number.

- Check public records at the county courthouse or town hall. The unlisted number may be included in, say, a permit application.

- Some corporations distribute to their employees internal phone directories that give the home addresses and phone numbers of each. These directories often include phone numbers and addresses not listed in the telephone company's white pages. Thus, if you know where your subject works or used to work, you might try to get the number and address from another past or present company employee who has a copy of the directory. Note that such directories are frequently obtained by personnel agency headhunters who use them to call around to see whether anybody is interested in moving to a new job.

- If the subject is an alumnus or alumna of a private school, university, or professional college, his or her home number may be listed in the alumni directory or a class reunion directory. The subject may have provided this information because it never occurred to him or her that the directory would be consulted by anyone except old classmates.

- If the subject is a college student or a member of a college faculty or support staff (or the spouse of same), check the campus directory; the home number may be listed here even if it is unpublished in the telephone company's white pages.

- If you can induce the subject to call you at a telephone line that has Caller ID, you may be able to discover his or her unlisted number depending on what type of call he or she makes and whether or not he or she uses the Caller ID blocking code (see section 4.34).

Finding Alternative Phone Numbers and Other Contact Information

- When you call Directory Assistance, always ask for any business listing in a person's name as well as the residential listing. Often the former will be listed when the latter is not, perhaps even at the same residential address. (And if you call the business number during off-hours, a recording may give you the unlisted residential number even if the business line is located elsewhere.)

- Just because one resident of the household has an unlisted number doesn't mean the others do. Check in the phone book for separate phone numbers under the names of other family members. You may find that Mr. X's wife has a home business that necessitates a separate business line in her own rather than in her husband's name. Note that over 17 per cent of U.S. teenagers today have their own phone lines— and are generally less likely than their parents to request an unlisted number.

- The subject may have a weekend or vacation home or a *pied à terre*. Although Ms. Jones keeps the phone number of her main residence unlisted, she may not have thought to do likewise with the number at her getaway cottage.

- The subject may have a home fax number, a personal (non-business) email address or Web page, one or more cellular or car phone numbers, or a beeper number. If your aim is to contact the subject outside his or her office environment (to see whether he or she might become a whistle blower), this alternative contact information (some of which is currently available using online people finders and even hardcopy phone directories) may serve your purpose even better than might the unlisted number. (After all, some potential sources might feel threatened or violated if called out-of-the-blue by a reporter who shouldn't, but does, have their unlisted home number.)

4.7 The Phone Number Is in Another Name

As we now know, a male subject's phone number may be listed under his wife's maiden name. It may also be in the name of another family member, a live-in lover, or a roommate. This may be simply for convenience—Janet agrees to handle the phone bills while Harold takes care of the utilities. Or it may be that Harold is ducking bill collectors, in which case both phone and utilities may be in Janet's name. It also may be that when Harold and Janet moved from their previous address, Harold owed the phone company hundreds of dollars. Getting the phone in Janet's name is thus a tactic to evade that bill and also avoid paying a deposit on the new phone service. In general, finding Harold under these circumstances will be a serious problem for tracers only if Harold met and became involved with Janet *after* skipping out on his last address (otherwise, one of Harold's previous friends, neighbors, or co-workers could be induced by a pretext question to describe her or give you her name).

Sometimes people will list their number under a variation of their name which you would not easily recognize, or even under a fictitious name. Using such a name means that a searcher cannot verify through Directory Assistance that the subject is living within the given area code (which *can* be determined if the subject has an unpublished number in his or her own name). However, if the account name (the name of the person who is billed) is nevertheless the subject's real name, you may be able to find him or her through a source inside the phone company. If not, the subject can often be found by going to various public records—such as tax assessment or voter registration lists (see section 4.22)—where the subject's real name may be listed. If you get the address from one of these lists, you can then go to a crisscross directory and find out the name and telephone number listed for that address. Chances are this will be either the fictitious name the subject is using or else the subject's wife's maiden name. Call the answering machine and see what name, if any, is given with the message.

If Mr. X is living under a false identity, tracing him through telephone and crisscross directories and county courthouse records will become extremely difficult if not impossible. You will need to focus your attention on people from his former life with whom he remains in touch. More on false identities can be found in section 7.6.

4.8 Subject's Listed Address Is Not His or Her Real Address

Phone customers who use a telephone answering service or a mail-receiving service may list the address of this company as their own address in the white pages or other directories. If you cannot visit the address, look in the crisscross directory to see whether the neighborhood is residential or business, and also to determine whether the particular building includes both businesses and apartments or is exclusively an office building (of course, an answering service or mail-receiving service might operate out of someone's private home, depending on the local zoning laws *and* whether or not the person is obeying those laws). You should also check the yellow pages to see whether any of the local answering or mail-receiving services are located at this address. If there is indeed such a service at the given address, note that the subject may have chosen it because of its proximity to his or her real home or place of work (in some parts of Manhattan, mailbox rental services are located on the street level every few blocks).

A residential telephone customer may also have a phone line at and a directory listing for a private home where he or she doesn't really live or spend any time. This could be done for a variety of reasons. For instance, Mrs. Smith may have a telephone installed in her own name at a friend's house in a neighborhood with good schools as part of a scheme to make her kids eligible to attend those schools rather than the blackboard jungle in her own neighborhood. (If she's going to be careful about this, it means putting her *real* home phone in someone else's name.)

Another example concerns Mr. and Mrs. Jones, the yuppie co-op owners who are temporarily renting their apartment to Ms. Price without the knowledge or permission of the co-op board, while themselves living at another address. The Joneses maintain the phone in their own name at the co-op while listing the number at their real place of residence under Mrs. Jones's maiden name. Ms. Price uses the phone listed under the Jones's name as her own phone (giving the number to her friends, for instance) but if anyone from the building management or the co-op board calls, she says she's the cleaning lady.

If you need accurate information about a residential address, never rely solely on the white pages. Cross-check the address against other records systems.

4.9 Subject Has No Phone

Almost 6 percent of American households lack telephone service. This includes about 200,000 Americans in isolated rural areas. It also includes low-income people in urban areas: A 1993 survey found that 20 percent of the homes in New York City's poorest neighborhoods were without phones. In some cases, this may not be simply because of poverty: Illegal aliens often don't apply for phone service because they fear the Immigration and Naturalization Service and also because their need for phone service for overseas calls to family members is adequately served by the many storefront phone parlors that have sprung up in immigrant communities in recent years.

Often, people without phone service in urban areas can be found using databases inclusive of the poor: voter registration lists, landlord/tenant court index, and so on. Those without phones in isolated rural areas may be found through the county tax rolls, Department of Motor Vehicles records, hunting license rosters, as well as voter lists.

4.10 Postal Change-of-Address Notices

When they move, most people file a change-of-address notice with the post office so that their mail can be forwarded. Until 1994, anyone could obtain a person's forwarding address by sending a request for this information, together with a money order for $3, to the postmaster of the station responsible for mail delivery at the subject's old address. This method has been abolished, but an alternative method is still available: You can mail an envelope with your mail-box return address on it to the subject at his or her old address with the words "Do Not Forward—Address Correction Requested" stamped on the envelope.

Although change-of-address notices are kept at the local post office for only a limited period, the data is not destroyed. It goes into the U.S. Postal Service's National Change of Address System, a database that contains permanent change-of-address information on more than 25 million relocating customers. This information is not available to the general public, but the Postal Service does sell the tapes and frequent updates to more than a dozen mailing list companies, who use the data to keep their own lists up to date. Information vendors then buy access to these mailing list databases and merge the data therein with other information to create a value-added product. *Note:* The Postal Service now allows anyone who files a change of address notice to opt out of the lists provided to mailing list companies.

In using any present or future system for tracing people by way of postal or magazine subscription (or any other) change-of-address notices, be aware that the address you receive may not actually be the subject's new address but rather that of a closed-mouthed friend or of a mail drop or mail-forwarding service.

4.11 Searching for Subject Using His or Her Previous Address

A person can't always have been in hiding. If you believe your subject previously lived in your city, check the back editions of the local phone directory (as described earlier in this chapter). Start with recent editions and work backward (or with a long-ago address and work forward). Remember to follow the procedures used with the current phone book (the wife's maiden name, the parents' names, and so on). If the subject appears in a recent or not-so-recent back edition, call the number and see who answers.

If you need to search backfile directories in another city, you might use Phonefiche's nationwide backfiles of thousands of telephone directories dating back to 1976 (these may be available for at least the cities in your own region at your public library).

City directories and crisscross directories are often essential in tracing a person back through the years as well as for certain specific details about his or her household. The back editions may be available at the public library or the local historical society, sometimes in microform. If you only find the current edition, contact the publisher to determine whether there is a hotline for obtaining information from back editions. If this hotline cannot be used by nonsubscribers, note that your library is a subscriber and one of the reference librarians might make the request for you.

Essentially, there are three methods for using back-edition directories in finding people: First, find out who lived with the subject at his or her last listed household, track them down at their current address(es), and persuade them to give you the subject's current address (or at least a recent address); second, contact the current residents of the subject's former house or apartment and see whether they know anything; third, question the subject's former neighbors or the shopkeepers in his or her former neighborhood. Note that these techniques are valuable not only in finding people but also in compiling detailed background reports and in writing biographies of celebrities.

Finding Former Household Members

If the given locality was covered by a city directory at the time the subject lived there, the directory may list all members of the subject's former household and provide information that will help find those members today, such as their occupations or former places of employment. If the given locality was not covered by a city directory, you can still find some of the names of household members using the crisscross directory:

- The numerical section in back editions of the local crisscross directory can be used to find any multiple listings (both same-surname and different-surname) under the subject's former phone number; in addition, it can be used to spot instances of duplicate service (two people sharing the same phone number but with lines in different apartments or houses within the same telephone exchange) and instances in which a person who shared the phone chose to list an address other than the actual household's (for instance, a P.O. box) or no address at all.

- The street listings in the back editions of the crisscross directory can be used to find the name of anyone in the household who at any point had his or her own separate telephone account/line with a listed number (unless that person chose not to give an address or gave an alternative address in the listings).

The record of who lives where can only get more detailed now that phone companies are offering such services as Ringmate, by which you can add up to two separate incoming numbers to your telephone line, each with its own distinctive ringing pattern and its own directory listing. Because this service is an inexpensive way to relieve parents from having to answer the phone when Todd calls Lisa, a significant expansion of telephone directory listings for teenagers is almost inevitable.

In addition to the presence of teenagers in a household, separate phone numbers or multiple directory listings for a single phone number may occur under the following circumstances (among others): married women retaining their premarriage names for professional reasons, roommates sharing an apartment, adults living with their parents (or vice versa), renters or sublessees who live in the home while the owner or primary tenant is away, and businesses being operated out of the home (note that 20 million Americans operate part-time or full-time home businesses today). In addition, a separate phone account under a different surname at a private home may be that of the family that rents the basement apartment or of an individual who rents a room in the house.

Because crisscross directories do not include people with an unlisted number—or household members with no separate listing or separate number—you may want to supplement your search with other types of street listings that do not have this limitation. Your board of elections will have street-by-street and house-by-house listings of all registered voters. These listings (often sold to political candidates in computer printout form or on diskettes that contain the data for an entire assembly district) will include any member of a household who is old enough to vote and has bothered to register. The Department of Motor Vehicles databases sold to private vendors in some states may provide a list of every licensed driver or car owner at a given address. (If DMV records are unavailable in your state, try the local parking violations bureau index for a list of every scofflaw at your subject's current and former addresses.)

The New Residents of Subject's Former Home

If no one was listed at the previous address except the subject—or if none of the former household members will talk—it's time to go to the second stage of your crisscross/city directory search. Obtain from the street directory the name and phone number of the new occupant of subject's previous home and also of the closest neighbors on the block.

First check out the new occupants of the subject's former home. These people may be renting or subleasing from your subject (with a new telephone number in their own name, of course); they may have bought the house or co-op apartment from your subject and have a current address for him or her; they may have bought the house from a third party who acquired it from your subject and who knows the subject's current address; they may be renting from the same landlord from whom your subject rented. In this last case, ask them to give you the landlord's phone number (or the number of the rental office or managing agent, in the case of an apartment house). If the subject skipped out owing several months' rent, the landlord may provide you with information from the subject's rental application form—or from a credit check the landlord once ran on the subject—in the hope that you will reciprocate by giving the landlord the new address when you get it.

If the subject's last known residence was an apartment, the new tenant will often know nothing about his or her predecessor. Sometimes, however, the new tenant is a friend of the previous one and obtained the apartment on the latter's recommendation. Indeed, the current tenant may be subleasing from the previous one. Or if the apartment is a co-op or condo, the new tenant may be directly renting from the old tenant, who is now the apartment owner (of course, in this case, you can probably get his or her new address from the co-op board or the building management).

Crisscross directories often do not give the apartment numbers but only the phone numbers for residents of large apartment buildings. Often this information is available, however, from the online or CD-ROM people finders. Another way to find out which tenant now occupies the subject's former apartment is to ask the super. (The super usually lives in the building; just call any tenant at random and ask for the super's name.) If the super won't help you, go back to the crisscross directory, which tells you the number of years each telephone number has been listed. Call up all tenants who moved in around the time your subject moved out. (Note that this approach will work only if the new tenant of the subject's former apartment has a listed phone number.)

Former Neighbors

Next, try the subject's former neighbors. The latest crisscross directory will tell how many years each telephone number has been listed at a given address, so you can figure out which neighbors were around at the same time as your subject. Start with the next-door neighbors and also those directly across the street (the latter might be the most likely to have noticed the name of the moving van company). If these people all moved in after the subject moved out, start with the nearest neighbors who resided on the block at the same time as the subject.

If a former neighbor of your subject had or has an unlisted number, you will not find him or her in a crisscross directory (on a residential street of single-family homes, a missing number in sequence in the street listings may be your tip-off to an unlisted number). In such cases, however, you might find the neighbor's name and address (if not his or her phone number) using one of the electronic people finders. You almost certainly can find this information in the voter registration lists, property tax rolls, and other public records arranged by street address.

The old hardcopy crisscross directory system breaks down for our purposes when the subject lives at an intersection of two or more streets. How do you easily find the name, address, and phone number of the subject's next-door and across-the-street neighbors whose houses face other streets? And how do you identify the subject's backyard neighbor, who may have known the subject much better than his or her next-door neighbors did? The online people finders solve this problem with street-map databases, based on the federal government's TIGER street files, that will depict the streets surrounding any given block in the United States. The people finders will even show you the quickest way to reach a particular block from your current location and point out the house that is your supposed destination with an arrow. If you prefer, you can buy a CD-ROM version such as Street Atlas USA.

When you start calling residents up and down the subject's former block, you will hopefully find at least one garrulous and gossipy person who remembers the subject well. If so, let this person ramble awhile, even if he or she is slightly annoying: You never know what clues you might pick up. For instance, he or she may recall that the subject had a serious weight problem. Later, when you get a tip that the subject is living in Portland, you might want to check with weight-loss clinics in the Portland area.

If most of the current residents on the subject's former block are people who moved in after he or she left (which is frequently the case if a neighborhood has changed its ethnic composition), you will need to use a back-edition crisscross directory to identify individuals or families who lived on the block at the same time as the subject. You can then look up these people in the local telephone directory or online or CD-ROM directory to find their new addresses.

Neighborhood Stores

You can find businesses of various types in the subject's former neighborhood by using Select Phone and Streets USA (or their online equivalents) in tandem. Because there may have been a high turnover rate of small retail businesses in the given neighborhood, you will also want to check the back-issue crisscross directory for the subject's last known year of residence there. (This will not only save you unnecessary calls to businesses that did not yet exist when the subject lived there, it also may help you identify local businesses—or the offices of local professionals—that later moved to other locations.) Based on what you've previously learned about the subject, you can decide which businesses or professionals are most likely to remember him or her. If the subject is a pet lover, call up the nearest vet's office. If the subject's wife is especially fashion conscious, check with neighborhood boutiques. You might also try local auto dealers, video stores, and dry cleaners. Business establishments that are centers of local gossip, such as beauty parlors, should always be called.

If the subject left town owing money to a local merchant, there are two possibilities: First, the subject later paid by mail, in which case the merchant may remember the address on the check or the return address on the envelope. Second, the subject never paid up, in which case the merchant may cooperate by making inquiries for you among customers and other store owners.

Checking with merchants may be a long shot in areas where most shopping is done in vast malls; still, there is often an equivalent of the old corner store (or country store) for convenience shopping.

4.12 Tracking a Person Through His or Her Family, Friends, and Ex-Spouse(s)

Most people have a hometown (or, at least, a town or city where they spent a considerable period of time during their early years), and many stay in contact throughout adult life with one or more members of their family who have remained in the hometown. Likewise, most people establish families of their own; these family units may not remain intact, but even the worst reprobate usually maintains some kind of contact with his or her children.

Finding a Person's Hometown and Members of His or Her Family

When attempting to track a subject through former next-door neighbors (as just described), always ask whether they recall where the subject grew up. If they don't, you can find this information or clues to it in various records. For instance, the name of the subject's high school—and sometimes the subject's place of birth—will be included on job applications and résumés. Credit-reporting agency databases will often have the place of birth and may have a string of addresses for the subject going back to his or her hometown days. In many cases, the subject's Social Security Number is the best clue of all: It is coded to reveal the state of issuance (see section 7.4, "Making Use of the SSN Code"), which probably is a state in which the subject lived as a teenager or young adult.

If the subject has listed himself as "John R. Doe III," you could search the online white pages (see section 4.2) for the father or grandfather, obtaining all listings for "John R. Doe," "John R. Doe, Jr.," "John R. Doe, Sr.," "J.R. Doe," "J.R. Doe, Jr.," "J.R. Doe, Sr.," and various other permutations. In addition, if the subject has a very unusual surname, or a very unusual spelling of a common surname, you might use Select Phone to compile a complete nationwide list of everyone with this surname or spelling. And if you know the subject's home state, you might generate a list of every telephone subscriber in that state with the subject's surname, even if it's a rather common one.

When you call the same-surname people cold, begin with those in the subject's hometown if you know it. Start with persons with the same first name and middle initial (your subject might be a "Jr." without you knowing it). This method is not guaranteed, but there is a good chance that, with a few calls, you will find someone who is at least a cousin of the subject and will be able to steer you to the immediate family.

If you know the subject's mother's maiden name (see 7.1, "What's in a Name?"), you might also call people with that surname in the subject's hometown or home region to find maternal grandparents, aunts, uncles, and cousins.

You may find that the subject's family left the area long ago and that they are apparently scattered throughout the country. Nevertheless, the hometown records may give you their names and perhaps clues to where they live now. Back-issue city directories may tell you the names of everyone who lived in the household while the subject was growing up—his or her siblings, parents, perhaps a grandparent. (The city directory may also have information from that period on the households of aunts and uncles.) As described earlier, back-issue crisscross directories and white pages can also be used to gather the names of at least some former household members.

Society-Page, Obituary, and Other Clippings

You might also obtain articles pertaining to the subject or mentioning the subject's name in the hometown newspaper's morgue (see section 6.9, "Morgues of Local Dailies") or electronic archives (see section 6.4, "Newspaper Databases"), as well as articles relating to the other members of the subject's former household (as listed in the back-edition city directories) and other local people with the same surname as the subject. The articles may include information about the arrest of one family member and the winning of a lottery by another, but you will be looking mainly for an overview of the family. A society-page article about the subject's marriage will provide the names of his or her parents (possibly including the subject's mother's maiden name) and other family members. An article about a sister's wedding will give her married name, and the list of guests may fill in gaps in your own list of family members. An article about the parents' silver wedding anniversary may also be useful. In addition, an obituary notice about a parent or other family member may provide the names of all the subject's siblings (including the married names of his or her sisters) and their cities of residence at the time of the funeral. It may also list the subject's surviving aunts and uncles on the deceased parent's side.

If a daily newspaper does not have a morgue or a general index for its pre-electronic years, it may at least keep a card file of the obituaries it has printed. Large metropolitan dailies generally do not print obituaries for ordinary citizens, but you may find a brief mention in the paper's vital statistics column; also, an ordinary person's death may be mentioned as a news item if the death was a murder, auto accident, drowning, or the like. If you obtain the date of death from such news items (or from the Social Security Death Index), you could then look for an obituary in a suburban daily or an ethnic or neighborhood weekly. The city directory will have told you the occupation of the father or mother and possibly where they worked; you could thus search for an obituary in a local or statewide trade, professional, or labor union newspaper or in the house organ of the company where the deceased worked. You should also look for death notices placed in any of the preceding publications (including the metro daily) by grieving family members, friends, or co-workers and listing the names and cities of residence of the survivors, or a thank-you notice from the family in a newspaper issue following the funeral.

If the deceased family member is a college alumnus or alumna, the alumni association's newsletter may have published an obituary. An obituary may also have appeared in the class anniversary book of the deceased's college class.

Note that many county or state historical societies, state university libraries, and so on have compiled collections of well-indexed obituaries going back to the early 20th century.

Genealogical Records and Vital Records

You will most easily find decades-old obituaries, engagement and wedding announcements, and other family news in the local newspaper backfiles if you first get the names of family members and the dates of their births, marriages, and deaths from vital records indexes, genealogical databases, and various published genealogical works.

The giant Web site at www.ancestry.com is the most convenient place to begin. Here you can search the Social Security Death Index and various state death indexes (see section 4.2), the Military Index (records on almost 100,000 soldiers who died in Korea and Vietnam), and the Ancestry World Tree (9.7 million names of deceased persons, including many who died in recent years). For sources that cover living individuals as well as the deceased, go to the Biographical Reference Materials database at this same site. First search "50,000 Bibliographic Sources from the Library of Congress" (to find the titles of family name books, town or county histories, and published genealogies at the LOC that might include information on the subject and his or her family). Next search the "Genealogical Library Master Catalog," which covers the same types of publications for libraries throughout the United States. Third, search the online version of the *Periodical Source Index (PERSI)*, which covers over one million articles from almost 5,000 current and defunct periodicals in the genealogy field dating back to the 19th century (articles are indexed by family surname, locality, and research method).

Next go to the Web site for the Church of Jesus Christ of Latter-Day Saints (the Mormons) at www.lds.org. The LDS has compiled in its Family History Library the largest collection of genealogical records on this planet. Its FamilySearch system, long available on CD-ROM at the church's Family History Centers, is scheduled to go online by the time this book is published. The current CD-ROM system includes (and the new online system will include) the following:

- The Family History Library Catalog, which covers the holdings of the Family History Library in Salt Lake City. The catalog gives a breakdown by locality of over 2 million microfilm rolls of local records, including birth, marriage, and death indexes; wills, deeds, and land records; church records (such as baptismal records) from churches of all denominations; and over a million books and maps pertinent to genealogical research. Each local FHC will have the microfilm records for its own locality; microfilm for other localities can be borrowed from Salt Lake City for your viewing—it's one way to search old courthouse records in Oregon if you're stuck in New Jersey.

  The catalog also includes a comprehensive list of family name histories and genealogies (this list can be supplemented by *Genealogies in the Library of Congress* and *Complement to Genealogies in the Library of Congress* or the online versions of these two works at www.ancestry.com). Not every name in the Family History Library records is provided, but the catalog does list the major families included in each family history (you should look not only under the subject's surname but also, if you know it, under the wife's maiden name, the subject's mother's maiden name, and so on).

- The International Genealogical Index (IGI), which lists more than 250 million deceased people in the United States and overseas. Similar surnames are grouped together in the IGI under standardized spelling, with entries providing the event type (for example, *B* for birth, *M* for marriage) and the year and place of the event.

- The Ancestral File, an index to 35 million names (mostly deceased persons) extracted from pedigree charts or family group sheets and filed by genealogy enthusiasts around the world.

Note that the LDS has about 2,500 Family History Centers scattered throughout the United States and Canada. If the launch of the planned Web site is delayed, you can use the CD-ROM FamilySearch at the nearest center. (A list of centers is available at the LDS Web site, or you can look under the LDS listing in your local telephone directory.) Even after the Web site is up and running, you might still find it more convenient to use the local center because it will have a library of print volumes on genealogy (including *PERSI*) as well as microform records pertaining to your community and region. Plus, you can obtain advice from staff members and your fellow patrons regarding search methods and sources. An alternative is to use the genealogy section at your public library, your local historical society library, or your municipal or county archives. These facilities may have relatively recent county or state vital records indexes as well as old county tax rolls and other records that can help you trace the subject's family ties.

Biographical Dictionaries and Obituary Indexes

Another quick way to get information about a subject's family is to look in the same-surname listings in the *Biography and Genealogy Master Index*

(*BGMI*) (see section 5.2, "Biography and Genealogy Master Index"). Your subject may be an obscure person, but he or she may have a notable father, mother, or sibling who is listed in a half dozen biographical dictionaries (including *Who Was Who* for a deceased family member). All it takes is one notable in the family, and you've got a wealth of information—including the hometown—for family backgrounding purposes. (If the subject's father is listed, the entry may include the names and dates of birth of all the subject's siblings, as well as the name of the mother or stepmother.) For obituaries of notable persons, see the *BGMI* and the *New York Times Obituary Index* (the latter includes 353,000 names from 1858 to 1968). For full indexing of *Times* obituaries up to the present—and for indexing of *Times* articles on deaths from accident or murder—see the *Personal Name Index to the New York Times Index* (described in section 6.7, "Print Indexes to Newspapers and Periodicals"). Also see the UMI Obituaries database at www.ancestry.com; it includes the full texts of hundreds of thousands of obituaries appearing in over 85 newspapers since 1990.

Probate Court Files

Another way of getting information about a subject's family is through the local probate court, which administers estates, trusts, and guardianships and includes the office of the registrar of wills. Here you may find detailed information about the family and its finances. For the names of your subject's children (as well as of your subject's siblings), look especially at the wills of the grandparents. Also check whether the subject or any of his or her siblings ever filed a motion for conservatorship over an elderly parent's affairs (this is handled by the state district court rather than by the probate court in some jurisdictions). In an investigation some years ago, I discovered such an action in New York State Supreme Court, listed under my subject's name as plaintiff. In the microfilm records, I found the names and addresses of all six of my subject's siblings (his co-petitioners), most of them in the metropolitan area. This information proved invaluable in tracing my subject's real estate dealings under straw names.

Miscellaneous Records That Identify Family Members

Securities and Exchange Commission filings will list stock that the subject controls, as an insider owner, on behalf of his or her spouse, children, grandchildren, and other family members. U.S. Department of Labor Form LM-30 may list business dealings of a labor union official's family members. Department of Motor Vehicles records will reveal all owners of cars at a given address; this may include a son or daughter who owns one of the family cars in his or her own name. Board of Elections rosters will include all registered voters at an address, which may include the subject's spouse and any children 18 or older (in some localities, you can search these rosters going back decades on microfilm, either at the city or county archives or at the board itself). Limited partnership filings may list several family members as owners of shares in a particular partnership and may include records of a transfer of shares from the subject to a son, daughter, parent, or other family member or to a trust established on their behalf.

Tracing a Subject Through His or Her Ex-Spouse

The full premarriage name of the subject's ex-spouse may be found in the marriage index in the county where the marriage took place, and often in the marriage column of a local newspaper (along with the names of the subject's former in-laws). In addition, you can learn the names of ex-spouses (including an ex-wife's maiden name if listed as a middle name or as part of a hyphenated surname) in back-issue city, crisscross, and white-pages directories for the period in which the couple were together. You may find ex-spouses' names in the divorce and annulment index at the county courthouse and in the "header" material in credit-reporting agency databases. If you look in the court plaintiff and defendant indexes under the subject's name, you may find a child custody or other case in which the subject and ex-spouse are listed as adversaries. You may also find cases before the divorce in which the subject and former spouse were jointly sued by a neighbor or jointly indicted for growing pot in the backyard.

If a subject's first wife has not remarried, she may be listed in the phone directory under either her maiden name or her ex-husband's surname. If she has remarried and is using her new husband's name, but you don't know what it is, you can often contact her through her divorce attorney, whose name and address will be in the court file. You may also try to contact her through her parents, whose names were in the hometown newspaper marriage clippings. If she and her new husband have a teenage child from her previous marriage living with them, that child may have a separate telephone listing under the subject's surname. In addition, the remarried spouse may have retained her previous married name within certain record systems (for example, a department store credit card or driver's license) simply because it was too much bother to change it. And if she reverted to her maiden name temporarily before remarrying, she might retain this name for some of the same records systems *after* her remarriage (or for *all* records systems after her remarriage if she's become a feminist as a result of the first marriage's unpleasant aspects). Generally, however, the records systems will have her new address regardless of what name she is using.

If you are having trouble finding an ex-wife's maiden name (as when the marriage was a common-law one and there is no marriage license on file), check the following possibilities:

- She and your subject may have lived together before they adopted the same last name. During that period, she may have had a separate listing for their telephone under her maiden name or a previous married name. Or the subject may have moved in with her in an apartment where the phone was already listed in her maiden name.

▪ A teenage child may have adopted a hyphenated name (mother's maiden name/father's surname) even if the mother never did so. Look for a separate listing of the previous household telephone number (or a separate number at the same address) under the child's name.

▪ Couples may use hyphenated names temporarily or on isolated occasions for various reasons; you may spot some public record in which your subject and/or his wife did so.

In searching for a subject's ex-wife, don't be blinded by male chauvinist assumptions. Your subject may be an obscure person, but his ex-wife (indeed, his current wife) may have become quite a successful person. Check the local newspaper index, morgue, or electronic archives or search the NEXIS or DIALOG nationwide newspaper/magazine archives for articles about her. Look for her under both her married and maiden names in BGMI and in Biography Index (the cited dictionary entries or articles, if any, will often include the names of her children). If she is a professional or a businessperson, you may also find her in one or more professional or trade directories or rosters (see section 5.5, "Biographical Material Not Listed in the Master Indexes").

Tracing a Subject Through His or Her Children

If the subject's children are grown, check for current local telephone listings under their names. Note that after the split-up of their parents and the remarriage of their mother, these children (if they ended up living with the mother) might have adopted their stepfather's (or mother's same-sex domestic partner's) name, their mother's maiden name, a hyphenated version of their mother's/stepfather's (or mother's/domestic partner's) name, or a hyphenated version of their mother's/real father's name (see section 7.1, "What's in a Name?"). If the children had lived primarily with their father, of course, they might have chosen yet other variations.

Contacting Former Spouses and Relatives

Note that a subject hiding from the police or from bill collectors often has left a string of legal or common-law marriages and children in his or her psychopathic wake. However tragic this might be, it makes the investigator's job easier: Bitter ex-spouses are excellent sources of information, especially if the subject has skipped out on child-support payments or just skipped out period, leaving his or her erstwhile partner to raise a houseful of kids alone. However, not all marital breakups are like this, and some divorced couples even remain close friends. The ex-wife or ex-husband you contact may be quite loyal to the subject. Even if not, the "ex" may refrain for the sake of the children from providing any information harmful to his or her former spouse.

Before contacting any relative, ex-spouse, son, or daughter of your subject, plan carefully what you will say to them. If your reason for finding the subject is benign, and if the subject is not in hiding, a relative may either give you the subject's telephone number or pass along a message that you want to speak with him or her. But if the subject is hiding out, you may need to employ a ruse to obtain the information you need.

Subject's Close Friends from Years Past

If you can't find family members, you can still possibly trace your subject through childhood or early adulthood friends with whom he or she might have kept in touch. High school or college yearbooks will give the names of classmates; by noting who was on the same sports team or in the same fraternity or sorority with the subject, you can compile a list of classmates most likely to have kept in touch with him or her. You will find many of these individuals through the online people-finder databases. They in turn will often know how to reach others on your list. You might also try the alumni directories or class reunion directories of these schools (colleges and prep schools always have such directories, as do many public or parochial high schools).

A clipping from the local newspaper's society page will give you the names of the members of the bridal party at the subject's wedding. In addition, the clipping may tell where both the bride and the groom were employed at the time of the wedding; employees at those firms may still be in touch with them.

4.13 Local Churches and Other Organizations

Check with the church secretaries at local churches of the subject's denomination—they may have records regarding a transfer of membership. If you want to contact members of a subject's former congregation who might have known him or her well, you may be able to get names from the church secretary. Churches will often tell you just about anything about congregation members (except their sins).

Make similar inquiries with the subject's former civic club or fraternal lodge and any other organizations to which the subject or other members of the household belonged. You might even check with the scoutmaster of the subject's son's former troop.

4.14 Former Employers and Co-Workers

Your subject's former place of employment can sometimes be found in a listing for the subject in a back-issue city directory or in the Federal Election Commission's databases (see section 10.10, "Federal Election Commission Records"). Try calling the firm's personnel office to see whether they have a recent address for the subject. If they can't help you, go back to the city directory and see whether anyone on the subject's former block worked at the same firm during the same time period. Such a neighbor/co-worker might have known the subject fairly well. Even if this person doesn't have the subject's current address, he or she may at least remember some potentially useful personal trivia, such as whether or not the subject has a dog, and the name, color, and breed of the dog. (This can be useful in finding the subject if he or she is living under an assumed name with an altered personal appearance; you identify your subject by the dog's appearance—and by whether or not the dog still answers to its old name.)

Sometimes the city directory or the FEC records only tell you the subject's occupation without giving any place of employment. In such cases, you can look in the electronic yellow pages (searching by Standard Industrial Classification [SIC] code might be helpful here) and *Thomas Register of American Manufacturers* (online version at www.thomasregister.com) to find the names of firms in the given locality that would be likely to employ people in the subject's job category. If you are trying to identify a place where the subject may have worked several years ago (or even a decade or more ago), you should look in old editions of the yellow pages and the *Thomas Register* at the public library and then cross-check against the latest online edition.

4.15 Professional, Alumni, and Other Types of Directories

Professional and trade organizations, college alumni associations, and the reference book industry publish thousands of directories each year for the purpose of helping people with mutual interests find or keep in touch with one another. These works give current or recent addresses for tens of millions of Americans.

To use these resources, you will need a little background information about your subject; for instance, his or her occupation or profession, college alma mater, hobbies, and so forth.

Check every heading in *Directories in Print* that might pertain to your subject. Then call your public library's telephone reference service and ask them to look in the most likely volumes. If your library doesn't have a certain volume, call a library in another city.

Is your subject a full-time or part-time college teacher? The three-volume *National Faculty Directory* lists over 670,000 college teachers at more than 3,800 American and Canadian junior colleges, four-year colleges, and universities. Always check the annual supplement, which includes tens of thousands of new and updated listings. If the subject has retired or quit teaching, you may still find him or her in a back issue.

Is your subject a lawyer? The 27-volume *Martindale-Hubbell Law Directory* (or its CD-ROM counterpart) gives the business addresses of over 900,000 lawyers and law firms worldwide (over 800,000 in the United States and Canada), divided according to town, city, state, province, and country. You can use the online Martindale-Hubbell Law Locator for free (www.martindale.com) to find any lawyer in the directory.

Is your subject a physician? The AMA's *Directory of Physicians in the United States*, based on its Physician Masterfile, gives the address of virtually every licensed medical and osteopathic doctor in the United States. You can search a continuously updated version of this information using AMA Physician Select, a free service at www.ama-assn.org.

The variety of available directories is extraordinary, covering even very obscure professions, trades, and hobbies; I suggest that you spend some time browsing through *Directories in Print* to get an idea of the possibilities.

If the comprehensive national directory for a given profession does not include your subject's name, look in *Directories in Print* for the names of local, regional, or special-focus directories for your subject's profession. For instance, nonpracticing law graduates (especially those who never passed the bar) are not listed in the massive *Martindale-Hubbell*, but some of them may be found in such works as the *Directory of Women Law Graduates and Attorneys in the U.S.A.* (more than 25,000 names).

College alumni associations are one of the largest sources of directory-type listings. Virtually every college and university has an alumni directory that gives the names and current addresses of most living alumni as well as annual listings of recently deceased alumni. Alumni associations need alumni addresses for fundraising purposes and often pay search agencies to find missing alumni and to keep the rosters up to date.

If you know which college the subject attended, simply call the alumni office and ask them to look up the subject's address in the alumni association's latest directory. If they don't give out such information, try the college library or the off-campus public library, which will usually have a copy. If the book provides only an outdated address, you might find a more up-to-date one through the national office of the subject's fraternity or sorority. (To find out which fraternity or sorority this is, you'll have to persuade the librarian at the campus archives to dig out the yearbook for the subject's senior year; see section 11.1, "Backgrounding a Subject's Educational Past.")

Note that many alumni directories list not only graduates but also matriculants who dropped out, flunked out, or transferred. Thus, if Jane Doe is not listed (or is listed at an out-of-date address) in the alumni directory of the state university from which she received her bachelor's degree, you may still find her current address (or at least a more recent address than you started out with) in the directory of the community college she attended during her first two undergraduate years. And if she's not in either of these, she may be in the graduate alumni directory of the university where she studied for her master's degree. Alumni associations vary widely in their commitment to keeping their mailing lists up to date; thus, the more colleges or universities your subject has attended, the greater your chances of finding a current address.

If you find that the subject's current address is not in the latest published directory, the alumni office might be willing to check its update files for you if they think you have a legitimate reason for requesting the information. You'll probably get a better response to such a request if you make it clear that an office address (if available) rather than a home address would be sufficient.

Prep schools, and also many parochial and public high schools, have alumni directories; check these if you don't find what you need in the college directories.

High school class reunion committees sometimes compile directories of members of the class in question. To find out whether your subject's high school class has produced such a directory, call the administration office of the school in question and ask for the name and phone number of the chairperson of the class reunion committee.

A number of Web sites now offer searches for former high school classmates. You might try www.classmates.com, which purports to cover 30,000 high schools. A directory of such services can be found at www.inil.com/users/dguss/wgator.htm.

4.16 Electronic Business Directories

Most small businesses and professionals in the United States are included in the many free yellow-page services online, such as www.bigyellow.com or wwww.bigbook.com, or in CD-ROM directories such as Select Phone. These directories enable you to search for business names that include, in some form, the first or last name (or initials) of the subject or the names of the subject's spouse or children (see section 8.27, "Corporate, Partnership, and D/B/A Files"). They also make it easy to find the office addresses (which may also be the home addresses) of millions of physicians, lawyers, veterinarians, chiropractors, podiatrists, psychotherapists, and other professionals and quasi-professionals (including consultants of various types and freelance writers or photographers), as well as persons in a variety of service trades, from hairdresser to plumber, who do business under their own names.

4.17 Membership Rosters

If you have sufficient information regarding the subject's occupation and interests, you can seek help from trade, professional, labor, charitable, religious, hobby, or sports organizations to which he or she might belong. Thousands of these organizations maintain membership rosters (although perhaps not in the form of a directory sold to the public) as well as mailing lists of financial supporters.

Two library reference works that will orient you to the vast world of membership rosters and membership/contributor mailing lists (including even some offbeat ones) are the *Encyclopedia of Associations* and the *National Trade and Professional Associations of the U.S.* You might also check the Web directory of organizations at dir.yahoo.com/Society_ and_Culture.

Even if an organization does not give out members' addresses, they may be willing to forward a letter in which you ask the subject to contact you (see section 4.31).

4.18 Subscription Lists

A former neighbor of your subject recalls that the subject played the fiddle and often attended bluegrass conventions. You go to the *Standard Period-ical Directory* and look under the subject category "Music and Music Trades," where you find the *American Fiddler News*. If you can get someone at this publication to check the mailing list, it might include your subject's current address. (Also, you might ask them to check the membership roster of the American Old Times Fiddlers Association, which publishes *American Fiddler News*.) Note that some people-finder Web services use databases that include magazine subscription change-of-address information.

4.19 Licensing Agencies and Certification Boards

In any locality of the United States, the city, county, and state governments license hundreds of professions, trades, and types of business activity. The roster of license holders is a good place to search for your subject if you can figure out which licenses he or she is likely to have. For a full discussion of licenses, see sections 10.11, "Permits and Licenses," and 10.12, "Professional Licensing."

4.20 Department of Motor Vehicles Records and Other State Records

An abstract of a person's driver's license (if available in your state) will give you his or her address at the time of license issuance or renewal.

If you think that your subject has moved out of state, the DMV may have records of license transfers that will tell you the state to which he or she moved. You can then request from the latter state (if its records are open) an abstract of the new license, which will include either the subject's current address or a more recent address than the one you started with.

Note that many people who don't know how to drive or whose licenses have been revoked will apply to the Department of Motor Vehicles for a nondriver's state I.D. card.

In 1994, Congress passed the Driver's Privacy Protection Act, which provides individual auto owners and drivers with the right to opt out of any state system for providing personal information about themselves to the general public. The states were given until 1997 to comply. Some states decided to keep the records of persons not choosing the opt-out option open to the general public; others passed restrictions even stiffer than those in the federal law. (For more on this complicated situation, see section 10.2, "Department of Motor Vehicles Records").

Ironically, Congress had earlier passed a bill that allows people to register to vote when they apply for a driver's license (the "motor voter" law). Thus, many of the driver's license applicants who opt to keep the information on their license private are at the same time helping to create a new publicly accessible record on themselves: Voter registration information is not only available at local boards of election but is also offered nationwide (subject to privacy restrictions in some states) through the Aristotle Industries database (www.governmentrecords.com) and various public records vendors. Note also that any DMV records sold in bulk to public records vendors before the activation of the new federal and state driver-privacy laws will be useful for many years to come (as value-added data in various online records) in tracking people by their past addresses.

In addition to automobile and truck drivers' licenses, you might check licenses for the operation of recreational vehicles and motor boats and also hunting and fishing licenses.

4.21 Unclaimed Property Lists

Each state has an office of unclaimed property that maintains lists of persons (and their previous addresses) to which such property belongs. In New York State alone, about five million names and addresses are included. Property on these lists includes checking and savings accounts, real estate, term deposits, tax refunds, stocks and bonds, dividends, safety deposit boxes, and so on. Reasons why the property has become lost might include a misspelled name on an account, a postal delivery error, a marital breakup, a sudden job relocation to another state, or a relative dying without a will. In most states, these lists are published in newspapers and have been made available in hardcopy or CD-ROM form at municipal offices and public libraries. As of early 1999, 43 states are providing the lists online at their state government Web sites. A directory of these sites and other contact information for all states is located at www.unclaimed.org/offices/index.html.

To search the Pension Benefit Guaranty Corporation's list of persons owed unclaimed pension benefits, go to search.pbgc.gov.

For a search of the Bank of Canada's list of unclaimed balances from Canadian banks, go to www.bank-banque-canada.ca.

Although most of the addresses on such lists are outdated, the one for your subject may be newer than the one with which you began your search. And even if it's an *older* address than the one with which you started, it may turn up a former neighbor who has kept in touch with the subject through the years.

You can search a vast database of U.S. and Canadian unclaimed property lists from states, banks, and other sources at www.foundmoney.net. The results for all matches to a name cost $20. Certain records in this database extend back to the pre-World War II years, making it an important resource for tracking birth parents and long-lost siblings and other relatives.

4.22 Miscellaneous Local Government Records

If you've narrowed your search to a single locality, you can check various public records at the county clerk's office, the municipal building, the register of deeds office, and so on. Your options may include the tax assessment rolls, the county water commission's roster of accounts, the roster of sewer charges, and the "grand lists" (the latter are lists of persons paying taxes on valuable personal property such as autos, boats, and airplanes). You also might check the judgment docket, the wage garnishment index, the Uniform Commercial Code (UCC) filings, the federal tax lien index, the courthouse plaintiff/defendant indexes, and the roster of municipal employees.

If your subject is a low-income person, the voter registration lists may be your best bet. (The Democratic party registers millions of welfare recipients and other impoverished people every presidential election year.) You can often find noncitizens this way because those with children in the public schools are eligible to vote in school board elections in some localities. (For an online search of voter lists from across the country, go to the Aristotle database at www.governmentrecords.com.)

To find both low-income and moderate-income persons, check the county or municipal courts that handle claims for less than $20,000. Certain plaintiffs (such as finance companies and hospitals) may have filed cases against thousands of people over the years. If the index lists cases only by plaintiff, the defendants may be listed in alphabetical order under the plaintiff's name. (Note that in some cities, there will be a separate index of hospital liens.) To find the subject's home address, you may have to search through the court file for an affidavit filed by a process server for the opposing side.

If a large percentage of your city's residents are apartment renters, try the housing court index. Look under the subject's name and also his or her spouse's name (including maiden name) or live-in lover's name. To search housing court indexes for an entire metro area or state, check with one of the tenant-screening services used by landlords; a list can be found at www.publicrecordsources.com.

The scofflaw index is a marvelous tool for finding people of all socio-economic brackets. In New York City, every car owner who has an unpaid city parking ticket is listed, together with the address on his or her car registration at the time the ticket was issued. In years past, I often used the multivolume computer printout indexes at the county clerk's office in Manhattan; these include separate volumes for scofflaws who received their tickets in New York City but reside in New Jersey, Connecticut, or elsewhere. Backfile volumes are available, so even if your subject has paid up, you can find a listing. (Current listings are now searchable at a computer terminal, but the older records are still extremely useful for tracing a subject's past addresses and finding his or her past neighbors.)

The backfile of scofflaw index volumes, if such exist in your city, can be located in the municipal archives. Although the addresses may be years out of date, even in the current index, they at least will give you a place to start.

For journalists in a central city, scofflaw indexes are a quick way to locate residents of the suburbs and exurbs who have unlisted phone numbers. A large percentage of these people work in the city, and many others come into the city to shop or dine, getting parking tickets in the process.

Skip tracers recommend looking at the county roster of dog owners. In many localities, you can obtain a copy of the entire roster for a small fee.

A good rule of thumb: Begin your search with the records systems that list the largest numbers of local residents on a citywide or countywide basis with addresses updated annually (the tax rolls, for instance). Work your way down to the narrower and often harder-to-search records systems.

For further descriptions of the various courthouse and municipal records and their larger uses in compiling background reports, see Chapters 8, 9, and 10.

4.23 Mail Drops and Mail-Forwarding Services

As noted in section 4.8, the subject's supposed home address may turn out to be a mail drop located in an office building. If so, the mail drop may also be a mail-forwarding service that forwards the subject's mail to just about anywhere in the world. You can determine whether the company in question provides mail forwarding either by looking at its advertisement in the yellow pages or by a pretext phone call. You might also look in *How to Use Mail Drops for Profit, Privacy, and Self-Protection* (see bibliography), which includes a list of such companies and is widely circulated among individuals with a secretive bent. Be aware that a small number of these mail drops/mail-forwarding services are actually run by, or sell their forwarding address lists to, firms specializing in skip tracing. (The latter do reverse traces on the mail drop customers, find out to whom they owe money, and then sell the forwarding addresses to creditors.)

4.24 If Subject Is a Full-time RV Traveler

Many retired persons spend part of each year in recreational vehicles (RVs), traveling around the country. Over one million of them are full-timers, traveling year round without a fixed home. Such people will either use a friend or relative's address as their mailing address or use a post office box or a mail drop/mail forwarding service. In addition, thanks to satellite communications, most will have cellular phones and many will have faxes and computers in their RVs. They may keep in touch with relatives through email and may even have a Web page that provides pictures of the latest tourist sites they have visited. Most RV travelers are very law-abiding and are rarely trying to hide from anyone. Generally, their friends and relatives will tell you how to contact them if you can provide a legitimate reason for your request.

4.25 Trailer Rental and Moving Companies

If your subject has recently moved, ask the neighbors (or the doorman or super, if it's an apartment house) what they remember. Did the subject hire a small van or U-Haul-type trailer and do the moving with the help of friends? Or did he or she hire professional movers? Did the movers arrive in a panel truck or in a large moving van? If no one remembers the rental company or mover's name, you'll have to start calling the various companies in both categories listed in the local yellow pages.

4.26 Locating Present, Former, or Retired Military Personnel

You can locate many active duty and Reserve/Guard military personnel through the locator databases at www.militarycity.com/newsroom/databases.html. In addition, each military branch has a locator service that will tell you the military unit and installation to which the subject is currently assigned. You should provide the subject's full name, date of birth, SSN, and any other basic data you have gathered.

To find those on active duty in the Army, write to the U.S. Army World Wide Locator, 8899 East 56th Street, Indianapolis, IN 46249. For those in the Army Reserve or Inactive Reserve—and those retired from U.S. Army active duty, the Army Reserve, or the Army National Guard—write to the U.S. Army Reserve Personnel Command, One Reserve Way, St. Louis, MO 63132. For current members of the Army National Guard, write to the State Adjutant General of the given state.

For those on active duty in the Navy or in the Navy Active Reserve, write to the U.S. Navy Personnel Command, U.S. Navy Locator, 5720 Integrity

Drive, Millington, TN 38055 (the Navy will provide the U.S. land-based unit location only). For personnel retired from active duty or from the Navy Reserve, and those in the Individual Ready Reserve and the Inactive Reserve, write to the same address.

For those on active duty in the Air Force or in the Air Force Reserve or Air National Guard, or retired, write to the World Wide Locator, Headquarters AFPC/MSIMDL, 550 C Street West, Suite 50, Randolph AFB, TX 78150. (The Air Force will not provide the location of overseas personnel.) For retired Air Force personnel, send a letter in a stamped envelope with the person's name; the World Wide Locator staff will fill in the address and forward the letter.

For those on Active Duty in the Marines or in the Marines Active Reserve, write to the Commandant, U.S. Marine Corps, HQMC, MMSB-10, 2008 Elliot Road, Room 201, Quantico, VA 22134. For inactive Reserve personnel, write to the U.S. Marine Corps Reserve Support Command, 15303 Andrews Road, Kansas City South Airport, Kansas City, MO 63132. For Marines retired from Active Duty or the Reserve, write to Headquarters-USMC-MMSR6, 3280 Russell Road, Quantico, VA 22134.

For those on active duty in the Coast Guard or in the Coast Guard Reserve, write to the U.S. Coast Guard Locator Service, G-PIM-2, 2100 2nd Street S.W., Washington, D.C. 20593. For those retired from either Active Duty or the Reserve, write to the Retired Military Affairs Branch, CGPC-ADM-3, U.S. Coast Guard, 2100 2nd Street S.W., Washington, D.C. 20593.

When you know the base or post at which the subject is stationed, you can check with the locator at that facility, who may provide the subject's unit or ship assignment and work phone number. A directory of military bases and other military facilities in the United States, with zip codes, telephone information numbers, and base/post locator numbers, is included in Lt. Col. Richard S. Johnson and Debra Johnson Knox's *How to Locate Anyone Who Is or Has Been in the Military: Armed Forces Locator Guide* (see bibliography).

For overseas personnel, the servicewide locators provide unit location by post office zip code only. Johnson and Knox's book provides a list of zip codes matched to overseas bases/posts.

The service locators will forward letters to current armed forces members at home or abroad. To take advantage of this service, you must provide the basic identifying information just mentioned. If you already know the base/post where the subject is assigned, you can send the letter in care of the local base/post locator.

Records on all personnel discharged from Active Duty or Reserves (all services) are kept at the National Personnel Records Center (NPRC), Military Personnel Records, 9700 Page Avenue, St. Louis, MO 63132-5100. The NPRC will not give out addresses. Under a few circumstances (such as a financial institution attempting to collect a debt), the NPRC will forward correspondence to the last known address. The NPRC will not forward correspondence for persons seeking lost family members; for this you must go to the government locator services described in section 4.30.

You can locate many war veterans through Web sites found at the various military/veterans directories, such as www.inil.com/users/dguss/wgator.htm (select "Military"). Some of the best sites, each with its own directory of other sites, are www.militarycity.com, www.shipmates.com, and www.militaryusa.com (the latter has a National Reunion Registry for veterans). Especially useful is the veteran and active-duty personnel verification service (includes over 15.4 million names dating back to the American Revolution) at members.aol.com/warlib13.htm.

Many other methods of locating discharged military personnel can be found in Johnson and Knox's book, which should be in every investigator's library.

4.27   Locating Licensed Pilots and Ham Radio Operators

You can obtain the address of a Federal Aviation Administration (FAA) licensed pilot at www.search3.knowx.com (select "FAA Airmen Directory"). To locate a licensed ham radio operator, go to the U.S. Amateur Radio Callsign Lookup Page at www.ualr.edu/~hamradio.html (this database is derived from FCC license records found at ftp://ftp.fcc.gov/pub/XFS_AlphaTest/amateur).

4.28 Locating the Homeless

For over a century, the Salvation Army has helped families find loved ones who have become homeless as a result of alcoholism or mental illness. The Salvation Army's Family Tracing Service (as it is now called) will not tell you where the missing relative is, but will act as a "postbox" until such time as the missing relative is willing to meet with you. Note that the Salvation Army does not usually become involved in searches for former spouses, missing spouses in divorce cases, friends, or an adoptee's birth parents, although an occasional humanitarian exception is made in such cases.

The regional addresses for the Salvation Army Family Tracing Service are listed here:

- **Eastern United States:** 440 West Nyack Road, (P.O. Box C-635,) West Nyack, New York, 10994

- **Central United States:** 10 West Algonquin Road, Des Plaines, Illinois, 60016

- **Southern United States:** 1424 Northeast Expressway, Atlanta, Georgia, 30329

- **Western United States:** 30840 Hawthorne Boulevard, Rancho Palos Verdes, California, 90274

The sharp rise in the number of homeless since the late 1970s has led to a plethora of private and local government agencies providing health care and counseling as well as soup kitchens and shelters. To a great extent, these agencies have taken over the Salvation Army's traditional role. To find the appropriate agencies in your locality, look in local community resource directories at your public library (in New York City, one such book is the *Directory of Alcoholism Resources and Services*) or go to www.ir-net.com for a directory of agencies nationwide that provide human services in areas such as substance abuse and mental illness. Such agencies are your most practical way of communicating with the homeless population if the Salvation Army can't help. (You might send each of them a photograph of your subject along with your request for help.) Another possible source of help for your search is the nationwide network of street newspapers for the homeless; a directory of these publications can be found at nch.ari.net/streetnews.

4.29 Finding the Addresses of Celebrities

Avid fans often want to find out the home addresses of celebrities of stage and screen. This is not very difficult. Numerous tourist maps show the homes of movie stars in Hollywood and Beverly Hills. For East Coast celebrity fans, Larry Wolfe Horwitz has written *New York City Starwalks*, which includes the addresses of about 1,000 stars of screen, stage, and TV, plus information about the restaurants and clubs where they hang out, the hair salons they visit, and so on. Horwitz found 5 to 10 percent of his targets by looking in the current phone book; they were often listed under their last names with only an initial for the first name. Horwitz's main tactic, however, was simply to walk around the trendiest neighborhoods in Manhattan and talk to shop owners, pizza and grocery delivery persons, building maintenance employees, and also neighborhood residents who had seen this or that celebrity walking the proverbial poodle.

Garbologist A.J. Weberman searched in old phone books for his celebrity targets. He found that many had been listed before they became famous. They later obtained unlisted numbers to fend off the fans and tabloid journalists, but they did not move to new apartments. Instead (like many other well-to-do but thrifty Manhattanites), they remained in their rent-controlled digs.

The home addresses of entertainers can occasionally be found in biographical dictionaries and directories such as *Who's Who in Entertainment* or *Christensen's Ultimate Movie, TV & Rock 'N' Roll Directory*.

Most famous individuals first achieved a listing in a biographical dictionary or directory when they were still only moderately well known. By the time they became sufficiently celebrated or notorious to fear stalkers and paparazzi, their home addresses were already easily available in numerous reference works.

Home addresses of the more secretive celebrities (including their vacation home addresses) often can be found in property tax rolls, condo ownership rosters, and voter registration lists.

If you're stumped, check out the fan-sponsored Web pages devoted to the celebrity in question or the email lists or newsgroups devoted to discussing his or her work. There's often at least one obsessed fan who's already ferreted out the address by some ungodly means.

Famous authors, scientists, journalists, or the like (who, unlike the famous people of stage and screen, are not usually hounded by paparazzi or stalkers) are often very easy to find. Their addresses are frequently listed in biographical works (for writers, see *Contemporary Authors* and *Contemporary Authors New Revision Series*). One of the best known science-fiction writers has had a listed phone number for his entire adult life—and pictures of his house can be found at the Web page of one of his fans.

Even if you only have the address of a famous author's publisher or agent, your fan letter may elicit a personal response from the author with his or her return address on the envelope or at the top of his or her letter. This tactic also might work with artists, composers, columnists, or other famous persons who work at home and therefore answer their correspondence from their home address.

4.30 Government Locator Services

The Social Security Administration (SSA) has one of the government's largest databases of names and addresses. You cannot obtain a person's address from the SSA, but you might try reaching your subject through its letter forwarding service. Write to the Social Security Administration, Office of Public Inquiries, 6401 Security Boulevard, Room 4-C-5 Annex, Baltimore, MD 21235. To use this service, you must give a clear humanitarian reason, such as a death or serious illness in the missing person's immediate family, or else you must be attempting to notify the person that money is due him or her (as from an inheritance). The SSA will forward your letter to the missing person in care of the employer who filed the last quarterly earnings report for him or her, or in care of the address at which he or she is receiving Social Security benefits. You should provide the SSA with the subject's full name and either his or her SSN or identifying information that can help the SSA find the SSN (date and place of birth, father's name, mother's full birth name). The letter you want forwarded should be sent to the SSA in a plain, unstamped, unsealed envelope showing only the missing person's name. Note that if you are simply seeking to find a missing family member, the SSA will not forward a letter from you but will send its own letter notifying the person of your desire to establish contact.

The Internal Revenue Service (IRS) may also forward a letter to someone if there is a compelling humanitarian reason or in cases where a lawyer or estate administrator directly controlling certain assets (or a commercial locator service working for this asset controller) is seeking to notify a person that he or she is entitled to the assets in question. The IRS must be provided with the missing person's SSN, which is also the person's taxpayer identifying number. Requests for this IRS service should be directed to the IRS district office serving the locality in which the requestor resides.

The Department of Veterans Affairs (VA) will forward a letter to any of the 5 million veterans listed in its files (that is, to any veteran who has ever applied for VA benefits). You should place your letter in an unsealed, stamped envelope *without* your return address on it. Place this envelope inside another envelope along with a note to the VA giving the name of the person you are trying to reach and as much identifying information as you have (date or year of birth, approximate dates of military service, and so on) and send it to the nearest VA regional office. This service is widely used by vets searching for servicemates or members of their former military units.

You can also get a letter forwarded to a retired federal civil servant. Write to the Office of Personnel Management, Employee Service and Records Center, Boyers, PA 16017.

The Federal Bureau of Prisons will locate a federal prison inmate for you; call the national Inmate Locator hotline at (202) 307-3126. This hotline will not provide information about state prison inmates; however, most state departments of corrections have their own locator services.

4.31 Locator Form Letters and Mailings

If you are an adoptee searching for a birth parent, or if you are searching for a long-lost relative, try sending a form letter to a broad array of government agencies, private organizations, and periodicals that might have the person in their files or on membership, mailing, or subscription lists. Explain in the letter your humanitarian need to reach the subject and provide any identifying information you have, such as full name, physical description, date and place of birth, SSN, mother's maiden name, spouse's name, and previous known addresses. State that you have enclosed a stamped envelope with a personal letter to the subject inside it and ask the organization or agency to either forward the letter or otherwise contact the subject on your behalf. Urge the organization or agency to write you or call you collect if they have any questions about your request.

Make plenty of photocopies both of this letter and of a handwritten appeal to the person you are trying to find, and buy stamps and envelopes. Go to the public library and sit down with the *Encyclopedia of*

Associations, Washington Information Directory, Standard Periodical Directory, and other relevant reference directories. Address your mailing to any and every organization, agency, or periodical that you think might have a past or present address for your subject. Be sure to send the form letter to the circulation departments of the highest circulation general interest magazines as well as to specialty publications that might attract your subject's interest (for example, if your lost brother is a biker, you obviously would send the letter to motorcycle magazines).

With the exception of the official government locator services (described in the preceding section), it's difficult to predict how any of these third parties might react. They may have a fixed policy regarding such appeals, or it may be up to the person who opens the letter (or his or her supervisor) to decide on the spot. Even if the organization usually ignores such requests, your letter might touch the heartstrings of the person opening the letter. Obviously, a lot depends on the care with which you word your appeal.

Unless told not to (as by the Department of Veterans Affairs), always include your return address on the envelope of the letter to be forwarded. If the third party forwards it to the address in its files, and the Post Office returns it to you marked "moved," you are one leg up: You now have a previous address for the subject and can use the crisscross directory and other resources to eventually find a more recent address (or possibly the current address) for the subject.

Another type of mailing could be sent nationwide to people listed in Select Phone or other locator databases who have the same surname and given name as your subject. If the surname is an uncommon one, or if you have narrowed your search to a manageable geographic area or areas (say, the state in which the subject was born and grew up, and the state in which he or she was last sighted), you might also send your form letter to everyone with the subject's surname regardless of their given name. Tell them you are looking for the subject and provide certain identifying information you have collected (such as year and place of birth, town where the subject grew up, and the high school he or she attended). Ask the addressee to get in touch with you if he or she happens to be the person you are looking for or knows how to contact that person.

You could send your requests by email, but this might lack the crucial personal touch. Always include, however, your email address as well as your phone number or mailing address in your form letter.

4.32 "Missing" or "Wanted" Posters on the Internet

The television show "America's Most Wanted" has helped law enforcement catch many fugitives. You can use the same tactic on a smaller scale, not to search for violent desperadoes but to find a missing teenager, an adoptee's birth parents, or the genial Romeo who absconded with your elderly aunt's life savings. You can do this by circulating information about the person you are seeking on Web sites and bulletin board systems nationwide.

The National Center for Missing and Exploited Children has significantly increased its recovery rate of missing children by this method, which targets a potential audience of millions of people. The center uses imaging technology to "age progress" photographs of the children to show what they might look like now, as opposed to when they were first reported missing.

Adult sons and daughters looking for the father who walked out on the family 20 years ago could also circulate age-progressed pictures. Obviously such an effort would not get the same level of online cooperation that a missing children's center receives; still, the searchers could send their appeals for help to Web sites, email lists, and newsgroups frequented by those computer users who, because of their special interests or their geographical location, would be most likely to have encountered the missing person.

4.33 Reverse Traces

As noted in section 4.1, many Americans are living under false IDs, sometimes as fugitives from the law. When the police or the FBI want to find one of these paper trippers badly enough, they first identify through database searches everyone who appeared for the first time in certain key public records systems (for instance, the motor vehicles bureau records of the state where the subject is rumored to be hiding) within a certain time frame following the subject's disappearance. Next, they narrow this list to include only those who, according to their driver's licenses and other available data, share certain physical characteristics of subject (for example, race, height, approximate age).

You don't have to be a police officer to use this method (or, at least, a truncated version of it). If you believe the person you are looking for moved to a certain city two years ago and is now living there under a false ID, examine that city's roster of water connects (and other utility connect records if available) and compile a list of all persons who had utilities turned on during the weeks following the subject's disappearance from his or her previous address. Then cross-check those names against the local crisscross directory or back-issue white pages to identify those who are new-to-the-directory subscribers as opposed to previous telephone subscribers at other addresses in the same locality. If you then go to visit (or conduct surveillance on) the homes of the remaining people on your list, you may find that one of them is in fact your subject living under his or her new identity. (Of course, a highly intelligent paper tripper would have prepared his or her disappearance carefully, either by purchasing or renting a new home and getting the utilities turned on months in advance, or else by waiting a couple of months after his or her disappearance before getting any new utilities under any name whatsoever. In addition, he or she would have avoided getting a telephone listing in the white pages, precisely to keep out of local and national crisscross directories.)

4.34 Caller ID

If you are calling around to find people who don't want to be found, they may hear about you from a former neighbor and become curious or angry. They may call your number just to hear what your voice sounds like and then hang up without saying anything. Or they may call pretending to be someone else and try to pump you for information. Or they may call anonymously with threats, obscenities, or heavy breathing. Caller ID (or else *69) may tell you the number from which the call was made. If you dial back immediately and ask for the subject, he or she may break down and talk to you. If your version of Caller ID tells not just the number but also the name of the line subscriber (or if you reverse the number using an online people finder), you may discover that it's a residential number listed under a name you've never heard of (perhaps the subject himself under his assumed identity, or perhaps a friend with whom the subject is staying), a business number (perhaps the subject's new place of work), or a pay phone. At least you now know which city the subject is in, and you can also assume the likelihood that the pay phone is in the same general neighborhood as the subject's home or business or somewhere along the route between them.

If you get a call from a fugitive or skip who has used the blocking code so that you can't learn the number he is calling from, put him or her on hold at some point in the conversation, using a mute button rather than a true hold button. You can then hear anything the subject might say to a third party or, at least, any background noise as from the TV or from squabbling kids or passing trucks (of course, you might pick up a certain amount of such background noise even without putting the subject on hold). This might provide important clues about the subject's location. Note especially the regional accent of anyone with whom the subject speaks or whose voice is otherwise heard in the background, any references to the weather, any community news items on the TV, and so on. (You can later sometimes pinpoint the probable location of the weather comments or local news or weather report through an Internet search.) Traffic noise in the background can sometimes indicate whether subject is calling from a downtown metro area or from a phone located beside a major highway or expressway. A popular TV sitcom star's (or network news anchor's) voice in the background might reveal the time-zone from which the subject is calling.

To take advantage of such clues, you may want to tape such calls (if this can be done legally in your state). You can then play back the conversation as many times as necessary.

Rather than waiting for the subject to call you with his harassment act, you can take the initiative. For instance, you might send a letter to the subject at his or her last known address (with "please forward" written on the envelope), requesting on some pretext that he or she call you. (Or you can transmit the message through someone who knows the subject's current whereabouts but isn't talking.) If the letter is forwarded or the message is passed on to the subject, and he or she calls you from a listed phone, you will learn the number and location from whence the call was made if the subject fails to use the blocking code. If the subject calls from an unlisted number, you will learn the number and location provided that your own phone has deluxe Caller ID and the caller fails to use the blocking code.

If you believe that Mr. Jones will probably use the blocking code, you might in your letter or message urge him to call you collect or at your "800" or "888" number. If he calls long distance collect, the number will appear on your bill. If he makes a local collect call, you will be able to obtain the number on request from the phone company. If he calls your toll-free number, you will learn the number from which he is calling because the blocking code doesn't yet work with toll-free numbers.

For more on Caller ID, see section 11.7, "Making Use of Caller ID."

4.35 If You're Completely Stumped

Consider the following:

- The subject may be in an institution. According to the 1990 census, over 3.3 million Americans (more than 1 in 100) are in a prison, juvenile detention center, old-age home, long-term care facility, mental hospital, or the like. Some of these institutions warehouse inmates or patients for decades or even a lifetime.

- The subject may have moved overseas.

- The subject may be living as a mountain survivalist or in a totalitarian religious cult, almost completely isolated from the outside world.

- The subject may be dead, but there may be no record of the death in the Social Security Death Index or in any state death index (this would be the case if the subject was murdered and the body buried in a swamp or, less luridly, if the death was simply never reported to the SSA because of bureaucratic laxness). However, you should never assume for sure that a person is dead on the basis of a database entry or even a death certificate. Scam artists will sometimes fake their own deaths (especially by going overseas to countries where public officials can be easily bribed to alter records). Apart from such schemes, the Social Security death index and many state death indexes are notoriously inaccurate, often listing as dead (through clerical or computer error or name confusion) people who, in fact, are alive and well in a retirement home or retirement community.

5.

Backgrounding the Individual: Biographical Reference Sources, Résumés, and Curriculum Vitae

5.1 Overview of Biographical Reference Sources

Millions of Americans are included in one or more "who's-who"-type biographical dictionaries or other reference works containing biographical data. There are thousands of such works: Never assume that a person is not listed, no matter how humdrum his or her life might be.

Biographical dictionaries generally contain one-paragraph entries with non-controversial basic information such as date and place of birth, names of parents, schooling, military service, job history, awards and other honors, names of spouse(s) and children, membership in professional or fraternal societies, published writings, hobbies, and office or home address.

Such information provides a springboard for further investigation. The date of birth may help you in obtaining driver's license abstracts and other public records concerning the subject. The name of a parent or former spouse may lead you to court papers regarding a divorce or probate of a will. Information about a subject's educational background may guide you to college yearbooks, a master's thesis, or a doctoral dissertation.

Because the biographical data on living persons is usually provided by the subjects themselves, some of it—even in the prestigious *Who's Who in America*—may be false or misleading. Indeed, because a subject will rarely want to advertise his or her warts, most "who's-who"-type profiles will be slanted toward the positive. The late Teamster leader Jimmy Hoffa never described himself in a biographical dictionary questionnaire as a "labor racketeer." Nor did he ever list, under awards and honors, his multiple indictments in federal court. Nevertheless, most subjects tell the truth about non-controversial basic facts such as when and where they were born, and this provides leads for further investigation and a chronology around which you can organize your research findings.

5.2 Biography and Genealogy Master Index

Always begin with Gale's *Biography and Genealogy Master Index* (*BGMI*), which indexes over 11 million biographical sketches from over 2,500 editions and volumes of about 900 source publications, both current and retrospective. Names of over four million living and deceased individuals are in this index. It lists not only each biographical work in which there is an entry for your subject, but also all editions in which the entry appears. Thus, you can trace the changes in the subject's entry from year to year, and you can glean from old editions various bits of information excised from the current one, such as former addresses and the names of former spouses.

The core of *BGMI* is an eight-volume base set published in 1980. Since then, annual updates have been cumulated every five years into subsidiary sets. Almost 500,000 citations are added each year. The entire *BGMI* is available on microfiche (under the name Bio-Base), on CD-ROM, and online from GaleNet and DIALOG.

An abridged print version covering 266 of the most widely available source publications may be on the shelves at smaller libraries. Because the full version of *BGMI* is so easily available, you should not restrict your search to the abridged version.

Some of *BGMI*'s source publications may be hard to find, especially the cited back editions (smaller libraries often discard them once the new edition is cataloged). If a publication is not available at your local library, get the research librarian to order the volume (or a photocopy of the cited entry) through interlibrary loan.

5.3 Marquis *Who's Who Index* and The *Complete Marquis Who's Who*

The annual one-volume *Index to Marquis Who's Who Publications* (first published in 1974) is available, as is the *BGMI*, in most research libraries. It will direct you to 300,000 biographical sketches in the current editions of *Who's Who in America* and 15 mostly regional and professional Marquis Who's Who publications. The Marquis publications are also covered by *BGMI*, which provides (unlike the Marquis Index) cumulative indexing of past editions.

You can conduct a far more efficient search using the online or CD-ROM version of the *Complete Marquis Who's Who* (see section 5.9), which enables you to instantly search the contents of 20 Marquis titles dating back to 1985 (a total of 788,000 sketches). Of course, if you have to find sketches that appeared only before 1985, you must use the print indexes and the back editions in the library stacks.

Note that two Marquis biographical dictionaries, *Who's Who in American Art* and *Who's Who in American Politics*, both recently acquired from R.R. Bowker, are not yet included in Marquis' electronic compendium, although both are available online from LEXIS-NEXIS and DIALOG (see section 5.9).

5.4 Biography Index

BGMI indexes only biographical dictionaries. For other types of biography-related books and for periodical articles of a biographical nature, you should consult the H.W. Wilson Company's *Biography Index*, a cumulative work going back to 1946. *Biography Index* issues quarterly updates, interim annual cumulations, and permanent two-year cumulations. It covers every biographical-type article (including interviews and obituaries) in more than 3,000 periodicals, together with over 2,000 works annually of individual and collective biography. In addition, it includes autobiographies, memoirs, journals, diaries, letters, bibliographies, and biographical information from otherwise non-biographical works.

Biography Index tells you whether an article or book contains a photograph of your subject. It also includes cross-indexing by profession or occupation (I recommend that you check whether any of the subject's colleagues or business associates are listed). Many public libraries have *Biography Index* from mid-1984 to the present on CD-ROM. It is also available online from mid-1984 to the present on CompuServe and WilsonWeb.

5.5 Biographical Material Not Listed in the Master Indexes

BGMI skips over many obscure but potentially useful biographical dictionaries. Indeed, one could say there is a vast un-indexed universe of such works beyond *BGMI*'s reach. Start with Robert B. Slocum's *Biographical Dictionaries and Related Works*. This is a standard guide describing 16,000 source publications. Even if you find your subject in *BGMI*, you might check in Slocum's (based on what you know about the subject's background) to see whether there are other books in which he or she is likely to be included. Slocum's describes obscure local who's whos (many of them are from decades ago, but they might include your subject's parents), society registers, vanity registers, state government handbooks, works of collective biography, genealogical works, and bio-bibliographies.

Among the thousands of titles that can be used to supplement the standard biographical dictionaries, certain types stand out as being especially useful for journalists and private investigators:

▪ Society registers provide a way of tracing the marriages, divorces, remarriages, yacht club memberships, and Ivy League academic credentials of America's upper crust. Preeminent is *The Social Register*, which, together with its supplement, the *Social Register Summer*, reports annually on the most prominent families nationwide. *The Social List of Washington* (the so-called "green book") covers society and officialdom in our nation's capital. Social registers have also been published for various states over the years (for example, *The Social Record of Virginia*).

▪ State government handbooks (often called "blue books" or "red books") may contain detailed biographical sketches of state legislators, judges, and officials. Back editions and current editions from across the country may contain upwards of 50,000 sketches of living Americans who are now serving or have served in any of the three branches of state government.

▪ College class anniversary directories (usually published on the 15th, 25th, or 35th anniversary) may include autobiographical sketches provided by the class members themselves. Such sketches can be quite elaborate, providing data available from no other published source. Reading between the lines, you can often pick up a clue about which of your subject's classmates might be willing to talk freely with you.

To find out whether your subject's class has published such a directory, call the college archives or alumni association. And also check whether the subject's prep school or parochial or public high school class has held a reunion and published an anniversary book.

▪ "Vanity" directories solicit biographical information from ordinary people and charge them a flat fee to be included (the fee may be disguised as the advance purchase price of a deluxe, gold-embossed copy). At any given moment, there are about 200 vanity directory publishers soliciting from the American public (often the mailings come from a British address to provide an aristocratic touch). Typically, such publishers will produce one or two editions of a work before replacing it with a new title. Thousands of such works have been published in the English language over the past century. They are of interest to an investigator for two reasons: First, they include people who would never get into a serious who's who on their own merits; and second, they often devote a relatively long entry to a local person who would rate only the briefest of entries in a serious who's who. Unfortunately, research libraries rarely buy vanity directories. Your best hope is that the proud listee has donated a copy to his or her local public library or the library of the college from which he or she flunked out in 1956. If you find a copy, the self-written entry on your subject may include the fact that he or she previously appeared in another vanity directory (as if this were an honor of the highest distinction). By going from one to the other, you may notice odd variations in your subject's life story that warrant further probing. The largest collection of vanity directories is at the Library of Congress.

- Local history buffs may have produced a biographical dictionary for your town, county, or state. Check with your county or state historical society.

- Family name books (also called genealogy books) sometimes contain biographical dictionary-style entries on various living family members as well as their antecedents. These books are often self-published in very small editions by a family genealogy enthusiast for circulation mostly among his or her relatives or the members of a particular family name association. To find such books, you can start with *Genealogies in the Library of Congress* (look in the supplements as well as in the base volumes) and *Complement to Genealogies in the Library of Congress* (the latter lists volumes that are *not* in the Library of Congress). (These resources are now online at www.ancestry.com.) You might also check the Mormon's Family History Library Catalog (www.lds.org). In any such search, be sure to look under the maiden name of your subject's mother as well as under your subject's original surname.

  To find the right family name volume (if the surname is a common one), you may need the help of an expert. Consult the *Directory of Family Associations* and also the *American Family Records Association—Member Directory and Ancestral Surname Registry.* These volumes match the names of hundreds of genealogists and family historians with the thousands of surnames they have researched.

  After you find the right family name volume, it may turn out to have only genealogical lists and charts. This of course is useful information, but you were hoping for a collection of biographical sketches. In such cases, contact the author—he or she may have files containing very detailed biographical data. (Even if the volume includes biographical sketches, I would still contact the author to see whether he or she has additional data.) You might also contact other members of the relevant family name association.

  Although your chances of finding a biographical sketch of your subject in a family name book are not great, it's worth a try. You could end up with a wealth of material about the subject and his or her children, parents, siblings, grandparents, aunts, uncles, and cousins. If the subject still lives in his or her hometown, surrounded by these relatives, information about the extended family could be quite important in researching the subject's business affairs.

- Professional, organizational, or alumni directories or rosters often contain a vast amount of biographical material. The *BGMI* does not index such volumes (nor does Slocum's list them) because the amount of biographical detail per entry is usually too sketchy. Yet, if you can find from such a directory where a person lives and works (and, from back issues, where they used to live and work), their year and place of birth, their college and year of graduation, and their spouse's name, you will have made a good beginning. Tens of thousands of such directories have been published over the past century; today, hundreds are published each year by college alumni associations alone. I have found that although each volume listing your subject may contain only one or two facts not included in the others, the amount of information builds up when you go through volume after volume. One individual I was tracking was listed in two alumni directories, two national faculty directories, a law directory, and a directory of consultants. By the time I finished looking through these, I had as much material as from a brief *Who's Who* entry. Such directories can also be useful in finding sources who will tell you their recollections of your subject: professional colleagues, former classmates, and others. In addition, some professional directories may contain full-blown biographical sketches of selected listees. *Martindale-Hubbell*, for instance, includes sketches on about 40,000 attorneys along with its roster of over 800,000.

In searching a professional directory or roster, examine not only your subject's entry but also those for his or her closest colleagues. And be sure to search the non-directory text in the volumes, which may include much more detailed information about both the subject and his or her colleagues. My favorite example is an edition, from several years ago, of the Special Library Association's annual directory. As well as having an alphabetical roster of member librarians and their work addresses, it lists members by city or state chapter and by specialty (which could help you identify members who might know or have known your subject well). Furthermore, the directory includes lists of SLA charter members, honorary members, Professional Award and Special Achievement Award holders, Special Citation recipients, SLA Hall of Fame members, SLA past presidents, current officers (both nationally and for each chapter and division), SLA committee members and officers, SLA representatives to other professional organizations, and a name index with page citations for each listing of each member's name.

If you want to engage in personal surveillance of your subject, professional directories such as the SLA often provide a listing of upcoming professional meetings and the city and hotel at which each will take place. Such directories will usually also provide subscription information for the group's newsletter, which might provide even more information about your subject's career in its current and future editions and in its backfiles.

▪ Major corporations and law partnerships sometimes publish in-house biographical works. For instance, LeBoeuf, Lamb, Leiby & MacRae, a New York law firm, publishes a biographical book that includes a half-page sketch on each of several hundred partners and associates (both in New York and in its regional and overseas offices) with a picture of each attorney.

- The annual bulletins of medical, law, and divinity schools have long included biographical sketches on all or selected faculty members and administrators. Recently, the Web sites at such schools and also at the broad range of American colleges and universities have begun to include such data. (For more on online faculty biographies, see section 5.9.)

- Newspapers, newsletters, and magazines published by national, state, or local trade unions, professional and trade associations, and other nonprofit organizations frequently publish detailed biographies of candidates for organizational posts, recently elected or appointed officers, and new members of the board of directors. Sometimes such information can be found at the organization's Web site, but it is usually removed after a few months.

- Boards of elections and nonpartisan citizens' groups such as the League of Women Voters have long published voter guides at election time that include biographical sketches of all candidates for local, state, or federal office who will appear on the local ballot in the given primary or general election. For the voter guides of past years, see the pamphlet files at your public library, municipal archives, or county historical society. (For online biographical information about candidates, see section 5.9.)

5.6 Back Editions of Biographical Dictionaries

If you have found an entry on your subject in the current edition of a biographical dictionary, don't neglect the entries for past years in this and other dictionaries. As noted earlier in this chapter, the older sketches may provide you with past residential and business addresses and the names of former spouses that are not included in the most recent entry. By going to these earlier sketches in the library stacks, you may be able (if your subject is consistently included) to use the back editions almost like a city directory.

Although *BGMI*'s indexing of back editions dates back only to 1974–75, a few standard reference works have their own cumulative indexes covering earlier years. For example, *American Men and Women of Science*'s index to its first 14 editions (1906 to 1979) includes listings for more than 270,000 living and dead scientists. In searching most biographical dictionary editions published before 1974–75, however, you will have to check each edition separately in the library stacks.

Often a subject who is not included in any current biographical reference work may have been included years ago because of a governmental appointment, electoral candidacy, or some other factor that temporarily qualified him or her. To find such sketches that are not indexed in *BGMI*, look first in *Directories in Print* and Slocum's to identify works in which your subject's name might have appeared given what you already know about his or her past. Let's say that you are backgrounding John Doe, a local campaign consultant. You know from the rather meager press clippings that he was a congressional staff aide for a brief period in the early 1970s for the late Congressman Mark Grouch. Looking in *Directories in Print*, you see a listing for the annual *Congressional Staff Directory*. Finding it in the public library, you note that it includes in its current issue over 3,000 biographical sketches, many of them rather detailed. You also note that it has been published since 1959. If you can get the back editions for the early 1970s from the library stacks, you will probably find a sketch of Mr. Doe.

5.7 Parallel Backgrounding Using Biographical Reference Works

Information your subject has failed to provide to the compilers of a biographical work may be contained in a sketch of one of his or her relatives, business partners, or close colleagues. In an investigation of a local attorney, I found biographical sketches that contained virtually nothing about what I was interested in—his connections to the Arab world. Then I found a sketch in a biographical dictionary about his closest friend from college days, who was described as a lobbyist for Arab governments and a partner in a Mideast trading firm, the name of which included my subject's surname. I was later able to confirm that my subject was indeed connected to this firm.

To use parallel backgrounding to the maximum, I suggest that you compile a list of your subject's known relatives, business associates, and the like early in your investigation and add names as you find them. Periodically check the biographical indexes to see whether they include any of the latest names you've collected. Also, as you search the indexes, develop a roster of persons who have the same surname as your subject or your subject's in-laws or (if you are backgrounding a married woman who uses her husband's surname) as your subject's parents. When you go to a biographical dictionary cited by the indexes, you should photocopy or download not just the subject's entry but also the surrounding same-surname entries and all entries with the same surnames as the subject's in-laws or parents. And your surname sweep should not be restricted to dictionaries in which the subject is listed. For instance, if he or she comes from a successful, highly educated family, you should *always* go to *The Complete Marquis Who's Who* and photocopy or download the same-surname entries even if your subject is missing from them. (If, in any of these procedures, one of the surnames you are checking is extremely common—for example "Smith"—you might want to narrow your selection by geographical location and other criteria.) Doubtless most of the persons whose sketches you find with your surname sweep will not have any connection to your subject, but if only one or two do have such a connection, their entries might contain valuable information indeed.

Note: If you happen to be using an expensive database vendor service, you can save money by photocopying the relevant same-surname entries from the print edition at the public library or by getting them from the library's CD-ROM version.

Parallel backgrounding is easiest when you find what I call a "high-yield" biographical dictionary—one that specializes in a category of people likely to include a high percentage of your subject's associates, relatives, and so on. In the case of a subject who comes from a successful, highly educated family, *The Complete Marquis Who's Who* would probably be high yield and thus should *always* be searched. But many other dictionaries might be high yield depending on your subject's background and current standing. For instance, I was once looking into the background of a Harlem businessman. The world of black New York politicians and businesspeople is unusually tight-knit—everyone has dealings with everyone else, and, because they live in the city that has long been the cultural center of black America, a large percentage of them are included in *Who's Who Among Black Americans*. I found myself returning to this book again and again.

If my subject were a prominent New York corporate attorney, *Who's Who in American Law*, *Who's Who in America*, and the biographical entries in *Martindale-Hubbell* would be high-yield sources of information on his or her colleagues, friends, and clients. If my subject also happened to be connected by birth or marriage to an old-money family, I would use *The Social Register* to ferret out the more subtle interrelations. If my subject's legal practice involved the handling of the private legal affairs of wealthy people, I would use not only *The Social Register* but also the Taft Group's annual directories, especially *Who's Wealthy in America* (which provides data on over 100,000 potential givers to charity).

High-yield dictionaries are most useful (and the usefulness of lower-yield dictionaries can be greatly enhanced) by full-text search capabilities available online or on CD-ROM (see section 5.9).

If a deceased parent of your subject was professionally prominent, Marquis' retrospective work, *Who Was Who in America*, might be invaluable for parallel backgrounding purposes. The print version is available in 13 volumes, including an index volume, and covers every deceased individual who ever appeared in *Who's Who in America* since its inception in 1896. (The electronic version, included in *The Complete Marquis Who's Who*, covers only back to 1985.) An entry in *Who Was Who in America* will provide you with information not only on the parent profiled therein, but also on the other parent, deceased or not (this information may include the mother's maiden name, a key identifier in backgrounding your subject's finances). The entry may also provide the names, dates of birth, and married names of your subject's siblings, information about where the family lived during the subject's childhood and youth, and data on the subject's aunts and uncles, stepmother or stepfather, and grandparents.

Note: If deceased parents—and also deceased siblings, uncles, aunts, or business associates—of your subject are not found in *Who Was Who in America*, look for them in other regional, local, or professional biographical works from past years as well as in obituary collections.

5.8 The Clues Hidden in Biographical Sketches

The fact that the information for biographical sketches is provided by the biographees themselves (which, in effect, is subject to censorship) can be turned to your advantage. Study the sketches for clues inherent in the information as presented: Are there any glaring or subtle contradictions among the versions of the subject's life that he or she provided to different directories (or to the same directory at different times)? Are there any unexplained time gaps? Does the subject list himself or herself as a board member of a corporation, bank, foundation, or nonprofit institution that you can't find in any standard directory? Does he or she claim a degree from a college that is not listed in the directories of accredited institutions? Does he or she list attendance at a college without claiming a degree? (If so, what happened?) Does he or she claim personal achievements that sound dubious on the face of it (for example, an alleged Rhodes scholarship for someone whose life before and after does not fit the pattern)? Note that some legitimate directories try to verify such claims; others let them pass unless they are embarrassingly obvious.

Politicians occasionally get caught listing exaggerated or false information in their campaign bios. You may find that your subject has done likewise in his or her biographical dictionary sketches (which is another reason you should develop an efficient filing system for the background information you collect).

5.9 Searching by Computer for Biographical Data

Online versions of biographical dictionaries/directories are not without their limitations. Many offer only the current edition, and those that cover earlier editions rarely do so for the years before the mid-1980s. However, by gaining access to an online vendor that offers hundreds of databases, you can conduct in a few moments a search of biographical works that would take hours if you were working with print volumes in the public library. And the full-text and cross-searching capabilities of both online and CD-ROM biographical databases enable you to find connections that would inevitably be missed in a print-based search. This is especially true with a work such as *The Complete Marquis Who's Who*. Prominent people tend to associate with other prominent people, and potentially prominent people tend to form associations with each other long before they become prominent. Thus any person covered in *The Complete Marquis Who's Who* is almost guaranteed to have significant present and/or past ties with several other persons profiled therein. Do you need sources for an article about the wealthy Mr. Smith? If he's in one or more of the Marquis works (and even if he's not), you can use 35 combinable search criteria in the CD-ROM version and various additional search methods online to find biographees who are the same age as Smith and come from the same home town, or who attended the same university as Smith during the same years Smith was there, or who worked at Corporation Y while Smith was one of its executives, or who today live in the same city as Smith and belong to some of the same professional or fraternal organizations, or who married women with the same maiden name as Smith's wife (this may help you find Smith's brother-in-law). If you are a reporter doing a friendly feature story on Smith, probably the majority of these people will be willing to talk to you. If you are an investigative reporter, your search may turn up Smith's bitterest enemy.

Online Vendor Searches

- **LEXIS-NEXIS.** For a comprehensive online search, begin with the *LEXIS-NEXIS People Library*, which offers a vast full-text compendium of biographical information, including (among others) *The Complete Marquis Who's Who, American Men and Women of Science,* the *Almanac of American Politics, Associated Press Candidate Biographies, BNA Labor Relations Reporter Arbitrators' Biographies,* BASELINE *Celebrity Biographies, Congressional Member Profiles, The Congressional Staff Directory,* Gale biographies (including *Who's Who Among Black Americans, Who's Who Among Hispanic Americans, Who's Who Among Asian Americans, Who's Who in Technology,* and others), *Martindale-Hubbell Law Directory, Standard & Poor's Register of Corporations, Directors and Executives, Who's Who in American Art, Who's Who in American Politics,* and the *Directory of Bankruptcy Attorneys.* The *People Library* also includes all biographical stories from the *New York Times* (from 1980 on), *Los Angeles Times* (from 1990 on), *Washington Post* (from 1989 on), and *People* magazine (from 1981 on), as well as a vast selection of biographical articles and obituaries from over sixty other newspapers and periodicals.

- **DIALOG and CompuServe.** Both of these database vendors offer *The Complete Marquis Who's Who; American Men and Women of Science;*

Standard & Poor's Register of Corporations, Directors and Executives; *Who's Who in American Politics*; and *Who's Who in American Art*. Both also offer access to newspaper and periodical full-text and abstract/index databases, which include a vast number of biographical profiles.

CD-ROM and Special Online Resources at Public Libraries

At major public libraries and some smaller ones, you can use the CD-ROM versions of many important biographical reference works and also the online subscription services of reference book publishers (for example GaleNet and WilsonWeb, both of which offer major biographical resources unavailable from the online vendors listed in the preceding section).

Biographical dictionaries and directories available on CD-ROM at your public library may include *The Complete Marquis Who's Who*, *Martindale-Hubbell Law Directory*, and *The Official ABMS Directory of Board Certified Medical Specialists* (the latter includes over 435,000 brief sketches).

Works available both on CD-ROM and from reference publishers' online services include *Contemporary Authors* (more than 100,000 detailed sketches; the online version is on GaleNet); and *Wilson Biographies* (about 40,000 sketches; the online version is on WilsonWeb). The latter compendium includes all the biographies and obituaries from *Current Biography* since 1940 plus sketches from about 30 Wilson biographical reference works covering such categories as writers, illustrators, songwriters, composers, musicians, artists, and film directors. *Wilson Biographies* also provides links to relevant index citations or full-text articles in some 4,000 biographical sources.

Miscellaneous Internet Resources

Much biography-related information can be found (usually for free) on the Internet:

- **Securities and Exchange Commission (SEC) filings.** A vast number of prospectuses, annual reports, and other securities documents are filed each year with the SEC (see section 8.14, "Securities and Exchange Commission Filings; State Securities Filings"). SEC filings since the mid-1990s are available directly from the SEC's in-house database at www.sec.gov/edgarhp.htm. Filings back to 1987 are available from DIALOG and LEXIS-NEXIS. In many of these filings, you will find career summaries (along with personal financial information) on corporate executives, members of boards of directors, investment advisors, and broker-dealers. (A portion of this personal data is included in the online and print versions of *Standard & Poor's Register of Corporations, Directors and Executives*—described earlier in this chapter.)

▪ **Electoral sites.** Many public-interest or partisan Web sites are devoted to disseminating information about candidates and elected officials at every level of politics. The best place to start is Project Vote Smart's site (www.vote-smart.org), which focuses on federal and state elections. As of November 1998, this site provided over 12,000 campaign biographies from the 1998 cycle, as well as candidate biographies for the 1996 cycle and biographies of officials elected in previous cycles who are still in office. Information from the 1992 and 1994 cycles can be requested through the project's hotline at 888-VOTE-SMART. Although most of the biographies in the Project Vote Smart database are very brief, they are supplemented by information on the candidate's or elected official's campaign finances, voting record, and stance on issues as well as evaluations of his or her performance (all of which, one might argue, is of a biographical nature). In addition, Project Vote Smart provides links to a vast number of other political sites, including individual campaign sites. At a minimum, you should always check out your subject's own site, which may contain a rather detailed biography. You might then contact his opponents to find out what he left out or lied about.

▪ **Campus Web sites.** Biographical sketches of faculty members, administrators, and trustees can be found at the Web sites of most universities, colleges, and professional schools. To find a campus Web site, go to the directory at dir.yahoo.com/Education/Higher_Education/Colleges_and_Universities/UnitedStates and select the link to the desired school's main page. Then either conduct a search for your subject's name or follow the site map to your subject's academic department's Web page (this page will often have links to the biographies of each of its members). Note that some departments may provide online biographies not only of their faculty but also of their recent and not-so-recent graduates who've made good; for instance, the "gallery of professionals" at the Ball State University Department of Telecommunications's Web page. Look also for the personal Web pages of faculty members and students. These may contain résumés and curriculum vitae. They may also include miscellaneous informal biographical facts that accompany pictures of the subject's summer trip or wedding, his or her ruminations or tirades regarding Washington politicians or a recent Hollywood film, his or her Web links to body piercing sites, and other quirky expressions of his or her personality.

Internet Directories of Biographical Resources

Yahoo!, the giant Internet directory, includes a comprehensive guide to biographical resources at dir.yahoo.com/Society_and_Culture/People. The initial menu allows you to choose from forty categories, including, among others, astronauts, athletes, authors, celebrities, chefs, journalists, poets, prison inmates, radio personalities, and semioticians. In each category, you will find a large number of links to personal Web pages (see the following section).

5.10 Résumés and Curriculum Vitae

Résumés and curriculum vitae (CVs) provide far more detail about a person's life than can be found in any biographical dictionary. And although only a small percentage of Americans have been profiled in dictionaries, probably over half of all Americans have compiled a résumé or CV at some time.

Investigators are sometimes able to get a copy of an old résumé of their subject's through a contact at a firm where the subject once worked. Some investigators have obtained an up-to-date résumé from the subject himself by way of a deceptive phone call, letter, or e-message (the investigator may pretend to be a personnel agency headhunter). However, you can often obtain the subject's résumé or CV in an above-board fashion from one or more of the thousands of employment-related Web sites, UseNet newsgroups, and email lists at which millions of Americans each year post their job qualifications. In many cases, you can also find the résumé or CV at the job seeker's personal Web page. And these online résumés usually contain twice as much information as did the pre-Internet snail-mail ones.

Online résumé and CV postings can be divided into two basic types: First are the postings by persons seeking a full-time salaried position. It will be worth your while to search for such a posting if you have information that your subject recently lost a salaried job and is searching for another one, is dissatisfied with his or her current salaried job, needs to relocate to another region for family reasons, or is a college senior or recent college graduate hunting for his or her first job in a field in which salaried jobs are the norm.

Typically, a person seeking a salaried position will post his or her résumé with several (or even dozens of) online résumé sites. The sites he or she chooses will, in most cases, include one or more of the giant résumé banks such as Career Mosaic (www.careermosaic.com). At any given moment, such a site may contain a quarter of a million résumés or more.

The résumés of salaried job-seekers are not always easy to find. This will especially be the case if the job-seeker is currently employed and doesn't want his or her employers to learn about the job search. Such a person will hesitate to post a résumé at his or her own Web page and will be likely to choose an online résumé service's restricted access option for postings. To make matters worse (from the investigator's point of view), some résumé services bar anyone from searching the résumés except subscribers (mostly corporations and job-placement agencies).

Another problem is that the résumés at most online résumé sites are accessed not by the person's name but by type of job, salary range, and geographic location. Thus, to find your subject's résumé, you must already know, apart from the subject's current location, some details about the subject's education, job training, and past job history. But such information may not be sufficient if your subject, unbeknownst to you, has decided to make a lateral career move from one field to another, or is seeking a job in a locality far from his or her current home because his or her spouse has already accepted a job there.

A final problem is that résumés for salaried positions (unlike the continuously posted résumés described next) don't always stay online for very long. If the economy is experiencing flush times, the qualified job hunter may find a job in a month or so, and then ask the job bank to delete his or her résumé. Even if the successful job hunter forgets to do this, most résumé banks will automatically remove a résumé after three to six months. However, a résumé may remain online longer (and the job hunter may repost it after its automatic removal) if the economy is in recession and even highly skilled job hunters have to search for many months. The résumé will also remain online for a lengthy period if the job hunter has a poor job history or has health problems that make most employers reluctant to hire him or her.

In most cases, you should begin by searching the largest résumé banks. You might get a friend in a job placement agency or corporate personnel department to help you do this because his or her firm will likely be a subscriber to several of these services. If you're going to search on your own, one of the best places to start is the directory and Web links at www.yahoo.com/Business_and_Economy/Employment/Résumés. This directory will lead you not only to résumé banks but to newsgroups, personal Web pages, and so on. In addition, always search for the subject's name using several search engines to find what you would inevitably miss by simply following directory links. And if you need a thorough search of newsgroups, go to the Usenet search engine at www.dejanews.com.

The second basic type of posting is the more or less continuous posting aimed at attracting freelance assignments, consulting contracts, research grants, clients for one's personal services, short-term project-by-project bookings, and the like. Persons who post their qualifications in this manner include self-employed professionals and freelancers of all types; actors, models, and others who work in industries where short-term work is the norm; and college professors with full-time teaching jobs who customarily seek consulting work or special grants on the side.

Because the résumé or CV postings of such persons are kept online for long periods at the same site or sites (much like the daily ads of a pizza delivery service in your local newspaper) and with few if any restrictions on who can view them, they are much easier to find than those of the salaried job-seeker.

Such postings are often found not only in résumé banks but also at Usenet newsgroups, professional or trade association Web sites, university or college Web sites, and personal Web pages linked to one or more of these résumé banks.

To get a sense of the vast quantity of biographical data available through continuous online résumé postings, go to dir.yahoo.com/Entertainment, then choose "Actors and Actresses." Following the links, you can search a résumé directory of aspiring young performers who have yet to make their mark, and then browse a directory of over 100 talent-agency sites, most of which have their own résumé collections (altogether, thousands of acting résumés). And acting is only one of hundreds of professions indexed by Yahoo! in this manner.

Note that the résumés or CVs of highly skilled and experienced free-lancers or consultants (not to speak of those posted by actors who have appeared in hundreds of plays and TV dramas and done hundreds of voice-overs) will often be far more detailed than those of persons searching for ordinary salaried positions. One example is a documentary film producer's résumé, found at www.dir.yahoo.com/Entertainment/Movies_and_Film/Employment/Individual_Résumés, which goes on for over twelve pages, listing virtually every film project he has worked on in various capacities during his entire career, every award he has won, every script he has written, every country he has visited, and so on. This everything-but-the-kitchen-sink approach is not at all unusual. College professors or scientists routinely post even lengthier résumés and CVs. (In perusing such a document, always look in the section entitled "Awards and Honors"; the subject may inform you that he or she has been profiled in a certain biographical dictionary or in one of the periodicals of his or her profession or specialty. This dictionary or periodical may be one that is not indexed or archived in any online database library and which you would never have thought to consult otherwise.)

5.11 The Use of Résumés in Parallel Backgrounding

The most important résumé to find, other than the subject's own, is that of his or her spouse. If they work together (as in their own consulting business or as a freelance editorial team), the spouse's résumé will provide solid direct information about the subject's own work history and achievements. If they have been married for many years, the spouse's list of past jobs (with addresses) may tell you the cities in which the subject also worked during the same years. And if the subject's spouse lists on his or her résumé that he or she now only wants to work in one particular locality (a locality that is beyond commuting range from the couple's current home), that will suggest to you that your subject (whose own résumé you have not yet found) may also be job hunting in the same locality. You could then conduct an online search for your subject's résumé using this locality as a keyword.

If your subject has a parent who is still of working age, you might search for any résumé posted by this parent. It could tell you the name of every community in which the subject lived while growing up and the financial circumstances of his upbringing. If your subject is middle aged and has one or more grown children in the workforce, their résumés might include the names and addresses of schools they attended, which in turn might reveal where the family lived in past years and its financial circumstances at the time. And you should also consider looking at the résumés of the subject's closest colleagues, including those who have worked as his or her top assistants and those who have functioned as his or her immediate superiors. (A comparison of Dr. Z's current résumé and those of his former co-workers on a long-disbanded U.S. government pest control study might provide the first clue that Dr. Z and his fellow bug scientists were really working on a top secret biological warfare project....)

6 ∙

Backgrounding the Individual: Newspaper and Periodical Searches

6.1 Overview

If your target is a celebrity or an elected public official, newspapers and periodicals are the obvious place to start your search for information. But the vast range of these publications, especially local dailies, can also provide a wealth of easily accessible data about tens of millions of non-celebrities, from stockbrokers to panhandlers. The back issues of America's newspapers and periodicals—and the knowledge and working files of the vast number of journalists working for these publications and for wire services—are a potential intelligence resource to rival the combined assets of the CIA and the former KGB.

You can most easily search newspapers and periodicals by computer. An ever-increasing number of publications are available online. You can search the entire contents of every issue of a newspaper for, say, the last five years, finding every mention of the subject and his or her associates. Indeed, you can do full-text global searches of hundreds of publications at once using large database vendors such as LEXIS-NEXIS.

The majority of newspapers (especially those serving smaller cities) and obscure periodicals (especially those of little or no interest to corporate, academic, or scientific searchers) are not yet part of the online libraries offered to computer users worldwide by vendors such as LEXIS-NEXIS and DIALOG. Furthermore, electronic archives of even very important national newspapers and magazines may be available online only for issues dating back less than a decade. To search the backfiles of your local daily for its pre-online years, you will need to use traditional low-tech resources. These include print or microform indexes and abstracts (although some of these are searchable online for recent years), newspaper "morgues," archival clippings files, and microform or bound-volume backfiles. The online databases, however, may guide you in your low-tech search. For instance, an online article may refer to a pre-online incident that the reporter read about in old newspaper clips while preparing his or her own article. Usually the reporter will give the date or at least the year of the earlier incident or article; you can then find the article on microfilm and perhaps learn from it about a still earlier incident or article.

6.2 Finding Serials on the Internet and Through Directories and Catalogs

In backgrounding a prominent businessperson, you may decide to search the daily newspapers in his or her state as well as local and national business and trade publications. But how do you find out which publications are online and from which vendors? And what if you want to search smaller dailies (and weeklies) in the subject's locality that are not online? or pre-online issues of the major local daily? or the backfiles of the latter's now-defunct rival? or obscure periodicals that relate to the subject's career, business, hobbies, and civic and religious involvement?

If a newspaper in a given city or town currently has a Web site, it will be listed at dir.yahoo.com/News_and_Media/Newspapers or at other news-paper Web site directories. To find currently published newspapers that may not have Web sites, search one or more of the various Internet yellow pages. To find out whether a newspaper's electronic archives are available online (and for how many years), go to metalab.unc.edu/slanews/internet/archives.html.

To find current Web pages of even very obscure specialized periodicals, go to dir.yahoo.com/News_and_Media/Magazines/Web Directories. One excellent resource listed there is the *American Journalism Review*'s magazine directory at ajr.newslink.org. If you want to search magazines (as well as newspapers and broadcast media) by geographic location, go to www.mediainfo.com.

To find more newspapers and periodicals, especially defunct ones, go to the Library of Congress's Serials Catalog (at lcweb.loc.gov/catalog/browse/locs.html). This resource includes titles from union catalogs as well as from the LOC catalog. Here you can search by subject and "corporate author" (organization, agency, committee, or association), which should help you find many local periodicals in which your subject might have been mentioned at some time. At the LOC Web site, you can also gain access to the Center for Research Libraries' online public access catalog, which includes union listings of many obscure newspapers and serials in libraries across the country (go to lcweb.loc.gov/rr/news/newscats.html). All of these resources should be supplemented by a search of the online library catalogs in the subject's own locality and by a phone call to the historical society in that locality.

Before going further, you might want to consult one or more of the following excellent directories or catalogs that can be found at your public library in print, on CD-ROM, or through online vendors accessible through the library's subscriber account:

- **Information Today's** *Fulltext Sources Online.* This directory lists over 4,500 journals, newspapers, newsletters, and newswires available online. It includes vendors, coverage dates, database codes, lag times (time between date of publication and date available online), title changes, and whether the coverage is selective or complete.

- *Gale Directory of Publications and Broadcast Media.* The print version is a three-volume set (with an inter-edition supplement) divided by city/state. This well-known reference work covers more than 30,000 newspapers and periodicals in the United States and Canada. It includes every type of publication except newsletters, house organs, publications issued fewer than four times a year, and publications issued by primary and secondary schools or houses of worship. Defunct publications are removed from the main body of entries and listed as "ceased" in the master name and keyword index.

- *Standard Periodical Directory.* This work includes annotated entries on 85,000 periodicals in the United States and Canada, divided into more than 250 major subjects and featuring a title index and cross-index.

- *Newsletters in Print.* This work describes more than 11,500 titles (almost every U.S. and Canadian newsletter published in a print or online version).

- *Newspapers in Microform.* This cumulative Library of Congress reference set (with annuals between cumulations) includes religious, collegiate, labor, and other special-interest papers, as well as general news dailies and weeklies. It also covers defunct and merged papers. Under the current title of a paper is listed its previous names and the names of papers that merged with it or split from it, with the dates of each change; for example, if you look under the *Anytown Courier-Herald* you will find that it is the successor to the *Anytown Courier* and the *Mist County Herald*, which merged in 1949. *Newspapers in Microform* tells which libraries, archives, or microform companies in the United States or overseas have copies of the given newspaper; it also indicates partial or badly broken runs. In most cases, the major public or university libraries (and also the historical societies) in the locality in which a given newspaper is or was published will have copies of the microform backfiles. If you are located in another part of the country, you can obtain the reels you need through interlibrary loan.

- **UMI's *Serials in Microform*.** This massive annual catalog lists more than 20,000 periodicals that the company offers for sale on microform. UMI also publishes a catalog of 7,000 newspapers it sells on microform. UMI's microform backfiles of a publication will often go back decades or even well into the nineteenth century. Both of the UMI catalogs can be searched online at www.umi.com.

- ***The Union List of Serials* and *New Serial Titles*.** These multivolume sets, available in major research libraries, include many obscure and long-ceased serials not listed in print anywhere else. They will tell you which libraries in your region have a particular serial.

6.3 Full-Text Searching

Database searches are conducted using key words or phrases supplied by you; for example, the full name of the person you are researching, or the names of businesses he or she is associated with, or the names of his or her closest cronies. If you don't know the full name, you can search by a partial name, by variant spellings, and so on. The database vendor's search engine will search every word of every text in the entire database collection (or any designated file or library thereof) and display the title and date of publication of each article in which the key word or phrase appears (along with the block of text in which it is embedded); you can then decide whether you want to open the text of a given article or download it.

The most obvious advantage of newspaper database searching is that you avoid the tedium of going through indexes and microfilm. Equally important, database searching enables you to find articles in which your subject is mentioned only in passing—those obscure, unindexable references that so often furnish a researcher with the best leads but are found only by sheer luck when perusing the headlines on microfilm.

Full-text-search capabilities also facilitate research into your subject's associates and business interests. Let's say you are compiling information about Moe G., a Midwest racketeer. Your search of the database that includes the leading daily in Moe's city (online since 1981) turns up six articles, from which you learn that Moe owns a trucking company and a nightclub and that he is alleged to control a Teamster local. The articles also tell you the name of the lawyer who won Moe's acquittal in a 1984 extortion trial and the names of Moe's codefendants. You then search the database for every article mentioning Atlas Trucking, the Starlite Lounge, IBT Local 4294, or any of the individuals mentioned in the six articles. You find 12 additional articles with this second search. Some have no probable connection to Moe (for example, the article about the death of Moe's lawyer's mother in a nursing home). Others spark your interest—for instance, the article about the Atlas driver arrested for armed assault in

1982. You can take your search through additional cycles if you believe the results will warrant the expense. (Understand that this example of a search restricted to one newspaper is somewhat simplified; in reality, you would be doing a global search of other publications in the database along with the local daily. You might also enter another database from another vendor that carries the city's rival daily. And you would surely search a variety of non-newspaper databases—for instance, the Dun & Bradstreet database for a credit report on Moe's trucking business and the computerized indexes of the local courts for the docket numbers of all civil cases involving Moe or any of his associates.)

6.4 Newspaper Databases

Online Full-Text-Search Newspaper Archives
The number of newspapers searchable online is constantly growing. As of 1998, major database vendors were offering over 250 daily papers from every region of the United States and Canada. The *Gale Directory of Publications and Broadcast Media* and *Fulltext Sources Online* (see section 6.2) will tell you which vendors offer which newspapers. If the paper you need is not listed in the print version of either directory, you might check the online version (the *Gale Directory*'s online version is updated daily).

The following vendors are recommended for full-text newspaper searches:

- Dow Jones News/Retrieval offers over 200 U.S. dailies, with archives in some cases dating back to the 1980s. These include the former DataTimes archival collection, with coverage ranging from big-city papers such as the *Houston Chronicle* to those in medium-sized cities (such as the *Des Moines Register*) to those serving smaller cities (such as the *Greensboro News & Record* in North Carolina).

- UMI's ProQuest Direct, which you can access at most large public libraries, also offers the DataTimes collection (along with over two dozen national newspapers that UMI previously covered) for a total of 150 newspapers. Currently, the DataTimes papers are available only back to 1995; full electronic runs of these papers—in many cases back to the 1980s—should be available by the year 2000, according to UMI.

- DIALOG—the online service most widely available at college libraries—offers through its "Papers" library almost 60 U.S. dailies ranging from the *Anchorage Daily News* to the *Wichita Eagle*.

- LEXIS-NEXIS, a division of Reed Elsevier, Inc., offers over 250 U.S. newspapers, including dailies from all regions and from cities of all sizes, national business and trade newspapers (such as *American Banker* and *Computerworld*), local business papers from dozens of cities, and national and state legal newspapers (such as the *National Law Journal* and *Michigan Lawyers Weekly*). Major national and regional newspapers of record can be searched back 10 years, 20 years, or more: the *New York Times* (since 1980), the *Washington Post* (since 1977), the *Los Angeles Times* (since 1985), the *Boston Globe* (since 1988), and the *Chicago Tribune* (since 1985).

A subscription to LEXIS-NEXIS is too expensive for most private individuals. You can search the NEXIS (news rather than legal) databases at some public libraries, however, to find citations for the articles in which your keyword is listed. If you have a home business, you can pay $25 for one-day usage and do your searching at home. However, if you choose to download the articles you find—as opposed to copying them from microform or from the bound volumes at your local library or obtaining copies through interlibrary loan—the cost could swiftly mount.

If your research task requires an unusually complicated search, you might consider using the LEXIS-NEXIS express service (the search is performed by the vendor's in-house staff; you are given a cost estimate before the search begins). Similar services are offered by public library search services—a professional librarian will search several database vendors for you using a single gateway.

Note that there may be differences in the amount of text from a given newspaper offered by different vendors. Not all vendors offer the complete electronic backfiles; nor do all vendors offer every single edition (city and final, all suburban editions, and so on) or even the full representation of a single edition (the vendor may have only the stories with the newspaper's byline). If full coverage is important to you, question the customer service representatives of the different vendors to find out who offers the closest approximation.

Internet Online Editions

As of 1998, over 600 U.S. daily newspapers (over one-third of the total) and about 200 weeklies had an online presence. The dailies included not only major national and regional papers such as the *Washington Post* and the *Chicago Tribune* but a wide range of small dailies from every state; indeed, 60 percent of the online dailies had print circulations of no more than 50,000. You can view the current editions of most of these papers for free on the Internet; however, access to their archives through the Internet is often a problem.

The world of these online editions can be accessed from a variety of Web directories. If you want a megadirectory to the many newspaper directories, go to lcweb.loc.gov/rr/news/lists.html. If you simply want a directory of newspaper Web sites by state, city, and type of newspaper, try dir.yahoo.com/News_and_Media/Newspapers (this directory includes not just dailies but also college papers, business and alternate-news weeklies, and other categories). If you want to concentrate on newspapers that offer extensive archives at their Web sites, try metalab.unc.edu/slanews/internet/archives.html. If you want a search service that will search multiple news sites, your options include (among others) totalnews.com, www.newsworks.com, www.newsindex.com (current articles only), and www.realcities.com (Knight-Ridder papers only). For finding local business weeklies online, try www.amcity.com. Online access to local alternative weeklies and campus dailies and weeklies is discussed in sections 6.15 and 6.19, respectively.

Although useful for finding current news items, the Web sites of individual newspapers are no substitute for LEXIS-NEXIS and other major vendors of newspaper databases. Many newspaper Web sites offer only the current online edition, which may not contain all the contents of the print edition. If a site offers archival access, this access may be limited only to the truncated online edition or to selected articles deemed most important by the editors. Even if the archives do include all or most of the news in the print edition, coverage may not go back more than a week or so. Some city dailies offer archives going back a year or two, and some campus dailies offer archives going back only to the beginning of the semester or the school year. It should also be noted that most online archives (and this includes the archives provided by commercial databases) do not contain the display advertising, legal notices, and other items that might be of crucial importance in backgrounding a person or business entity. Some online newspapers do contain classified advertising from the current edition, but this material is generally not archived.

On the other hand, online editions may contain certain original material not included in the print edition or in the traditional electronic back-files available through NEXIS or DIALOG. Such supplemental material may include the portions of important articles that were cut from the print edition because of lack of space, expanded neighborhood news, expanded local business news, an expanded letters to the editor section, the full texts of press conferences and speeches, and various types of background reports.

If you want to download articles from many source newspapers, you should use one of the Internet subscription services that provide free searching and that allow you to download the articles you find for a very modest fee. NewsLibrary (www.newslibrary.com) offers fifty U.S. daily newspapers with coverage in some cases back to the 1980s. The Electric Library (www.elibrary.com) also offers an impressive list of papers, including many ethnic weeklies as well as dailies and newswires.

Full-Text-Search Newspaper Databases on CD-ROM

The backfiles of many newspapers are available on CD-ROM. Although often updated less frequently than their online counterparts—and usually offering less-than-full coverage of the news text of the editions included—CD-ROM databases for major national newspapers and often for your local newspaper can be searched for free at your local public library.

Newsbank, Inc., offers the full text of 51 U.S. newspapers; the archival disks in some instances date back to the early 1980s. One option your library may have is Newsbank's Nationwide News, which provides full-text articles (but not the complete editions) of seven national and regional newspapers: the *Atlanta Journal/Constitution* (from 1983); *Boston Globe* (from 1985); *Chicago Tribune* (from 1985); *Christian Science Monitor* (from 1990); *Dallas Morning News* (from 1984); *Los Angeles Times* (from 1985); and *Washington Post* (from 1986). UMI's ProQuest offers the *New York Times*, the *Wall Street Journal*, *USA Today*, and the *Washington Post*. DIALOG OnDisc offers CD-ROM versions of the *Boston Globe, Detroit Free Press, Los Angeles Times, Miami Herald, Newsday, Philadelphia Inquirer, San Francisco Chronicle*, and *San Jose Mercury News*.

"Hidden" Newspaper Databases

Many of the online newspaper databases offer full-text coverage back only to the middle or late 1980s; very few provide coverage for issues before 1981. However, a given newspaper might have earlier issues stored electronically that have not been offered for sale through an online vendor because the demand is not sufficient. Also, some newspapers have had electronic archives for years but have not yet signed an agreement with a vendor to sell them online.

If you need access to any of these "hidden" databases, call the newspaper's library. They may occasionally do courtesy searches for serious researchers. Some publications have a reader call-up service, linked to the in-house database, through which you can get at least the date of the article you need.

You can also try contacting the staff reporter whose beat corresponds most closely to what you are working on, get him or her interested in your research, and obtain printouts from the electronic library—and photocopies from the clippings morgue that predates the electronic library—in return for a promise of access to the fruits of your investigation.

Full-Text-Search Newswire Databases

Most people think of the wire services as organizations with correspondents in Washington and Moscow who cover the Big Picture. But the wire services' state and regional bureaus—and their stringer correspondents—generate a vast amount of news at the grassroots level. The Associated Press (AP) employs more than 3,000 staffers in 143 domestic and 93 overseas news bureaus; as a news cooperative, it also draws on the resources of its 1,800 newspaper members and 6,000 radio-television members. United Press International (UPI) also has a network of bureaus and stringers.

Wire service databases can be accessed through LEXIS-NEXIS, including AP and UPI's world, national, business, and sports wires (since 1977 and 1980 respectively), UPI's state and regional wires (since 1980), Canada NewsWire (since 1992), Southwest Newswire (since 1984), States News

Service (since 1984), Central News Agency (since 1984), Gannett News Service (since 1989), and the Jewish Telegraphic Agency (since 1991). LEXIS-NEXIS also offers foreign wire services (such as Reuters) and several publicity, business, financial, and government newswires. DIALOG offers AP News (since 1984), UPI News (since 1983), Federal News Service (since 1991), BNA Daily News (since 1990), and several other wire services.

Wire service databases may help you find many local and regional news items that could never be found by searching local unarchived newspapers or local and regional newspapers whose own online archives do not date back as far as those of the wire services. If any local item from a given day was important enough to make the wire, you can be sure that it was covered at the same time by the local daily or weeklies. You can then go to the microfilm of the local papers and probably find articles with much more detail than what the wire service stringer reported.

Note that if newspaper archives or clippings files contain an article bearing a wire service dateline, you should (if the article's topic is especially important to your research) check the wire service archives for the full text (newspapers very often print only the first few paragraphs of lengthy wire service articles). This is especially important if the wire service article comes from a local bureau staffer or a local stringer who knows the "territory" as well as the local media reporters do, and who may have included in his report certain facts or incidents ignored by the local daily.

Online and CD-ROM Newspaper Abstracts and Indexes

The Information Bank, produced by the New York Times Company and available through LEXIS-NEXIS, offers abstracts of *New York Times* articles from 1969 (as well as the full text of the *Times* from 1980 on). It also selectively abstracts dozens of other national and regional newspapers.

UMI selectively indexes and abstracts 29 national, regional, and ethnic newspapers. Coverage since 1989 is included in DIALOG file 483 (Newspaper Abstracts Daily) and coverage from 1984–88 is in DIALOG file 603 (Newspaper Abstracts). UMI's ProQuest also offers Newspaper Abstracts on CD-ROM (coverage of nine major newspapers since 1989).

The National Newspaper Index (DIALOG file 111) provides front-to-back indexing of the *New York Times*, *Christian Science Monitor*, and *Wall Street Journal* from 1979 on, and selective indexing of the *Los Angeles Times* and the *Washington Post* from 1982 on.

These resources are chiefly useful today in searching the period between the earliest year covered by indexing and the earliest year for which full-text searching is available.

NewsBank Electronic Information System and NewsBank Library

The NewsBank Electronic Information System provides selective indexing of newspapers in over 450 U.S. cities, including the state capital and largest city of each state (for NewsBank's coverage of periodicals, see section 6.5). Your public library may have part of this collection, which is on CD-ROM back to 1981 with microfiche coverage back to 1970. All articles included are locally written; the index does not include wire service or syndicated articles. Issued concurrently is the NewsBank Library, which offers the full text on microfiche of over 2 million of the indexed articles dating back to 1970. A CD-ROM version of the NewsBank Library, with over 40,000 full-text articles per year, is available back to 1991 only.

NewsBank's research tools can extend the range of your search significantly beyond the current limits of online databases. The system is available at over 6,000 libraries nationwide.

6.5 Periodicals Databases

Online and CD-ROM Full-Text Search of Periodicals

Major Database Collections: LEXIS-NEXIS offers over 2,000 general-interest, business, and trade periodicals online, including hundreds of newsletters. Most of these can be searched full-text through the LEXIS-NEXIS News and Business Library (you can either search the entire library or narrow your focus to a particular type of publication or region of the United States). In addition, LEXIS's specialized law libraries (including the Environmental Law Library) include relevant titles from the News and Business Library.

ProQuest Direct, the UMI online service available at many public libraries, provides the full text of over 1,400 general-reference, business, and scholarly periodicals (back to 1986).

The Northern Light Special Collection (www.northernlight.com) includes thousands of full-text magazines and journals dating back to 1995. Northern Light provides free searching of its databases and requires no subscription fee. You pay only for what you read (the prices of articles typically range from $1 to $4).

Interactive Editions: Hundreds of national magazines, following the lead of newsweeklies such as *Time* and *Maclean's*, have developed online interactive editions at their Web sites. These editions often include letters to the editor and comments by writers (in response to reader queries) that would never be included in a print edition. In addition, these editions can include entire articles or portions of articles that were cut from the print edition because of lack of space (some online magazines, however, offer *less* text than is found in the print edition).

Electronic Journals: Another new development is the Internet electronic journal (or *e-journal*); examples range from scholarly and scientific publications to quirky e-zines. Some of the e-journals are exclusively electronic; others have a print version as well. To find directories, listings, collections, and reviews of e-journals, go to gort.ucsd.edu/ejourn/jdir.html. For links to almost 4,000 e-zines in the United States and abroad, go to www.meer.nt/~johnl/e-zine-list/index.html.

Periodicals on CD-ROM: Many news magazines and other popular magazines are available on CD-ROM. For instance, *Newsweek* offers a quarterly cumulation of its weekly editions with multimedia additions to the text (including, among other things, recorded radio interviews with news makers).

The full texts of articles included in ProQuest's Periodical Abstracts database are available in page-image or full-text-searchable CD-ROM format.

Online Abstracts and Indexes of Periodicals

Begin with UnCover (uncweb.carl.org/uncover), a database of article information (citations and very brief descriptions) taken from over 18,000 journals and periodicals dating back to 1988.

For more detailed information on individual articles, try ProQuest's Periodical Abstracts database, which provides abstracts and indexing of over 2,000 general-reference, business, and scholarly periodicals back to 1988 (with selected titles dating back to 1986); also try ProQuest's ABI/Inform, which provides abstracts and indexing for over 1,000 business-oriented titles (with coverage in some instances back to 1971). Both of these databases are accessible through ProQuest Direct, an online service available at many public libraries, as well as through DIALOG. Note that there is an overlap of titles, so if you need a pre-1988 search of a Periodical Abstracts title, always check ABI/Inform.

The IAC Magazine Database (DIALOG file 47; formerly the Magazine Index) includes indexing/abstracting of more than 450 popular U.S. and Canadian magazines, with some records dating back to 1959.

The online versions of *Readers' Guide to Periodical Literature* (dating from 1983) and *Readers' Guide Abstracts* (from 1984) are available on WILSONLINE and CompuServe. These databases cover 240 popular magazines; the abstracts, averaging 125 words in length, cover every article indexed in *Readers' Guide*.

Numerous other indexes and abstracts are available through DIALOG and other database vendors (see section 11.3, "The Subject's Published Writings," for scholarly and scientific journals and section 14.2, "Publicly Held Companies and Other Large Established Businesses," for business periodicals). If the index in question does not include the name of your subject, articles mentioning him or her may be found by looking under the names of his or her closest associates or business entities (parallel backgrounding). If the index in question does not include personal names at all, a search of appropriate corporate, organizational, or subject listings may turn up articles in which your subject is mentioned and even featured.

NameBase (www.pir.org) is a selective index of personal and organizational/corporate names appearing in magazine and newspaper articles, as well as books, that deal with the intelligence community, political conspiracy, drug trafficking, and the like. NameBase includes rather thorough indexing of certain specialized magazines such as *Covert Action Quarterly*. Although the quantity of indexed articles in NameBase is relatively small, the quality of its information makes it a crucial resource for many investigative journalists.

Note: Indexes and abstracts of periodicals remain very important even in this age of full-text electronic archives. This is true not only because the indexes/abstracts may cover a decade or more of pre-electronic runs but also because many periodicals publishers retain all electronic rights and will not allow their full text to be sold by online vendors, and because some of the purported full-text databases are in fact still index/abstract-based databases with selective full text for the most recent years only.

Periodical Indexes and Abstracts on CD-ROM with Various Full-Text Retrieval Products

ProQuest offers its Periodical Abstracts and ABI/Inform databases (see "Online Abstracts and Indexes of Periodicals" earlier in this chapter) on CD-ROM. In addition, it offers a collection of CD-ROMs that include the electronic page images, cover to cover, and the ASCII text of hundreds of the titles included in Periodical Abstracts and ABI/Inform back to 1988.

The NewsBank Electronic Index to Periodicals, available in many public libraries, is a comprehensive CD-ROM index of 100 general-interest magazines beginning with the January 1988 issue. NewsBank also offers cover-to-cover microfiche and CD-ROM editions of selected periodicals from this list.

CD-ROM versions of Magazine Database as well as of *Readers' Guide to Periodical Literature* and *Readers' Guide Abstracts* are also available at many public libraries.

6.6 Full-Text Copy Services and Interlibrary Loan

If the index/abstract resource you are using does not include a microfiche or optical-disk article retrieval system, you will need to go to the bound volumes of the cited publication in the library stacks (or to the library's own microfilm copy). If the library doesn't have the publication in question in any format, you can obtain it (or a photocopy of the particular article) through interlibrary loan.

Another option—if you need the article quickly—is to go through a commercial copy service. You can order virtually any article indexed by DIALOG through an online service called DIALORDER, which will route you to the appropriate company (one of about 80 full-text copy services) for copies of articles from the periodical or newspaper in question.

If you are using a non-DIALOG index, contact the vendor or publisher regarding such services (hardcopy indexes may include a copy service telephone number in the front of the book).

6.7 Print Indexes to Newspapers and Periodicals

The New York Times Index

The *New York Times Index* is the grand old lady of newspaper indexes. Much larger and more detailed than any other index, it provides coverage back to 1851 and has been published in roughly its present index/abstract format since 1913. If your subject has been prominent in a part of the country distant from New York, don't automatically assume that his or her name is not included. The *New York Times* is America's newspaper of record—truly national in scope—with bureaus or stringers in every region.

The *Times Index* is an annual, with monthly supplements cumulating quarterly. Unless you access it through a database (or use the personal-name print index described later in this section), you must search the volumes one by one. I find this index useful chiefly for parallel and indirect backgrounding (see sections 1.3 and 1.4). Indeed, its hierarchical, topic-oriented mode of organization and its chronological abstracting of articles on each topic will give you a unique sense of your subject's interrelations with the people and institutions surrounding him or her. Let's say that you are backgrounding a Teamster official, and you want to know about his rise in the union in the 1970s. Regardless of whether there is any mention of this official in the *Times Index*, I would suggest that you photocopy everything under the headings for Teamsters Union and Organized Crime for every year during that period. Take the material home for careful study because it is likely to contain a wealth of leads to unindexed articles, old court files, and the subject's former associates or opponents. (As you learn more about the subject, you should consult these photocopies again from time to time to see whether you've missed anything.)

Personal Name Index to the New York Times Index

Searching for references to an individual (or his or her associates) in old volumes of the *New York Times Index* can be tedious. Entries for individual names merely refer you to subject entries; thus, you have to look up a name at least twice within each annual index. For editions of the *New York Times* since 1969, of course, you can conduct a full-text search for any name in the *New York Times Abstracts* (1969 to present) or in the *New York Times—Fulltext* (1981 to present), both on DIALOG. For editions before 1969 (or for later editions if you lack access to DIALOG or other vendors that carry *New York Times* abstracts/archives), you can find personal name references quickly using a remarkable reference work, the *Personal Name Index to the New York Times Index*. The base set is 22 volumes, covering 1851 to 1974. A supplemental set brings things up to the present and also corrects errata and adds names missed in the base set.

Both sets are organized alphabetically by personal name—you only have to look in two volumes (one for the base set, one for the supplemental set) to find every listing of your subject's name.

The *Personal Name Index* lists each reference to a person's name in chronological order, providing the year and page in the *Times Index*. The *Times Index,* in turn, usually provides enough information (including context) for you to decide whether or not you need to see the full text of a particular article on microfilm.

Although the *Personal Name Index* is not an index to the full text of the *Times,* skillful use of it can help you find articles in which unindexed references to your subject (or mention of his or her activities without mention of his or her name) occur. Simply look under the names of your subject's closest associates, especially those who are better known than your subject (or were better known during the years in question). For instance, I decide to background New York City Councilman X. I know that, in the early 1960s, he was an aide to Congressman Y. I do not find him in the *Personal Name Index* for those years, but I do find Congressman Y. Checking in the *Times Index*, I find that several of the articles on Congressman Y concern a bribery scandal. I then look at the text of the articles on microfilm and discover that the future Councilman X's name was mentioned several times in connection with the scandal. This stimulates me to try to learn more about this all-but-forgotten incident.

Print Indexes to Other Daily Newspapers

UMI offers print indexes of the following newspapers: *American Banker* (since 1971); *Atlanta Journal & Constitution* (since 1982); *Boston Globe* (since 1983); *Chicago Sun-Times* (1979–82 only); *Chicago Tribune* (since 1972); *Christian Science Monitor* (since 1945); *Denver Post* (since 1976); *Detroit News* (since 1976); *Houston Post* (since 1976); *Los Angeles Times* (since 1972); *Minneapolis Star & Tribune* (1984–85 only); *Nashville Banner & Tennessean* (since 1980—only on microfilm); *New Orleans Times-Picayune* (since 1972); *St. Louis Post-Dispatch* (since 1975); *San Francisco Chronicle* (since 1976); *USA Today* (since 1982); *Wall Street Journal* (since 1955); and *Washington Times* (since 1986). These indexes are not as detailed as the *New York Times Index* (which is also available from UMI). If your subject is not listed, look under the subject headings with which his or her name is most likely to be linked and then search the most promising articles on microfilm.

For other indexes to daily papers, check Scarecrow Press's three-volume *Newspaper Indexes: A Location and Subject Guide for Researchers.* Many of the listings in this set are of interest only to historians and genealogists, but contemporary newspapers are also included. You will find that many of the indexes only offer spotty coverage or coverage of a single brief period. Some are listed as unpublished in-house indexes or as being in preparation. Some are little more than obituary card files. *Newspaper*

Indexes is incomplete in many respects; if you don't find a particular newspaper listed, you should check with the paper's librarian (or the local historical society if the paper is defunct).

If your library does not have the microfilm backfiles of a newspaper whose index you have searched, you can obtain the microfilm reels or copies of specific articles through interlibrary loan.

Indexes to weekly newspapers specializing in investigative journalism are covered in section 6.15.

Print and Microform Magazine Indexes

Magazine Index, a microform version of the IAC Magazine Database (DIALOG file 47), is still available at some public libraries; its coverage of hundreds of magazines dates back to 1959. For earlier coverage, consult the *Readers' Guide to Periodical Literature*, which has indexed the nation's most important weekly, monthly, and quarterly general-interest magazines since early in this century. It is an annual work with cumulative supplements between volumes, and today it covers 240 periodicals. Although it is available online dating back to 1983, you must search the annual volumes for previous years. *Readers' Guide* can be useful in filling in the gaps in what you find in *Biography Index*, a resource described in section 5.4.

The rather stodgy list of publications in *Readers' Guide* is supplemented by *Popular Periodicals Index* (about 35 magazines), *Access: The Supplementary Index to Periodicals* (about 120 magazines and weekly newspapers), and *The Left Index*. These works include a number of publications specializing in investigative and advocacy journalism.

Print Indexes of Business Newspapers and Periodicals

The print indexes of business newspapers and periodicals (see section 14.2, "Publicly Held Companies and Other Large Established Businesses") are rich in biographical data about individuals in *all* fields, not just in business, dating back several decades.

6.8 Leveraging Database/Index Search Results to Find Non-Archived and Non-Indexed Articles

From Big Fish to Little Fish (and Vice Versa)

An article in a certain large daily that you found using a LEXIS-NEXIS full-text search (or through a search of index/abstract databases or their print equivalents going back decades) may be based on (or may have triggered) articles in relatively obscure newspapers that are not included in any database or print index. If there is no cross-reference within the given article, you can usually figure out which newspapers are the most likely prospects. For example, if the *New York Times* published a short article in the middle 1980s on the antics of a right-wing extremist in Iowa, the *Times* stringer may have followed up on a much more detailed story or series in the small daily covering the town in which this individual lived at the time. You will know from the *Times* article the probable time period in which the story or series in the Iowa newspaper would have appeared. Thus, if you fail to gain access to this paper's morgue (see section 6.9), you may be able to find the story or series fairly easily in the paper's microfilm back-files at the public library.

When you are following the news trail from one publication to another, keep in mind the following:

- A major local or regional story, although covered in major newspapers in other regions, will usually be treated in greater detail in the newspapers of its own region.

- A local story will often be treated in greater detail in a small local daily or weekly than in a major metropolitan daily 50 miles away.

- A local daily may be taking its story from a rival local daily or from a local weekly that treated the story in greater detail.

- Newspapers rarely give proper credit to each other.

Finding the Trigger Events

Although your local newspaper's online archives may date back only five years or so, you may find pointers to much earlier articles. If an incident occurs that transforms a person suddenly into a major focus of local or national news (for example, his or her election to public office or indictment for murder), it will trigger news coverage of all aspects of his or her life (and references to earlier reported incidents involving him or her) going back to childhood. It will also help you to find follow-up articles in the time period between the trigger event and the earliest date for which online searching of the newspaper is possible.

High Achievers

If a person is a consistent high achiever, by either local or national standards, expect the density of news coverage (and the frequency of trigger-event articles) to increase as his or her career rises to its peak. If your subject has *passed* his or her prime as a news attractor, however, your best tactic (especially for offline searching) is to start at the subject's career peak and use the pointers you find to guide you to news items from previous and subsequent years.

6.9 Morgues of Local Dailies

Morgues (systems of cross-referenced and cross-filed clippings files) were, until recent decades, the main way reporters and editors accessed the back-files of their own dailies. Today, most newspapers use digital archiving and full-text searching to supplement or replace their clippings files. (Many of these databases are then leased to vendors who sell online access to the general public—so, in essence, when you perform a full-text search of a newspaper database, you are accessing its "electronic morgue.") But the majority of newspaper backfile databases, whether available commercially online or not, do not date back more than 10 years. For earlier news items, reporters must rely on the old-fashioned clippings libraries. The best organized of these libraries will contain every mention of your subject, his or her business firm, and so forth, going back many decades.

Even if an index to your local paper exists, access to the morgue is of great value. First, it will save you the tedium of going to microfilm at the public library. Second, a morgue that has a really thorough system for clipping the daily editions will be much more complete than any index. Third, the morgue may contain court papers and other documents gathered by reporters in the course of their investigations. Fourth, it may contain clippings from the local weekly, ethnic, or "underground" papers (which usually couldn't afford to maintain their own clippings morgues in the pre-computer era) as well as from rival dailies in the city and surrounding region. Fifth, the newspaper may have obtained the clippings files of defunct local dailies and merged these files into its own.

Some newspapers allow limited morgue access to scholars, freelance journalists working on books, or researchers from public-interest organizations. If not, contact one of the newspaper's staff reporters or part-time stringers (or a freelancer who often writes for the paper's weekly magazine or Op-Ed page). Interest him or her in your investigation and arrange an exchange of information, including morgue clippings.

6.10 If There's No Index or Morgue

Don't despair. A longtime reporter may remember an article on your subject and the approximate date. Or you may learn through one of your subject's former neighbors or from a biographical dictionary the approximate date of an event in the subject's life that might have been reported (for instance, the subject's marriage or the marriage of one of his or her children). In these cases, you will have to do some searching through the microfilm or bound copies, but at least you've narrowed your search within reason.

An event covered by an unindexed local paper may also have been covered by a larger, regional paper that does have an index. Learning the date of the event from the indexed paper, you then go to the microfilm or bound volumes of the unindexed paper.

Federal, state, and local court indexes will tell you about civil and criminal cases involving your subject that may have been reported in the press. The press coverage of such cases is crucial because it may touch on matters that the rules of evidence, rulings by the judge, and the prudence of the opposing parties kept out of the court record. A particular case may drag on for years, but the most important news articles usually appear at predictable times. In a nonsensational criminal case, this will be the newspaper issues immediately following the arrest, the grand jury indictment, the trial jury verdict, and the sentencing. If the case was a high-profile one, you will need to search through the newspaper issues for the entire period from arrest to sentencing, but look especially for articles regarding the opening arguments and the summations (and don't forget the post-trial appeals process!).

For civil cases, news coverage is most likely to come when the case is first filed (especially if the plaintiff calls a press conference) and thereafter either when the jury announces its decision or the parties to the action announce an out-of-court settlement. To find these dates, examine the docket sheet at the courthouse.

If these methods fail to turn up any articles, consult a local muckraker's clippings files (see sections 6.27, "The Amateur Muckraker," and 15.1, "Finding the 'Experts'").

6.11 Searching the Internet for Unarchived Articles

Even if a local newspaper has not placed its electronic archives online, you still may find articles from that paper on the Internet. First, the paper may place selected articles that it is especially proud of on its Web site from time to time. Second, it may give permission to local civic groups or city agencies to post certain articles at their own Web sites for public interest reasons. Thus, when you search for your subject's name on the Internet using several search engines, you may find articles on him or her that appeared online in these ways. As an experiment, I searched for information on the new police chief of an upstate New York town. Although the local daily's archives were not available online, I was able to find several relevant articles (some by searching under the chief's name, some by searching under that of the newspaper) that had been placed online by city officials pursuant to their search and selection process.

Note that an unarchived article about the subject may be available at the personal Web page of the staff or freelance reporter who wrote it. The article may also be posted at the subject's own Web site; for instance, if the subject is a lawyer hungry for new clients, he or she may have posted local news articles about his or her successful trial cases.

6.12 Suburban News

Your subject may work in the city but live in a suburban community (or a smaller nearby city) that has its own daily newspaper. The archives of some suburban papers, such as *The Record* in Bergen County, New Jersey, are searchable online going back a decade or more. Such papers may be the best source for news about a subject's social life, civic activities, and grass-roots involvement in electoral politics.

An area's major metropolitan daily may produce special editions for various suburbs to compete with the suburban-based dailies. Generally, a major metropolitan paper's article on a suburban event that you find in the paper's index or through a database search will have been treated at greater length in the edition for that suburb than in the metropolitan edition or in editions for other suburbs. Indeed, the article may have appeared *only* in the given suburban edition. Although you will be able to find the article in a properly organized morgue, you may not find it (or may not find the full version) on microfilm or in the electronic database if these resources include only a single edition.

6.13 News from the Community Where the Subject Has His or Her Second Home

Your subject may spend several months of the year, and perhaps most weekends during the rest of the year, at his or her seasonal or weekend home and may be deeply involved in the life of the surrounding community. In the newspaper for this community, you may find articles about your subject's involvement in an environmental cause (or his or her arrest for drunken driving) that you would completely miss if you searched only the newspapers in his or her community of primary residence.

6.14 Defunct and Merged Dailies

The importance of newspapers in the United States has declined substantially since the advent of television. If you are backgrounding a prominent person of middle age in any medium-sized or large American city, it is quite likely that at least one local daily newspaper—a newspaper that possibly reported on your subject's activities during his or her early years (for instance, as a high school sports star or a scholarship recipient)—has gone out of business or merged with another newspaper since your subject became an adult. Indeed, a local daily may have gone out of business or merged with another since your subject's rise to prominence (say, within the last 10 years). To find the names of these defunct and premerger papers, see section 6.2.

The backfiles of a defunct newspaper, whether on microfilm or in bound volumes, are often available at the public library or historical society of the community in which it was published, or in the in-house library of a surviving local daily, and there may be an index of some kind. In addition, the defunct paper's morgue may have been sold to a surviving daily or donated to the public library or county historical society. Usually the public library or historical society will microfilm these clippings at some point and develop its own name/topic index to the microfilm reels.

6.15 Local Weeklies

In every metropolitan area, you will find flourishing weeklies, both of the free-distribution variety and of the paid subscription/newsstand type, aimed either at the entire city or at a particular city neighborhood or suburban community. You will also find weeklies specializing in ethnic or alternative-lifestyle news.

A few weeklies will have excellent clippings files for past years, organized like those of the dailies. Most weeklies lack comprehensive clippings files, but they may keep files on ongoing local political conflicts or the paper's most important investigative pieces through the years. In addition, a staffer may remember an article on your subject and be willing to dig out the back issue in which it appeared.

Never underestimate the weeklies, including the smallest. Major investigative pieces by large dailies frequently are based on spadework performed by the weeklies, and the latter may treat a story in much greater detail (and with much less pulling of punches) than any large daily would.

The *Alternative Press Index* and *Access: The Supplementary Index to Periodicals* cover feisty metropolitan weekly newspapers such as New York City's *Village Voice*, as well as defunct or still-existing counterculture newspapers that, in their heyday, uncovered vast quantities of scandalous (and still relevant) material about people in high places. Several counterculture weeklies not covered by these two reference works are indexed in *The Left Index*. Most of the indexed counterculture publications have been microfilmed by UMI; its Alternative Press collection (which, for the years since 1986, includes over one hundred publications) is available at many research libraries.

If you are investigating a crooked politician, landlord, or businessperson, the alternative press is often the best place to start. Note that a similar investigative vigor is displayed, in some localities, by city magazines (such as *New York*) and state magazines (such as *Texas Monthly*). You can find profiles of hundreds of such periodicals in *Regional Interest Magazines of the United States*.

For an online search of current editions and short-term archives of alternative weeklies, see the Association of Alternative Weeklies (AAN) Web site at www.aan.org, which provides links to about 100 publications. For links to city and state/regional magazines, see the *American Journalism Review*'s

Web site at ajr.newslink.org. For archives of the best-known alternative weeklies and city/state magazines going back several years, see LEXIS-NEXIS and other online vendors.

6.16 Ethnic and Minority Weeklies

Virtually every ethnic group in the United States has its own weekly or weeklies. African Americans alone have about 300 newspapers (mostly weeklies) throughout the country. Jews also have at least one weekly for each metropolitan area in which there is a significant Jewish population. Smaller ethnic groups may have one or two papers giving nationwide news. The New York–based *India Abroad* has regional editions in six North American cities and reports in detail when any member of the Indian-American community wins a civic award or is convicted of a crime. (Note that *India Abroad* has a very well-organized clippings morgue for its pre-electronic years.) Native American communities also publish a number of newspapers, such as *The Tundra Times*, serving the 80,000 Eskimos, Aleuts, and Athabaskans in Alaska.

Nine African American newspapers, mostly weeklies, are covered by the *Black Newspaper Index* (1979 to present). Selective abstracts from these newspapers can be accessed through UMI's Newspaper Abstracts database (1984 to 1988) and UMI's Newspaper Abstracts Daily database (1989 to present), both available on DIALOG.

Ethnic NewsWatch, a CD-ROM product, offers a collection of about 400,000 full-text articles, reviews, and editorials from over 200 publications of all ethnic and minority groups in the United States. The general ethnic categories covered include African American, Asian/Pacific, European/Eastern European, Hispanic, Jewish, Arab/Middle Eastern, and Native American. About 7,500 news articles are added each month. The start dates for coverage of most of these publications range from 1991 to 1996. The online version of Ethnic NewsWatch is available from LEXIS-NEXIS, Northern Light, and other vendors.

6.17 Professional and Trade Publications

Articles that feature or mention your subject may have appeared in a professional or trade publication. If it's an interview in a publication read only by the subject's colleagues, he or she may have spoken far more freely than if being questioned by a reporter from the major media. To find the most likely publications, look under the appropriate topic headings in *Associations' Publications in Print, Standard Periodical Directory*, and *Newsletters in Print*. Also check *Ulrich's International Periodicals Directory* because the subject may have talked most frankly of all to a foreign trade publication.

To find additional trade and professional publications, look in the *Encyclopedia of Associations* and the *National Trade and Professional Associations of the U.S.* If an association is listed, it probably has, at the least, a newsletter for its members. Simply call the association's research director and ask for the names of its local, regional, and national publications and where library backfiles might be located.

Many trade and professional newspapers and periodicals are indexed in works such as the *Business Periodicals Index* or can be searched online using the major database vendors. Others must be searched issue by issue, unless they include an annual index at the end of each year. Fortunately, many have a short section in each issue devoted to news about members. If your subject is prominent in his or her trade or profession, it may be worth your while to spend an hour or so going through back issues.

Even if you don't find any direct information about your subject in a professional or trade periodical, you will at least find the names of many people in the subject's field who will know him or her personally or by reputation. In addition, you may find articles about the company for which the subject works or about one or more of his or her closest colleagues or associates.

Indexes of professional and trade association Web sites can be found at dir.yahoo.com/Business_and_Economy/Organizations (select "Professional" or "Trade Associations"). Often such Web sites will include the current issue of the organization's newsletter or magazine, and sometimes a few recent back issues or selected articles from recent back issues. These Web sites may also provide links to other online publications relevant to the given profession or industry.

6.18 House Organs

The house publications of companies or nonprofit organizations for which your subject has worked may include noncontroversial background information on his or her career. For instance, such publications may tell about job promotions or professional honors that the subject has received. Possibly, there will be a section of personal news in each issue telling about marriages of employees, births of their children, and so forth. (If not in the firm's public organ, this material is often included in a staff newsletter produced by the personnel department.) Equally important, house organs will give you the names of many of the subject's past and present co-workers.

The *Magazines and Internal Publications Directory* (volume two of the *Working Press of the Nation* series) describes over 1,200 house organs. The most recent editions of a house organ can sometimes be obtained from a company or nonprofit organization's public relations department (or at the organization's Web site); the backfiles will usually be available in the in-house library. (Nonprofit organization's libraries are often open to the public; corporate libraries can sometimes be accessed by a college business major preparing a term paper.) For house-organ backfiles in public libraries, check the *Union List of Serials* and *New Serial Titles*; also conduct a corporate author search of the Library of Congress's Serials Catalog (lcweb.loc.gov).

6.19 Campus Newspapers

Over 500 student-run college and university newspapers are currently online, although often in truncated editions. In many cases, these newspapers offer limited backfiles (the current week, semester, or school year). Some offer archival access back to the mid-1990s. A directory with links to over 400 campus newspaper Web pages is found at http://dir.yahoo.com/ News_and_Media/College_and_University/Newspapers. At this site, you can also check separately for business school and medical school newspapers. Note that a keyword search by school may turn up more than one publication. For instance, I found that the Columbia University Web site offers not only the *Columbia Daily Spectator* but also a business school paper and a paper sponsored by the journalism school (these, however, are by no means the only student newspapers published at Columbia).

The nonelectronic backfiles of a campus newspaper may be found in bound volumes at the newspaper's office or on microfilm at the campus library. Clippings files regarding selected topics or individuals may be found at the campus library's archival division. These resources may be useful in gathering information from years or decades past on students, faculty, administrative staff, alumni, visiting scholars and speakers, and even non-university-affiliated residents of the surrounding community. For more on campus newspapers, see section 11.1, "Backgrounding a Subject's Educational Past."

6.20 Alumni Newspapers and Magazines

If you know which college your subject attended, contact the editor of the alumni newspaper and magazine. Many of these publications maintain clippings files of back-issue articles. As boosters of their school, they may be delighted to furnish journalists with clippings that show what high achievers their alumni are. Even if they don't have clippings files, the editor may recall an article on your subject. You should also try the university archives, which may have clippings files more comprehensive than those at the alumni office.

When searching the bound volumes of an alumni magazine, note that brief biographical notes and obituaries are often organized under class headings. If your subject is a member of the class of 1956, you can quickly search through the listings for that class in each issue.

Many alumni publications are now online, some offering several years in backfiles (for instance, the Cornell University alumni magazine can be searched back to 1989). Of course, the online versions may not contain all of what's in the print version. A directory of and links to alumni organizations can be found at http://dir.yahoo.com/Education/Organizations.

6.21 Trade Union Publications

In the United States and Canada, there are hundreds of labor union newspapers, magazines, and newsletters published by international unions, by state or local AFL-CIO councils, or by individual unions on the district or local level. In some unions, each local will have its own publication. District councils (the locals of a given union within, say, a given metropolitan area) may also have a publication. The backfiles may have valuable information on your subject if he or she was or is a union officer, an active rank and filer, or a management figure who has clashed with the union.

Don't neglect the dissident newspapers put out by rank-and-file groups at odds with the union bureaucracy. For instance, *Convoy Dispatch*, the Teamsters for a Democratic Union monthly, is an excellent source on the misdeeds of old-line Teamster officials on every level.

Backfile collections of trade union newspapers can be found in university libraries, especially if the university has an industrial relations department. To find the nearest library with back copies of a particular publication, see the *Union List of Serials* and *New Serial Titles*.

For a giant directory of thousands of trade union Web sites (from locals to regional councils to international union headquarters), go to www.mgbgs.com/labor.shtml. Links to other union Web directories can be found at dir.yahoo.com/Business_and_Economy/Unions.

Information on many obscure trade union publications, past and present, can be found through a corporate author search of the Library of Congress's Serials Catalog at lcweb.loc.gov.

6.22 Sports, Hobby, and Other Specialty Publications

Is your subject a collector of ancient coins? a breeder of prize-winning dogs? a rock climber? an ardent participant in bridge tournaments? Look in *Associations' Publications in Print* as well as *Standard Periodical Directory* for periodicals relevant to your subject's field of interest. Investigative journalist Steve Weinberg found relevant material for his biography of billionaire Armand Hammer in publications as obscure as *Arabian Horse World*.

To find the Web pages (and online editions, if any) of specialty magazines, go to the index of directories at dir.yahoo.com/News_and_Media/Magazines/Web_Directories. Also see the directory of sporting and hobby magazines at dir.yahoo.com/Recreation/Magazines.

6.23 Publications of Fraternal, Civic, and Charitable Organizations

If a biographical dictionary lists your subject as holding membership (or a volunteer or paid position) in any fraternal, civic, or charitable organization, look in *Associations' Publications in Print* for the name and address of that group's newsletter or bulletin (or go to the organization's Web site). Note that many associations (such as the Boy Scouts) have state or regional as well as national publications. Some also have local newsletters. In general, the most detailed information about an active local member will appear in the local or state publication rather than in the national one.

6.24 Religious Publications

Ever-growing numbers of religious newspapers and periodicals are published in the United States. American Catholics, for example, have no less than 155 diocesan newspapers. If your subject is in the clergy or is a lay person active in church affairs, his or her activities are almost certain to have been covered in denominational publications on some level, whether national, regional, state, or local.

Weekly church bulletins handed out at the Sunday services often include news about members of the congregation, such as births, marriages, participation in a mission-work team, election to the church governing board, or appointment as a Sunday school teacher. If one of your subject's children is being baptized or confirmed on a particular Sunday, that, too, will be in the bulletin. For many blue-collar families, these publications may be just about the only place they are mentioned in print. Church bulletins are usually on file in the church office, often going back decades.

For news of the clergy and prominent lay persons active in the church, you might check the archives of the online church news services. These include the Religious News Service (with its daily news reports), the Lutheran News Service, the Episcopal News Service, United Methodist Information, ChurchNews International, and the Catholic News Service, all available through CompuServe.

For access to religious news on the Internet, go to Zondervan Publishing House's vast Web directory at www.zondervan.com.

6.25 Genealogical Periodicals and Indexes

If there is a periodical devoted to persons with the subject's surname or the subject's mother's maiden name, it may contain biographical information about the subject or some of his or her relatives. *The Directory of Family One-Name Periodicals* lists 1,600 of these publications. Many other genealogical periodicals are indexed (by individual as well as family name) in the *Periodical Source Index* (*PERSI*), which also covers local history periodicals; always check the *PERSI* supplements as well as the base set. *PERSI* is available online at www.ancestry.com. Photocopies of articles indexed in *PERSI* can be ordered for a small fee from the Allen County Public Library Foundation in Fort Wayne, Indiana; the order form is at http://www.acpl.lib.in.us/database/graphics/order_form.html.

6.26 The Reporter: His or Her Sources and Files

The main object of searching through newspapers and periodicals is not simply to compile more and more clippings; rather, it is to find live sources: the people behind the news stories who know the things that didn't get printed.

Clippings will lead you to basically four types of people: the reporter who researched and wrote the article; the people mentioned in the article as participants in the reported events; the people whom the reporter quotes as sources (whether participants, eyewitnesses, or experts with background information); and the reporter's unnamed informants.

If the reporter is an expert on your subject (for instance, the longtime reporter on the labor beat who has written several articles about the carpenter's union official you are investigating), get whatever background information and advice he or she is willing to provide and, if possible, gain access to his or her private clippings files and a referral to his or her chief sources. (Contrary to the TV depiction of reporters, most are not jealous of their files and sources unless a major scoop is involved. In approaching reporters, remember that it's in their interest to cooperate with you if your research can fill in gaps in their own work.)

Sometimes the reporter may not know very much, as, for example, when an article was only one of many hurried pieces written on a tight deadline. In such cases, you may want to see whatever documentation the reporter has retained, but your main objective will be to get the telephone numbers of the sources who provided most of the information.

6.27 The Amateur Muckraker

The amateur muckraker is the freelance writer or citizen-researcher devoted to gathering all the scandalous clippings (and gossip) on everyone in town (or at least on particular groups or individuals who have incurred his or her wrath). At their best, muckrakers can be an almost miraculous source of information on evildoers, and you should urge local reporters to put you in contact with them. For a full discussion, see section 15.1, "Finding the 'Experts.'"

6.28 Library Clippings Collections

Hundreds of libraries around the United States have newspaper or periodicals clippings files donated to them by private researchers or compiled by library staffers. A good example of the treasures you might find is in the North Carolina Collection at the University of North Carolina's Wilson Library in Chapel Hill. The library staff began collecting these clippings from newspapers across the state in the 1920s. Photocopies of all clippings through 1975 were compiled into 364 volumes, which are divided into biography and subject collections. The biography volumes, organized alphabetically by name, contain clippings on thousands of North Carolinians. They include profile articles, interviews, and obituaries as well as news articles centered on the individual's activities. You can access further information on an individual by looking in relevant subject articles. In the mid-1990s, the UNC library staff completed a second set of volumes to cover the years 1976–1989, including 99 volumes (plus an index) for the biography section. The biographical and subject indexes to this second set (as well as indexes to selected portions of the first set) can be searched at www.lib.unc.edu/ncc/online.html.

To find similar collections elsewhere, see *Prospect Researcher's Guide to Biographical Research Collections*, which lists more than 1,000 genealogical, biographical, and other special libraries (cross-referenced by subject and geographical area). See also the tips given in section 11.2, "Backgrounding an Individual Using Archival Collections," and in section 15.4, "The World of Research Filing-Cabinets."

6.29 Reprints/Reproductions of Newspaper and Periodical Articles

Individuals and organizations have a healthy instinct for self-promotion. An article on your subject in an obscure publication—which you would never have found on your own—may have been reproduced and widely circulated by the subject or an organization with which he or she is closely affiliated. One activist whom I know sends out a newsletter every few months composed mostly of reproductions of articles from newspapers in cities and towns of all sizes around the country in which he and his organization have staged protest rallies. If I decided to write a profile on this individual, I would first ask him for all the back issues of his newsletter. I rather suspect that I would end up with far more articles on him with this simple request than if I used a NEXIS search.

This individual is putting the text for many of the articles about himself on his organization's Web page. He is also sending the articles that present his organization in the most favorable light to reporters along with his press releases (and to his supporters along with his fundraising appeals).

The more he circulates these copies, the more he is guaranteeing that some of them will be preserved in reporters' clippings files as well as in the personal files of his supporters and the organizational files of his opponents—and eventually in some archival collection.

Tactics such as these are used not just by activists but also by people engaged in self-promotion for business or professional reasons (such as Dr. Z, the chiropractor down the block, who is always seeking publicity for his self-published diet book or his weekly radio talk show). In addition, the deeds of even the most unassuming person may be trumpeted by a proud employer. (Thus, if you happen to gain access to the in-house newsletter backfiles of the company where your subject works or used to work, you may find a reprint from an unarchived local weekly praising the subject's work on an annual charity fund drive or announcing that he or she has been chosen by a local professional society as its Person of the Year.)

6.30 Broadcast Transcripts, Abstracts, and Indexes

Two companies, Journal Graphics (www.tv-radio.com) and Burrelle's Information Service (www.burrelles.com), dominate the broadcast transcript field, offering wide coverage of national television and radio news programs, public affairs programs, and talk shows. To find the transcripts you need, consult the indexes published by both companies (Journal Graphics's index is cumulative back to 1968).

Journal Graphics transcripts from 1990 on are available online from Dow Jones (along with transcripts from several other sources); Burrelle's transcripts (from 1996) can be accessed using LEXIS-NEXIS.

Broadcast News, a CD-ROM database produced by Journal Graphics, provides over 44,000 full-text transcripts annually from more than 50 broadcast news and public affairs programs; it is found in many large public libraries.

Abstracts of the transcripts from about 90 TV programs are included in UMI's Newspaper & Periodical Abstracts database, available on DIALOG.

The *Television News Index and Abstracts*, found in many research libraries, covers the national evening news on all three major networks back to 1972 (and in microform back to 1968). It includes an item-by-item description of each program—you can then order a video cassette of a given segment or of the entire program from Vanderbilt University's Television News Archive. The entire index and abstract database, including special reports and periodic news broadcasts, can now be searched at tvnews.vanderbilt.edu.

Links to a variety of Web sites from which you can search U.S. and Canadian radio and TV archives (including the Pacifica Radio Archives, which contain over 40,000 recordings) can be found at the JournalismNet site (www.journalismnet.com).

7 ·

Collecting the "Identifiers"

To conduct a thorough background check, three items are most important: the subject's full name, correctly spelled, including a full middle name and correct generational designation (such as "Jr." or "III"); the subject's date of birth; and the subject's Social Security Number (SSN). Without the first, it is sometimes difficult to follow the paper trail even on the simplest level (especially if the name is a common one). Without the second and third, it is difficult to find public records filed according to these identifiers.

In addition, there are a number of secondary identifiers, such as place of birth, which are important under certain limited circumstance; information on such identifiers is also included in this chapter.

7.1 What's in a Name?

Without any deceptive intent, many individuals leave a confusing paper trail because of marital name changes or informal name variations. When you first see your subject's name in a newspaper article or phone directory or on a mailbox, you should not assume that this is the full name under which most records regarding the subject's past are filed. Indeed, there may be no single form of his or her name that covers most of the available documentation.

Middle Names, Nicknames, and Aliases
Your subject may be commonly known by his or her middle name, a nickname, or a shortened form of his or her first or middle name (such as "Dell" for "Delmore"), and your subject may give any of these as his or her first name in a telephone listing or when introducing himself or herself in social situations. John Quincey Public may receive utility bills as Quincey

Public, receive MasterCard statements as John Q. Public, sign his name on checks as J. Quincey Public, and be listed in the phone book (and also be known to most acquaintances) as Quince Public. In searching through phone or crisscross directories and county courthouse indexes, this may be only a minor annoyance because Public is such an uncommon surname. But if your subject's last name is Smith, you will have to get things clear. This is all the more necessary if the subject has more than one middle name and varies their use according to whim (for example, John Gerald Wellington Marshall Smith, who is always one step ahead of the bill collectors!).

To make matters even more confusing, some people don't have a middle name; and others, such as Harry S Truman, may have only a middle initial.

In your earliest interviews with persons who know your subject, find out whether he or she is usually called by a first or middle name, what his or her past and present nicknames are, and whether he or she has ever used any pseudonyms or aliases. Also note carefully any evidence of name variations in newspaper clippings about your subject.

Generational Designations

Confusion may result when a father and son have the same first and middle as well as last name. This is supposed to be cleared up by the use of "Jr.," "III," and "IV." But your subject and those with whom he shares the name (grandfather, father, son, or grandson) may not use the generational designations consistently. For instance, if the father and son live in different cities, the son may not bother to include "Jr." or "III" in his telephone listing. Or he may drop the "III" because it sounds pompous. Someone searching for the son may see "Jr." after the father's name in the phone book and thus mistake father for son. Confusion may also result when the father and son live in the same household and the telephone listing for one or the other lacks the proper designation.

Maiden Names, Married Names, and Other Variations

If a married woman uses her husband's surname, you will still need her previous name or names. Records from before her marriage will be listed by her maiden name or her previous married name, and she may still use her maiden or previous married name in her professional career. If your subject is her husband, be aware that he may be using her maiden name (or the name of one of her parents) as the "straw name" to conceal his ownership of a real estate parcel. The question of maiden names and previous married names is dealt with in detail later in this section under "Finding a Subject's Previous Names" and "Finding the Maiden Name of a Subject's Mother" (also see section 4.12, "Tracking a Person Through His or Her Family, Friends, and Ex-Spouse(s)").

In this era of frequent divorce and remarriage, joint custody of children, two-career households, "blended" families, and legally recognized gay and lesbian partnerships, name variations can become extremely complicated.

- Wives frequently use hyphenated surnames, and the practice has also been adopted by some husbands. Although this can sometimes be convenient for genealogists and skip tracers, it can also be quite confusing. The wife may put her name first, the husband may put his first, she may put his first, he may put hers first, both may put his first, both may put hers first. In addition, either or both spouses may vary the usage according to the situation or their mood. In filling out a job application, for instance, the husband may drop the hyphenated name to avoid being regarded as a flake.

- The husband may give up his own surname for his wife's.

- Husband and wife may choose an entirely new surname to share, which can be an amalgamation of syllables from both names or an entirely new name with a shared symbolic meaning.

- The wife may retain her maiden name for all purposes, social and business, and may be listed in the phone book *only* under that name. Or she may use her maiden name for professional purposes (especially if she was established in a profession such as medicine or law before her marriage) and her husband's name for social purposes. Or she may use both names *without* a hyphen, as does Hillary Rodham Clinton. Or she may shift from maiden name to married name (or vice versa) for certain special purposes such as establishing an alternative credit history if she has a bad credit rating under the other name.

- When a teenage child is living with a mother who has remarried, the mother may use her new husband's surname while the teenager continues to use (and has a telephone listing under) the father's surname. Or the teenager may use the father's name in some situations and the mother's new husband's name in other situations (for other variations on this, see section 4.12).

- Parents may choose for a child, at birth, a surname in the maternal rather than paternal line, a hyphenated surname with either the husband's or wife's name first, or a surname that is an amalgamation of the parents' surnames.

- Parents may choose a surname at random for their child. According to the *Wall Street Journal*, February 11, 1987: "Parents are making use of little-known laws that allow them to bestow on their children the surname of their choice. Short of a curse word or a series of numerals, the choice in most states is unlimited."

- When an unmarried couple is living together, the woman may use the man's surname or a hyphenated version of the two names in certain social situations or in signing an apartment lease (hence ensuring that the "married" name will appear in the building lobby's directory). But she may continue to use her maiden name or the name of the husband from whom she is separated or divorced in other situations. In the case of one couple I tracked, this was complicated by the fact that both were using "political" surnames at meetings of, and in their writings for, an extremist sect. Over a 10-year period, the woman used, often interchangeably, her lover's political surname, her lover's real surname, her ex-husband's surname, her own previous political surname, and her maiden name.

For further information on maiden names and women's adult names, maiden or not, see the next section.

Common-Law and Statutory Name Changes

If you are tracing a subject's name backward in old telephone books and the trail runs out, it could be that the subject has changed his or her name. Immigrants from Europe in earlier generations often "Americanized" their names. Many African Americans in recent decades have replaced their "slave names" with Arabic, West African, or Swahili names. Cult members (such as the Hari Krishnas) change their names on the instructions of their guru. Persons who have suffered public disgrace change their names to facilitate building a new life. Actors adopt names that will enhance their box office appeal. And some people change their names on a whim.

The laws regarding name changes vary from state to state. In New York, the right to change one's name for legitimate purposes is a common-law right that can be exercised by simply beginning to use the new name in all transactions and having it recognized by friends and associates. This right, which includes that of the mother of an illegitimate child to adopt the name of the putative father for herself and the child, does not require court permission. However, the law provides for statutory name change (by order of a court) as an affirmation of the common-law right. This process is distinct from name changes pursuant to marriage, adoption, divorce, or annulment.

Court-approved name changes are typically recorded at the county courthouse (unless the courthouse has become completely computerized) in a ledger book that gives both old and new names. The number of such name changes per year is usually quite small.

Whether a person uses the court method or the common-law method, he or she will need to notify various ID-issuing agencies, his or her bank, and so forth. When a person notifies the Social Security Administration of a name change, that change is recorded but the person keeps the same SSN as before. The SSN thus becomes a convenient way by which an investigator can establish the link between the subject's old and new names.

Note that some people who adopt a new name (especially those who do so through the common-law method) might only selectively notify public and private record-keeping agencies, thus continuing to use the old name in various transactions. Even if a person does notify the most important agencies, there will be a time lag before the new name fully replaces the old.

If you can't find any record of a name change, the person with the suspiciously short paper trail may be using a false identity based on a fraudulently obtained ID (see section 7.6, "How to Detect a False Identity").

Finding a Subject's Previous Names

For information about the previous name of a subject who has legally changed his or her name (whether through the name-change processes described in the first section of this chapter or pursuant to a marriage, divorce, or remarriage), a good place to begin is at one of the online information broker's sites that provide access to "above-the-line" information from credit-reporting agencies and other sources likely to have compiled name-change data. Such a search has a high likelihood of success because most people adopting a new name will inform their bank, credit card providers, and the like.

If you believe that your subject obtained his or her new name through a court order, but it's not recorded at your county courthouse, try to figure out from your knowledge of the subject's past which other jurisdictions are most likely. You can order from any county courthouse a search of its name-change register (see the *Public Record Research System—PRRS—*for contact information) and, if that search is successful, a certified copy of the name-change court order or certificate.

If your subject went the common-law route in obtaining a new name, or you can't find any information in online databases, look in old crisscross directories. If you see that the telephone number of the previous listee at the street address where the subject now lives is the same as the number now listed under the subject's name, this possibly may indicate that the name previously listed at that address is the name your subject formerly used. (If the subject had *not* changed his or her name and was merely trying to evade harassment from bill collectors or crank callers, he or she would most likely have changed the number as well as the name listed in the directory or would have obtained an unlisted number.)

As noted earlier in this section, the former name of a married woman can often be found by picking up the local phone directory. Many married women continue to use their premarriage names in the telephone directory business listings or in the white pages, often in hyphenated combination with the husband's name. In addition, premarriage names (or a reversion to the premarriage name after a separation or divorce) may often be found in the same way as other legitimate name changes—by looking in the street listing sections of back-edition crisscross directories.

Finding the Maiden Name of a Subject's Mother

Your subject's mother's maiden name is often important as a secondary identifier (for example, as an aid in complicated or very broad database searches or as an identity verification item when personal information is requested over the phone). It can also be important in gathering information about the subject's past, his or her business dealings with relatives, and so on.

You should begin your search at online information broker sites. If you don't find the maiden name there, you can consult the most relevant and accessible of numerous print directories and other resources. College alumni directories and class anniversary directories (and similar directories for public, private, and religious high schools) give both the maiden and married names of women graduates. The alumni or class anniversary directory of a husband may also give the wife's maiden name. Society guides (such as *The Social Register*) provide both names, as do biographical dictionary entries (a married woman's own dictionary profile will give this information, while her husband's profile and profiles of her grown children may also include it). Other possible sources include state or county vital records indexes (see section 10.1, "Vital Records"), old newspaper obituaries and society page wedding notices, family name books, and genealogy charts. (*Note:* If you use genealogical records in your search, be aware that the maiden name is not necessarily the birth name. The subject's mother may have taken the name of a stepfather at some point in her childhood.)

Many married women in America select their maiden name as the basis for their middle initial. For other women, and for most men, the middle initial stands simply for the middle name (or one of the middle names) they were given at birth (for example, Mary C.—for Catherine—Smith). If your subject's mother uses her maiden name as her middle name, then it will appear on any application or form she has filled out that requires the full spelling of her middle name. Generally, bank and credit card applications request that the applicant provide a full middle name; what a person puts down will appear later in the giant databases accessed by information brokers (all the more reason to start your search at these brokers' Web sites).

As already noted, many women continue to use their maiden names after marriage or may create a hyphenated or unhyphenated combination of their maiden and married names. In addition, some divorced women revert to their maiden names. The trick is to determine which women are doing this and which are using a middle name or new surname *other* than their maiden name (for instance, a name from a previous or subsequent marriage or an entirely new name adopted by a common-law or courtroom process).

If you are interested in the subject's mother's maiden name only as a secondary identifier in searching records pertaining to the subject's own finances (and not for parallel backgrounding), the definition of the mother's maiden name becomes, simply, the name her adult children routinely provide in applications to banks or other entities that routinely make such information available to credit-reporting agencies and other giant repositories of personal data, and during proof-of-identity checks when accessing personal information from a bank, credit card company, phone company, or the like. Thus, you might first look for the information you need in records directly pertaining to the subject rather than in records of his or her mother.

Finding Nicknames and Aliases

Alumni directories, class anniversary directories, high school and college yearbooks, and newspaper and periodical archives may provide you with information about the subject's current or former nicknames. You can also (when appropriate) get such names from one of the subject's past or present friends or associates.

The judgment docket at your county courthouse sometimes lists AKA's beside a person's name. These may include personal aliases as well as business names and property ownership "straw" names.

Criminal court records and newspaper crime articles often give the aliases and nicknames of persons charged with crimes.

Making Sure That You Have the Right Person

In the early 1980s, Edward H. Heller of Brooklyn practiced law at 230 Park Avenue in Manhattan. Meanwhile, another Edward H. Heller, also of Brooklyn, practiced law at 250 Park Avenue. When the former was convicted of grand larceny and disbarred, the latter wrote a letter to the *New York Law Journal* to clear up the confusion, signing his name "Edward Harris Heller."

The innocent Mr. Heller's problem was no different in essence from that of the many Americans who are mistakenly arrested each year—or denied credit—because of name confusion in databases rife with small errors that are really big errors.

Never assume that you have the right person unless the middle *name* (not just the middle initial) fits; the address (including street number) fits; and the date of birth and SSN fit (the latter is especially important in avoiding mistakes in generational designation, as when the John Smith of 221 Elm Street, arrested for indecent exposure, turns out to be John Smith, Jr., the emotionally disturbed son who lives in John Smith, Sr.'s basement).

If you are writing for publication and are making your own assertions rather than relying on an official statement from police or prosecutors, always call the person about whom you are writing to verify his or her identity.

7.2 Obtaining the Birth Date

"Real" Versus Operative Birth Date

In following a person's paper trail, you can become confused if you don't distinguish between the "real" birth date and the operative birth date. The "real" date is that found on the birth certificate. (I have put "real" in quotation marks because, before the sexual revolution of the 1960s, dates on birth certificates were frequently fudged to disguise the fact that a child was born less than nine months after his or her parents' wedding.) By contrast, the operative birth date is that used in a person's adult life as an identifier. The two are frequently different because there are so many reasons to deliberately misreport one's age. The initial misreporting may occur early on, as in the case of teenagers who added a year to their age in order to join the Marines during World War II. More often, people misreport their age later in life to avoid age discrimination when applying for a new job, to retire or qualify for benefits early, to delay retirement, or simply for vanity's sake. Often, the "new" birth date may become operative in one set of records but not in another (say, in the subject's personnel records at a new job, but not in his or her medical records). If the "new" date is used on a credit application, it may be part of an attempt (also involving a shift from a married to a maiden name, the listing of a new address and phone number, and so on) to set up an alternative credit history.

The operative date of birth is therefore best defined as the one recognized by any particular records system as an identifier for the subject's records. In the following sections—unless we are speaking of the birth certificate and other early-in-life documentation—*date of birth* is used in the sense of *operative* date of birth.

Birth Indexes and Birth Certificates

In the county courthouse of the county where your subject was born, there may be a birth index that you can look through to find his or her date of birth. This birth index may also be on microform at the local public library or local historical society. The New York Public Library's genealogy division, for instance, has the city health department's annual birth indexes from 1917 to 1982.

If you know the state but not the county in which a person was born, contact the state's bureau of vital statistics (usually part of the state health department). In some states, you can get the birth records searched and obtain a copy or abstract of the birth certificate. For more information on how to deal with county and state vital statistics registrars, see section 10.1, "Vital Records."

Church Records

A subject's date of birth may often be found in church baptismal and christening registers, which are usually open to the public.

Credit-Reporting Agency Databases

The operative birth date is header material on credit files; as such, it should be readily available from credit-reporting agency databases that can be accessed through an information broker.

Biographical Dictionaries and Professional Directories

Although some of these reference works provide only the year of birth, others provide the full date. For instance, *American Men and Women of*

Science generally includes the date of birth for its 123,000-plus entries. The *Martindale-Hubbell Law Directory* gives only the year of birth in its roster listings but includes the date of birth in biographical sketches of about 40,000 attorneys.

Note that with the year of birth alone, you can still order a search of many records systems (for instance, some military personnel records); it's just a bit more difficult.

Miscellaneous Public Records

A subject's date of birth may be found on his or her marriage license and in Motor Vehicles Bureau and voter registration records.

The date of birth of a deceased person can be found in the Social Security Death Index, which is searchable at www.ancestry.com. The Social Security Death Index and the records to which it can lead are especially important if you are looking into a subject's family background or are doing some parallel backgrounding of the subject's deceased business partner.

Military Rosters

The date of birth is included in the annual registers of Army, Air Force, Marine, Coast Guard, and Army National Guard officers. The Navy register gives only the year of birth. The back editions of these rosters can be found in large research libraries.

Applications for Jobs, Loans, and So Forth

A date of birth, accurate or not, will be on every application the subject has ever filled out for a job, loan, rental of a house or apartment, or admittance to a college. A landlord or former employer may be willing to dig out such an application from his or her files.

Date of Birth: No Great Secret

Some investigators will call a subject, claim that they want to include him or her in an occupational directory (or to register him or her for a lottery prize), and get various basic items of personal information (including birth date) in a few moments. This type of deception is not recommended for journalists. I simply want to stress the point that, because the date of birth is so commonly asked for, most people are not secretive about it.

7.3 Finding the Social Security Account Number

As header material on his or her credit file, a subject's SSN was, until recently, easily available from credit-reporting agency databases accessible through an information broker. Now most of the largest credit-reporting firms are only releasing the first six digits of a person's SSN. (You can still get complete SSNs from a limited number of credit-reporting firms, but they may not have the one you need.) However, you don't always need credit-reporting agency records; you can often obtain your subject's SSN while checking various public or private records that you would check anyway. Following are some of the places the SSN might be found.

Driver's License Abstracts

In some states, the SSN is always the same as the driver's license number or is listed on the driver's license in addition to the driver's license number. In other states, the use of the SSN is optional, or it is not used at all.

Voter Registration Records

In some localities, the SSN is included on voter registration cards as a safeguard against vote fraud. Voter registration records are kept at the local board of elections and are almost always open to the public. The use of the SSN for this purpose has declined in recent years, so look in older records if available.

Court Records

The SSN may be found in civil court records; for instance, when an apartment rental application including the SSN is attached as an exhibit to a motion or affidavit in a landlord/tenant case. If your subject has ever been convicted of a crime, you may find his or her SSN in the criminal court file. If the subject has ever filed for personal bankruptcy, the case file will include his or her SSN. If the subject has ever been served with a subpoena or summons, the SSN will probably be included on the copy of this document in the court file.

Income Tax Records

The SSN is the same as a person's taxpayer identifying number (TIN). Thus, whenever tax records of an individual are made public in court (see section 8.13, "Federal and State Income Tax Returns and Related Information"), you can find his or her SSN.

Disclosure Statements and Other Filings

The SSN may be included in financial disclosure statements required from elected and appointed public officials, high-ranking civil servants, and candidates for public office.

In addition, you may find the SSNs of officers of nonprofit corporations on the 990 forms filed by these organizations with the IRS.

Applications for Jobs, Housing, and So On

The SSN, like the date of birth, is required information when a person opens a bank account, rents an apartment, or applies for a job, loan, mortgage, or credit card. If you are investigating an obnoxious local cult, you may find that landlords or businesspersons will give you access to cult members' apartment rental or job applications.

Discarded Personal Records

The SSN is sometimes found on health insurance bills (here the number may be divided into three sets of three digits each, rather than the SSN's 3-2-4 division), brokerage account statements, and so forth. Canceled checks may have the SSN (or driver's license number including the SSN) scrawled on the back if the subject had to show ID when cashing the check. The SSN may also be on correspondence received from the IRS. The subject may routinely discard such things with the garbage. The use of "garbology" as a research technique is described in section 11.4, "The Subject's Garbage."

Military Records

Present, former, and retired members of the Armed Forces, Reserves, and National Guard are identified by their SSN. Although the Privacy Act of 1974 prevents the government from giving out the SSN when you request someone's service record, you may find the SSN on discharge papers filed at the county courthouse.

Until the mid-1970s, the SSN was listed beside each officer's name in the register of officers for each service. The Army National Guard register included SSNs as late as 1980. Back issues of the service registers may be found at your nearest federal depository library.

Multiple SSN Holders and Other Special Problems

Before 1973, all a person had to do to obtain an SSN was to fill out an application; no ID was required. The result was that millions of people ended up with more than one SSN either under a variation of their name or under an entirely new name. Reasons for doing this included, among others, a desire to put distance between oneself and a poor credit history, to avoid debtors and court judgments, to evade industry blacklists, and to engage in fraudulent activities. But whenever a person obtained an alternative SSN in this manner (as opposed to officially requesting a *replacement* SSN) the old number would continue in the SSA's records and the alternative SSN holder would have the option of returning to the use of his or her original SSN at a later date.

After 1973, it became more difficult to obtain an alternative SSN because the SSA began requiring verification of identity for the issuance of any new cards. If you still wanted to obtain an alternative SSN, you had to gather and present fraudulent ID, thus in effect constructing a new identity.

Over the years, some individuals have attempted to obtain an official replacement SSN. Today's SSA regulations make this quite difficult to do (as opposed to changing the name on one's card or getting a replacement card, both of which are easy). Applications for an SSN change are given serious consideration, however, under special circumstances (for example, a battered woman fearful of being found by her estranged husband).

Even if your subject has at some point obtained a new SSN fraudulently (or has "borrowed" the SSN of a legitimate holder), his or her previous SSN does not disappear magically from all records systems pertaining to him or her. For instance, if the old SSN was already established as the identifier on his or her health insurance policy, it could continue as such indefinitely. Thus if you snoop around in the mysterious Mr. X's trash and find a letter from an HMO addressed to a variant of his name and with an SSN included as the identifier—and if this SSN is different from (and appears from its numbering to have been issued earlier than) the one you are aware of him using—you may have found the key to unlocking his past.

The problem of tracking people by their SSN is compounded by a variety of deceptive or fraudulent practices involving this so-called universal identifier. Some people will "accidentally on purpose" switch two digits on their SSN (or even make up a fictitious SSN) if they are opening a temporary new bank account that they don't want bill collectors or the IRS to know about. Others will list an SSN taken from stolen or forged Social Security cards (illegal aliens frequently do this). Con artists have been known to expropriate a stranger's identity and SSN (as by learning the SSN and other identifying information through a telephone ruse and then applying for a new card in the victim's name), so that John Doe who has an impeccable credit rating in Connecticut becomes John Doe the deadbeat in Oregon. Participants in the so-called underground economy may use a false identity (and an SSN issued in that name) for certain banking transactions while continuing to use their real identity and SSN on other occasions. These are only a few of the problems that make it difficult to track people by their SSN alone.

7.4 Making Use of the SSN Code

Have you been unable to find out where your subject grew up? Do you suspect that he or she has given false information about his or her past? The SSN contains coded information that often will help shed light on such matters.

The nine-digit SSN is divided into an area number (the first three digits), a group number (the middle two digits), and a serial number (the last four digits). Both the area number and the group number are useful for our purposes.

Area Number

The Social Security Administration has always assigned area numbers by state, and the area number at the beginning of your subject's SSN will fall within one or more series of consecutive numbers assigned to a given state. Before 1973, the SSN was assigned to the individual by the field office where he or she applied, and the area number represented the state in which that field office was located (which was not necessarily the state in which the applicant was then living). Since 1973, the SSN has been assigned by the SSA's central headquarters in Baltimore, and the area number represents the state in which the applicant under the new system was living (or claimed to be living) at the time he or she filed the application.

With the single exception of area number 232, no two states share the same area numbers, although several present and former U.S. territories share area numbers. The higher series of area numbers assigned to some states following a nonadjacent lower series are the result of population growth—the given state simply ran out of numbers (or is projected to run out of numbers) within the originally assigned series.

The majority of today's adult native-born Americans obtained their SSN in high school or shortly thereafter. Thus, the subject's area number quite likely indicates the state in which he or she grew up. (The subject's family may have moved one or more times during his or her childhood, but most families that move tend to stay within the same state or region.) If you lack any information about your subject's past except for this one clue, you might search the online white pages or CD-ROM directories such as Select Phone for persons with the subject's surname who are currently residing in the state in question. One or more of them may be related to the subject and may confirm that the subject once lived or still lives in the state.

Even if you don't want to bother tracking down your subject's relatives, the area number of the subject's SSN may at least give you an indication of whether or not the subject is being minimally truthful about his or her past. If a subject claims to have grown up and attended college in Hawaii, but the SSN is coded for North Dakota, you may have grounds for suspicion.

As of November 1998, area numbers have been allocated or issued within only two ranges: 001–728 (with 666 omitted for obvious reasons) and 750–763. (For future changes, check the SSN area number allocations chart at www.ssa.gov/foia/stateweb.html.) Any supposed SSN that begins with an area number outside these officially allocated ranges is invalid.

The following is the SSA's November 1998 list of area numbers and the states to which they correspond:

001–003	New Hampshire
004–007	Maine
008–009	Vermont
010–034	Massachusetts
035–039	Rhode Island
040–049	Connecticut
050–134	New York
135–158	New Jersey
159–211	Pennsylvania

212–220	Maryland
221–222	Delaware
223–231	Virginia
232	North Carolina
232–236	West Virginia
237–246	North Carolina
247–251	South Carolina
252–260	Georgia
261–267	Florida
268–302	Ohio
303–317	Indiana
318–361	Illinois
362–386	Michigan
387–399	Wisconsin
400–407	Kentucky
408–415	Tennessee
416–424	Alabama
425–428	Mississippi
429–432	Arkansas
433–439	Louisiana
440–448	Oklahoma
449–467	Texas
468–477	Minnesota
478–485	Iowa
486–500	Missouri
501–502	North Dakota
503–504	South Dakota
505–508	Nebraska
509–515	Kansas
516–517	Montana
518–519	Idaho
520	Wyoming
521–524	Colorado
525	New Mexico
526–527	Arizona
528–529	Utah
530	Nevada
531–539	Washington
540–544	Oregon
545–573	California
574	Alaska
575–576	Hawaii
577–579	District of Columbia
580	Virgin Islands
580–584	Puerto Rico
585	New Mexico

586	Guam, American Samoa, Northern Mariana Islands, Philippine Islands (that is, the former and present Pacific territories)
587	Mississippi
588*	Mississippi
589–595	Florida
596–599	Puerto Rico
600–601	Arizona
602–626	California
627–645	Texas
646–647	Utah
648–649	New Mexico
650–653*	Colorado
654–658	South Carolina
659–665*	Louisiana
667–675	Georgia
676–679*	Arkansas
680*	Nevada
681–690*	North Carolina
691–699*	Virginia
700–728	Assigned before July 1, 1963, to railroad workers covered under the Railroad Retirement Act, irrespective of the state in which the worker applied
729–749	Unassigned
750–751*	Hawaii
752–755*	Mississippi
756–763*	Tennessee

* *New areas allocated but not yet issued.*

Note that the California area/group numbers 568-30 through 568-58 were issued to Vietnamese and other Southeast Asian refugees between 1975 and 1979, as were SSNs within 574 (Alaska), 580 (Puerto Rico and the Virgin Islands), and 586 (Pacific territories).

Note that the area number 232 is shared by West Virginia and North Carolina.

Possible red flag: If a job applicant uses an out-of-original-sequence area number in the range 587–699 (numbers allocated in recent years to states with rapidly growing populations), you should make sure that this area number is already in use. (None of the area numbers in the out-of-original-sequence 750–763 range are being used yet, although they have been allocated to states that may need them soon.) If the applicant seems too old to have been originally assigned an SSN with this area number, you might inquire why and how the applicant functioned in the job market without an SSN during his or her earlier years.

Definite red flag: If a youthful applicant uses an area number in the long-frozen Railroad Retirement Act range, you have a right to say to that applicant (paraphrasing former Vice Presidential candidate Lloyd Bentsen), "You, sir, are no railroad worker."

Group Number

The SSA provides a chart (updated monthly) at www.ssa.gov/foia/highgroup.htm showing the latest group number issued in relation to a given area number. For instance, we see for 001–003 (New Hampshire) that, as of November 1998, the latest group numbers yet issued are 92, 92, and 90, respectively. To determine whether the group number on a suspicious SSN is fraudulent, however, you need to understand how group numbers are assigned.

Within each area, the group numbers range from 01 to 99 but are not assigned in consecutive order. Group numbers issued first consist of the *odd* numbers from 01 through 09 and then the *even* numbers from 10 through 98, within each area number allocated to a state. After all the numbers in group 98 of a particular area number have been issued, the *even* groups 02 through 08 are used, followed by *odd* groups 11 through 99. In the case of New Hampshire area number 001, it currently appears that odd group numbers 01, 03, 05, 07, and 09 followed by the even group numbers from 10 to 90 have been used up and even group number 92 is partially used up. Thus, if the SSN you are examining has the area number 001 followed by even group numbers 02 through 08, even numbers 94 to 98, or odd numbers 11 to 99, you should definitely flag this SSN for further investigation.

Rule of thumb: If a youthful applicant provides an area/group number that, according to the chart, was probably issued long before the applicant entered the job market—or if a middle-aged applicant who has apparently been in the job market for decades provides an area/group number that could only have been issued quite recently—you should flag that application for further checking.

As noted earlier, the SSA issues a monthly chart of the latest-issued group numbers. If you obtain the backfiles of these charts, especially of the last chart issued in each year, you can pin down the date of issuance of any post-1950 SSN to an approximate year. Indeed, there is a software program based on the SSA group charts, and the Informus Corporation's version can be accessed for free (go to www.brbpub.com/links.htm). Here you can learn instantly whether an SSN number has been validly issued and, if so, the state and approximate year in which it was issued.

Miscellaneous Information about SSNs

- If a supposed SSN has a 000 area number, a 00 group number, or a 0000 serial number, it is definitely not a valid number. If a supposed SSN has either less than or more than nine digits, it is also not valid.

- The faster the population of a state increases, the faster each group number within each active area number will fill up. This means that you will be able to pin down the year of issuance of SSNs a little more precisely in high-population-growth Nevada (two group numbers filled per year in some recent years) than in North Dakota (a state whose population has remained stable for many decades and where a group number often takes at least two years to fill up).

- Beginning in 1987, federal law required parents to obtain SSNs for any child five years old or older if the parents wanted to list that child as a dependent for income tax purposes. In 1992, this requirement was extended to children one year old or older. Many parents since then have obtained SSNs for their children immediately after birth. The inferences you might draw from SSNs should be adjusted accordingly if you are analyzing an SSN issued after 1986.

- The reliability (as an identifier) of post-1973 SSNs should be some-what greater than those issued before 1973: Only with the advent of the new system were SSN applicants required to provide any proof of identity. This greater reliability probably holds true for post-1973 SSNs issued to average Americans, but there has been an increase over the years in various forms of identity theft and identity fraud among some elements of the population (especially among illegal aliens or aliens on visas that do not allow them to work in the United States, but also among scam artists of various types). The SSA and private identity verification services, however, are now using some very clever computer programs to spot fraudulent SSN use.

- An SSN is not reassigned when its holder dies. Rather, it is used to administer Social Security benefits to the holder's dependents and survivors.

7.5 Secondary Identifiers

A *secondary identifier* can be defined as any item of identification that is used less often than the big three (full name, SSN, and birth date). Secondary identifiers can include anything from the subject's mother's maiden name and the subject's place of birth to the subject's tattoos and eye color. The functions of secondary identifiers include the following (among others):

- To aid in a search of databases or other records when one or more of the primary identifiers are imperfectly known (for example, the year of birth but not the month and date) or are not known at all

- To aid a search when primary identifiers are bringing up confusing results as a result of input errors or an excessive number of hits (six hundred John Smiths, for instance)

- To serve as telephone or email verification items when a person requests access to sensitive information about himself or herself

- To be used as questions on applications for credit, a job, a rental apartment, and so on, so that the applicant's background and identity can be thoroughly checked

- To serve specialized needs whenever basic identifiers can't do the job (for instance, fingerprinting might be used to weed out applicants for public school janitorial positions who have criminal records)

When a person applies for a loan or a job, the secondary identifiers requested on the application will include such items as birthplace, mother's maiden name, and present and past residential addresses.

When a person makes a telephone request for personal information from a bank or utility company, he or she may be asked to provide, along with the primary identifiers, such items as current and former home addresses, place of birth, and mother's maiden name. The person will also be asked to provide his or her bank account and bank branch numbers or his or her utility account number.

Physical identifiers are important in searching for a missing person as well as in law enforcement. Physical identifiers may include height, weight, eye and hair color, scars, tattoos, fingerprints, and physical handicaps.

Note: When you are searching for a missing person, try to get as many identifiers as possible, not just the primary ones, from the subject's family, friends, and acquaintances. If you need the information as part of a background check on a person whose location is already known, be aware that secondary identifiers can often be obtained by looking through a person's trash.

7.6 How to Detect a False Identity

The Paper Tripper

If the records of a subject's past go back only a few months or years, it may be that he or she is "paper tripping," that is, using a false identity based on the birth certificate of a dead person. Paper trippers usually pick the identity of someone who died in infancy or early childhood and whose date of birth, sex, race, eye color, and so on, as recorded on the birth certificate or other available documents, fit the impostor. The impostor obtains a copy of the birth certificate and uses it to obtain a Social Security card, a driver's license, and other ID. This is possible because there is no nationwide cross-register of birth and death records and also because some states and counties do not require rigorous proof of identity from an applicant before issuing a birth certificate.

Careful paper trippers will select the identity of a dead person who was born in one state and died in another; this ensures against their being unmasked as a result of any future statewide correlation of birth and death records. To guard against accidental discovery (as by an encounter with a sibling of the dead person), they may search through old newspapers to find reports of accidents in which entire families perished (for example, an auto crash or a household gas leak or fire) and then adopt the identity of one of the victims. Note, however, that such accidents are relatively rare, and law enforcement authorities have caused the relevant birth records to be flagged.

One indication that a person might be an impostor is if his or her SSN does not fit plausibly with his or her reported age (for example, the man in his fifties who has an SSN that could not have been issued before the 1990s). Your suspicions might increase if you were to learn that the subject recently obtained a driver's license in your state after getting a learner's permit and passing the test for new drivers, rather than by simply exchanging a license from another state for the in-state license. And your suspicions might really soar if you learned from information broker databases that the subject lacks any credit history or any other data trail before his recent appearance on the local scene.

In checking out a suspected impostor, you should always order a search of the central death index in the state in which he or she claims to have been born (failing this, search the county records in the county of birth listed on the birth certificate). Although, as noted earlier, many paper trippers prefer to use the identity of a child who was born in one state and died in another, this is not always easy to do (the majority of families who move from one town to another stay within the same state) and, indeed, your subject may have been too lazy to take this extra step. However, if you don't find a record of the suspected death in the state in which the child was born, you might conduct a multi-state death index search. Do *not* use the Social Security Death Index for this search.

Also try to find the parents or other relatives of the presumably dead child. Once you have the child's date and place of birth (which the impostor would have given out to various public and private database compilers pursuant to obtaining his or her new SSN number, bank account, driver's license, and credit cards), you can check the birth register or obtain a copy of the birth certificate to find out the parents' names. You can then track down the parents, the surviving siblings, or various relatives (using the techniques described in section 4.12, "Tracking a Person Through His or Her Family, Friends, and Ex-Spouse(s)") to solicit their help in exposing the impostor.

Stolen, Forged, and Unofficial Social Security Cards

Some users of false ID are too lazy to adopt the paper-trip method. They prefer to just steal a Social Security card or purchase a stolen card for short-term use. In such cases, you can simply check the name in online databases that include credit-reporting agency header material (including the first six digits of the person's SSN) to find the SSN's real holder. If the name on the card is an unusual one, however, you might find it easier to just look up the person in a nationwide online white-pages directory and then call him or her directly.

Another short-term alternative to paper tripping is the forged card. The forger (or the customer, when he or she orders the forged card) may pick a nonexistent area number. Or, if the forger or customer knows enough to get the area number right, he or she may pick a group number that has not yet been assigned to anyone or that is otherwise suspicious (as explained earlier in this chapter). If the forger or the customer picks a number that has already been assigned, you can locate the legitimate assignee using the header databases. If the forger picks a number that was assigned to a person who is now deceased, you can tentatively determine this using the Social Security Death Index, which can be searched by SSN as well as by name.

A variant on the forged card is the unofficial plastic or metal copy of a Social Security card that can be ordered from a mail order company. Supposedly, a card-holder purchases the unofficial copy to carry in his wallet while the official copy is left at home, safe from pickpockets. This in itself is perfectly legal, both for the supplier and the customer. But many persons who order such cards provide the mail order company with a false SSN to put on the card, and the mail order company will often be less than scrupulous in checking whether the SSN is for real. Of course, the person providing the false SSN runs the risk that the company he is dealing with is selling its customers' names and addresses to private investigators and bounty hunters who conduct reverse traces (see section 4.33, "Reverse Traces").

8.

Credit and Financial Information

8.1 Credit-Reporting Agencies and Other Database Sources

The amount of information collected by credit-reporting agencies is staggering. Experian's credit profile database alone has information on 170 million people, including data on their credit card payment history, lines of credit, and secured loans. It also has public record information on tax liens, judgments, and personal bankruptcies. Equifax and Trans Union, the two other major national agencies, have equally vast consumer files; Equifax's include gossip from a subject's neighbors as well as arrest and conviction data. Regional or local credit bureaus (about 1,300 nationwide) often have more detailed files than any of the big three on individuals and small businesses in their locality.

The Fair Credit Reporting Act restricts the dissemination of credit information about individual consumers. To obtain such information, a client of a credit-reporting agency must have a "legitimate business need." Banks, department stores, insurance companies, credit card issuers, employers, and landlords fall into the category of clients with a legitimate need, although even they must obtain a signed release from the subject of the report under some circumstances.

Be aware that under the 1996 amendments to the Fair Credit Reporting Act, it is now a federal felony to procure a credit report under false pretenses. Several states also offer stiff criminal penalties. In addition to the prospect of jail time and large court fines, you could also be sued by the consumer whose file you obtained.

Under the 1996 amendments, information brokers who provide consumer data at secondhand or provide a gateway to consumer credit information must exercise caution that the users of their databases have a legitimate purpose. Many information brokers only provide their services to insurance companies and other businesses with a routine legitimate need. Others allow casual users into the system, but those users may find certain databases closed to them unless they can certify a legitimate need.

Be aware that credit reports from the major credit reporting agencies are rife with error. According to a 1991 Consumers Union report, almost 50 percent had one or more inaccuracies, and almost 20 percent had errors that could seriously impair a consumer's ability to obtain credit. More recent surveys have confirmed this finding. Typical errors include the mixing of data from the files of two people with the same name and the inclusion in a consumer's file of data reflecting the fraudulent use of that person's identity and SSN by an impostor.

8.2 Alternatives to the Individual Credit Check

There are three basic ways to compensate for the restrictions on consumer credit reporting while staying completely within the law and adhering to journalistic ethics. First, the portions of the credit reporting agency file on an individual obtained from public records (for example, from Uniform Commercial Code [UCC] filings and judgment docket listings) are available directly from state or county records or from database vendors who are not part of the credit reporting industry.

Second, the Fair Credit Reporting Act does not restrict the dissemination of business credit information. Thus, if you are backgrounding a businessperson, you can run a comprehensive online credit check on his or her known business entities. Experian (www.experian.com) and Dun & Bradstreet (www.dnb.com) offer credit reports on over 10 million U.S. businesses; both services offer credit card pay-as-you-go access for casual users as well as subscriber rates for high-volume users.

Experian's "snapshot reports" on a firm include tax liens, judgments, and bankruptcies in all states for $15 per business searched. These reports also include a firm's payment record with suppliers, its payment trend behavior, and its financial services history. Much more detailed background credit reports are also available, as are UCC searches (for 43 states) and corporate registration searches (for 42 states).

D&B offers a variety of reports on businesses large and small, including business background reports and credit check reports. It also offers nationwide searches of business registrations, lawsuits, liens, judgments, UCC filings, and bankruptcies.

Such reports—especially the payment histories—can give you a better picture of a subject's overall financial status than any individual credit check would provide: Mr. Jones may always pay his household bills on time, yet his business may be on the brink of bankruptcy. For more information on backgrounding a business, see Chapter 14, "Businesses and Nonprofit Organizations."

The third way to compensate for consumer credit reporting restrictions is simply to do some leg work—dig into real-estate mortgage records at the register of deeds office, search the plaintiff/defendant index and case files at your local courthouse, interview former associates of your subject, and so on. In doing this, you may miss some things that are in the credit bureaus' files, but you will collect much information—especially from case files that the credit bureaus rarely consult—that may give you an excellent picture of the subject's finances.

8.3 Uniform Commercial Code Filings

Whenever an individual or a business entity borrows money or leases property or equipment using personal (nonreal) property as collateral, the lender or lessor fills out a UCC financing statement and files it with the designated government office. Some states require central filing at the state's Department of State. Others have a system of dual filing at both the local and state level. Generally, local filings are done at the same office at which real estate documents are filed.

Any local search in a dual-filing state should be followed by a search of the statewide records because local UCC filings are often done in the wrong local jurisdiction (this is especially true in a metropolitan area with complicated jurisdictional lines).

You can search the UCC records of most states using online public records vendors. At the minimum, you should check the records for the subject's state of residence and for any state in which the subject conducts business or has a vacation home. If the subject resides in a multistate metropolitan area, check each state in the area (for example, check New Jersey and Connecticut for any down-state New York resident). One place to begin is at the KnowX Web site (www.search3.knowx.com), which offers single-state and all-state UCC searches by debtor's name for $1.00 and $1.50, respectively (the detail records are $6.95 each or $15.00 for as many as you'd like per search session). Be aware that these are searches of all online UCC records accessible through KnowX, not all UCC records in general (and certainly not all records predating the given state's development of an online system).

You can do your own direct online searching in two ways: First, register for dial-up access to the state UCC database (if such access is available for the state in question). Second, go to the state Web site (if one exists) that offers free public access to the UCC database. For information on dial-up access, consult the *PRRS*. For directories of state Web sites offering free access to UCC records, go to www.inil.com/users/dguss/wgator.htm (select "Companies, Corporations, and UCC Listings") or www.brbpub.com/pubrecsites.htm (see "State Sites").

An alternative to online searching is to mail in a UCC-11 form (Request for Search) along with the designated fee. You will receive, within a few days, an abstract of all UCC statements statewide in which your subject is listed as a debtor. (In several states, you can request this information over the phone or by fax.) If the staff at a given state office does not perform searches for the general public, you can, of course, visit the office and do your own searching.

A UCC financing statement will tell you the name(s) and address(es) of the debtor(s) and creditor(s), the date on which the financing statement was filed, and whether or not the obligation has been satisfied (paid in full); the statement will also describe the asset offered as collateral. This collateral may be something tangible (a car, truck, a computer, or a debtor company's inventory) or it may be intangible (a patent, a franchise, or the debtor company's accounts receivable).

The UCC statement will not tell the amount of the loan, but if the collateral is a car of a certain year and model, you can obtain a rough estimate of its value (and hence of the loan) by calling the manufacturer or a used-car dealer.

Not all of a subject's debts and obligations will be reflected in the UCC records; there must be collateral involved. You will not find information here regarding most credit card debts, retail installment purchases, non-collateral bank loans, and so on. Although information regarding mortgages and other debts involving real property as collateral are mostly to be found in county real estate records (see section 8.7), you may find some information in the UCC files about the subject's real estate holdings if fixtures in a building owned by the subject have been accepted as loan collateral.

If a debt recorded by a UCC filing is satisfied, the UCC statement will be discarded after a statutorily fixed period. If the debt is not satisfied, the statement will remain in the records indefinitely.

The UCC filings should be regarded as a guide to further investigation. For instance, if the collateral offered by the borrower is an airplane or yacht, this will lead you to Federal Aviation Administration, U.S. Coast Guard, and state registration records. If the collateral is a painting, this may lead you into an examination of the subject's relationship to the world of art dealers, galleries, and museums. If the collateral is a racehorse, you will want to learn more about the subject's involvement in the world of horse breeding and racing. (The racing world has specialized databases through which you can find out when the subject bought the horse and from whom, the name of the horse's sire, the track records of both horses, and a list of other horses the subject owns.)

If the creditor is a private individual rather than a bank or finance company, this may reflect a significant personal or business relationship of the debtor's that you might not otherwise have learned about. If more than one debtor is listed on the financing statement, you may have found the name of a business partner of your subject or possibly a relative who acted as guarantor for the subject's loan.

If the UCC records reveal that the subject obtained a recent loan from a particular bank, this may be the same bank at which the subject has his or her main checking and savings accounts. If the loan comes from a finance company rather than from a bank, this may indicate that the subject has a mediocre credit rating.

The most detailed information on UCC filings is contained in *The Uniform Commercial Code Filing Guide,* a five-volume work (also on CD-ROM) with quarterly updates covering all UCC filing offices nationwide. This work is available in large research libraries and online from WESTLAW.

8.4 Judgment Books

Money judgments obtained against your subject in the local courts are usually on file at the county clerk's office. Recent judgments may be listed in a computer index; older judgments are listed in annual ledger books (with separate books for judgments against individuals and corporations). The ledger books are permanent records—you can access them going back as far as you like.

In New York City, each judgment book entry tells the amount of the judgment, the name and address of both the creditor and the debtor (and often of the creditor's attorney), the date of filing of the judgment, the court in which the judgment was obtained, the docket number of the case, and the date of satisfaction (if any). If the judgment was also obtained against another individual or individuals, a partnership, or a corporation, this information is recorded in the entry for your subject.

The judgment books, which also include city and state tax liens, are a rich source of leads. For instance, the individuals listed along with the subject as the targets of a judgment may be business partners you had not known about. A judgment obtained against a subject by a hospital may be your first clue that he or she has a serious medical problem.

If the state attorney general is listed as the creditor, this may mean that the state has obtained a judgment against the subject because of nonpayment of a fine resulting from an enforcement action penalizing him or her for illegal activity.

Other judgments may provide the names of a subject's former customers, clients, vendors, or spouses. In researching an article some years ago, I checked the Manhattan judgment books and found the name and address of a woman who had obtained a judgment for several thousand dollars against my subject (a Manhattan restauranteur) in a dispute over an item of jewelry she had lost in his restaurant. As it turned out, she and the restaurant owner had many friends and business associates in common; I was regaled with extremely interesting gossip.

The judgment books in the county clerk's office will cover actions in state district court (often called *superior court*) and in the county or municipal courts; the books may also record judgments from other localities. Federal court judgments generally are recorded separately at the federal district court. Once you have the docket number, you can obtain the case file.

Note that a judgment may be obtained as part of a fraudulent conspiracy between creditor and debtor. Let's say that Mr. X has borrowed large sums with the intent to declare bankruptcy and thus evade payment. He gets a crony to obtain a large judgment against him. When bankruptcy is declared, the crony has a secured prior lien and is paid first out of money that otherwise would go to legitimate creditors after tax debts are satisfied. Later, the crony returns the money to Mr. X minus his or her own cut.

Judgments obtained in recent years can be searched online for various localities within 39 states. You might begin your online search at www.search3.knowx.com, where the cost is $6.95 for each detail record viewed and $15.00 to view as many detail records as you like per search session. In the majority of cases, these online records will include only those judgments against businesses. However, personal judgment records are available online for many urban areas (for instance, the county-level files in Los Angeles, Philadelphia, and Houston). And, of course, you can search in person at the county courthouse for judgments against individuals, or you can order a search by mail from the courthouse staff or (for older records) pay a document retrieval service (see www.courtrecordsources.com) to obtain the information for you.

A search of the online judgment index may be useful even if it does not include judgments against individuals. For example, you may find, in the business judgment records, information about business entities controlled by your subject (or your subject's spouse) which will shed an important light on your subject's personal financial situation.

Be aware that a hands-on search may be necessary (even if the online database includes judgments against individuals) to find all relevant information, especially information about judgments that have been satisfied and judgments (satisfied or not) from many years past.

8.5 Tax Lien Files

Tax lien records give the amount owed, the date of perfecting (the date the lien was obtained), and the date of satisfaction, if any. They are retained as long as the lien is unsatisfied. Following the date of satisfaction, the information will be removed from the file/database after a fixed period.

Corporate and individual tax liens are generally maintained in separate files and sometimes even at separate locations. Some states require business liens to be filed at the Secretary of State's office and individual liens to be filed at the county level.

The amount of the subject's tax liens may give you some clues regarding the subject's annual income, business difficulties, and so on. If Mr. A is known by you to have a modest-paying civil service job, but the IRS is after him for $250,000 in back taxes, this indicates some other sources of income that you will want to track down. If Ms. B has accumulated several personal or business liens over the last few years, it may suggest that she is having other personal financial difficulties and that her catering business is barely keeping afloat. In addition, the addresses listed on the liens, as you trace them through the years, may provide you with previously unknown former residential or business addresses of your subject.

Tax liens and other liens (mechanics, chattel mortgage, and so on) from various state and county offices across the United States can be searched online, although the majority of such online databases accessible to the general public contain business liens only. At the KnowX Web site (www.search3.knowx.com), you can search by name of debtor (taxpayer or grantor) or name of creditor (grantee). The cost is $6.95 for a single detail record and $15.00 for as many detail records as you want per search session. Study carefully the KnowX table of sources and effective dates to make sure that a particular state or county database will have the information you require. For instance, you should determine how far back the records go, when the database was last updated, and whether the database contains personal as well as business liens.

8.6 Wage Assignments (Wage Garnishments) Index

The wage assignments/garnishments index is usually located at the county clerk's office, with indexing by date and alphabetically by assignor (the person whose wages have been assigned). In New York City, the index gives the amount originally owed, the names of the assignor and assignee, and a file number. This information may lead you to a judgment obtained locally or to an out-of-town judgment. In some localities, the assignor's place of employment at the time of the wage assignment will be part of the public record. If not, you can perhaps obtain this information from the assignee.

8.7 Recorder of Deeds Office

The telephone white pages list your subject as living at a suburban address; checking in the crisscross directory, you see that this is a private house. You want to know whether the subject is the owner or a renter. If an owner, how much did he or she pay for the property? What is the amount of each mortgage and who is/are the mortgagee(s)? Is the subject in default on his or her mortgage payments and facing a foreclosure action? If the subject is a renter, who is his or her landlord?

The real estate files in the recorder of deeds office are your key to answering such questions. First, you must obtain the block and lot number of the property from the plat maps or from a CD-ROM. Next, check the index of mortgages and conveyances either in the ledger books or on CD-ROM for a brief description of each transaction regarding the property; the index will tell you who the current owner is and when and from whom this owner purchased the property. Some localities do not record the sale price, but you can often estimate it from the recorded real estate transfer tax if your state has such a tax. (Note that before 1965, a federal transfer tax allowed for estimates within about $1,000 of the sale price.)

Recorded with each transaction will be a file number (reel number or liber and page numbers) so that you can access the actual deeds, surveys, and certain other documents (depending on the locality, these documents may include copies of mortgages and leases) on microform. Examination of deeds and other documents may be necessary to figure out who the grantor and grantee really are if straw names are being used (this will be more common in real estate speculation than in ordinary transactions involving the purchase or sale of a home). In addition, the file may reveal varied information for backgrounding purposes: the name of a parent (if the subject inherited the property), the name of a spouse or ex-spouse (if he or she is listed on the deed or mortgage), the name of the subject's attorney, the name of the lending institution (this may be the bank where the subject has his or her main account), and a specimen of the subject's (and possibly of the subject's spouse's) signature.

In general, mortgage payments are the dominant financial obligation in the lives of moderate-income homeowners. The size, position (for example, first or second), and timing of a mortgage may provide clues to many aspects of your subject's life. For instance, if the subject and the subject's spouse took out a second or third mortgage on their home in 1996, this may reflect business difficulties they were experiencing at the time, a major uninsured medical expense, the need to pay for a child's college education, and so on. (It also may suggest a negative equity in the property, especially if it is coupled with a decline in the appraisal price.)

If mortgage documents are available in the files at your local recorder of deeds office, they may help you gain a better understanding of the subject's overall financial situation. For instance, a blanket mortgage document will inform you about other real estate the subject owns; a package mortgage may tell you about the subject's personal as well as real property; a reverse mortgage will reveal to you that the subject and his or her spouse have received cash in a lump sum (or are receiving cash monthly) that they will not have to pay back until they sell or move; and a Veterans' Administration (VA) mortgage will alert you that the subject or the subject's spouse is a veteran, with all the government benefits that flow from that status and indirectly affect the subject's net worth.

The recorder of deeds office will also have an index of liens against real property by block and lot number. These may include mechanics' liens (resulting from nonpayment for services, labor, or materials for which the subject contracted during the construction or repair of a house or other structure on the lot) and also liens resulting from violation of city or county ordinances (for example, pest control liens and sidewalk, lot, or fence liens).

Also at the recorder of deeds office you will find the *Lis Pendens*—public notices of pending litigation that inform prospective buyers of a given property that a lien may be placed on it in the future. Here you will learn about mortgage foreclosure, tax foreclosure, and property condemnation proceedings, and also about divorce and inheritance cases in which the opposing parties are contesting the division of real property.

If foreclosure proceedings on the subject's home have been started, don't jump to the conclusion that the subject is about to be evicted into the street: Only about one in seven of these proceedings results in a judgment (and, in turn, only about one in seven judgments results in eviction). However, such proceedings do suggest that the subject is experiencing financial difficulties at the moment, perhaps because of a job layoff or a major medical problem.

The recorder of deeds office may have an alphabetical roster of owners, with listings of all properties owned by each of them. The clerks who compile these lists may be aware of corporate names used by a local landlord or developer and hence will list the property under his or her personal name as well as the corporate name. If the recorder of deeds office does not have such a list, the local real estate directory, available at your public library or at a real estate broker's office, may include this information for commercial and apartment rental properties (you look under the address and get the owner's name, then look under the owner's name and get a list of all the other properties he or she owns). This information can also be obtained at www.firstam.com (described later in this section).

In looking for residential properties owned by a subject, you will be looking for three things: the primary residence, a secondary (weekend or vacation) residence, and non-owner-occupied residences. The latter might include rental income properties or a house bought for an elderly parent. Note that a family home might be owned by a family limited partnership to protect against seizure in case of legal or financial problems.

If you need an out-of-town search of real estate records (for instance, to see whether the subject owns any properties elsewhere in your region or to find out about the mortgage on his or her vacation home), you can get this through a name search of real estate databases.

The big name in real estate records searching is First American Real Estate Solutions (formerly TRW REDI), which provides access to filings from over 300 county and municipal government offices in 34 states (call 800-426-1466 or go to www.firstam.com). Information available from one of its property profile reports typically includes the legal description, site address, parcel number, assessed value, deed book and page, lot size, sales date, sales price, year built, zoning and mortgage information, number of rooms, and living area in square feet. It may also note the presence of a pool, spa, decks, patios, and fireplaces; it may even describe the views. A single-property profile report costs $7.95.

First American RES's data is also available on CD-ROM and microfiche and in print directories targeting specific localities. These products can often be found in the business section of larger public libraries.

You might also use KnowX (www.search3.knowX.com) to search real estate records. KnowX's real property search options include foreclosures, refinances, tax records, and transfer records; each category can be searched by owner's name or by address. If you can't find a listing under your subject's name, use KnowX's people-finder service at the same Web site to locate your subject's address and then search by the address in the real property database. Note that (as with the First American RES service) not all states are included in the database, nor are all counties within a given state included. The cost is $6.95 per detail record or $15.00 for as many detail records per search session as you like.

Note that counties, cities, and states across the country are rapidly placing real estate and tax assessor records on free government Web sites. The process is most advanced in Florida, Massachusetts, and Texas. A directory of these Web sites can be found at www.inil.com/users/dguss/gator.htm.

Aerial Photographs of Subject's Home and Neighborhood

First American RES's real-estate data resources include a collection of low-altitude aerial survey photos of neighborhoods and communities across the country. Do you want to know if a subject has a swimming pool in his or her backyard, and if so how big it is? Want a peek inside the carefully guarded mansion of Swami Sam the cult leader? Want an overview of a particular block so that you can better plan your surveillance of George the Bigamist? With these photos, you can look at the homes of a subject and his or her neighbors, almost as if you had rented a helicopter.

To find the largest collection of aerial photo records of sites in the United States, check with the U.S. Geological Survey. Its EROS Data Center in Sioux Falls, South Dakota (edcwww.cr.usgs.gov) houses millions of aerial photos of the United States as well as satellite photos. To search for and order photos of a particular location, use the Photo Finder interface at the EROS Web site. You might also consult the Aerial Photography Summary Record System (APSRS) database and its contributor database (photos available from sources other than the USGS); this system comprises a master index of over 12 million aerial photos taken by over 500 federal, state, and local government agencies and private companies. The entire index is available on CD-ROM for $57. For information on ordering, go to mapping.usgs.gov/www/products/mappubs.html.

Aerial photographs can be especially important when used in tandem with street and contour maps, which are now available both on the Web (at people-finder sites) and on CD-ROM covering the entire United States. Back in the 1980s, I recall discussing with an attorney about setting up surveillance of a cult leader's farm from a hilltop. The attorney said he'd driven by the property and that it all seemed to be flat country. I later found out from a member of the cult leader's security detail (after this individual defected) that, in fact, there was a hilltop of sorts (owned by someone who intensely disliked the cult) and that the cult leader had been very worried about this incipient threat to his privacy. The attorney and I could probably have made the cult leader's worry a reality if we'd only been able to turn on a computer and instantly examine a contour map of the quadrant in question.

8.8 Condominium and Cooperative Ownership Lists

First American RES offers information about condos and co-ops in various localities. For instance, *The Record and Guide Quarterly* reports on condo sales in Manhattan and includes both a buyer's and a seller's index. First American RES's real estate directories covering New York City and other localities include a listing of all condo owners alphabetically by name; you can thus see quickly whether a subject's apartment falls into this category (and if he or she got stuck with a bad investment when the real estate market crashed). As to cooperatives, First American RES's directories can tell you whether a building has gone co-op, but they do not provide information on individual co-op owners. Because a large percentage of the occupants of New York cooperative apartment houses are rental tenants left over from pre-cooperative days, or are tenants renting from nonresident co-op owners, you shouldn't jump to conclusions about a subject's financial worth just because he or she happens to live in a co-op building. However, if an occupant lived in the building before the co-oping occurred (which you can determine through the crisscross directory), he or she may have bought at an insider price. Depending on the present market value of the apartment, he or she may have more equity than you might think from looking at other personal worth and income indicators.

Note: In a co-op, buyers have shares in a cooperative corporation; in a condo, they have a deed to their apartment and own it outright. Co-op boards have far more control over such matters as whether you can rent out the apartment, establish a bed-and-breakfast, and so forth. Information on a co-op's rules, insider prices, and so on can be found in the files of the state agency that regulates cooperatives.

8.9 City or County Property Tax Records

Property tax records are usually listed by date and by block and lot numbers. After you have a list of the properties your subject owns, you should check the assessment rolls (land value and the total value for each lot), the tax abatement books (amounts of abatements for each block and lot), the tax rolls (assessed valuation, quarterly tax, total tax, abatements, and arrears), and the tax registers (balance due, charges, and payments).

Increasingly, county assessors are including in these records the market-value estimates from which the assessed values are derived. In most counties, the water-meter charges and the sewer rental charges are filed in the same office as the tax assessment rolls.

Do not judge the owner's equity by the amount of taxes paid because property tax rates vary widely and often irrationally. As of 1993, the owner of a house valued at $200,000 in New York City would pay $1,574 in property taxes, while the owner of a co-op valued at $200,000 would pay $3,273. Also, do not judge equity by the assessed value because this often differs widely from the market value: Some towns in New York State (which does not require periodic reassessments) have not updated their property valuations in 30 years or more. Even with periodic reassessments, wide differences are often found in assessed values and equalization rates between communities of comparable socioeconomic status.

Always check to see whether the subject has filed a challenge of his or her tax assessment with the county's Board of Assessment Review; such a challenge can generate a significant paper trail, especially if the property owner is dissatisfied with the board's decision and appeals to the county court or state district court. Also, if the subject is in arrears on his or her property taxes, check whether the city or county has instituted foreclosure proceedings.

Don't forget the property tax records on the subject's weekend or summer home, which will probably be located in another county or state. (A recent trend is to buy a vacation home at a location hundreds of miles from the primary residence. For example, New Yorkers may have vacation homes or condos at Hilton Head, South Carolina, rather than in the Hamptons on Long Island.) Note that many prosperous urban residents choose to live in rental apartments; their vacation home may be the *only* home they own (indeed, they may end up living in it year-round while telecommuting to their "virtual office" in the city). Note also that some suburbanites will own a city apartment either as a *pied-a-terre* or for the use of an elderly parent, a child in college, and so on.

Property tax records may be searchable on CD-ROM at the local tax assessor's office. In addition, tax assessment records from the most populous counties in most states are available from online services such as First American RES and KnowX. If you want to search online tax assessment records for free, a directory of county and state Web sites offering this information can be found at www.inil.com/users/dguss/gator.htm (select "Property Records").

8.10 Bankruptcy Court Records

If your subject has recently filed for relief under the bankruptcy laws, you're in luck. The case file, kept at the federal bankruptcy court while the case is open (and thereafter at the nearest Federal Records Center), will provide a quite detailed picture of the subject's income, liabilities, and assets—including personal property such as automobiles, computers, and stamp collections. (In 1992, a recession year, there were about one million individual bankruptcy filings in the United States.)

There are two types of individual bankruptcy filings: Chapter 7, which involves immediate liquidation of most assets in return for exemption of such necessities as a person's equity in his or her home and car and cancellation of most of his or her debts (which may be much larger than the liquidated assets); and Chapter 13, which involves reorganization of the person's debts and payment of all or part of the debt in installments over three years. Generally, a Chapter 13 filing provides an investigator with more useful information than does a Chapter 7 filing.

Be sure to inspect bankruptcy records for corporations with which your subject has been connected. These records may reveal his or her corporate salary at the time of bankruptcy, how much stock he or she owned in the corporation, and so forth. Chapter 11 bankruptcy proceedings are often the result of a well-thought-out scheme to defraud a corporation's vendors and other creditors. If your subject is a principal in the corporation, you should examine his or her role carefully.

As of 1999, all federal bankruptcy courts in the United States have adopted the online Public Access to Court Electronic Records (PACER) system through which you can search both the index and the docket for 60 cents a minute. You must register for each court individually, but all such registrations can be done at the same time by calling the PACER Service Center in San Antonio, Texas at (800) 676-6856. At this same telephone number, you can sign up for access to the U.S. Party/Case Index, which covers all bankruptcy courts. (Alternatively, you can obtain access to the U.S. Party/Case Index through a gateway service such as KnowX at www.search3.knowx.com.)

In deciding how much to rely on the PACER system at a particular court (or on U.S. Party/Case Index search results obtained from that court's PACER system), you should first find out how far back the given PACER system's case records go, whether or not it includes closed as well as open cases for the years in question, and what the policy is on purging cases from the system. If you are conducting a deep background search, you will of course want to look at older bankruptcy indexes that were never, or no longer are, included in PACER. These older indexes will be available on microfiche or in a card file at the bankruptcy court clerk's office.

The majority of bankruptcy courts have adopted, along with PACER, a Voice Case Information System (VCIS) for providing case index information to the public. VCIS, however, will only tell you about open cases.

Note: In searching bankruptcy files, you should be interested not just in cases in which your subject is the debtor but also those in which he or she (or a business that he or she owns) is a creditor. In filing his or her claims, a subject may reveal significant bits of information about his or her finances and business affairs (not the least being the subject's relationship to other creditors as well as to the debtor). Also, if the creditor's relationship to the debtor is a complex one, the documents filed by the debtor may include many direct and indirect leads regarding the creditor's own business affairs. (You might just call up the debtor and see whether you can induce him or her to discuss the case.)

8.11 Probate Court Records

The local probate court is also a vital source of financial information if your subject has inherited any money or property. Wills offered for probate are kept on public file, as are other records pertaining to the protection and transfer of the estate. Important documents to look for include the estate appraisal and the reports filed by the administrator or executor regarding payments to the heirs. If the will is contested, much information will become part of the public record that otherwise would remain private. Probate court records are generally indexed by the name of the decedent; thus, to find all records that might shed important light on your subject's finances, you will need the names of any deceased grandparents, parents, in-laws, or other close relatives who might have left property to the subject, as well as the locations of the probate courts that handled these cases. (The Social Security Death Index is useful for this purpose.) Note that if the decedent owned real estate in a state other than the one in which he or she lived at the time of death, a separate probate may be necessary in the nonresident state.

8.12 Court Records of Civil Suits

Frequently, the court records of civil lawsuits are the richest single source of information about an individual. For a quick online search, go to www.search3.knowx.com, which provides access to the online indexes of many circuit, district, small claims, chancery, municipal, state, and superior courts throughout the country. (For more information, see Chapter 9, "Court Records.")

8.13 Federal and State Income Tax Returns and Related Information

If the Internal Revenue Service (IRS) has settled a claim against a subject for less than the amount originally owed, IRS Form 7249-M will be filed at the regional IRS office for one year and thereafter in Washington. This form, which is available for public inspection, contains rather detailed information about the subject's salary and other income, assets, and liabilities.

If the subject's dispute with the IRS found its way into the U.S. Tax Court in Washington, the case file will contain a wealth of financial documentation, including income tax returns, affidavits, depositions, and court testimony concerning the subject's financial affairs. The case file is publicly available, but you'll have to go to Washington to examine it (or else hire a Washington researcher). To interpret it, you may need an accountant's help.

If the subject is involved in civil litigation and his or her personal finances become relevant, federal and state tax returns may be produced during pretrial discovery and possibly entered in the case file; they may also be entered as evidence at trial. Be on the lookout, especially, for divorce cases involving alimony, child support, child custody, or property division; tax returns are often key evidence in such cases.

If the subject is indicted on white-collar criminal charges such as securities fraud or income tax fraud, the prosecution may enter federal and state tax returns and other personal financial documents as evidence.

8.14 Securities and Exchange Commission Filings; State Securities Filings

A publicly held corporation's registration statement, prospectuses, proxies, Form 10-Ks (annual reports), and other Securities and Exchange Commission (SEC) filings are crucial sources of financial data about the firm's top officers, directors, insider owners, and beneficial owners of 5 percent or more of the shares. The data disclosed will include salaries of top officers and payments to directors as well as any personal financial transactions, gifts of stock, and so forth that might create a conflict of interest for officers or directors. In addition, you will find out the number of shares each officer or director owns as well as the number of shares each holds in trust for his or her spouse, children, or grandchildren.

In Form S-1 registration statements, look at the sections on Management and Executive Compensation. Especially note the Summary Compensation Table (salaries, bonuses, stock awards, and stock option exercises) and the subsections on Employment Contracts, Profit Sharing, Retirement Plans (this section will include a Pension Table), and Security Ownership. Also note any details you find regarding top executives' medical benefits, life insurance, accidental death and dismemberment insurance, long-term disability plans, and so forth.

Pay careful attention to the information regarding executive stock options, which are pledges by a company to issue a fixed number of shares to an executive at a fixed price for a fixed period. Although most corporations issue stock options to their top executives, the options are not always clearly reported as compensation expenses in the company's annual reports to its stockholders. Stock options are the major device by which a chief executive officer can inflate his or her income far beyond his or her reported salary, even when the company is not doing well.

Note that some filings (for instance, Form 10-K) may include the full texts of employment and stock options agreements with top executives.

SEC filings for most of the nation's 11,000 publicly held companies can be searched online for free through the SEC's EDGAR system (www.edgar-online.com). By going to people.edgar-online.com/people, you can search the entire system for the name of a particular executive, director, and so on. (EDGAR also enables you to extract the entire Executive Compensation Table from a document without having to search the document.) Although the most important filings of a company since at least May 1996 will in most cases be available on EDGAR, the SEC does not require electronic filing of certain documents regarding individual finances. Thus, for instance, Forms 3, 4, and 5 (security ownership and transaction reports from corporate insiders) are still filed on paper. (*Note:* You can obtain a search of SEC stock ownership records compiled from Forms 3, 4, and 144 at www.search3.knowx.com.)

You can obtain a search of SEC corporate ownership information from pre-EDGAR years (as well as current information) through the DISCLOSURE/Spectrum Ownership database, available from DIALOG (file 540). Searching by individual name, you can find every instance in which a person has been reported as an insider owner or 5-percent beneficial owner of shares in any of the companies in the database. The database will tell you the number of shares he or she holds, the rank of this holding among those of other reported insiders, the filing date, and the type of insider (for example, chairman of the board, officer, director, trustee, beneficial owner as trustee, and so on; there are 24 relationship codes for types of insiders). Especially interesting is the ownership summary of total shares held by corporate insiders and the total market value in millions of dollars.

In addition to regulating publicly held companies, the SEC monitors and requires filings from 12,000 broker-dealers and 5,000 investment companies. Each individual broker, as well as the top officers of investment companies, must provide financial information regarding his or her business affairs in periodic statements to the SEC.

Additional financial information regarding brokers and investment company officers—and also corporate insiders—may emerge in an SEC investigation of securities violations. To find out whether your subject (or a company in which he or she is involved) has ever been the target of such an investigation, consult the *Securities Violations Bulletin*, an SEC quarterly publication that is consolidated into volumes. Look in the index (or search on LEXIS) for the subject's name and the names of relevant companies. If you find anything, write to the SEC for copies of the opening and closing reports of the investigation. If you then want other documents referred to in these reports, you may have to make a Freedom of Information request.

Comprehensive information on a broker's disciplinary record and financial missteps (including regulatory actions, criminal charges and convictions, consumer-initiated arbitrations and civil proceedings, bankruptcies, outstanding liens and judgments, and several other items) are available through the NASD Regulation Public Disclosure Program at www.nasdr.com.

Note that the SEC regulates only those companies that trade stocks across state lines. State securities offices, however, regulate companies trading stocks within individual states. Like the SEC, these offices require public filings that may reveal information about the finances of a company's officers and directors. Many companies that file reports on the state level will never be required to file with the SEC. The state securities offices thus offer, at least in part, access to financial data regarding a different layer of the business community.

8.15 Financial Data on Civil Servants, Elected Officials, and Government Appointees

Salary information is available for millions of Americans working at city, county, state, school district, or federal jobs. On the local and state level, there may be a salary roster giving each employee's base pay, overtime pay, and total pay for the year. If not, the job title of a civil servant, and the salary range for that title, will surely be on the public record. In addition, the city or state's pension plans and health insurance plans will be a matter of public record, so you can find out, in general, what kinds of benefits your subject and his or her fellow employees are entitled to.

On the federal level, the Freedom of Information Act entitles you to be told the job title, grade, salary, and duty station of most civilian employees. To obtain this information on your subject, contact the department or agency at which he or she is employed. If your subject is a former federal employee, write to the National Personnel Records Center, Civilian Personnel Records Correspondence Section, 111 Winnebago Street, St. Louis, MO 63118-4199. State that you are requesting the information under the Freedom of Information Act and sign and date your request.

All elected officials on the federal level and most elected officials on the state and local levels must file periodic financial disclosure statements. In addition, about 10,000 federal political appointees, ranking civil servants, and congressional aides must file disclosures. Laws regarding disclosure by state and local legislative aides and executive appointees vary from locality to locality (in New York City, disclosure statements from all city employees earning over $30,000 per year are filed with the city clerk's office), but in general, the salaries of such people are a matter of public record.

For salary and expenses of members of the U.S. House of Representatives, their staff members, committee staffers, and other House employees, see the quarterly *Report of the Clerk of the House*. For similar information on U.S. senators and Senate staffers and employees, see the biannual *Report of the Secretary of the Senate*. For salary information on approximately 3,000 top federal appointees, see *U.S. Government Policy and Supporting Positions* (the so-called "Plum Book"), the full text of which is available at www.access.gpo.gov/plumbook/toc.html.

8.16 Financial Data on Candidates for Public Office

Every candidate for federal office and most candidates for state or local office must file campaign financing reports with a designated agency. On the federal level, statements are kept by the Federal Election Commission (FEC); on the state and local levels, they are kept by state and local boards of elections. This holds for candidates in party primaries as well as for general election candidates. Over a million Americans have filed such reports while pursuing public office over the years. Campaign financing reports frequently reveal the names of contributors (both individual and corporate) with whom the subject has had or will later have a close and often secretive business relationship. Vendors used by the subject's campaign committee and consultants hired to help out with the subject's campaign may also fit into the picture of the subject's ongoing business relationships (such information from Lyndon LaRouche's FEC filings in 1979 helped prove his secret control of a well-known computer software company and his business and political ties with several known associates of organized crime).

For online access to FEC databases dating back to the 1980 electoral cycle, go to www.tray.com. For links to campaign finance filings on the state level, go to www.compaignfinance.org.

More information on FEC filings is provided in section 10.10, "Federal Election Commission Records."

8.17 Government Statistics and Other Indirect Indicators

If you think your subject is living beyond his or her means, you might attempt a rough estimate of his or her income using government wage and salary data.

The U.S. Labor Department's Bureau of Labor Statistics (stats.bls.gov) issues numerous online and print reports that tell, for instance, the average earnings and other compensation data for hundreds of occupations and trades broken down by area of the country and type of firm. Take some time to browse through the BLS databases, but see especially the National Compensation Surveys (broken down by metro area) prepared by the BLS's Office of Compensation Levels and Trends (go to stats.bls.gov/compub.htm). Print versions of many BLS reports and periodicals can be found at a local research library; the best collections will be at the designated regional libraries of the Federal Depository Library Program. If you want to order BLS publications online, go to stats.bls.gov/opborder.htm.

For still more detailed information, contact your state's labor information office. State labor departments often track as many as 1,000 occupations on the county as well as the state level, using the quarterly unemployment contribution reports from every employer in every county as a basis for their statistics.

If the subject belongs to a labor union, its contract with the subject's employer will stipulate wages, linkage of wages to years of service, overtime rates, hours, and various benefits. Union contracts are often available from either the state or the federal labor department. The Bureau of Labor Statistics has a massive file of these contracts (including almost every agreement covering bargaining units of 1,000 or more workers); copies can be ordered for free if the agreement is less than 100 pages. (Order information is at stats.bls.gov/cbaccess.htm.) Contracts for your own area, including those for smaller bargaining units, can be found at your regional Department of Labor office. In addition, the Federal Mediation and Conciliation Service (www.fmcs.gov) maintains files of collective bargaining agreements searchable by company name.

Data for estimating a person's earnings is also available from many other sources. For instance, the National Center for Education Statistics (NCES) compiles an annual survey of "Salaries, Tenure, and Fringe Benefits of Full-time Instructional Faculty" covering colleges and universities in every state with information by rank, sex, tenure status, and length of contract (go to nces.ed.gov/Ipeds/facultysalaries.html). The reports provided by individual schools can be obtained from the NCES, the state board of higher education, or the school itself. Other excellent sources of earnings reports are the nation's professional and trade organizations, many of which publish detailed salary and benefit data according to job category, region, and other indices; for example, the American Payroll Association's biennial *Survey of Salaries and the Payroll Profession*.

Familiarity with the local statistics on wages, salaries, and fringe benefits may help you avoid hasty assumptions. For example, attorneys are generally regarded as a high-income group, especially by fans of the TV show *L.A. Law*. Yet many attorneys in your region (especially those working as public defenders or assistant D.A.s) may earn less money than do unionized blue-collar workers in certain job categories. When using wage statistics, be aware that most people have other sources of income in addition to their primary jobs (see the next section), and earnings from primary jobs may fluctuate. Millions of people work overtime at irregular, unpredictable intervals, thus boosting their annual income significantly. Millions more work at trades that involve seasonal layoffs. Others work two full-time jobs, often keeping this fact secret from one or both of their employers.

Note that you can't estimate someone's financial stability just by looking at how big their house is. They may live in a mansion and drive a Mercedes, but still be on the verge of bankruptcy. But one thing is relatively certain: If an individual or couple owns a middle or upper income co-op and had to win co-op board approval to get in, they almost certainly were in good financial shape at the time they were accepted by the board (and for some years before that time). Co-op boards conduct extremely rigorous financial checks and are fanatically picky regarding who they allow to become shareholders. This observation does not always apply, however, to condo owners, nor does it apply (in New York, with its strict tenant protections) to previous tenants who were allowed to buy in automatically when the building went co-op.

A detailed knowledge of the co-op market in your city might enable you to extrapolate even more. For instance, in the most desirable residential neighborhoods in Manhattan, co-op boards often have restrictive formulas that require the buyer's net worth to be at least twice the purchase price.

8.18 Investigating Secondary Income Sources

Millions of Americans do part-time moonlighting (for example, police officers who double as private security guards). A person working at a moderate-income job may have sizable investments as a result of savings through the years, an inheritance, or a dead spouse's life insurance. A homemaker may be boosting the family income through a part-time job or office temp work; a teenage child may have an after-school job, or summer jobs, that also help the family as a whole. Also, the family may be benefiting from some special situation (such as a rent-controlled apartment in New York City that costs only 10 percent of the family's annual income). To make matters even more confusing, there's the problem of the underground cash economy: The subject you believe is living beyond his or her means may gain extra income from growing marijuana on the family farm. Or the extra income (exaggerated in your mind) may actually be the modest receipts from weekend yard sales.

These are only a few of the possibilities for which you should keep alert. A person you know to be retired may have started a second career and thus be receiving a full salary in addition to his or her pension. A family with its own private residential home may be renting out part of it to another family, whether or not they are allowed to do so under zoning regulations, or they may be operating a part-time bed-and-breakfast. A family with a vacation home in a popular resort may be making big extra income by renting it out at the height of the summer or winter season. A tenured college professor may not need to pay for his or her kids' college tuition because the tab is picked up by the college (this can boost the professor's family's income enormously compared to that of non-faculty neighbors). Just about anyone could be collecting royalties from a book or a song or a patent, either as a result of his or her own work or that of a parent or other relative. A person who is in poor financial circumstances now may be on the brink of a new income level as a result of an impending inheritance from a dead or dying relative.

Note: To check on patents, you can search the Patent and Trademarks Office database by name of inventor at patent.womplex.ibm.com (a free service of IBM). For copyrights, go to lcweb.loc.gov/copyright. If you don't believe the subject ever invented or published anything personally, search for the name of a parent or dead spouse from whom the subject might have inherited the rights.

In investigating someone's income (and his or her finances in general), take nothing for granted. Always assume that there's still something you don't know about.

8.19 Bank Account Records

A bank will not tell you how much money a subject has in his or her accounts or any other details without the subject's permission. However, someone with a clear need to know—such as a potential employer or landlord—may be told whether or not the subject has an account at that branch and whether or not the account is "satisfactory" (that is, is not overdrawn). In addition, someone who calls the bank and claims that he or she has been given a check by the subject (say, for $1,000) may be told whether or not the subject's balance will cover it. (This ruse will not work if the caller is unable to furnish the subject's account number as listed on one of the subject's checks.)

8.20 Loan, Job, and Apartment Rental Applications; Résumés

In assiduously researching a subject's background, you may from time to time come across a copy of a loan, job, or apartment rental application filled out by the subject in the recent or not so recent past. Such a document may provide interesting details about the subject's salary history and other financial matters, but you should never accept such information at face value. People filling out such applications naturally slant the truth to present themselves in the most favorable light, and a large percentage of them actually lie about one or more facts.

You may not find your subject's salary history in the résumé he or she posts online, but he or she will surely have emailed or snail-mailed a version containing this information to prospective employers at one time or another. If you happen to obtain a copy of such a résumé, be aware that any information therein should, like the information on an application, be regarded with some skepticism. (For information about finding a subject's résumé online, see section 5.10, "Résumés and Curriculum Vitae.")

Unscrupulous investigators will sometimes call a subject and pretend to be a personnel headhunter. They will sweet-talk the subject (with promises of a high-salary position) into sending a résumé to a so-called job agency that is really a mail drop. An easier method, which enables the investigator to obtain résumé-type information over the phone without setting up a mail drop, is to call the subject in the guise of a salesperson for a fictitious credit card company and offer a card with very low interest rates and a very high credit line if the subject will answer a few quick questions over the phone. These questions, of course, will focus on the subject's salary history, present and past employers, present and past job titles, and so on. Often the subject will not only supply each answer in detail but will even volunteer additional information in his or her eagerness to obtain the promised credit. (If some creep tries this tactic on *you*, call the cops.)

8.21 Credit Card Records

Records of credit card transactions are confidential. If your subject is an elected official, political appointee, or civil servant, however, you can make a Freedom of Information request (under federal or state law, as appropriate) for access to the records of the government credit card(s) he or she uses.

8.22 Financial Information from a Subject's Garbage

A word of warning to readers: If you throw out credit card receipts, monthly credit card statements, bank statements, or canceled checks (on which you may have written your unlisted telephone number or your credit card number), a private investigator (or a thief) can sift through your garbage (see section 11.4, "Subject's Garbage") and obtain these documents.

After a snooper has obtained your bank account and credit card account numbers (and also has obtained basic identifying information such as your SSN, date of birth, residential zip code, telephone number, and mother's maiden name), he or she can call up the customer information numbers at both institutions, pretend to be you, and sometimes find out (depending on the institution's procedures) such information as your current bank account and credit card account balances, your total and available credit limits (including cash advance limits), the value of your money market accounts, and so forth. Often, the snooper won't need to speak to anyone; he or she will just get the information from the automated account information system using a pay phone.

If your garbage also contains old telephone or gas and electric bills with account numbers on them, the unscrupulous snoop—if he or she is trying to determine whether or not you are experiencing financial difficulties—will call up the telephone or utilities company in your name to find out how much you owe, how many months behind you are in your payments, and whether or not you are or recently have been on a deferred payment plan.

Moral of the story: Don't throw out financial documents without shredding them first.

A garbologist who sticks to the clues in the garbage itself may find vital information about financial difficulties in a person's life (such as bounced check notices, utility bill overdue notices or disconnect warnings, envelopes from creditors stamped URGENT FINAL NOTICE, and letters from a landlord warning that the rent is overdue or that eviction proceedings will soon commence). This information could set you to looking for the reasons for these financial problems in civil court records and elsewhere. On the other hand, the reason may be right there in the same garbage: a pile of old lottery tickets, discarded racing sheets and turf magazines, airline receipts for a recent round trip to Las Vegas or some other center of casino gambling, hypodermic needles and syringes, an unusual number of booze bottles, empty prescription medicine bottles that suggest that someone in the household has an expensive-to-treat illness, numerous mailings from fly-by-night investment houses or phony pyramid or franchise schemes (indicating that the person is on a special mailing list for suckers), or literature from a cult notorious for its financial predation on its members and supporters.

Note: Most Americans are constantly being deluged with offers from credit card companies, which they promptly throw out. These offers provide clues about a person's credit situation because they are targeted to narrow segments of the market based on confidential credit information. If a person is being offered pre-approved gold cards with high credit limits, it probably means that he or she is in good standing. But if the person is offered only secured cards with a low credit line, it's a sign of previous credit difficulties.

Also note: If the subject tossed out his or her payroll check stubs in the garbage, do not assume that the name on the check stub is that of the company employing him. It may instead be the name of a company that processes payroll checks for thousands of other companies.

8.23 Financial Information on Nonprofit Employees and Consultants

Federal 990 forms filed with the IRS by charities and other tax-exempt organizations may contain salary and expense disbursement information regarding the organization's top officers and also the amounts paid to outside counsel and consultants. If the organization is the recipient of federal grants, it must file additional information about the finances of officers and consultants with the agency or agencies providing the grants.

You should also check the tax-exempt organization's annual filings with the state's department of state.

Note: Top officers of a nonprofit organization may receive a much higher income than reported on the 990 form. This additional income may come from a second salary paid by a profit-making (non-tax-exempt) arm of the organization, or it may come in the guise of a no-show job for the subject's spouse or one of the subject's children.

8.24 Financial Information on Labor Union Officials and Employees

Forms LM-2 and LM-3, filed by union locals and higher union bodies with the U.S. Department of Labor, will tell you the salaries and disbursements paid to each union officer regardless of amount, and information about each union employee who received more than $10,000 from the union in the given year. These reports also list all direct or indirect loans of more than $250 made by the union to any union officer, employee, or member, or to any other person or business.

Form LM-30 is a detailed financial disclosure form that union officers and employees must submit if they or their spouses or children have business dealings with a firm whose employees are represented by the union in question. It may include important information about a union official's outside sources of income, his or her investments and debts, and so forth.

Form LM-2 is what you examine to find out the salaries of union leaders, but there's a catch: Some union fat cats rake in more than one salary by being president of more than one local, by serving as an officer of a district council, or by serving on the board of the international union in Washington, D.C. To find out the total salary, you must obtain the separate LM-2s filed by each of these entities.

A union leader's LM-2 forms can now be requested online from the Labor Department (go to www.dol.gov/dol/esa/public/regs/compliance/olms/rrlo/ordern.htm).

8.25 Financial Information on Philanthropists and Other Wealthy People

Numerous reference works have been published to help charities and charitable institutions identify potential donors. To gain background financial information on the wealthy, just go to the Taft Group's *Who's Wealthy in America* (profiles of over 100,000 individuals, including data on their stock ownership). By looking at back editions, if they are available at your library, you can trace changes in the subject's stock and real estate holdings. Other Taft books that are now out of print but are widely available in libraries and are useful for backgrounding include *Who Owns Corporate America* (comprehensive listings of over 75,000 insider stockholders); *Owners and Officers of Private Companies* (information on 105,000 individuals that you won't find in any SEC filings); *Major Donors* (data on over 16,000 philanthropists and their major gifts); *Guide to Private Fortunes* (a three-volume set profiling thousands of generous donors); and *New Fortunes* (profiles of prospective donors with a net worth of at least $2 million). All but the last two of these titles were annuals, so the backfiles can be used, like those of *Who's Wealthy in America*, to get a sense of how an individual's fortune has grown or shrunk.

Other capsule information on wealthy donors can be found at the libraries of the Foundation Center and in various reference directories (see section 14.3, "Investigating a Nonprofit Entity").

Information on ownership of yachts and summer estates can be found in *Social Register Summer* (for more on yacht ownership, see the *Register of American Yachts*).

No study of a wealthy individual or family would be complete without a search of the SEC's EDGAR (go to people.edgar-online.com/people) and of the DISCLOSURE/Spectrum ownership database on DIALOG (see section 8.14, earlier in this chapter).

8.26 Ownership of Airplanes, Boats, Cars, and Other Valuable Personal Property

Using many online vendors, you can find out whether or not your subject owns an aircraft or a large boat. For instance, go to www.search3. knowx.com and select the "Assets" search option. This option enables you to search the Federal Aviation Administration's aircraft database (all civil aircraft owned by individuals, businesses, and government agencies) and the U.S. Coast Guard's watercraft ownership database (all merchant and recreational vessels greater than 37 feet in length and registered with the Coast Guard). Both databases can be searched by individual owner's name or corporate owner's name. (If Subject A's corporation owns a small jet, you may be on your way to exposing yet one more of the perks through which he or she is cheating the corporation's stockholders. If Subject B, a prominent politician, turns out to be the owner of a large boat with a name like "Monkey Business," grab your camera and head for the docks.)

To find out about your subject's ownership of other valuable personal property (including, perhaps, a boat too small to be listed with the U.S. Coast Guard), you should look in the "grand lists" at the county clerk's office. You should also check with the state agency that registers recreational vehicles (from snowmobiles to dune buggies), mobile homes, and motorized pleasure craft. And don't forget the Department of Motor Vehicles (DMV) auto registration files: Family cars are an important element in the net worth of ordinary working families, while ownership of a late-model Mercedes or Cadillac may be the only significant remaining asset of a high-living deadbeat. DMV databases, if still open to the general public in your state, can provide a list of the cars registered in the name of a subject or any member of a subject's household together with the liens on any of these vehicles. (If you can't get any information from the DMV, you can drive by the house, take pictures of the family cars, identify them by make and year, and then estimate their remaining value.)

Note that security interests in a trailer or motor home may be filed (depending on the laws of the particular state) under the motor vehicle title statute, under the UCC as a fixture filing, or (if the trailer is attached to the ground and of a certain minimum size) under the real estate title recording statute.

8.27 Corporate, Partnership, and D/B/A Files

If you know of businesses that the subject owns or is affiliated with, you may find much valuable information in the state or county business files (see section 14.1, "Businesses, Legitimate and Otherwise"). For instance, if the subject is a limited partner in a real estate investment, the partnership agreement may contain information about how many shares he or she owns. It may also contain information about shares owned in the names of the subject's spouse and children. And the list of limited partners may include the names of business associates of the subject about whom you would not otherwise have learned. (If you do a little paper trailing of some of these associates, you may learn about other ventures in which your subject is involved.)

If you don't know the names of any of the subject's business entities, try checking under his or her surname (for example, the Richardson Organization) or under his or her first or middle name (for example, Judy's Boutique, Inc.). Next look under the first names and middle names of the subject's spouse and children, especially his or her daughters (for example, the Lucille Cab Company). In all of these examples, you should check under each family member's nickname, and you might even check under the family cat's name. You should also examine the file on any business that includes the subject's (or the subject's spouse's) initials either in capital letters or in phonetic form. For instance, in searching for local real estate companies controlled by one Lawrence Cole, check the records for any entities with names such as LC Enterprises, Elcee Corporation, or El Cee Incorporated.

Business registrations are generally the easiest of all public records to find online. Experian (www.experian.com) offers searches of business registration files in 42 states and fictitious business name (D/B/A) files in all 50 states (but not every county in every state). Another firm offering searches of these records is KnowX (www.search3.knowx.com). In addition, some state governments have placed these records online at free Web sites for the convenience of the business community and the general public. For directories of these state government sites, go to www.inil.com/users/dguss/gator.htm (select "Companies, Corporations, and UCC Listings") and www.brbpub.com/pubrecsites.htm (see the "State Sites" listing).

To find tax-exempt entities that your subject might have established over the years, look in the IRS's *Cumulative List of Organizations*. Try combinations such as the following: the Johnson Foundation, the Johnson Family

Foundation, the James and Sarah Johnson Foundation, the Sarah and James Johnson Foundation, the James I. and Sarah E. Johnson Foundation, and so forth. Note that the *Cumulative List of Organizations* can now be searched online at www.irs.ustreas.gov/prod/bus_infor/eo/eosearch.html.

9.

Court Records

9.1 Introducing the Court System

Researching court records is a complicated matter because of the wide variety of courts and records systems. If you are starting out as an investigative journalist, one of your first steps should be to familiarize yourself with each court located in or having jurisdiction over your city, county, and greater metropolitan area. You should also learn how to use the court indexes to maximum effect (I am referring not only to the electronic indexes of recent cases but also to the old, pre-electronic indexes in the courthouse basement).

The trial courts in any locality are divided into local courts and district state courts on the one hand and federal courts on the other. Each has civil and criminal divisions and a system of higher courts to which appeals are made.

The lowest level of a state court system is the village, town, city, or county court, which handles relatively minor matters—say, claims of up to $20,000 and misdemeanors such as prostitution and driving while intoxicated. These local courts, which usually do not offer jury trials, go by many names: magistrate's court, district court, city court, or superior court. Some may have specialized jurisdictions; for example, small claims court (to handle claims of $2,500 or less), traffic court, and landlord-tenant court. These courts exist in every state, although their names and functions may vary from town to town within a single state according to local custom.

The next level is the state courts, which offer jury trials of larger monetary claims (say, claims of over $20,000) and the more serious criminal offenses. Anyone disputing a city court judge's decision will also come here for a *trial de novo* (new trial). These state courts, each of which may have jurisdiction over one or more counties, are referred to, variously, as the district court, superior court, county court, circuit court, or state supreme court (note the overlap in terminology with the municipal courts). Various specialized divisions are usually included in this level of the court system; for instance, the probate court (also known as surrogate's court), which handles the probate of wills, administration of estates, and appointment of guardians; and family court, which handles child custody cases and various other marital and family disputes (and, in some localities, juvenile criminal cases).

The federal court of original jurisdiction is the U.S. district court, which may cover an entire state or several counties within a state (for example, the U.S. District Court for the Southern District of Iowa). Most federal district courts have more than one court location (or "division"); for instance, the Iowa southern district has a Council Bluffs division, a Davenport division, and a Des Moines (headquarters) division. Federal district courts handle suits brought by or against the federal government and other civil cases involving federal law. They are also the trial courts for all federal criminal violations.

The U.S. bankruptcy courts handle all bankruptcies of individuals and businesses. Generally, they follow the same territorial lines as the U.S. district courts, but within these lines the bankruptcy court may have fewer court locations or divisions. For instance, the U.S. District Court for the Northern District of New York (NDNY) includes four divisions, while the U.S. Bankruptcy Court covering the same area has only two divisions. Federal district courts and bankruptcy courts will usually have their headquarters at the same court location (Albany for the NDNY).

9.2 Working with Your Local Court Indexes

Each court keeps indexes of all civil and criminal cases brought before it. Federal court indexes today are fully computerized and can be searched online or at terminals in the courthouse. In many state court districts, the indexes can also be searched at in-house computer terminals, although the process of putting these indexes online for the general public is going more slowly than in the federal courts. For older records at any court, you will still need to conduct a manual search. The older records may be on microfiche, on index cards, or even in bound computer-printout volumes. *Note:* In working with federal district court records, either online or offline, always check whether there is a single index for all divisions of that court, or whether each division's index must be searched separately.

Computerized systems allow you to search the entire court index instantly by plaintiff or defendant's name, docket number, type of case, and so on without any need for an alphabetized list. Of course, you may have to try several variations of your subject's name before you find the cases you are looking for, and the information in the index entry may fail to include the names of certain of the plaintiffs or defendants in a multiplaintiff or multidefendant case. Indeed, your ability to find the name of a particular person depends (as it does in manual systems) on the amount of detail in (and the accuracy of) the database.

In the traditional court index, criminal court cases are listed by defendant; bankruptcy cases, by petitioner (either debtor or creditor); probate actions, by the decedent's name. Civil suits are listed alphabetically by either plaintiff or defendant, although some courts have both a plaintiff/defendant and a defendant/plaintiff index (or else one index that merges both in a single alphabetical listing, in which each case appears at least twice—this is called a "party index"). In general, the plaintiff/defendant or defendant/plaintiff index lists only the first-listed plaintiff and first-listed defendant in multiparty cases.

Some computerized indexes will list *all* parties (if a system combines index and docket information in a single database, it almost certainly will be all-party searchable). Fully developed digital systems, however, are not available in every trial court; and where they do exist, the coverage usually doesn't extend back very many years. If you want the names of those 10 other plaintiffs in the 1985 product liability suit *Barnett et al. v. Ace Toys*, you will need to go to the docket sheet or the case file.

Finding all the local civil suits involving your subject in a nonelectronic index requires considerable ingenuity if there is no cross-index or if indexing is restricted to the first-listed parties. Yet this type of search—which is often necessary to find closed or dormant cases from past decades—is of vital importance in investigative journalism. This is especially true in tracking a corrupt politician or an organized crime figure; the conspiracies in which such people are involved often go way back, and today's trickery may be understandable only in the light of courtroom revelations from a decade or more ago.

Following are some methods you might find useful in finding cases involving your subject in older nonelectronic indexes in which the cases are listed alphabetically by first-named plaintiff only, with no cross-indexing by defendants. These methods will also be useful in finding cases in electronic indexes that include only first-named parties.

- Look up all cases in which the state or city is the plaintiff. Depending on local practice, these may be listed under "People of————," "State of————," or "City of————," or possibly under the official designation of the state or city attorney (such as "Anystate Attorney General," "Anystate Department of Law"). Under the most commonly used of these government plaintiff headings, you may find hundreds of defendants listed in alphabetical order.

- Flip through the plaintiff indexes, looking for examples of plaintiffs who file massive numbers of cases. In the metropolitan and state district court indexes of any large city, hundreds of defendants may be listed alphabetically opposite the name of the city hospital corporation and other public and private entities that deal with consumer debt problems on a large scale.

- Go to the judgment books (see section 8.4, "Judgment Books"). If a private or governmental plaintiff has obtained a judgment against your subject in the local courts, the case file number will be listed alongside the subject's name.

- Whenever you find the subject listed as one of several plaintiffs or defendants, check the names of the other parties separately in the index to find other cases that might include your subject as a party.

- Whenever you find a case involving the subject, look on the docket sheet and in the case file for references to other lawsuits. Especially look for countersuits or cross-suits. Examine the transcript, if any, of the subject's deposition or court testimony to see whether he or she was asked about previous litigation. Also check directly with the other parties (or their attorneys); they may be aware of cases you would otherwise miss.

- Look in newspaper and business periodical databases and clippings files for reports of any lawsuits involving the subject.

- Check for "bad blood" suits. If you learn from the plaintiff index that your subject once filed a suit against Mr. X, check to see whether Mr. X ever filed suit against your subject on another matter, either before your subject's suit or afterwards.

- Use the federal court party index to find possible leads to state court cases indexed only by plaintiff. A person who sued your subject in federal court might also have sued him or her on a related or entirely separate matter in state court.

- Follow clues that emerge from other aspects of your investigation. For instance, check in the plaintiff index under the names of the subject's ex-spouses or ex-lovers, former business partners (especially in businesses that went bankrupt), political rivals, and others. They may have sued your subject or a close associate of your subject. Any time you find an antagonist or associate of the subject listed as a first-named plaintiff or first-named defendant, check the docket sheet or the case file to see whether the subject was one of the unindexed parties. (All this should apply to any businesses linked to the subject as well as to individuals.)

- Check the bankruptcy court index to see whether the subject or his or her business has ever been involved in a bankruptcy proceeding, either as debtor or creditor. Debtors in bankruptcy cases must file with the court a list of all outstanding judgments against them and all pending litigation in which they are involved in any jurisdiction.

9.3 Finding Cases in Other Jurisdictions

Your subject may have moved around a lot or may do business in many states simultaneously. How can you identify cases involving him or her in localities other than your own?

Online Court Indexes and Dockets

Begin with the federal courts. There is now a U.S. Party/Case Index that allows you to search, by party name, for open and recently closed cases in almost all the federal trial and appeals courts (as well as in the bankruptcy courts) nationwide. To register for this online service, call the PACER Service Center in San Antonio, Texas at (800) 676-6856.

For more information about a case, you will need to access the given court's online system. Court indexes/dockets from all 190 U.S. bankruptcy courts and from nearly all of the 300 U.S. civil/criminal district courts are now searchable using the online Public Access to Court Electronic Records (PACER) system. PACER generally costs 60 cents per minute. To sign up for PACER at various individual courts, contact the PACER Service Center.

As an alternative to PACER, some federal courts are now placing their records on Web sites or making them accessible through RACER, an Internet-friendly system. For links to federal court Web sites and to courts using RACER, go to www.brbpub.com/pubrecsites.htm.

Note that cases closed before a particular district court's index was computerized are usually not included in the electronic database, and cases may be purged from the online index after about four years.

If a case has been assigned a number beginning with the letters "MDL" (which stands for MultiDistrict Litigation), you will know that the judicial panel on multidistrict litigation in Washington, D.C., has consolidated this and other cases into a single action. Typically, such consolidation is effected to handle numerous product liability suits involving the same product and the same defendant manufacturer(s).

Federal court cases are only a tiny fraction of the total number of cases filed on all levels of the American court system. The real heart of court-records searching is at the county level (county and municipal courts plus state trial courts). For detailed information on how to obtain index and file searches of these courts in every county in the United States, consult *Find Public Records Fast* or the *PRRS*. Both of these BRB publications will tell you what is online and how far back the computerized records go; they also cover mail and telephone search requests and provide a city/county cross-reference index.

If you need to search multiple state courts around the country, it is advisable that you do so through an online public records vendor who can provide a gateway to the various court databases. One place to begin is at www.search3.knowx.com (select "Lawsuits"), where you can search the online indexes of thousands of court jurisdictions nationwide. You should also search, at the KnowX site, judgment and lien indexes around the country, which provide pointers to lawsuits you would otherwise miss. Once you find a relevant case, you can order a copy of the case file either from the court itself or from a court record retrieval service (see www.publicrecordsources.com).

Searching with LEXIS

If you can afford it, try searching for your subject's name in LEXIS. This giant collection of legal databases covers most of the decisions handed down by the nation's federal and state appeals courts since the last century. It also covers trial court decisions for recent years in various states, as well as decisions in the U.S. Tax Court and other specialized federal courts. You can search court decisions by state (for example, the LEXIS Maryland Library) or by type of case (the LEXIS Family Law Library).

Author Steve Weinberg used LEXIS and its competitor, WESTLAW, in researching his unauthorized Armand Hammer biography. He located about 300 cases involving Hammer or close associates and relatives of the oil tycoon. Reading over the judges' decisions, Weinberg selected certain cases that seemed to warrant further digging. He then went to the various courthouses or Federal Records Centers to examine the case files and photocopied selected portions

The cases searched with LEXIS will represent only a fraction of those filed nationally each year, most of which either don't go to trial or don't get appealed. A case that does get appealed is often a richly complicated one, however, and the case file may be full of juicy revelations.

Your Local Law Library

As an alternative to LEXIS, you can search the case law digests in your county bar association's law library. For federal court cases, see *West's Federal Practice Digest*. For state cases, see the various state digests. For New York State, you would go to *West's New York Digest 4d* (for cases since 1978), *West's New York Digest 3d* (for cases from 1961 to 1978), and *Abbott New York Digest 2d* (cases before 1961). Both *West's* and *Abbott* have plaintiff/defendant and defendant/plaintiff tables. Note that case law digests give comprehensive coverage only of appeals court decisions. Trial court rulings may be covered, however, if they involve significant points of law.

Newspapers and Periodicals

You can often find court cases involving your subject in newspaper and periodical databases. A case with general news interest will usually be reported in the daily press; cases with specialized news interest may be reported in regional or local business or trade publications. A search of these databases often will turn up several cases not found in LEXIS or WEST-LAW. For instance, a divorce case involving a certain movie star may have zero interest as case law and thus not be reported in any legal database, but you may find a hundred references to it in NEXIS or DIALOG databases covering tabloid newspapers and popular general-interest magazines.

9.4 Obtaining the Civil Case File

In many courts, there will be separate civil indexes for individuals and corporations. The index will tell you the date the case was filed, the name of the first-listed plaintiff, the name of the first-listed defendant, and a docket number. It will also tell you whether the case is still pending or whether it is closed. You can then fill out a requisition form and give it to the clerk in the file room, who will bring you the file.

Always tell the clerk that you want *all* the folders in the case file, including any supplemental folders with depositions in them. If certain of the documents listed in the docket sheet of an open case are not in the case folder(s), they are probably in the judge's chambers. To make an appointment to examine them, call the judge's law clerk.

If the case is closed, the file may be on microfiche or stored in an archive at another location. The files of closed federal court cases are usually sent to the regional Federal Records Center. To access the files there, you must first get the case locator numbers of the file boxes from the originating court. Note that after a period of 20 to 30 years, records at the Federal Records Center are transferred to the National Archives and Records Administration's regional archives.

Don't expect to find too much beyond the original pleadings in the court file of your average closed case. Of all civil cases, about 97 percent nationwide are settled with very little court involvement. Often in an out-of-court settlement, the parties will agree to keep secret the conditions of the settlement, including the amount of money paid by defendant to plaintiff (this is especially important to defendants in product liability and medical malpractice cases). The agreement may also include a court order sealing all records of the discovery process and perhaps even the entire court file. (During the early 1990s, some states moved to reverse this widespread practice, barring secret settlements and the sealing of discovery records in cases involving potential threats to public safety and health. Of course, such legislation cannot unseal records sealed before the passage of the legislation.)

If a case is appealed, all or part of the trial court file is sent to the appeals court. Locating the portion you need can get rather complicated (especially if an appeal is on its way from a lower to a higher appeals court). The portion of the file at a particular appeals court can usually be examined there by a news reporter. After the appeals court decision, the file is sent back to the trial court's file room (and from there to the court archives) unless there is a further appeal. The briefs filed with the appeals court (which sometimes bring out facts not found in the trial court case file) may be sent to a depository library eventually.

From this discussion, you might think that chasing down court papers can be extremely time-consuming. Fortunately, there is often a shortcut. You call one of the subject's opposing parties in the case (or their attorney). The attorney may have the complete file in his or her office, if the case is still open. If the case is closed, the attorney may still have the file, or the client may have taken it home. Note that this file will frequently have deposition transcripts and documents produced under discovery that are missing from the courthouse file.

9.5 Studying the Case File

You may find that a case that began several years ago is still open, yet the folder contains almost nothing except the original affidavit of service, the plaintiff's complaint, and the defendant's reply. In such instances, the plaintiff may have simply decided not to pursue the case. Or there may have been a delay because of a crowded court calendar or the dilatoriness of the plaintiff's attorney. (For these and other reasons, civil cases often don't go to trial until several years after being filed.) If a case is being vigorously pursued, however, the folders may be filled to overflowing with motions, countermotions, and other legal documents. Some of these will contain useful facts; others will be (for your purposes) legal mumbo jumbo. The case docket sheet is your guide to the case file—it lists in chronological order all papers filed, appearances, process served, orders, and so on. Although the docket can be confusing to a nonlawyer, a good rule of thumb is always to examine the original pleadings (the plaintiff's complaint against the defendant and the defendant's reply) and attached exhibits, any affidavits dealing with the substance of the complaint, and any pretrial discovery materials (especially depositions). Get these records while you can: Most such cases will be settled before trial, and the settlement may include the sealing of the court file.

If the trial has already occurred, the transcript (if one was ever made) will probably not be included in the file unless the case was appealed. If you want the transcript and can't get it from any of the parties, you will need to order it from the court reporter at a cost, possibly, of thousands of dollars. For this, if for no other reason, appeals cases are extremely important for an investigator: The party who is appealing must order a transcript and usually will file it (or significant portions of it) with the appeals court.

Many states are now using videotape (albeit to a limited extent) to supplement or even replace the court reporter's transcript. The cost to the court for a videotape of the day's proceedings is minimal, and copies are often deposited in the case file.

9.6 Pretrial Discovery

Often, the most valuable material will surface during pretrial discovery—the process by which each side seeks information from the other to clarify issues and strengthen its own case. For an investigative reporter, this material may be more important than the trial transcript itself because pretrial discovery is much more freewheeling than a trial in respect to the questions that can be asked and the evidence that can be collected. The reason for this is that pretrial discovery is not limited by the rules of admissibility at trial, the judge's rulings about specific evidence or testimony, or the plaintiff's and defendant's desire to avoid laying certain facts before the jury. During pretrial discovery, all sorts of things come out that a jury would never be allowed to hear.

Pretrial discovery involves the following procedures that are conducted according to federal or state court rules of civil procedure:

- **Discovery and inspection of documents:** A party to the action serves process on another party demanding the production of business correspondence and other documents relevant to the issues at law. In a corporate suit, thousands of pages of correspondence, internal memoranda, and financial records may be produced for inspection and copying. In a libel suit, the plaintiff may demand to inspect and copy the reporter's notes, article drafts, and any documents on which the reporter's allegedly libelous statements were based. Documents produced under discovery will not be found in the court file unless they are filed in support of a motion or as deposition or trial exhibits. If the documents produced are not covered under a permanent protective order, however, you may be able to examine them after the settlement or trial at the offices of the attorneys for the party that conducted the discovery and inspection.

- **The posing and answering of interrogatories:** A party to the action serves written questions on an opposing party, which the latter must answer in writing under oath. Interrogatories are often used as a way to identify documents that will then be demanded under an order to produce.

- **The taking of oral depositions (also known as Examinations Before Trial, or EBTs):** In a deposition, a person answers questions under oath from the attorneys for one or more parties, and the proceedings are recorded by a court reporter. The person questioned (called the deponent) may be a party to the action or a nonparty with knowledge of relevant facts. In cases that are settled before trial, the deposition is the closest thing to actual court testimony you will find. Some of the questions posed in a deposition will be designed to gain broad background information (thus, the deponent's attorney may complain on the record that the attorney taking the deposition is on a "fishing expedition"). Depositions can go on for days, generating thousands of transcript pages. Unfortunately for journalists, these transcripts are not always filed with the court, although brief excerpts may be included in support of a motion or brief. The rules of procedure regarding public access to deposition transcripts vary widely in both state and federal jurisdictions. For instance, in some jurisdictions, transcripts of depositions and exhibits marked for identification therein must be filed with the clerk of the court for public inspection unless there is a protective order. In other jurisdictions, they are not filed *except* by judicial order.

If the court file does not contain much in the way of pretrial discovery facts, it at least may give you an idea of what types of documents were produced and what lines of questioning were pursued. (Indeed, a motion to compel production of documents may itemize exactly which documents are being demanded.) You can then try to get access from a friendly party. However, you may find that the party who is the target of a particular discovery process has obtained a court order stipulating that access to documents, deposition transcripts, and interrogatory answers will be limited to the parties in the case (or sometimes just to the parties' attorneys) and the judge. On occasion, however, this will only be a temporary order; the materials will show up in the court file or can be easily obtained from one of the parties after the case is settled.

9.7 Dealing with a Subject's Opponents at Law

The attorneys for your subject's opponent may be your best source for copies of depositions and other pretrial discovery materials as well as the trial transcript. Often the attorneys will let you examine or copy documents if you have information to trade, if they think you might write an article favorable to their client's viewpoint, or if they're simply curious to see what you might dig up.

After the appeals are over and the case is closed, the attorney may give many of the documents generated by the case to the client, who will take them home and toss them in a closet. If you want to know about a subject's divorce, and your state bars public access to divorce filings, you might approach the ex-spouse to see whether he or she would be willing to dig the papers out of the closet. (The case file in a legal battle over division of property, child support, alimony, and so forth can be extremely revealing about the finances of one or both parties.)

Even if you don't need their help in obtaining deposition transcripts and other documents, it's still useful to talk with the subject's opponents at law. They may give you much valuable information off the record. While backgrounding a certain businessman a few years ago, I found a single case in the court index in which he was being sued for fraud. Meeting with the plaintiff's attorney, I was treated to a fascinating lecture on the subject's corporate veil and his ties to organized crime, based mostly on private investigators' reports and confidential internal documents of the subject's business entities. I learned more about the subject in that one session than during weeks of earlier research.

9.8 Criminal Court Records

Arrest and Conviction Records

Criminal records are kept by county and municipal courts and state trial courts (which all send data regarding convictions to a central state repository) and by federal trial courts. Each criminal court will have an index that gives the defendant's name, the charge, the disposition (if any), and the case file number.

Public access to arrest and conviction records varies from county to county as well as from state to state. In general, if a person has been convicted of a felony or misdemeanor (or if the case is still pending), this information can be found in the criminal court index. However, in some localities, you will need a release to obtain a records search. If the person was acquitted or the case was dropped, the record usually will be expunged.

In attempting to directly search criminal records, there are two basic approaches: searching the records of the state repository, and searching at the county (trial court) level. If you search the state repository (assuming that these records are available without a release), you will miss many cases—the trial courts at the county level are often negligent or tardy in forwarding data to the state repository, and some state repositories do not accept misdemeanor or lesser felony records. On the other hand, if you just search the records in the subject's home county, you may get reliable results for that county, but you'll miss the subject's felony conviction in a neighboring county. Experts at backgrounding suggest that you always search both the state repository and the trial courts of those counties where the subject is most likely to have gotten into trouble.

The *PRRS* describes the procedures for obtaining a criminal records search from every county and every central state repository in the nation, and tells which jurisdictions will provide information only by mail and which will provide it by phone. It also gives the separate procedures for obtaining misdemeanor and felony records and tells which jurisdictions require a release. Finally, its city/county cross-references help you match any city or town with the county courthouse that controls its criminal records.

On the federal court level, you can now search for your subject's name in the nationwide U.S. Party/Case Index to find out whether he or she is or recently has been a defendant in a federal criminal case. You can then obtain further online information from the court in question through PACER or RACER. However, this approach will not enable you to find older cases, which may require a search of microfiche or index-card records.

LEXIS Searches

Another way to access criminal records is with a full-text search for the subject's name on LEXIS. If the subject ever appealed a conviction to a state or federal appeals court anywhere in the country, LEXIS will probably have the appeals decision. You might search the LEXIS state libraries for any states in which the subject has lived or worked. You might also check the LEXIS Federal Sentencing Library, the Racketeer-Influenced and Corrupt Organizations (RICO) Act case law file within the LEXIS General Federal Library (this covers both criminal and civil RICO cases), and the Military Justice Library.

Credit Agency Files

Information on a person's problems with the criminal justice system may be included in the below-the-line portion of his or her credit agency file. Under the original Fair Credit Reporting Act, a credit agency had to cease reporting this information to its clients after seven years. However, thanks to a law passed in 1998, a criminal conviction record can now be revealed to clients indefinitely, although records of arrests, indictments, and dispositions other than conviction are still subject to the seven-year rule. It should be noted that the new law includes a provision to the effect that the laws of individual states, if more restrictive than the federal law, supersede the latter. Thus, if state law includes the seven-year rule for criminal conviction information, that rule will remain in effect.

You should not try to get access to information on a person's criminal record from a credit reporting agency, directly or indirectly, unless you have a valid reason for the information as defined by the Fair Credit Reporting Act.

Internet Postings, Hot Lines, and So Forth

In the current tough-on-crime climate in America, a surprising amount of information on the records of criminals and former criminals has entered the public domain at Internet Web sites and from various state and federal hot lines and other public notification and locator services.

- **Prison inmates and ex-inmates.** If you think your subject is or has been a federal prison inmate, you can call the Inmate Locator Line at (202) 307-3126. Give them the subject's name, and they will tell you whether this name is in the database, which covers inmates back to 1982. If the name is in the system, the locator service will provide you, over the phone, with conviction, sentencing, and parole information and will tell you where subject is or was incarcerated. (For inmates released before 1982, you should write to the Office of Communications and Archives, Federal Bureau of Prisons, 320 First Street NW, Washington, D.C. 20534, and provide as much identifying information on your subject as possible.)

The Departments of Corrections in most states also have locator systems, and a few have provided information about convicted criminals on their Web sites. The most interesting Web site is that of the Florida Department of Corrections (www.dc.state.fl.us/index.html), which includes locator information on individual inmates as well as inmate release and inmate escape information. You can search by criminal offense category as well as by name. Several other states provide more limited information or instructions on how to obtain a criminal record. A directory of these sites can be found at www.inil.com/users/dguss/wgator.htm (select "State Parole Boards, Inmates, Criminal Histories, and Prison Information").

Web pages devoted to alerting citizens about convicts up for parole are also emerging; see www.parolewatch.org, which monitors the New York City criminal justice system, and www.state.nj.us/parole/elig.htm, which covers New Jersey.

▪ **Sex offender information.** Information on convicted sex offenders is publicly available in every state, thanks to the federal Megan's Law. How this information is made available to the public is up to the individual states. Several states have placed their registries online (the North Carolina registry includes information on over 2,000 individuals). Other states have hot lines you can use to check a name over the phone. Still others make the data public through press releases. California has produced a CD-ROM database on over 60,000 offenders which can be viewed at sheriffs' offices (you can search by physical traits such as hair color and height, as well as by name; photographs are also included). Some city and county authorities have placed the information about offenders in their localities online even if the state has not yet done so.

Private citizens have also placed information about sex offenders at various Web sites. In California, a group put the state sex offender database just described on the Web at www.sexoffenders.net (the state authorities did not allow any use of the mug shots). Another Web site (pedowatch.org/pedo-search.htm) provides a database of arrest information on pedophiles that you can search by suspect's name, city, or state.

A directory of sex offender Web sites from various states and cities is found at www.inil.com/users/dguss/wgator.htm (select "Sex Offender Registries").

▪ **Online wanted posters.** The "Nation's Most Wanted" Web site at www.mostwanted.com includes fugitives from around the country. Local police departments and state police are also putting mugshots and warnings about fugitives online (such as the New York Police Department's directory of desperadoes at www.ci.nyc.ny.us/html/nypd).

A Web directory of almost 70 federal, state, county, municipal, and privately sponsored Wanted sites is found at www.inil.com/users/dguss/wgator.htm (select "Wanted Lists"). The directory includes both criminal fugitives and deadbeat dads.

When There Was No Conviction

As noted earlier, an arrest and prosecution record may be expunged from the judicial system's records if the person was acquitted or the charges were dropped. In such cases, you will have to go beyond the ordinary criminal court records to find anything. The previous section pointed out that some of this information may be available (for up to seven years) from credit agencies if requested by a prospective employer or landlord, a bank, and the like. Here are a few suggestions for how a journalist might obtain arrest and indictment information without violating the privacy laws that regulate credit reporting.

First, try the police or sheriff's department arrest logs and jail books. These records, if available to reporters in your city or county, will tell you the offense the person was charged with and the date of arrest. In addition, the jail book will tell you whether the subject made bail and how. These records are sometimes not expunged along with the court records, either because there is no policy of doing so or because of inefficiency. The problem is that the records are filed chronologically, so if you don't know the approximate date of the arrest, it will often be difficult to find the entry.

Second, consult local newspaper databases and clippings morgues. If all police and court records have been sealed or expunged, these resources may be your only practical way to find out about a subject's arrest(s), but be aware that it's a hit-or-miss method—especially in cities with high crime rates where a majority of arrests are never mentioned in the press.

Third, test the memory of a longtime crime reporter or someone in law enforcement (or someone retired from law enforcement) who specializes or once specialized in tracking the type of criminal activity in which you believe your subject has engaged.

Fourth, check with your state or city Crime Control Commission, if there is one. It may have clippings files on organized crime (such as the files maintained by the Chicago Crime Commission ever since the 1920s), and its research director may have a long memory.

Fifth, check other special clippings libraries when appropriate. The Anti-Defamation League of B'nai B'rith and the Southern Poverty Law Center both maintain massive collections of newspaper clippings on arrests and convictions for hate crimes and hate-related violence dating back years (the ADL files go back at least to the 1940s). The library of the Drug Enforcement Administration (DEA) in Washington has extensive clippings on drug raids and drug arrests, including the DEA's daily "press book" compiled from newspaper clippings sent to Washington by 19 field offices.

The National Criminal Justice Reference System, the Justice Department's information clearinghouse, has a large collection of books, government reports, and newspaper and magazine articles on organized crime that it will search for you for a modest fee.

Sixth, look for evidence of the subject's possible arrest record or the subject's ongoing criminal activity in indexes and files of civil cases and administrative proceedings. Here's a list of some of the types of cases that might provide direct or indirect information:

- Actions by the state attorney's office seeking an injunction or other civil remedy against a person's alleged illegal activity. Such an action may precede an indictment or follow an unsuccessful indictment.

- Civil RICO actions filed in federal court against a person and his or her associates either by the government or by a private plaintiff. These filings also may precede or follow criminal indictment.

- Civil rights suits filed by criminal defendants against the police officers who made the arrest and against the county, city, or state government.

- Suits filed by crime victims or their families seeking monetary damages from an alleged rapist, hit-and-run driver, and the like. Such suits may be filed parallel to a criminal action or after the authorities have failed to obtain a criminal conviction.

- Eviction proceedings filed by landlords (often with the encouragement of prosecutors) against tenants because of alleged drug dealing, prostitution, gambling, and other criminal activities in an apartment, store, or house rented by the tenant; often the case file in such a proceeding will include information about arrests made on the premises.

- Forfeiture proceedings in federal, state, or county courts. Federal law enforcement authorities are empowered to seize the cash, autos, planes, boats, and even the homes of suspected drug traffickers. In many states, laws have been passed that also authorize such seizures of property. In many instances—and this is true on all levels of law enforcement— the person whose property has been seized during or after an arrest is never brought to trial, much less convicted. Yet the forfeiture action filed by the authorities with the appropriate court, the challenge (if any) filed by the person from whom the property was seized, and the resulting civil forfeiture hearing may remain part of the open court record.

- Administrative proceedings and disciplinary hearings by various regulatory, licensing, and professional agencies or boards. The district attorney may have failed to win a conviction against Dr. X for sexual assault against a patient, but Dr. X's license may nevertheless have been lifted as a result of a proceeding before the state medical board. And the files of that proceeding, if you can get them, may contain most of what was in the sealed criminal file (and more). Administrative proceedings on every level are a gold mine in this respect. For instance, the Federal Securities and Exchange Commission, the various state securities commissions, and the National Association of Securities Dealers (NASD) all maintain records on investigations of and disciplinary action against stockbrokers. These records can be searched online using the LEXIS Federal Securities Library and the LEXIS State Securities Library. You can also obtain information on investigations and disciplinary actions regarding a particular broker (and criminal charges and convictions against him or her, if they relate to securities trading) by accessing the NASD disciplinary database at www.nasdr.com.

- Any lawsuit in which the subject was deposed or in which he or she testified at trial. In the deposition (if not in the trial), the subject may have been asked about previous arrests, prosecutions, and convictions.

- Civil lawsuits in which the subject was a defendant. A large percentage of civil cases essentially revolve around a plaintiff's seeking civil remedies for what are alleged to be illegal activities, especially fraud. Often the complaint in such a case presents as clear a picture of the defendant's criminal mind as any prosecutor could provide (the plaintiff's attorney becomes, in effect, the prosecutor). Thus, if you are unable to get the court file on the prosecution of George Roe for selling forgeries of Renaissance paintings, the civil case filed against him the previous year by the purchaser of one of his so-called Old Masters will give you a pretty good idea of why Roe decided to plead guilty to a misdemeanor rather than face a jury of his peers on felony charges.

The Official Case File

You can access the case file in a criminal case using the index case file number. Generally, the case file will contain the information sheet and complaint against the defendant, the arrest and search warrant applications, the indictment, the bail affidavit and receipt, subpoenas for witnesses, motions and answers, the exhibits list, the judge's instructions to the jury, and the verdict and sentence. The file may also include the trial transcript, the transcript of the defendant's bail hearing (which may include detailed testimony from police officers about why they think the defendant is too dangerous to be set loose), and the transcripts of witness depositions taken before trial.

Public access to the case file will vary from locality to locality and according to the disposition of the case. Generally, while a case is current, the file can be examined by reporters, although you may have to go through the prosecutor's office to do so. If the case was dropped or the defendant was acquitted, the case file will usually be sealed. But even if the defendant was convicted, you may need a release to examine the case file.

Appeals Briefs

If a criminal case is appealed to a higher court, the briefs prepared by the prosecution and the defense will remain part of the public record regardless of whether the trial court case file is sealed. These briefs, often 50 pages or more in length, may be your best window on the indictment and the trial. Even if you have access to the trial court case file, you should look at the appeals briefs because they sometimes bring out facts or viewpoints not contained in the original trial record. Federal court appeals briefs usually end up in the Library of Congress or a local law library or archive designated as a depository (for example, the library of the Association of the Bar of the City of New York). Likewise, briefs from state appeals court cases will often be found in a university law school or bar association library in the state in question.

Subpoena Records

The records of subpoenas issued to witnesses in a grand jury investigation or trial may be available depending on the locality. If so, contact the subpoenaed persons to ask whether they would be willing to discuss the testimony they gave.

Prosecutors' and Defense Attorneys' Files

Both sides will usually have extensive files that go beyond anything in the official court file, including much evidence inadmissible at trial. A prosecutor seeking publicity may allow reporters to see portions of this file (for example, portions of wire-tap transcripts in an organized crime case) or will brief reporters on what's in the file. Defense attorneys may also cooperate with a reporter, especially if the defendant was the victim of egregious prosecutorial or police misconduct—the reporter is given inside information as a way of exonerating the defendant in the court of public opinion, if nowhere else. Of special interest in the defense team's files will be the reports of private investigators hired to gather evidence for the defense.

Contacting the Victim

If you find an old newspaper article about a subject's arrest but no article about the disposition of his or her case—and the court records are sealed—you can always try to obtain information from the victim. Often (except in cases of surviving rape victims) the article will give the victim's name. The victim or the victim's surviving relatives will probably recall many details about the case (they may even have portions of the court file), and they may have closely tracked the subsequent activities of the defendant. If your state has a victims' rights statute, the subject's victim may have obtained copies of the sentencing reports and may also have gained access to ongoing information about the subject's parole applications and hearings, the conditions of his or her parole, and so forth.

Don't restrict your inquiries to victims of violent crimes. I have found that the dupes of a white-collar scam can be unremitting in their thirst for revenge against the person who scammed them, even a decade or more afterward.

When Your Subject Is Not the Defendant

A criminal case file or trial transcript often becomes important in tracking someone other than the defendant. Generally, your attention will be drawn to such a case by an old newspaper article rather than by the court index. Your subject, according to the clippings, may have been an unindicted co-conspirator, may have testified for the prosecution in exchange for immunity in this or another case, or may simply have been a witness who was questioned at length about his or her past during cross-examination. Indeed, your subject may even have been the purported victim of the crime. In 1981, one Richard Dupont, a former gay lover of attorney Roy Cohn, was prosecuted in New York for harassing Cohn. Dupont's attorney, John Klotz, turned the trial into a probe of Cohn's own criminal activities, providing future researchers and historians with a remarkably detailed portrait of New York's premier power broker. When I interviewed Klotz afterward, he told me about evidence he had not been allowed to present during the trial (and questions he had not been allowed to ask witnesses) about Cohn's criminal activities. I also spoke with Dupont, who gave me a wealth of accurate details about Cohn and also about Cohn's lovers, business partners, and organized-crime clients.

9.9 Other Specialized Court Records

For housing court records, see section 4.22, "Miscellaneous Local Government Records"; for bankruptcy court records, see section 8.10, "Bankruptcy Court Records"; for U.S. Tax Court records, see section 8.13, "Federal and State Income Tax Returns and Related Information."

10 ·

Backgrounding the Individual: Miscellaneous Records and Resources

10.1 Vital Records

Vital records include the indexes and certificates for births, marriages, divorces, and deaths. Access to these records differs from state to state; often county authorities have a policy less restrictive than the state's.

Issuance of birth and death certificates is handled by the state vital records bureau in most states. However, certificates are also issued by about 7,000 local registrars throughout the United States. As for marriage and divorce records, the state's vital records bureau may keep a central index of marriages and divorces but usually will refer you to the appropriate county or city for a copy of the certificate.

The *PRRS* will tell you how to order state and county vital records in all 50 states. It will also inform you how many years back the state's centralized records in each category go (earlier records will be found at the county level) and what the privacy restriction are on the release of these records. A guide produced by the U.S. Department of Health and Human Services gives much of the same information; it can be downloaded from www.cdc.gov/nchwww/data/w2w12_98.pdf.

State vital records bureaus are geared toward meeting the needs of people who want certified copies of their own records (or the records of close family members) and already know the date of the given event and other identifying details. A journalist, however, is not usually interested in obtaining a certified copy of the certificate, only the information it contains. The index alone may have what he or she needs (date of birth and mother's name). If the journalist needs more information, he or she can request an abstract of the certificate.

The following procedure is suggested for obtaining vital records about your subject and his or her family. First, if the recorded event(s) occurred in your own county, go directly to the county authorities who, as noted earlier, may be less restrictive about access than are the state authorities. Until recent decades, marriages and divorces were often recorded in index books at the county or city clerk's office; today, local marriage and divorce indexes are often computerized.

Local birth and death records may be found either at the county or city clerk's office or at the county or city health department. If your county no longer issues birth and death certificates, it still may have the old indexes available for public inspection. In addition, the old indexes may be available on microform at the local public library or historical society.

If an event occurred after the county stopped maintaining records in the given category, or if you don't know in which county the event occurred (or if it occurred in another state), you will have to contact the vital records bureau at your state's (or the other state's) health department.

In about 10 "open record" states, there are no restrictions on obtaining vital records at the state level. In some of these states, you can get information over the phone, and if you want a copy or an abstract, you can order it over the phone and pay by credit card. (Elsewhere, you have to write a letter, enclosing a check or money order.)

Sometimes there are restrictions at the state level on releasing certified copies of birth certificates because of concerns over ID fraud. This is why you should check whether it's possible to get an abstract of the birth record (which could not be used as readily for fraudulent purposes) or simply an index search.

In some states, copies of birth and death certificates are not supposed to be provided to anyone except the person to whom the birth record pertains or the members of the deceased's immediate family. In many counties in these states, however, no proof of identity is required of anyone making a request in person, by mail, or over the phone. Indeed, persons requesting certificates by mail or telephone (as opposed to those appearing in person) often aren't even asked to fill out an application.

If you can't find the subject's birth record in either the state or county indexes, this may mean you have been given a false lead about the subject's place of birth. It may also mean that a record of the birth was never filed. In such cases, look for the birth information in local church baptismal and christening records, which are almost always open to the public.

The easiest way to find the date and place of death of a subject's parents is to look in the Social Security Death Index at www.ancestry.com. If the information is not there (which is usually the case if the parents died before 1962, the year in which reporting became mandatory), try the state death index (up-to-date death indexes from several states are available through genealogy Web sites). You might also obtain information on an individual's death from newspaper obituaries or funeral notices, cemetery records, church funeral records, or the local coroner's office.

A new category of vital records is emerging in cities with ordinances allowing the registration of gay and lesbian domestic partnerships. Indeed, some daily newspapers are now publishing announcements of gay and lesbian unions in their wedding and engagement pages.

For more tips relating to vital records, see sections 4.12, "Tracking a Person Through His or Her Family, Friends, and Ex-Spouse(s)," and 7.2, "Obtaining the Birth Date."

10.2 Department of Motor Vehicles Records

Historically, Department of Motor Vehicles (DMV) records have been available to the general public in most states. In 1994, however, the U.S. Congress passed a rather murky law placing certain restrictions on the general public's access to these records. (More on this law later in this section.) Yet in most states, these records continue to be available without restriction for purposes relating to lawsuits, insurance background checks, and the like. In some states, the records continue to be available to casual requesters.

Driver Records

An abstract of a subject's driver's license may provide his or her date of birth, license number (in some states, this is the same as, or includes, the SSN), address, sex, physical characteristics, and driving restrictions (if any).

A subject's driving record may provide information on his or her license suspensions and revocations as well as his or her convictions for moving violations (including drunk driving). The driving record may also include information on accidents (date, location, and report file number). Note that driving-record information is maintained on any individual found guilty of a moving violation in a given state, whether or not he or she is a resident. Hence, an investigator should check the records in states in which the subject has traveled frequently for business or pleasure in recent years, as well as in the state where the subject resides. (*Note:* This extra checking is not necessary when the subject has a commercial driver's license because his or her out-of-state violations will show up in the home state records.) After the investigator obtains an abstract of the subject's driving record, he or she can search the court records on each violation as well as the state police accident reports, records of insurance coverage at the time of the accident, and so forth.

Vehicle Records

The DMV also offers searches of license plate numbers (tags), vehicle identification numbers (VINs), and records of vehicle ownership and liens. This information can be obtained from the DMV office in person or by mail, phone, or fax. Online vendors (see www.publicrecordsearch.com) offer multistate or all-state searches of these records. Give them the license plate number, and they can find the owner's name and address. Give them the

VIN, and they'll find the year, make, and model of the vehicle and the names of any lien holders. Give them the subject's name and address, and they'll come up with a list of all registered vehicles he or she owns.

Privacy Restrictions

In 1994, Congress passed the Driver's Privacy Protection Act (DPPA) which allows motor vehicle drivers and owners a measure of control over the dissemination of personal information about them contained in state DMV records. They can now opt out, if they wish, from their state's system for providing DMV records to database vendors and the general public. However, in states where this option is offered without being heavily publicized, few people actually choose it; and the records of those who do opt out still remain available for certain DPPA-defined "permissible uses" (for example, the uses to which such information is put by businesses seeking to verify the information on job or insurance applications, parties suing the person, and so on). Furthermore, the DPPA privacy option does *not* cover information on vehicular accidents, driving violations, and driver's status, although some states restrict public access to these items on their own.

States were given until 1997 to comply with the DPPA. Some states reacted by passing laws even more restrictive than the federal one (thus rendering an opt-out provision unnecessary); others decided to adopt the opt-out provision while continuing to allow the general public and database vendors access to DMV records of non-opt-out drivers and owners. Some states adopted one policy for vehicle records and another for driver records. (Several states even challenged the constitutionality of the DPPA; as of early 1999, the issue appears to be headed to the Supreme Court.)

This patchwork of laws has impacted on the availability of DMV records from online brokers. For instance, if a gateway service promises access to DMV records in all states, it is addressing its customer base of insurance companies, private investigators, and other major clients, *not* casual users. A journalist or other casual user will find that the records are hedged, state by state, with restrictions. If a given state sells its DMV records to list vendors only for permissible uses such as those enumerated in the DPPA, the casual user may not be allowed to search those particular records without certifying that he or she is engaged in a permissible use.

Readers of *Get the Facts on Anyone* should be aware that the very purposes for which they are consulting this book and considering such a records search may fall within the DPPA "permissible uses" for release of records of drivers and vehicle owners who have chosen the privacy option. For instance, release is authorized "in connection with any civil, criminal, administrative, or arbitral proceeding in a federal, state, or local court or agency or before any self-regulatory body, including the service of process, investigation in anticipation of litigation, and the execution or enforcement of judgments and orders, or pursuant to an order of a federal, state, or local court." Consult your attorney about how best to proceed under such circumstances.

Warning: In California, where DMV records have long been off limits to the general public, a request for information on a person's driving record will trigger a letter to that person from the DMV informing him or her of your request.

Guidebooks

Brief information on how to obtain DMV records in each of the 50 states is contained in BRB's *Find Public Records Fast*; more detailed information (including privacy restrictions) can be obtained from BRB's *The MVR Book*.

DMV records use special codes and abbreviations, which differ from state to state. To decipher these records, see BRB's *The MVR Decoder Digest*.

10.3 Selective Service Records

Under the current selective service registration law, any male born in 1960 or later is required to register at his local post office when he reaches the age of 18. The completed registration form, including name, date of birth, SSN, address, and phone number, is sent to the Selective Service Board data center in Illinois, where a number is assigned to each registrant. This number, the first two digits of which are the registrant's year of birth, may one day become an important identifier if the draft is reinstituted. At present, however, the registration forms and numbers have little significance, especially since the Selective Service Board does not reveal the registrant's address (or any other personal information) except to law enforcement authorities. The only thing the board will tell you is whether or not the subject is in compliance with the registration law. To get this information, you must write to the board and include the registrant's full name, date of birth, and SSN.

The old registration system, in effect until 1975, produced quite useful records for investigators. The individual registered with his county draft board and was given a number and a draft classification. His classification records were kept at the local board and were open to the public. After the draft was abolished, these records were sent to regional Federal Records Centers around the country, where they are still available to the public. (To obtain them, you must supply the registrant's full name, date of birth, and home address at time of registration.)

The classification records include the individual's Selective Service number, birth date, every classification (1-A, 4-F, and so on) he ever held, the date the notice of classification was mailed to him, the date of his Armed Forces medical exam, the fact of whether he passed or failed, the date (if ever) that he entered the Armed Forces, whether he enlisted or was drafted, and the date he left the Armed Forces (assuming that he was discharged before the old registration system was abolished). There are gaps in these records, however: The date of leaving the Armed Forces is not always included in the records of World War II veterans; men who enlisted before they reached the age of 18 (the time at which draft registration was required) are not included at all, even if they became career soldiers; and women in the Armed Forces are not included.

In the days of the draft, personnel managers and bank loan officers often found the Selective Service number useful in checking the accuracy of an applicant's statements about his past. This was because the Selective Service number contained (as does the SSN) coded information. Even today—if you come across a Selective Service number in an old court document or apartment rental application—it can be useful in finding out where a person grew up. The Selective Service number consists of four groups of digits connected by hyphens: The first group designates the state or territory of the United States where the individual first registered; the second group corresponds to the number of the county draft board within that state or territory; the third group corresponds to the last two digits of the year of the registrant's birth; the fourth group is the registrant's local draft board registration number.

The following numbers correspond to each state and territory:

1	Alabama	24	Montana
2	Arizona	25	Nebraska
3	Arkansas	26	Nevada
4	California	27	New Hampshire
5	Colorado	28	New Jersey
6	Connecticut	29	New Mexico
7	Delaware	30	New York
8	Florida	31	North Carolina
9	Georgia	32	North Dakota
10	Idaho	33	Ohio
11	Illinois	34	Oklahoma
12	Indiana	35	Oregon
13	Iowa	36	Pennsylvania
14	Kansas	37	Rhode Island
15	Kentucky	38	South Carolina
16	Louisiana	39	South Dakota
17	Maine	40	Tennessee
18	Maryland	41	Texas
19	Massachusetts	42	Utah
20	Michigan	43	Vermont
21	Minnesota	44	Virginia
22	Mississippi	45	Washington
23	Missouri	46	West Virginia

47	Wisconsin	52	Hawaii
48	Wyoming	53	Puerto Rico
49	District of Columbia	54	Virgin Islands
50	New York City	55	Guam
51	Alaska	56	Panama Canal Zone

10.4 Military Service Records and Discharge Papers

You can obtain a subject's service record by sending a copy of Standard Form 180 ("Request Pertaining to Military Records") to the appropriate records center. Form 180 can be downloaded or a printout obtained at www.nara.gov/regional/mpr.html. For records of discharged, deceased, and retired military personnel, send the form to National Personnel Records Center, Military Personnel Records, 9700 Page Avenue, St. Louis, MO 63132-5100. For the records of active-duty personnel as well as reservists and members of the National Guard, send your request to the appropriate address listed on the back of Form 180. Note that you will have to wait between three and six months for your request to be filled.

On Form 180, state that your request is being made pursuant to the Freedom of Information Act; otherwise, your request will not be honored. Ignore the notice on Form 180 that you need to get the veteran's signature on a release authorization (in fact, such a release is necessary only if you are requesting health records or detailed personnel records that are not part of the service record usually released).

If possible, you should provide the subject's full name, correctly spelled, service number or SSN, approximate dates of service, and branch of service. The subject's date and place of birth may also he helpful. If you do not have all this information, the NPRC staff may still be able to find the records.

The NPRC currently holds over 50 million military personnel records. An estimated 18 million records were destroyed in a 1973 fire, including most of the records on Army personnel discharged before 1960 and about two-thirds of the records on USAF personnel discharged before 1964. Although about 3.1 million of these records have been partly reassembled from other sources, no one knows exactly what is missing—there was no index. If you believe that your subject's records were probably destroyed in this fire, you should provide on Form 180, along with the information listed above, the subject's place of discharge, last unit of assignment, and place of entry into the service (if known).

The information available from the NPRC under a Freedom of Information request includes date of birth; dates of service; dates of rank/grade changes; awards and decorations; duty assignments; current duty status; civilian and military educational level; marital status; and the names, sex, and age of the subject's dependents. Releasable records also include court-martial records if unclassified and a photograph if available. You should request each of these items specifically in a statement appended to Form 180. Note that the NPRC will *not* provide you with the subject's SSN, address, or telephone number. The NPRC also will not release disciplinary, discharge, or medical records without the veteran's written consent or the written consent of the next-of-kin of deceased veterans.

If the subject's military records were completely destroyed in the 1973 fire, try to obtain his military discharge papers. These are available at the county clerk's office of the county in which the subject filed them. The trick is to figure out which county that might be. Your best bet is the subject's hometown or the town in which he ended up when discharged. Note that the Army sends copies of discharge papers to the Adjutant General of the veteran's home state.

You will find at www.publicrecordsources.com a list of several firms that specialize in checking military records. For detailed advice on how to conduct a search of military records on your own, see *How to Locate Anyone Who Is or Has Been in the Military* (listed in this book's bibliography).

10.5 Telephone Company Records

To access records of a person's toll calls, you will need an inside source at the phone company. If you don't have such a source, you might call the billing office and pretend to be the telephone subscriber, or call the special number for toll records and pretend to be a billing office employee. Such tactics, which require considerable knowledge of phone company procedures and terminology, are *not* recommended by this writer.

If your subject is a government official, you can make a Freedom of Information request to examine the toll records of all calls made from or charged to his or her office phone or official car phone, or all calls that were charged to his or her government-issued telephone credit card. You can then reverse the numbers and see whether the subject is calling his or her broker or engaging in other personal business to an unreasonable extent on the taxpayer's time and at the taxpayer's expense.

10.6 Medical Records and Other Medical Information

The Public Record
Authorization from a patient is required to get his or her medical records from a hospital or a physician's office. However, bits and pieces of a

subject's medical history can sometimes be gleaned from the public record. The subject's driving restrictions may be included in an abstract of the subject's driver's license (see section 10.2). The subject's driving record may list multiple drunk-driving incidents, suggesting an alcohol addiction; it also may list accidents in which the subject was involved (the accident report by the investigating officer, available from the state Department of Public Safety, may tell whether the subject was seriously injured). Registration records from the draft era may reveal whether the subject failed his Armed Forces medical exam and was given a 4-F status, although the specific medical reasons will not be provided. Income tax returns filed by the subject as evidence in a local court case or in U.S. Tax Court litigation in Washington may reveal large deductions for medical expenses. Aircraft pilot licensing files may contain medical information, as may various licensing files for occupations such as cosmetologist or optometrist.

In some states, workers' compensation claims records can be obtained without a signed release (if not, you may at least be able to determine whether the subject has filed a claim). These records, if available, might include the original injury report with date and type of injury and the work-related disability resulting therefrom. If the claim is contested by the insurer, or the board's determination is appealed by the claimant, more information might be available.

Typically, workers' compensation claims are filed at the state compensation board by name of claimant. Newer records are computerized, older records are on microform. In ordering a search, you may have to furnish the claimant's SSN and date of birth (especially for microform records). In a few states, the records are filed by name of company, in which case you must know where the subject worked in order to access these records. The *PRRS* will tell you the telephone and fax numbers and mailing addresses in all 50 states for obtaining these records (and the restrictions on access, which, in most states, are quite strict).

Some states sell their workers' compensation databases, with periodic updates, to database vendors. At www.publicrecordsources.com, you can find a list of the database vendors and document retrieval services that specialize in workers' compensation claims records.

In searching state and federal court indexes, you should keep alert for any case in which the subject's medical condition might have been an issue (for instance, a product liability suit, a suit against a health insurance company by a policy holder, a personal injury suit alleging negligence by an auto driver, or a medical malpractice suit). Frequently in such cases, the plaintiff will have to undergo a pretrial physical or psychiatric examination. The results of this exam may be filed as an exhibit to a pretrial motion or reply; it also may be presented as evidence at trial. The plaintiff may be questioned at length about his or her medical history in pretrial interrogatories and depositions and in court testimony. Likewise, physicians who have examined or treated the plaintiff may be questioned in depositions and at trial.

Further information on medical problems can be gleaned from county judgment dockets. You may find that several judgments or liens against a subject have been obtained by physicians or hospitals because of nonpayment of bills. The judgment docket entry will give you the case file number, and you can then retrieve the file from the county or state court file room. Such cases will possibly give you the dates of the subject's visits to a doctor's office or the dates of his or her hospitalization, which may fit together with other information you have gleaned. Once you have the name of a doctor the subject has visited, you can look in *The Official ABMS Directory of Board Certified Medical Specialists* (or check the ABMS verification service at www.certifieddoctor.com) to find out what the doctor's specialty is and also what subspecialty certificates he or she has been awarded. If a doctor is not listed with the ABMS, it may be that he or she is practicing in a specialty without board certification. In such cases, his or her claimed specialty can be found in the yellow pages or by a call to the doctor's office.

Note: You can sometimes gather information about a patient's probable medical condition simply from the name of the hospital that has sued him or her (for instance, the Hospital of Joint Diseases).

Criminal cases involving aggravated assault, driving while intoxicated, and so on will include information about the injuries suffered by the victim and also possibly information about the psychiatric problems or other mitigating medical problems of the alleged perpetrator. In addition, information about the victim's medical condition may be revealed in a sentencing hearing, while information about either the victim's or the perpetrator's medical condition may come out in a parole hearing.

Newspapers and Other Publications

Searches of newspaper databases and clippings morgues may turn up a story about an automobile accident, assault, or other incident resulting in serious injury to the subject at some time in the past. In-house newsletters at the subject's place of employment (or the subject's spouse's place of employment) and church bulletins at the subject's church may include information about a serious illness involving hospitalization of either the subject or a member of the subject's family, and may tell what hospital the patient was in.

Medical Garbology

Examination of a subject's trash (see section 11.4, "The Subject's Gar-bage") may turn up discarded medical or hospital bills (especially dunning notices) and correspondence from the subject's HMO. The trash may also contain discarded correspondence or newsletters from (or at least discarded envelopes with the return address of) organizations devoted to fighting a particular disease; but don't jump to the conclusion that the subject has this disease: He or she may be concerned about it because of its effect on a loved one.

The subject's trash might also include discarded prescription bottles (if the label is intact, it will tell you the name of the patient, doctor, and pharmacy as well as the medication and dosage amounts and instructions); discarded instructions or warnings regarding the medication (either from a sample package or from the printout instructions provided by the pharmacy); and medical junk mail on purported cures (probably sent to the subject because he or she is on mailing lists culled from the records of past purchases or inquiries regarding prescription medications for the given ailment).

Also look for cigarettes, booze, and other evidence of substance abuse. If a person is over 50 and smoking three packs a day (assuming that the smoker is your subject and not some other household member), you can infer that he or she is in lousy physical shape and is probably on the brink of (or already being treated for) at least one major health problem.

Nonprescription medications, herbal preparations, vitamins and other supplements, and unusual foods (or evidence of unusual dietary regimens) that you observe in a subject's garbage may also be clues to a serious medical condition. For help in deciphering such evidence, consult the *Physicians' Desk Reference of Non-Prescription Drugs*, the *PDR for Herbal Medicines*, and any of several alternative medicine manuals that include details on the use of vitamins, supplements, and special diets in relation to specific symptoms or illnesses.

Note: Herbal medicines are mostly used for less-serious forms of an illness, but some individuals may be "self-medicating" for a more serious condition because they don't trust doctors or can't take the side effects of the mainstream prescription drugs. For instance, many Americans take Saint John's wort for mild forms of depression, but some may take it inappropriately for major depression.

Marketing and Insurance Databases

Metromail has developed Patient Select, a spin-off from its National Consumer Database, to provide marketers of health-related products with mailing lists targeting persons who suffer from specific diseases. The Medical Marketing Service provides a similar database that targets persons with such common ailments as allergies and yeast infections. The information comes not from confidential medical records but from information provided voluntarily by consumers when responding to questionnaires or advertisements. Although these databases are intended for the health products industry, some of the more arcane online information brokers are also reported to have access.

The Medical Information Bureau (MIB) provides hundreds of insurance companies nationwide with medical information on over 15 million persons. A manual for private investigators has stated, apropos of the MIB, "We are getting into some networks of information that the insurance industry wishes no one but them knew about . . . ."

10.7 Welfare Records

Welfare records are not open to the public. However, your subject might file copies of his or her welfare checks or various welfare documents in a court proceeding (for instance, a family court case regarding child support payments). Welfare records would definitely be entered as evidence in a welfare fraud prosecution.

10.8 Immigration and Naturalization Records

U.S. Immigration and Naturalization Service (INS) records on individual immigrants are usually not available to the public. They become part of the public record, however, if filed by either the government or the immigrant in a deportation trial or in a suit launched by the immigrant against the INS in federal district court.

When an immigrant becomes an American citizen, a notice is filed with the county clerk's office in the county where he or she was naturalized. This record is public information. It may include the subject's age, address, and occupation when naturalized; date of naturalization; date of arrival in the United States; and former nationality.

10.9 Voter Registration Records

Voter registration records are generally kept by the county or city board of elections (AKA the election commission or the registrar of voters). You can check the enrollment books of registered voters, which list all registered voters in each state assembly district and their party affiliation or independent status. The lists are often arranged by street address, as in a crisscross directory. Even if the subject is not listed, his or her spouse may be listed, as well as their children of voting age who live at home. Note that, in many localities, these records are now on CD-ROM, so you can check instantly by name or street address at the board of elections' computer terminals.

The enrollment books from decades past, which may be available in the city archives or the county historical society if not at the board of elections, are an excellent way to trace changes in the composition of the subject's household and to gather the names of ex-spouses and of children no longer living at home.

You should also examine the registration records for individual voters (these may be on microfilm) and the precinct registration books that are used on election day. These resources are not always open to the general public, but if they are (or if you can get access to them as a campaign worker during the election season), you may find all the addresses at which

Mr. Jones has lived (including his apartment number) since he first registered to vote locally and also the dates on which he switched his registration from one voting district or precinct to another. You may also find (depending, of course, on the variations in local record compiling systems) Mr. Jones's telephone number, SSN, current party affiliation, previous party affiliation (and the dates of the affiliation change), occupation, and business address.

Do not neglect the precinct registration books. These will reveal which general and primary elections Mr. Jones voted in over the years, and which elections he missed. (This is especially important in backgrounding candidates for public office; you may find that your local "good government" liberal or superpatriotic conservative almost never bothers to vote.) The precinct registrations books will also include specimens of the subject's signature over the years, which might be helpful in establishing links between the current and previous identities of an impostor.

Some localities will not take mail-in requests for information, requiring that inspection of the voter rolls be done in person. However, the voter registration data is sold to vendors who make it available for various purposes. Almost all states allow use of their voter rolls online for political-electoral search purposes; about half allow use of the voter rolls for commercial purposes such as skip tracing.

Aristotle Industries, a Washington, D.C., public records vendor, offers an online and CD-ROM database incorporating the voter rolls from almost all states. It covers 4,000 counties and municipalities and includes enhanced features such as listed telephone numbers, national change-of-address data, removal of dead voters, and identification of "supervoters" who vote in most primaries and general elections. Casual users can search the Aristotle online database at www.governmentrecords.com provided that they sign a contract agreeing not to violate the restrictions that a given state puts on commercial use of any information coming from its own voter rolls. The cost is $10 per search for a single state, $25 for a multistate search.

An Aristotle CD-ROM covering a particular locality may be available at a political party headquarters or candidate campaign headquarters in that locality. In addition, many daily newspapers have the Aristotle CD-ROM for their state or metro area.

10.10 Federal Election Commission Records

The giant Federal Election Commission database of contributions and contributors to all federal election campaigns since the 1980 election cycle can be searched at www.tray.com. You can look up contributors by name, by employer, by occupation, and by zip code for each election cycle or for every election cycle in the 20 years that are covered so far. The database includes all contributions of over $200 to candidates, party committees, or political action committees (PACs).

Your subject may never have contributed money to any federal campaign. But if he has, you will find the date and amount of each contribution; the candidate, committee, or PAC to which each contribution was made; the city and zip code in which the individual resided at the time of each contribution; and the employer for which the individual worked (or, at least, the occupation in which he or she was engaged) at the time of each contribution. Unfortunately, the database does not include street addresses—the names are entered into the database only by town and zip code. (To find the street addresses, you must search the microfiche records at FEC headquarters or order specific microform or photocopied records by mail.)

When searching the individual contributor records, you should search by surname only (unless the name is a very common one). This will ensure that you find any listings for your subject under a nickname, a middle name without the first name, and so forth. Such a search will also enable you to find other contributors in the zip code who have your subject's surname. Some of these persons may be members of your subject's household or relatives who live nearby. (Online people-finder services such as infospace.com can help you ferret out these connections.)

The FEC's records regarding employers and occupations are incomplete because many committees submit their reports without this information (or simply give an occupation without an employer name), citing the "best efforts" loophole in the federal campaign finance disclosure law. Nevertheless, the contributor's place of work or occupation will be included in the majority of cases. You can thus use the FEC database like an old-fashioned city directory to compile a list of the places your subject has been employed since 1979–80 (or at least the type of work he or she has done) and also to compile a list of people who worked for the same employer in the same city at the same time that your subject did and who thus may have known your subject well. If your subject is an employer, you can use the FEC records to compile a list of people who worked for him or her over the years but no longer do so. Suppose that you see that an employee named Mary Dorn of your subject's software company gave a $500 donation to a local congressional campaign in 1992 but is not listed among the firm's employees giving money in subsequent years. You search under her name and find that in 1996 she again made a donation (this time for $700), but the 1996 record lists her as living in another city and working for a firm that you know is unrelated to your subject. You can infer from the size of her donations that Ms. Dorn was probably in a fairly high management position at your subject's firm, and thus would have important knowledge about its inner workings.

The FEC database is also useful in finding out whether your subject has any hate-group affiliations. Often people with bigoted beliefs are very close-mouthed in the presence of outsiders—you find out about their ferocious inner life only from the FEC filings. For instance, you may discover that the mild-mannered Mr. Deeds, who is always ever so polite to black and Hispanic customers in his store, has donated thousands of dollars in the last three presidential elections to the candidate of the super-rightist Thunderbolt party.

Note that the campaign finance records for state campaigns are also being placed online. Examples include the Web sites of the New York State Campaign Finance Consortium (www.timesunion.com/capitol/contributions) and the Florida Division of Elections (election.dos.state.fl.us/campfin/contrib.htm). Links to these and other state campaign finance databases can be found at the Campaign Finance Information Center Web site at www.campaignfinance.org.

10.11 Permits and Licenses

A wide variety of professions, trades, vending operations, and service-type businesses require a license from the city or state government or from a quasi-public commission or agency. You can get a list of the licenses required in your locality from the state and municipal government handbooks, but let's take New York City as an example.

If a subject operates a grocery or restaurant in New York City, he or she must have a permit from the City Department of Health. If the subject operates a liquor store or bar or sells alcoholic beverages in his or her restaurant, a license from the State Liquor Authority is required. If the subject is a teacher, he or she should have a certificate from the state Department of Education. If the subject earns his or her living as a real estate salesperson or broker, barber, hairdresser, cosmetologist, billiard-room operator, private investigator, or apartment referral agent—or if the subject is a notary public or sells hearing aids—he or she must have a license from the Division of Licensing Services of the state's Department of State. If the subject is a taxi driver, he or she must have a chauffeur's license from the state Department of Motor Vehicles and a taxi driver's license from the City Taxi Commission. If the subject owns a handgun, he or she must have a permit from the Police Department. If the subject is a master plumber, he or she must have a license from the city's Master Plumber's License Board; if the subject is an electrician, he or she requires a license from the city's Electrical License Board. If he or she carries a press card, it will have been issued by the Police Department. If he or she is involved in any of 54 different trades or types of business—from auctioneer to weighmaster, from bowling-alley operator to street vendor of hotdogs—he or she should have a license from the City Department of Consumer Affairs.

This list of licenses, permits, and certificates (similar to the requirements in other cities) is only the tip of the iceberg. *The City of New York Official Directory* lists no less than 1,600 licenses required within the city by various local, state, and federal agencies for the conducting of various trades or professions or for the sale of various products or services.

Violations of law by licensees in any regulated area may result in summonses issued by city or state inspectors, or civil or criminal actions initiated by state or city attorneys. In addition, complaints against a licensee may be filed by irate consumers with the City Consumer Affairs Department, the State Attorney General's office, a professional licensing board, or the Better Business Bureau.

Across the nation, new types of licenses are constantly being created by legislators to meet new social needs. For instance, in 1994, following several tragic boating accidents, Alabama became the first state to require motorboat operators to be licensed and to adhere to the same drinking rules as automobile drivers.

Many state licensing records regarding businesses and trades can be searched online at free government Web sites; see the following section.

10.12 Professional Licensing

Professional licensing laws are a confused patchwork from state to state. A recent congressional study found that although 700 professions require state-level licensing in one or more states, only 20 professions require licensing in all states. In addition, the examinations and other licensing requirements may vary widely in their rigor. Thus, a person whose license has been revoked in Vermont may either move to New Hampshire, which has no licensing requirements, or Connecticut, where the licensing body will overlook the earlier revocation (you should always check the previous state's records). Likewise, a person who cannot pass the licensing exam or meet other licensing requirements in his or her home state may move to a state with an easy exam or no exam at all, or a state that has loopholes in the other requirements.

By submitting to the licensing procedure, a person creates yet another paper trail for you to follow through his or her life. For instance, consulting *McKinney's Consolidated Laws*, we find that a licensed cosmetologist in New York State will have filed, at one time or another, an application for a trainee license, an application to take the licensing exam, an application for a permanent license, a physician's certificate stating that the applicant is free of disease, a photograph to accompany the license application, a diploma from a licensed training center, a copy of any license received in another state or in a foreign country, and change-of-address notices.

Just how much of such paperwork is open to public inspection varies from state to state. Hopefully, you will be able to find out whether complaints have been filed against the subject and if the subject has ever been the target of any disciplinary action such as license suspension or revocation, a reprimand, or a fine. Depending on the profession and the laws of the particular state, complaints may be filed with the State Attorney General's office, the professional licensing board, or the private association representing that profession or trade on the county or state level.

Occasionally, you may find that complaints have been filed and investigations conducted on all three levels. A complaint to the State Attorney General may result in a civil suit by the state or a criminal prosecution. A complaint to the regulatory board may result in an administrative proceeding followed by various appeals (and perhaps a suit by the licensee against the board). A complaint to the local professional organization may result in a more informal investigation, perhaps leading to the licensee's suspension or expulsion from the organization.

Many state governments have placed their public-access licensing records (including especially their professional licensing records) online at free government Web sites. For instance, the New York State Department of Education's Office of the Professions, which regulates 38 professions, has placed its licensing and disciplinary records online at www.nysed.gov/prof. (You can go to "Online License Verification" to see whether an individual is in fact licensed; go to "Summaries of Professional Discipline Cases" to search alphabetically by name a list that provides the city, license number, and profession of each offender together with the calendar number and action date of each disciplinary action involving the individual in question.) An excellent directory of state licensing agency Web sites is available at the Webgator directory (www.inil.com/users/dguss/wgator.htm). For state-by-state instructions on obtaining professional, trade, and business licensing records (including the phone numbers for the offices handling each type of license and the Web addresses for hundreds of free state government sites), see the *PRRS*.

11·

Backgrounding the Individual: Special Problems and Methods

11.1 Backgrounding a Subject's Educational Past

You may spot a bachelor's, master's, or doctoral degree on a subject's wall. Or you may learn about a supposed degree from his or her acquaintances or a biographical sketch in a vanity directory. Verifying the degree is a twofold process: First, you find out whether the college is a legitimate one, and then you find out whether the subject really graduated. This is an important step in backgrounding: A congressional study has estimated that upward of 500,000 Americans have obtained false academic or professional credentials from diploma mills, credentials brokers, and other suppliers of instant status.

Checking Out the College
Make sure that you have the name of the institution right. Some diploma mills use look-alike names so that people will confuse them with legitimate schools; for instance, "Darthmouth College" instead of Dartmouth College, or "Boston City College" instead of Boston College.

After you have the correct name, check out the school in one of the standard reference guides at your public library, such as *The College Handbook* or *Lovejoy's College Guide*. If it's not in these books, look in the American Council on Education's annual *Accredited Institutions of Postsecondary Education*. Note that the accreditation status of a school can be changed at any time, so to be absolutely certain about the status of a marginal school or a school you can't find in the preceding reference works, check with the regional accrediting association that covers the state in which the institution is located.

In the United States, only six regional groups, operating under the umbrella of the Commission on Recognition of Postsecondary Accreditation (CORPA), are accepted as having the authority to accredit an entire college or university. These are the Middle States Association of Colleges and Schools, New England Association of Schools and Colleges, North Central Association of Colleges and Schools, Northwest Association of Schools and Colleges, Southern Association of Colleges and Schools, and Western Association of Schools and Colleges.

The situation is different for professional training aimed at achieving certification or licensing in a particular profession. Here each profession has its own accrediting agency or agencies for schools, departments, or programs serving that discipline. These entities—about 50 in all—are approved by CORPA or the U.S. Department of Education.

Lists of and contact information on the regional accrediting agencies and the professional and other specialized accrediting bodies can be found at www.ed.gov/offices/OPE/Students/Accred.html or in *Lovejoy's College Guide*.

Professional training programs may operate either as independent institutions (for example, a college of optometry) or as departments or special schools within a regular college or university (for example, a university's engineering department or theology school). In the latter case, there may be differences between the standards of the regional and professional accrediting bodies. On the one hand, the professional accrediting body may fail to accredit the given college department, even though the college as a whole is accredited by the regional body. (The student's bachelor's degree thus is legitimate for all general purposes, but he or she might experience some difficulty obtaining a job in or getting into a higher degree program in the chosen field.) On the other hand, the professional agency may accredit the relevant department, even though the regional accrediting body has refused to accredit the college as a whole. To check the professional accreditation status of a school, department, or program, look in *Accredited Institutions of Postsecondary Education* or contact the accrediting body in question.

In checking the accreditation status of any college that is not well known, it is important that you focus on the years of the subject's attendance. A school that is fully accredited today may not have been accredited when the subject studied there in the early 1970s. Likewise, a small school that has lost its accreditation in recent years because of a loss of income (and hence a decline in the quality of its faculty, library services, and the like) may have offered an adequate education when your subject attended it in the late 1950s.

Never accept an obscure school's claim that it is accredited; diploma mills will lie. And be cautious regarding regional or professional accrediting bodies other than those approved by CORPA or the Department of Education. A number of unrecognized accrediting agencies have been set up to provide alternative accrediting for unaccredited schools. Although some may attempt sincerely to impose standards, others are just mail drops for diploma mills.

Apart from the question of accreditation, nontraditional forms of education are burgeoning. This trend reflects recent changes in technology (such as the Internet) and also such phenomena as adults going back to school in increasing numbers and college-age youngsters looking for a no-frills education. Because of such changes, traditional forms of alternative education (such as the correspondence courses and evening adult education programs offered by many established universities) have now been supplemented by accredited "electronic colleges" offering residence-free undergraduate and even graduate programs online. In addition, an increasing number of traditional colleges (as well as alternative colleges) offer minimal residency requirements, generous credits for life experience or for passing an equivalency exam, and learning contracts in place of required courses. For detailed evaluation of accredited alternative schools and programs, see the latest edition of John Bear's annual *College Degrees by Mail and Modem*.

If you are suspicious that a school might be a diploma mill, contact the state board of higher education and the regional accrediting agency for the state and region in which the school's offices or mail drop are located. One or both may have received complaints about the school. Another option is to contact the school itself, pretend that you want to purchase a degree—and see how they respond.

Also, you can check the diploma mill's Web page, if it has one. It will probably be a couple of pictures of generic ivy-covered buildings, a short sales pitch, and nothing else. Diploma mills are small-time scams and it beggars belief that anyone would spend the vast sums necessary to develop a fictitious fully developed Web site with faculty, departmental, and student directories, Web pages for campus organizations, course descriptions, and an online library catalog. (Of course, a diploma mill operator could simply download portions of a legitimate college's Web site, globally replace the college's name, and thus present a temporarily convincing fake. Always be suspicious if a college Web site cannot be accessed through the standard college Web directories, especially www.ed.gov/offices/OPE/Partners/ed.html.)

Note: Diploma mills are moving targets; when laws are passed against them in one state, they move to another and open under a different name. In the 1980s, many were in California; in the 1990s (until a new law was passed), some were in Wyoming.

Checking Out the Degree

After you have determined that your subject's college is legitimate, you will want to know whether the subject's relationship to the college—and his or her degree—are for real. For unofficial confirmation, you can look in the alumni directory; for official confirmation, contact the college registrar's office. No college will give you details on a former student's academic records without his or her written permission, but the majority of schools will confirm whether the subject ever matriculated and what degree, if any, he or she received and in what year. (Some schools will tell you a bit more, such as the subject's major field of study, participation in intercollegiate athletics, awards and honors, and so forth.) Note that people who falsely claim college degrees on resumes or job applications will often list a school they attended but from which they never graduated rather than pick a school at random.

The Public Record Research System (see the bibliography at the back of this book) will tell you the address, phone number, and fax number at each college for obtaining confirmation of a student's attendance and degree. It will also tell you what identifying information must be provided (some schools require the former student's SSN and graduation date), whether information can be obtained over the phone without a written request, and the varying restrictions on release of information.

How Good Is/Was the College or University the Subject Attended?

Colleges and universities vary in quality, not only overall but also in terms of particular programs. Because reputations change slowly in higher education, you might get a relatively accurate idea by looking at current evaluations even if the subject graduated from the school a decade or more ago. The best guides are the College Board's *The College Handbook* (preferred by college admissions counselors), *Lovejoy's College Guide*, and Peterson's *Four Year Colleges*. All have been published annually or biannually for several decades; thus, you can check the volume for the year your subject graduated (in a library that has the back editions) if you need the most accurate information possible. In addition, *U.S. News & World Report* publishes each year a special report, "America's Best Colleges," which ranks colleges and universities by reputation among top educators as well as by objective standards. A similar annual report is published by *Maclean's* for Canadian universities and colleges. Also valuable for backgrounding a recent college graduate are the various specialized evaluations of his or her college. For instance, the new American Academy for Liberal Education (AALE) evaluates liberal-arts schools and programs according to their fidelity to the traditional Western civilization curriculum. Other organizations or authors have produced quirky ratings of schools according to how welcoming they are for minorities, whether or not they adhere to Christian fundamentalist morality, whether or not they have reputations as "party schools," and so on. Graduate programs are ranked in the *U.S. News & World Report* and *Maclean's* annual studies. However, the most authoritative information on U.S. research-doctorate programs comes from the National Research Council of the National Academy of Sciences, which provides rankings in 40 separate disciplines. The NRC produced comprehensive assessments in 1982 and again in 1995. Its massive 1995 report is available online at www.nap.edu/readingroom/books/researchdoc.

Defining the Years of Attendance

To trace a subject's college career, you first need to know which years he or she was really in attendance. If the subject graduated in 1984, it does not necessarily follow that he or she matriculated in 1980 and went through the standard uninterrupted four-year grind. Although this was the typical pattern until the 1980s (except during the two world wars), there have always been students who dropped out temporarily for a variety of reasons. And today, it is financially very difficult for most students to complete their studies in four years: The average student in the California State University system, for example, now takes five and a half years.

If the college will not give you the subject's dates of attendance but only the date of graduation, look in the alumni directory. Occasionally, these books will list the years of actual attendance, but more often, students are listed as members of the class with which they entered; for example, "class of 1973" refers to the year the subject would have graduated if he or she had matriculated in 1969 and taken an uninterrupted four-year course of study. Thus, you will know to search the school's yearbooks, student directories, and other publications for the years between the class year minus four and the graduation year.

Most alumni directories will not tell you whether a student transferred from another school, although if he or she was on campus overall for less than four years, this was probably the case. (Note, however, that since the early 1990s, some colleges have begun to offer accelerated three-year bachelor's degrees.) The college may release information regarding transfers, but if not, you might check with all colleges within commuting distance of the subject's hometown. Many students spend their first two years at a commuter college while living at home for financial reasons (if they need to drastically improve their grade-point average, the school will probably be a two-year junior college) and then will transfer to a college or university in another locality. You might also check the national membership directory of any fraternity or sorority to which the subject belonged because most students who join these organizations do so during their freshman year. Note that many campuses will have "stray-Greek" organizations for fraternity or sorority members who joined societies at their previous schools that are not represented at the transfer school; in such cases, the yearbook of the transfer school may have a stray-Greek fraternity or sorority page that will list the society to which each stray Greek belongs.

Student Directories

In addition to helping you pin down a subject's years of attendance, student directories can be used like city directories to trace where a subject lived each year, either on or off campus (sometimes this can help you find a subject's former roommate). In the case of a university divided into separate schools or colleges, the back issues of the directory may tell in which division the subject was enrolled at the beginning of each year, thus revealing any sudden shifts in career goals, such as from engineering one year to liberal arts the next.

Yearbooks

College yearbooks often contain many details about a subject's campus activities and friends. Backfiles of the yearbook will be available at the college library (usually in the campus archives) or at the yearbook editorial office.

A typical yearbook includes sections on sports teams, fraternities and sororities, campus publications (newspaper, yearbook, and humor and literary magazine staffs), honorary societies, student government, music and drama, and religious and political clubs. For each organization, team, club, and so on, there will be a group picture with a caption giving the name of each person.

Look first in the yearbook for the subject's senior year. Here you will find his or her class picture together with information regarding degree, major, scholarships, fraternity or sorority membership, and possibly the name of the subject's hometown and the high school he or she graduated from. There will also be a listing of the subject's campus activities, honors, and affiliations with the year or years of each. You can then go to the editions for the designated years, look up each cited activity or organization, and get a list of the other students in each picture. In this way, you can rapidly collect the names of those former classmates most likely to remember the subject well, such as the subject's sorority sisters, field hockey teammates, or co-workers on the campus newspaper.

Some yearbooks have a name index that lists each page in which the subject's name or picture appears; this can make your search much easier, especially if there is no senior class picture of the subject or only a picture with no summary of activities. (Some seniors will have nothing but their degree and major listed, not because they were inactive on campus but simply because they failed to fill out the form sent to them by the yearbook staff. In such cases, simply look in the name index for each edition published during the subject's years of attendance to obtain the missing information.)

In recent years, African American and Hispanic students on some campuses have begun to publish their own separate yearbooks. In such cases, information on a minority student will be divided between the ethnic and the campus-wide yearbook, so consult both. You may also find that some schools now have a separate yearbook for students in degree-granting adult education divisions; such students were not usually represented in the traditional yearbook.

Other recent changes reflect the rising costs of publishing and also the decline of student involvement in traditional campus rituals. For instance, some schools have replaced their hardcopy yearbooks with magazines, CD-ROMs, or even video yearbooks. Some yearbooks are only published in years when there is sufficient enthusiasm. Some have been replaced by "senior books" when there are insufficient orders from non-seniors. In addition, a much smaller percentage of students bother to have their pictures taken for the yearbooks nowadays. It is doubtful, however, that yearbooks are on the way out (more likely, once they become digital, we will see them flourish as never before).

Note: Professional schools (medicine, law, nursing, pharmacy, and so on) will have separate sections in some yearbooks; look in this section for the student's class picture.

Faculty Directory

Back issues of the faculty directory will provide the names and departments of professors who were teaching at the school during the subject's years of attendance. The teachers most likely to remember the subject will be those in his or her departmental major. Also, if the subject was on a sports team, the coach may remember him or her quite well. If a professor or coach you want to contact has retired or moved to another school, get his or her new address from the online national white pages, from his or her former department, or from the latest full edition and supplements of the *National Faculty Directory*. If you can't find someone whom you believe is retired, you might look in back editions of the *National Faculty Directory* or in out-of-print directories such as the *Faculty White Pages* (last published in 1993) and the *Faculty Directory of Higher Education* (last published in 1988) to find the last school at which he or she worked.

Campus Newspapers and Periodicals

The campus newspaper for the relevant years may have published articles regarding the subject or articles, letters to the editor, or op-ed pieces by him or her. Larger colleges or universities have daily newspapers that cover campus life quite thoroughly. In backgrounding several followers of Lyndon LaRouche, I found much information in Columbia University's *Daily Spectator* on their activities as campus protest leaders in the 1960s.

Campus papers are usually available on microform in the college archives; the microform for the years you need can be borrowed through interlibrary loan.

The staff of the college archives may have compiled a newspaper index or clippings files. These are likely to be organized by subject only, but you can zero in on articles mentioning a particular person if you already know a bit about his or her college career from the yearbooks or conversations with former classmates. Even without a clippings file, you might be able to find some things quickly on microform; for example, if you know that the person was on the basketball team, just look through the sports pages for the basketball season.

If I were backgrounding the college career of a current celebrity, I would find out who the editors of the campus paper were during his or her years of attendance; they will be more likely to remember any newsworthy events regarding my subject than most other students would. Also, some of these former editors will have become professional journalists and thus will be naturally sympathetic to a fellow journalist or a biographer.

Note that universities and the surrounding cultural milieu give rise to a great variety of newspapers, periodicals, and newsletters that are dutifully cataloged by the staff of the campus archives. The subject's university may have two rival campus-wide dailies; it may also have Jewish, black, or gay/lesbian newspapers as well as newspapers for the law school, engineering school, evening students, and so forth. There may be a conservative organ (such as the *Dartmouth Review*) and an environmental newsletter. In the 1960s, there was often a campus Students for a Democratic Society (SDS) chapter newsletter and assorted other organs of protest. Usually there has been a succession of literary and humor magazines. In addition, most large college communities have one or more off-campus weeklies (offshoots of the former counterculture or "underground" press, in many cases) that report closely on campus happenings for a readership that includes many students and faculty.

Checking Out a Subject's Thesis or Dissertation

Every university will have in its library stacks the master's theses and doctoral dissertations of graduate students to whom it granted degrees. (*Note:* Not all master's degree programs require a thesis.) Some university and college libraries, especially those of schools that require a thesis from every senior, will also keep copies of senior honors papers and senior theses.

Many theses and dissertations have an acknowledgments page in which the author thanks his or her adviser, the members of the dissertation committee (and other professors), friends, parents, spouse and children, the department secretary, and so on. Often 20 or more names will be mentioned. The acknowledgments are especially valuable in finding the names of ex-spouses and ex-lovers. Also look for any mention of grants or scholarships received by the subject.

If you cannot visit the subject's college library, you can still easily find details about his or her dissertation. Look in *American Doctoral Dissertations* and the *Comprehensive Dissertation Index* at your local research library. These indexes indicate whether the subject indeed has the doctorate he or she claims to have. You can then consult *Dissertation Abstracts International* and *Masters Abstracts International*, which contain abstracts (usually written by the authors themselves) of dissertations (dating from 1938) and theses (dating from 1962).

Using DIALOG or CompuServe, you can access UMI's Dissertation Abstracts Online, which provides an index to the subject, title, and author of almost every dissertation accepted at a U.S. university since 1861 and master's theses since 1962. This database also provides dissertation abstracts (from 1980) and theses abstracts (from 1988). As of 1998, the total number of dissertations in the database was 1.5 million. Many research libraries have this database on CD-ROM.

UMI also offers online the full text of all dissertations or theses submitted to it since 1997. As of early 1999, the total number of these documents exceeds 100,000. To search by author and key word the index/abstracts of these full-text documents, and to purchase documents for downloading, go to www.lib.umi.com/dissertations.

If you need the full text of an earlier dissertation or thesis, you can order the microform or a photocopy from UMI (go to www.umi.com for details). If a particular dissertation or thesis is unavailable from UMI, you can get it through interlibrary loan from the library of the university that awarded the degree.

High School Background

A subject's high school years can be researched just like the college ones. The yearbooks can often be found at the local public library or the county historical society; if not, a serious researcher can sometimes gain access to the backfile at the high school itself. The same goes for the weekly high school newspaper and other student publications.

As at colleges, the most important yearbook is the one for the subject's senior year, which will contain a summary of his or her activities for all four years. If a student transferred from another high school during his or her junior or senior year, this will often be noted to explain the lack of listed activities.

11.2 Backgrounding an Individual Using Archival Collections

Although mostly used by scholars, archival materials can be invaluable to an investigative reporter. Such materials may include unpublished manuscripts, scrapbooks, newspaper clippings, leaflets, court documents, self-published pamphlets, personal correspondence, official papers and correspondence of an elected official, internal documents of a political party, internal memoranda of a corporation, oral history tapes and transcripts, photographs, home movies, and video or audio cassettes of TV and radio appearances.

A subject may have donated his or her personal papers to a library either for the sake of posterity or as a tax write-off. A person doesn't have to be famous to do this. Some libraries actively seek the papers of ordinary people for their sociological value. They also seek the papers of people who, although not well known to the public, played an important behind-the-scenes role in (or were well-placed observers of) significant historical events.

Although the chances that your subject has donated his or her papers to an archive are relatively small, there is a much greater chance that papers concerning your subject, or memos or letters by or to your subject, are contained in the archival papers of a notable person with whom the subject was once associated. If I were backgrounding a longtime business agent of an Ohio Teamster local, I would want to know where the papers of the late Ohio Teamster leader and international president Jackie Presser are kept. (Conversely, if I were Presser and still alive, I would be very interested to know that an investigative reporter who once dogged me had donated his files to the University of Missouri.) If I were backgrounding someone who once worked in a minor appointive post in the Carter White House, I would check the indexes of the Carter Presidential Library. If I were backgrounding a longtime local Democratic county chairman, I would go to the state university library and look at the papers of the late governor whose rise to power was engineered by that county chairman.

Let's say you are investigating Harry, the former radical who is now a neoconservative pundit. You know that Harry was once a disciple and top aide to Max Swift, the Trotskyist leader. You check the RLIN database (described in the next section) and discover that Max, who died several years ago, had donated his personal papers and correspondence to the radical history collection at New York University. You also ascertain from the database that a finder's aid has been prepared for Max's papers describing each box and folder and itemizing the most important individual documents in each. You obtain a copy of the finder's aid through interlibrary loan and learn that Max's papers include two folders of correspondence between Max and Harry as well as a draft of a never-published article by Max denouncing Harry after their quarrel. You go to New York City and examine the collection, finding that Max's unpublished article is a bitter tirade that, among other things, accuses Harry of stealing money from the movement and compulsive philandering.

Archival Databases and Other Guides

The best way to find archival material nationwide is through the two major library subscription databases: the Research Libraries Information Network (RLIN) and the Online Computer Library Center (OCLC). If you type in the name of the individual or organization you are researching, you may be surprised how many "hits" you get. Unfortunately, RLIN and OCLC provide only relatively brief descriptions of any given archival collection (although individual documents or letters of special importance may be noted); if your subject's name is not in the description, you will not get a hit even if the particular collection contains a large amount of information about him or her. To find material beyond what's listed under a subject's name, search under the names of his or her better-known colleagues or under the relevant organizational titles. In the case of Harry, you would search for material under "Socialist Vanguard Party," "Max Swift," or "Olga Strong" (Max's wife). You would also search under topic key words such as "Trotskyism" or "U.S. Left." Next you would call each library listed as having significant collections on Swift, Trotskyism, and so forth and ask for the archivist who best knows the collection or who prepared the finder's aid; he or she will probably recall whether the collection contains significant material on Harry. You might also contact the eccentric former "Swiftie" who donated his files to New York University: first, because he might have personal recollections of Harry; second, because he will know his own collection better than any librarian would; and third, because he might have boxloads of additional documents in his basement.

You should also look in the Library of Congress's *National Union Catalog of Manuscript Collections* (NUCMC). (The online version, and a gateway to portions of the RLIN database, is at lcweb.loc.gov/coll/nucmc/ nucmc/html.) If you're searching the print version, you will also find useful the *Index to Personal Names in the National Union Catalog of Manuscript Collections* (the latter includes about 200,000 personal and family names). Unfortunately, it is often a decade or more before collections from local libraries are listed in *NUCMC*.

To find material that is not contained either in *NUCMC* or in the other databases mentioned, look in the subject index in the *Directory of Archives and Manuscript Repositories in the United States* (or search the online version at lcweb.loc.gov/coll/nucnc/nucmc.html) and also search *Subject Collections*. Compile a list of repositories most likely to have relevant holdings and call the archivist at each or search their online catalogs.

Another useful work is *ArchivesUSA*, available in print or on CD-ROM at most research libraries, which indexes over 110,000 special collections at over 5,000 repositories, with links to over 1,700 finding aids.

Federal, State, and Local Government Archives

For federal government archival collections, see *The Guide to Federal Records in the National Archives of the United States*, the NARA Information Locator (NAIL), and the NARA Library Online Catalog, all of which can be accessed at www.nara.gov. Also see the *National Inventory of Documentary Sources in the United States: Federal Records*, which lists finding guides to the National Archives and Smithsonian Institution collections as well as to the seven presidential libraries.

Staff members at the various National Archives collections and at the presidential libraries will search for what you need and send you photocopies for a modest fee.

Each U.S. state has its own archives, often part of the state library. Guides or catalogs to your state's archival holdings may be available online at the state government Web site. For links to archival and manuscript depositories in each state, go to lcweb.loc.gov/coll/nucmc/director.html.

Whether you are a journalist or a private investigator, note that the municipal or county archives, often located in the same building as the public records you routinely check, are a potential gold mine. Such archives may include the annual lists of city employees and their salaries going back decades; minutes of old zoning board meetings bearing the secrets of many a never-revealed scandal; local newspaper clippings files organized by year, neighborhood, municipal department, and name of elected official or civic leader; "vertical files" containing old pamphlets and leaflets; and old audits and reports on questionable dealings between city officials and the private sector.

Oral History

Well over a million Americans from all walks of life have been interviewed as part of oral history projects. Thousands of these projects are sponsored by universities; by county, city, or small-town historical societies; and by corporations, trade unions, or churches desiring a record of their organizational life. Participants in these projects include the most unlikely people: For instance, the late Jackie Presser taped his recollections for a University of Nevada project.

Oral history transcripts or tapes (usually audio tapes but also occasionally video) are available at the library of the institution sponsoring the project. Well-funded university projects usually have transcripts (of which about 30,000 are listed in the *Oral History Index*), but your local county historical society probably can't afford this—you'll have to listen to the tapes and take notes. The purposes of oral history projects vary widely. If a person is interviewed only about a certain peripheral aspect of his or her life, the transcript may run less than fifty pages. If a person is asked to give an account of his or her entire life, the transcript may fill several volumes.

Finding tapes on a particular person is not very different from finding other archival material. Let's return to the case of Harry. You can search RLIN and OCLC for any tapes by Harry or by any of his former comrades (including Max and Olga) or by any of his later right-wing associates who might have recounted anecdotes involving him. You can also search by key word for tapes regarding the history of the U.S. Left, Trotskyism, the Socialist Vanguard Party, and the protest movements on the college campus where Harry had his moment of glory in 1968.

Although such a search will tell you whether material relevant to your research has been entered into RLIN or OCLC by archivists at libraries connected to the system, it will not help you find tapes at small-town historical societies outside the system. To find the most promising of the latter collections, see the *Directory of Oral History Collections*.

11.3 The Subject's Published Writings

The majority of today's books are written by part-time authors, who make their living either in related writing fields such as journalism or who write to communicate their professional findings in science or scholarship or simply for the love of writing. At any moment, hundreds of thousands of Americans are churning out fiction, nonfiction, or verse manuscripts, and these hopefuls may come from any walk of life. Most of them will receive only rejection slips from America's major publishing houses. But many would-be authors, undaunted, will turn to the thousands of small publishers (including vanity publishers). Others will self-publish their own books and pamphlets using home computers and desktop publishing software. Meanwhile, vast numbers of amateur and professional writers each year will publish articles, research studies, book reviews, short stories, poems, or letters to the editor in hundreds of thousands of publications ranging from nationally known newspapers and magazines through the most obscure and unindexed church newsletters, science-fiction fanzines, or high school literary magazines.

Never assume that your subject is not among the millions of Americans who have been published in one form or another at some time or another. As an experiment, I asked a friend to check with her family members. She came up with a list of over a dozen siblings, aunts, uncles, and cousins who had written for publication. Their output included bible lessons for a religious newspaper, a college textbook in education, a work on family genealogy, recipes for a cookbook, a self-published autobiography, and, in the case of one uncle, communist pamphlets in the 1940s.

Finding an Author's Books

How do you track down a subject's books, including out-of-print, small press, vanity press, and self-published books? One quick way is to search the subject's Web page (more on this later in the chapter). Another way is to look in biographical dictionary entries about the subject. A large proportion of book authors and other writers find their way into such dictionaries. This is true even of rank amateurs: The very energy that propels them to finish a book may also have propelled them into prominence in business or some other field. And however peripheral their writing is to their main career, they will proudly list (in the questionnaire they fill out for the dictionary editors) even that unreadable self-published autobiography distributed to only a few dozen friends and relatives.

Serious authors are just about the most exhaustively covered category in the biographical dictionary business. The chief publisher of biographical reference works on writers, with fairly comprehensive listings of each writer's published titles, is The Gale Group. Its *Dictionary of Literary Biography* (over 180 volumes so far) contains biographical-critical entries on even very obscure American writers in a wide range of categories: novelists, poets, dramatists, screenwriters, short-story writers, ethnic writers, magazine and newspaper journalists, children's writers, literary scholars and critics, humorists, science-fiction writers—the series even includes a volume on beatniks. Gale also publishes *Contemporary Authors* (163 volumes so far) and *Contemporary Authors New Revision Series* (64 volumes so far), both of which are available on CD-ROM. These and hundreds of other reference works are indexed in Gale's *Biography and Genealogy Master Index* (*BGMI*) (see section 5.2), which includes over a million citations to biographical entries on 400,000 living and dead authors (these figures do not include the hundreds of thousands of people in *BGMI* who did or have done occasional writing while following a career in some other field and whose writings may, as noted earlier, be mentioned in their entries).

Several other key reference works and databases will help you compile a full list of books and pamphlets written by your subject:

- R.R. Bowker's *Books in Print* includes entries for over 1.3 million books—virtually every English-language book in print from every press, in every genre, on every subject. This nine-volume work, found at most bookstores and public libraries, includes both author and title indexes. It is kept up to date between editions by *Books in Print Supplement* and *Forthcoming Books*. Many public libraries and bookstores have Books in Print Plus, a CD-ROM version of *Books in Print* and its previously mentioned companion volumes as well as the five-volume *Subject Guide to Books in Print*. The online version of *Books in Print*, which also includes *Books Out of Print*, is available from DIALOG and LEXIS-NEXIS. An Internet version of *Books Out of Print*, covering over 900,000 titles that have gone out of print or indefinitely out of stock since 1979, can be searched for free at www.bowker.com.

- H.W. Wilson's *Cumulative Book Index* (*CBI*) has annual volumes dating back to 1969 and multiyear volumes dating back to 1928. *CBI* is available on CD-ROM and online from WILSONLINE at your public library for easy searching of any author's name.

- LC MARC, the commercial version of the Library of Congress's computerized catalogs, contains bibliographic records for every book in English cataloged by the LOC since 1968. (Books in other languages are covered beginning at various points from 1973 through 1980.) Updated weekly, LC MARC is fully searchable by author, title, subject, and so on. LOC records for English language books before 1968 (and some foreign language books up through 1980) can be accessed through REMARC. Both databases are available through DIALOG. The LOC catalogs are also available for free on the World Wide Web at lcweb.loc.gov/catalog/online.html. For complicated searches, you may be better off using the more powerful DIALOG search software.

- *The National Union Catalog*, the Library of Congress's catalog of books reported from other libraries that are not yet in the LOC, is being put online for the years from 1982 to the present (the completed portion can be accessed at lcweb.loc.gov). For coverage before 1982, you will have to use the print volumes.

- BRS's Books Information database, available through CompuServe, includes indexing of pamphlets, books from small publishers, books published in English overseas, and other hard-to-find publications.

- Copyright registrations of books and other works since 1982 can be accessed through the Library of Congress catalog at lcweb.loc.gov/copyright or telnet://locis.loc.gov. You can also use DIALOG with its superior search capabilities.

Using these resources, you will probably find the titles of any of your subject's books if they were published under his or her name and if the copyright was registered with the U.S. Copyright Office. (Note that many self-published works bearing a copyright symbol are never formally registered.)

Yet another way to find a subject's obscure books or pamphlets is by simply calling up him or her and asking for a list. Ned the Nazi may be the most paranoid person in the state of Arkansas, but if you phone him at his rural bunker and say you're interested in his writings, he'll probably react like any other proud amateur author—talk your ear off and then send you a complete collection of his out-of-print scurrilous pamphlets by Federal Express at his own expense.

If, however, Ned refuses to discuss his writings with you, run his name through RLIN or OCLC. Pamphlets bearing his name may have been cataloged by an archive of right-wing nativist publications.

What to Look for in a Subject's Writings

Whatever their literary or scholarly merit, a subject's writings may furnish personal background information unavailable from any other source and may thus justify the often arduous search to find them. This is most clearly the case when a subject has written his or her autobiography or memoirs. Once, after spending weeks collecting information on a New York businessman, I discovered to my chagrin that most of this information had been readily available all along in the subject's self-published autobiography. Although most subjects of backgrounding have not written autobiographies, their books or articles on other topics may tangentially reveal many facts about themselves and their close associates, and also may provide a window on their values and psychological makeup. In addition, that short story or poem they dashed off for a local newspaper contest may reveal secret desires and unresolved psychiatric traumas in disguised form.

To squeeze the maximum amount of personal information out of any book written by your subject, you must search systematically from cover to cover. The acknowledgments page may give you the names of relatives, friends, and colleagues of the subject; his or her agent and editor; and foundations or government agencies that provided financial aid for his or her research. The page that faces the title page may include a list of the subject's previous books. The dedication may provide you with the first name of the subject's spouse or live-in lover. Indeed, the dedications of successive books may be the archeological strata of your subject's relationships. (A famous science-fiction writer once dedicated a novel about a sexy android to 31 women, apparently his most fondly remembered sweethearts. Alas for any future biographer: He did not provide their last names.)

The preface or foreword may include autobiographical remarks (or, if written by someone else, appreciative comments on the subject's work mixed with a few tidbits about the subject's personal background). The bibliography may include several of the subject's articles that you hadn't heard of before. The works by others that the subject chooses to list in the bibliography or cite in the footnotes or endnotes may provide a window on the subject's unspoken ideological biases.

Often the most important resource is the book's index, which may include numerous page references to the author and to organizations and individuals linked to the author, including those listed in the acknowledgments. Although the index of an autobiography or memoir by the subject will be the most useful, the indexes of books in other categories may lead you to implicitly autobiographical passages both in the text and in the notes. This is especially true of works of journalism and contemporary history that include memoir-type material in passing. A good example is *The Rise of the Right*, William A. Rusher's excellent history of American conservatism from the 1950s through the 1980s. Rusher, publisher of *National Review*, was a key player in this history, and the index has hundreds of references to Rusher himself, his magazine, and his closest associates. Thus, although the book appears at first glance to be history rather than autobiography, it actually includes in scattered form a rich autobiographical profile of its author. The presence of such material cannot always be inferred from the title or library classification of a book.

Reviews and Criticism

To find reviews of your subject's books, use the *Book Review Index* (*BRI*). This standard reference work published by Gale includes a bimonthly index and annual cumulations. *BRI*'s latest annual cumulation includes over 146,000 review citations for about 75,000 works reviewed in over 600 periodicals and newspapers. There is a master cumulation for 1965–84 in 10 volumes, including 1.6 million citations, and also master cumulations for 1985–92 and 1993–97. *BRI* from 1969 to the present is available online from DIALOG and on CD-ROM, offering over 2.5 million citations to reviews of about 1.5 million titles.

Many scholarly and scientific periodicals that review books are not indexed in *BRI*. Such reviews, however, can be found in the specialized indexes covering these periodicals, which can be searched through DIALOG.

When you go to the cited magazine or newspaper issue to photocopy the review, look at the letters-to-the-editor section for subsequent issues: An unfavorable review of the subject's book may have elicited an indignant reply either from the subject or from a friend or admirer; a favorable review may have flushed out a subject's detractors and enemies to express even fiercer indignation.

For quotes and summaries of critical opinion about an author—including material from books of criticism as well as periodicals—see the various biographical/critical dictionaries published by Gale. Also see H.W. Wilson's *Book Review Digest* (*BRD*), which provides excerpts from and citations to reviews of over 6,500 English-language books each year. *BRD*'s retrospective volumes date back to 1907 and can be easily searched with the cumulative author/title index. The contents of *BRD* since 1983 are available online and on CD-ROM. *BRD* is also easily searchable dating back to 1975 with the *Book Review Digest Author/Title Index* (print only).

Note: If you plan to interview your subject, familiarity with the critical reviews of his or her writing is essential: First, because it shows that you take his or her work seriously; and second, because nothing will get a writer talking faster than an opportunity to fulminate against his or her critics.

A Subject's Miscellaneous Writings

In backgrounding any professional or serious amateur writer, the following reference works from the H.W. Wilson Company should be checked: *Essay and General Literature Index* (over 250,000 essays published between 1900 and the present; print version from 1900, and online and CD-ROM versions from 1985); *Short Story Index* (over 150,000 short stories published between 1900 and the present; print only); and *Play Index* (over 35,000 plays published from 1949 to the present; print only).

Finding a Subject's Newspaper and Periodical Articles

Your first step should be to search the relevant full-text, abstract, and index databases (see sections 6.4, "Newspaper Databases," and 6.5, "Periodicals Databases"). For publications not included in any database—or for issues of a publication that predate its database coverage—your options will include print indexes (such as *Readers' Guide to Periodical Literature*); clippings files; article, book, and résumé bibliographies; and special bibliographical works. In the case of journalists who have written full time or as regular freelance contributors for an unindexed newspaper or magazine, just look for their byline in each issue on the microfilm or in the bound volumes. In backgrounding scholars and scientists as well as journalists, you should look at their personal Web pages; here you may find the full texts of the articles they are most proud of (or links to those articles elsewhere) and a résumé that provides a comprehensive list of their articles.

Such searches may turn up hundreds of articles written by a given individual. This can compensate for the often paltry courthouse paper trail that intellectuals (as opposed to real estate developers and politicians) leave. The articles of a prolific writer comprise a rich chronological record of the topics in which he or she has been interested and the collaborators with whom he or she has worked. In the case of a journalist, you can gain a fascinating record of the lives he or she has touched and the enemies he or she has made. This provides interesting options; for example, the Lyndon LaRouche organization, seeking negative information in 1984 about NBC investigative reporter Brian Ross, called up all the mobsters and Teamster hoodlums he had pilloried over the years.

Critics of a Subject's Articles

While searching for a subject's articles, also keep an eye out for replies, which may appear in a letter-to-the-editor format or as a full-blown article.

Often such replies will be indexed under the subject's name; if not, they can be found by looking through the next few issues of the publication following the appearance of his or her article. The essay or report you thought was so brilliant may have been subjected to devastating criticism. If the criticism is less than devastating, at least you've gained the name of someone who dislikes or envies the author.

A Subject's Scientific and Scholarly Articles

In your public library, you will find the various H.W. Wilson scientific, scholarly, and professional indexes, including *Applied Science & Technology Index, Art Index, Biological & Agricultural Index, Business Periodicals Index, Education Index, General Science Index, Humanities Index, Index to Legal Periodicals, Library Literature,* and *Social Sciences Index.* Most of these works provide coverage dating back to early in the century, often under a succession of different titles. Several of them lack a separate author index, but electronic versions enable you to search for an author's name for the years covered by the database (unfortunately, none of the H.W. Wilson databases begin earlier than 1981). All are available at public libraries on CD-ROM; online access can be gained through CompuServe or WilsonWeb. To search all Wilson databases at once for any author's name, use the Wilson Name Authority File.

Note: The preceding Wilson products now include abstracts as well as indexes and have changed their names accordingly.

Through DIALOG, you can access indexes with somewhat broader coverage of recent years than the Wilson indexes provide (and often beginning much earlier than the online versions of the Wilson ones) in every major field of scholarship, science, and technology, and in every major profession. Some of the most important are listed here:

- **Arts & Humanities Search** (indexes 1,300 of the world's arts and humanities journals, plus relevant material from 5,000 other journals; 1980 to present)

- **ERIC** (over 700 periodicals of interest to educators; 1966 to present)

- **Legal Resource Index** (over 750 law journals; 1980 to present)

- **MEDLINE** (over 7 million records from over 3,700 biomedical journals; 1966 to present)

- **Scisearch** (over 8 million records from 1974 to present, representing the vast majority of the world's significant scientific and technical literature)

- **Social Scisearch** (over 2.5 million records from 1,500 social science journals plus social science material from 3,000 journals in other fields; 1972 to present)

- **Philosopher's Index** (indexing and abstracts from over 270 journals; 1940 to present)

- **Religion Index** (indexing and abstracts from over 500 journals and 450 multiple-author works; 1949 to present)

Several of these and other scientific and scholarly databases on DIALOG are also available in print form; for example, MEDLINE corresponds to three printed indexes: *Index Medicus, Index to Dental Literature,* and *International Nursing Index.* Both MEDLINE and ERIC can be searched for free on the Internet, but you're probably better off using DIALOG's search software. Some of the preceding databases cover not just journal articles but also monographs, multiple-author books, conference papers, conference panel discussions, book reviews, and other special modes of scholarly and scientific communication. Of special interest on DIALOG, if you are backgrounding a scientist's work, is the Conference Papers Index, which covers over 100,000 scientific and technical papers presented at over 1,000 conferences annually since 1973.

Note that a subject's entry in the *Directory of American Scholars* (defunct since 1983) may include a brief bibliography of some of his or her earlier articles. In addition, you can look in the bibliography of any of his or her scholarly or scientific books or articles. Scholars and scientists are usually careful to include all of their own previous articles, research studies, and books relating to the given topic. (Obviously, to gain the biggest list, you would look at the subject's books or articles in his or her main specialty rather than his or her forays into other fields.) For instance, research psychologist Theodore X. Barber's *Hypnosis: A Scientific Approach* contains in the bibliography a list of over 60 articles by Barber.

A search of the subject's published writings through the years will provide several types of information to supplement what you find in biographical dictionaries or professional directories. For instance, an article will usually identify the university, think tank, or government or private-industry laboratory with which the subject was affiliated at the time of writing; this may fill in gaps in what you know about his or her job history. By noting the names of the subject's co-authors on various articles, you will learn who some of his or her closest colleagues and mentors have been at various career stages. You should also note the names of graduate students or junior scientists whose contributions to the subject's research articles were acknowledged in an apparently grudging manner (some of them may feel their work was ripped off or that the subject otherwise took advantage of them, and they may be willing to talk about it).

An article or book may also include information about government or foundation grants the subject has received. The preface to Dr. Barber's hypnosis book discloses that his research from 1956 to 1976 was supported by grants from the National Institute of Mental Health (MF-6343c, MY-3253, MY-4825, MH-7003, and MH-11521). After you know the funding source, you can find details on a government grant through Freedom of Information requests, and you can find details on foundation grants through Federal 990-PF forms or foundation annual reports. Note that grants on federal research projects are preceded by a review of the application by a committee of government scientists. After the research study is completed, another committee of scientists will write a peer review summary report. This report is available from the grantor agency.

Also note that scholarly and scientific indexes usually cover letters to the editor and other communications disagreeing with an article or report. These polemical pieces can sometimes be scathing (as can attacks on the subject's works found in the proceedings of scientific conferences). The indignant letter writer or outspoken panelist may become your best source in unmasking the pretensions of a pseudoscholar or pseudoscientist.

In searching scholarly and scientific literature (especially if you extend your search beyond the top journals with the highest standards), you will frequently find a large amount of flimflam. Scholars and scientists are under constant pressure to publish or perish (even if they are primarily teachers rather than researchers). The result of this pressure (and of the need to pad curriculum vitae bibliographies to qualify for a better post) is that professors often churn out research articles on trivial topics (or, in the humanities and social sciences, shallow opinion pieces requiring no research). A virtual industry of unrefereed scientific journals and obscure scholarly journals has arisen to abet this practice. In the sciences today, at least 40,000 journals produce a million articles a year, a vast percentage of which is of dubious value.

The various tricks involved include publishing a study in unnecessary installments (with each installment counting as a separate article), publishing two versions of the same findings in different journals, allowing colleagues to piggyback their names onto your articles as co-authors while you also piggyback onto theirs, and of course putting your name first on a study for which your graduate students did all the work. The most extreme padding occurs in the so-called team reports churned out by certain scientific laboratories. These labs will be working on many studies at once, and sometimes a dozen or more lab scientists will be listed among the co-authors of a given study even though the contributions of most of them were minimal. Department heads and research supervisors, in particular, get their names added to scores of articles—a kind of scientific *droit du seigneur*.

Unpublished Academic and Professional-School Writings

Dissertations, theses, and senior honors papers from universities and four-year general colleges are discussed in section 11.1. Almost entirely overlooked by indexers and abstracters of such works, however, are equivalent papers from the many professional and specialized schools that provide narrower types of education. These schools range from colleges of optometry or naturopathy through Bible colleges, most of them accredited by

Department of Education–approved bodies representing the given profession or belief system. The equivalent of theses or honor papers at these schools are often available at the school's library. A journalist might visit such a library to find out what a certain popular televangelist had to say about the Book of Revelation while he or she was a Bible student 20 years ago, or what a local naturopath being sued for malpractice asserted in his or her study of a certain exotic herb 10 years ago.

Anonymous and Pseudonymous Authors

Many books are published under pseudonyms, but the reason often doesn't involve any great desire for secrecy. A prolific author may decide that two books under one name in a single year won't sell as well as two books under separate names. A mainstream novelist may decide to write his or her trashy thrillers under a pseudonym so as not to undermine his or her "literary" reputation. Often you can find the truth simply by looking in the *Cumulative Book Index* where the author's various pen names are cross-referenced with his or her real name. Library catalogs usually have this information, taken from the Library of Congress catalog system. The Library of Congress record for Wall Street commentator Adam Smith's *Powers of Mind*, for instance, tells us that his real name is George J.W. Goodman.

Things are not so simple if an author is really determined to conceal his or her identity. The Library of Congress Copyright Office's Application Form TX does not require the copyright claimant to reveal the name of the work's author. In some cases, the claimant of an anonymous or pseudonymous work is, in fact, the unadmitted author of the work; in other cases, the claimant is an employer or other person for whom the work was "made for hire" or someone who simply purchased the contractual right to claim legal title.

Registration details on all active copyright and mask-work registrations on file at the U.S. Copyright Office from 1978 to the present is available on DIALOG (or you can search using the government's software on Telnet; go first to lcweb.loc.gov/copyright). The copyright database includes, among other things, monograph and legal document records. The former provide information on the initial registration and renewal of a work; the latter provide information on assignments and other information regarding ownership status.

To search copyrights before 1978 or to conduct complicated post-1978 searches, you either must go to the Copyright Office in person to conduct a manual search or pay $20 an hour for a search by a staff member. If you are searching for the identity of an anonymous or pseudonymous author, you should check all successive Form TXs, supplementary registrations, and records of transfer of copyright ownership pertaining to the work in question. You should also examine the entire portfolio of works published under the given pseudonym: Clues to the author's identity may be found in the records for one of these works that are not found in the records of the work you first researched.

If an author is trying to conceal his or her name (for instance, on a self-published manual on how to grow marijuana) and also to retain control of the work, the copyright claimant may be the author's attorney or spouse (especially a wife under her maiden name), or a corporation or unincorporated business set up by the author or an associate. In such cases, the standard backgrounding techniques in this book may enable you eventually to discover the author's identity.

Some anonymous or pseudonymous authors will fail to register their self-published book or pamphlet with the Copyright Office (although they will probably put a copyright notice on the title page anyway). However, such works will usually have the name of a publisher on the cover or the inside cover, and this publisher—even if it's just a one-book operation—will be a registered business. In addition, if the book is sold mail-order from a post office box, you can find out from the post office who rented the box (see section 14.1, "Businesses, Legitimate and Otherwise").

If you're still stumped, look for clues in the book itself: the printer and/or typesetter's name, the printers' union bug, the credits for a cover artist or other illustrator (or an artist's signature on one of the illustrations), and the photo credits. Any of these clues may lead you to someone who knows the author's identity.

11.4 The Subject's Garbage

This resource has produced some interesting if smelly results through the years. A private investigator's examination of the trash of Skadden Arps Slate Meagher & Flom, a major Wall Street law firm, led to the arrest and conviction of two individuals for securities fraud. Freelance journalist A.J. Weberman's probe of the garbage of Bella Abzug during the Vietnam War led to the revelation that Abzug and her husband owned stock in two major defense contractors. Jack Anderson's snooping in J. Edgar Hoover's garbage turned up empty booze bottles that called into question Hoover's sanctimonious demand that all FBI agents be strict teetotalers. In the early 1980s, I gained much information on Lyndon LaRouche's organization through my garbage rounds. (Landlords in Manhattan would sometimes call me at the newspaper *Our Town* when anything interesting turned up in the garbage of a LaRouche follower living in one of their buildings.) Once when a LaRouchian couple moved out of an apartment, leaving behind heaps of papers and trash, I spent a happy afternoon, crawling around in a dumpster on the street in front of the building, collecting bank statements, phone bills (with lists of long-distance numbers called), and supposedly top-secret internal memos of the LaRouche organization.

The *National Enquirer* was criticized for going through Henry Kissinger's garbage. The tabloid's reply: How can Kissinger complain about privacy when he ordered the bugging of his own staff's phones at the National Security Council?

For tips on this unusual technique see A.J. Weberman's *My Life in Garbology*, the full text of which can be downloaded from www.garbology.com or www.weberman.com.

Weberman cautions against trespassing on private property. Pick up garbage only from public sidewalks. With millions of homeless people sifting through garbage cans all over the United States today, it's unlikely that anyone will challenge you (at least not in an urban neighborhood) if you dress as if you, too, are homeless. Weberman's own specialty was to go to the Manhattan townhouses of the rich and famous where the garbage cans were either on the sidewalk or in an alley. To make sure that he had the right can, he'd sift through a bag in search of a piece of junk mail with the subject's name on it.

People generally put out their garbage the evening before (or early in the morning of) the scheduled pickup. If you want to snatch the garbage from in front of your local cult leader's mansion, call the sanitation department and ask on what days of the week (and at what hours) the garbage is picked up on that block. If you want to raid the office trash of a local business, note that the trash from commercial buildings is usually picked up by private carters. You can find out the pick-up schedule by chatting with one of the building maintenance employees or with a pretext call to the building superintendent or the carting company.

If you're lucky, you might find prescription bottles, canceled checks, and other medical or financial information in the subject's trash (see sections 10.6, "Medical Records and Other Medical Information," and 8.22, "Financial Information from a Subject's Garbage"). Other things you might find are junk mail and old copies of magazines to which the subject subscribes. The magazines may reveal the subject's hobbies and other interests (which might be important if you decide later to interview him or her and need to establish rapport). The junk mail may *indirectly* reveal such interests; for example, a letter from a magazine asking him or her to subscribe may indicate that he or she already subscribes to a similar magazine on the topic or has purchased products relating to the magazine's interests. It is well known to any consumer that if, say, you purchase mountain-climbing equipment in a store, you will almost immediately start receiving letters from mountain-climbing magazines. Letters from an environmental group asking the subject to join or to donate money may indicate that the subject has already joined or donated money to a similar group. Discarded copies of an organizational newsletter will strongly suggest that the subject belongs to the given organization (a "Dear Member" letter will settle the question). Before making such inferences, however, always make sure that the item is addressed to your subject rather than to someone else in the household.

The trash may also tell you where the subject went to college because alumni associations continuously pester grads with fund-raising appeals and booster mailings, as do professional and trade associations, churches, and so on. Also look for personal correspondence—you might just find a letter from one of the subject's lovers that you didn't know about, a letter from his or her lawyer regarding a dispute you didn't know about, or a letter from his or her parole officer asking why he didn't show up last week.

11.5 License Plate Surveillance of a Subject's Visitors

Jeannie arrives at her boyfriend Tom's house earlier than expected. While parking her car down the block, she observes a seductively dressed blonde exit Tom's front door, get in a Toyota, and drive away. Jeannie would like to know who that woman is, but she doesn't want to ask Tom and thus tip him off that she knows he has extracurricular visitors.

Russ the anti-Klan activist has stationed himself on a hill above the cow pasture of Roy the Grand Dragon. Through his binoculars, he observes several cars and pickup trucks pull up in the yard. Angry-looking men enter the house where they remain for several hours. A klavern meeting? Naturally, Russ would like to know the identities of the visitors, but he is certainly not going to stroll down the hill and ask them.

If Jeannie and Russ manage to get the license plate numbers of the cars in question, they may get the answers to their questions (or at least clues to the answers) from the state Department of Motor Vehicles (DMV). Motor vehicle registration information is available to casual requesters in some states. In other states, Jeannie could obtain the name and address of the car's owner through her attorney, if she decided to sue Tom; and Russ could obtain the information on his targets if he were investigating them for a civil rights attorney pursuant to a possible suit. (For a discussion of DMV privacy restrictions, see section 10.2.)

License plate searches involve two basic pitfalls. First, the license plates may have been switched so that you end up with information on the wrong car. To guard against this, note the car's make, year, and color so that you can later check this against what you receive from the DMV.

Second, the driver of the car—the person you are trying to identify—may not be the owner of record. Jeannie, for instance, discovers that the owner of the Toyota is a man; she now must determine whether the mysterious woman driver is his wife, girlfriend, sister, daughter, or whatever. Russ finds out that the owner of one of the cars at the klavern meeting is a rental agency. He must now persuade someone at the agency to tell him who rented the car that day.

Depending on the circumstances, other sources of confusion might arise during Russ's ongoing license plate research regarding right-wing extremists. One of the cars he observes may turn out to be stolen. Another, apparently that of an out-of-state visitor to a Klan meeting, may actually belong to a local guy who's registered his car in another state to get lower insurance rates.

In spite of these limitations, license plate checks can be quite useful. Essentially, there are two types of surveillance involved: You can stake out a residence or business and see who visits, or you can do a drive-through or walk-through (go to the company parking lot and gather all the license plate numbers—especially of cars that have company parking stickers, as explained later in this section). Do not use a pen and notebook; this might call unwanted attention to you if you're on foot—and it requires a partner if you're driving. I recommend a tiny microphone clipped to your shirt collar so that you can dictate the numbers and vehicle descriptions into a tape recorder. Also, wear earphones so that any observer will think you're just listening to music and that the movement of your lips is singing rather than dictation.

Both types of surveillance may help you find potential sources. A stake-out of visitors at a subject's house (from a parked car down the street) may give you the name of a maid or relative. A walk-through of the parking lot of a subject's small construction company may give you the license plate numbers of all workers in the front office. The uses of such information are only as limited as your imagination and initiative.

When examining parked cars up close, don't miss the information presented in the form of stickers and medallions on the windows, bumpers, and trunk. Registration and inspection stickers are only the tip of the iceberg here. The dealer's medallion will tell you who originally sold the car, and where. Parking-permit stickers may tell you where the car's current owner lives (a township or village parking sticker), where his or her vacation home is located (a private beach sticker), where he or she works (a company parking lot or university faculty sticker), and where he or she goes to school (a high school or college student parking sticker), as well as the fact that he or she has a bit of clout at city hall (a VIP parking sticker).

In addition, a car may have a trade union sticker, a college sticker (if there's no campus parking sticker to go with it, this is probably a proud alumnus's car), an ethnic celebration sticker (such as "Erin" or "Italia"), and an auto club membership sticker (usually an indication of middle-class status). Still other stickers (especially bumper stickers) may reveal which national parks the owner visited on his or her most recent vacation, what his or her favorite charity is, which candidates he or she voted for in the last presidential election, and his or her ideological beliefs (either right wing or left wing) regarding feminism, world peace, or street crime.

License Plate Codes

License plate letters and numbers—and also the plate colors and embossed captions and symbols—contain coded information. Thus, while observing license plates, you can decide on the spot which vehicles to check out further. You can also learn information from the license plates that might not be contained in the abstract of registration. For instance, in several states, the license plate letters reveal the county or congressional district in which the car was registered. Depending on the state, a plate may also reveal such information as the use or weight of the vehicle, the first letter of the owner's last name, the owner's occupation or professional status, his or her membership in a particular private organization or Native American tribe, and his or her status as a veteran, government official, handicapped person, or diplomat. Almost always, the plate will tell you whether the car belongs to a rental or leasing agency.

New York State license plates are a fascinating example of this coding. The dozens of codes include DCH (chiropractor), DAV (disabled veteran), TV (television industry), NYP (press), RX (pharmacist), and PBA (Patrolmen's Benevolent Association). If a New York plate has three numerals followed by a dash and a "Z" plus two other letters, the car is registered to a rental or leasing company.

License plates may also reveal whether a car belongs to the state government and even may identify the particular government department. Who was using the car at a particular time—or who the car is assigned to on a regular basis—should be publicly available information, although you might have to make a formal request under the state's sunshine law.

Federal government license plates are coded for dozens of departments and agencies; for instance, "J" means Justice Department, and "D" means Defense Department. But many government cars will simply have the letter "G" before the numbers, which means Interagency Motor Pools System.

A detailed description of the coded information for all 50 states, the District of Columbia, the federal government, and Canada's provinces is contained in Thomson C. Murray's *The Official License Plate Book* (see bibliography).

11.6 Finding Your Subject in Books and Dissertations

Millions of living Americans are mentioned in books and dissertations, either in passing or as the subjects of small portions of the text. Finding these passages is important not just for the information they contain but also because the author or his or her sources often know much more than was printed. Begin by checking the *Biography Index*, which, among other things, indexes biographical information from otherwise nonbiographical works. Next, if your subject has a background in politics, big business, national security, or organized crime, check NameBase (www.pir.org), an online name index compiled from a wide array of books by investigative journalists.

To go beyond these two resources, you will need to apply the principles of parallel and indirect backgrounding (see sections 1.3 and 1.4). First, make a list of notable persons, organizations, and events with which the subject has been associated. Second, search the online catalog of the largest library (or the library with the strongest relevant subject collection) in your locality for titles of books that might have information regarding each name or event. Third, go to that library and search the name indexes of all the books on your list that are available; be sure also to examine any lists of interviewees in a book's acknowledgments or appendix to see whether the subject's name (or the names of any of the subject's closest associates) crops up. Fourth, see whether the library has copies of any other likely books mentioned in the bibliographies of the preceding books but that you missed in your earlier searching. (If you have direct access to the stacks, you might also do a little intuitive browsing in the relevant subject areas— I've often found crucial books this way.) Fifth, contact the authors of books that mention the subject or the subject's associates to see whether they have any further information (including interview notes or tapes); also contact the authors of the most promising books not available in the library to ask them if they mentioned in print or have any background information on your subject. If an author is dead or can't be located, call a library that has the book in question and try to persuade one of the librarians to check the name index for you. If the book contains citations that interest you, borrow it or get a photocopy of the relevant pages through interlibrary loan.

If you want to extend your search to doctoral dissertations and master's theses, use Dissertation Abstracts Online to find the likeliest titles. Note that any dissertation or thesis accepted by a university in your locality will be available in that university's library; photocopies of most dissertations and many theses nationwide are available from UMI (see section 11.1). Before ordering a photocopy, make sure that the dissertation was not published at some point (the book, including revisions and updates not in the original dissertation, might be available in a local library). After you get the dissertation or book, pay special attention to the lists of unpublished source documents and interviewees in the bibliography and appendixes. If you feel that any of the material in the dissertation requires further probing, contact its author with your questions and your requests for access to research notes, telephone numbers of people he or she interviewed, and so forth.

11.7 Making Use of Caller ID

The Caller ID service involves the use of a small display screen that shows the telephone number from which an incoming call originated and (if you choose the deluxe service) the subscriber to whom that number is assigned. It is now available in most parts of the country, and its biggest early drawback—the fact that it showed only the numbers for incoming calls originating within the subscriber's own calling area or state—has now been overcome: The Federal Communications Commission (FCC) has ruled that all telephone companies must transmit a caller's number to out-of-state calling areas for Caller ID display.

In response to privacy issues, the phone companies have provided per-call blocking, a service by which a caller can prevent his or her number from appearing on the Caller ID subscriber's display screen by entering *67 before dialing the number (the letter "P" or the word "private" then appears on the screen along with the date, time, and daily numerical order of the call). Some states also allow or require per-line (or all-call) blocking to be offered to the public. With this type of blocking, the caller's number is automatically withheld unless the caller unblocks his or her line by entering *82 before making a call. Some states only allow per-line blocking for subscribers with unlisted numbers; others allow it only for people who can demonstrate that Caller ID puts them in danger.

How is Caller ID useful for a journalist? An investigative series often produces threatening or harassing phone calls, or calls from impostors trying to find out who the journalist's sources are. Caller ID will tell you the phone number from which the call is made and the name of the subscriber; you can then use an online crisscross directory to find out the address at which the phone is located. (*Note:* In some states, you can get Call 54, a service that allows you to obtain both the name and the address by calling 555-5454.) Caller ID is not just sensible self-defense: It can also help you fill out the list of your subject's known associates. Some of them may later become sources (especially if you are investigating cults, an area in which today's true believer is tomorrow's defector).

Caller ID is also of value if you are dealing with an anonymous source who is not yet ready to tell you his or her identity. Learning the identity surreptitiously and then gathering a little background information will enable you to decide whether or not the person's information should be taken seriously.

The usefulness of Caller ID is believed to be sharply limited by the fact that crank callers and other secretive callers often operate from pay phones or use per-call or per-line blocking. This perception is not altogether accurate. First, a person disturbed enough to engage in telephone harassment or to play compulsive secrecy games may lack sufficient impulse control to use the blocking code or a pay phone consistently. Second, there is the laziness/ignorance factor: Surveys in several states have shown that per-call blocking is used in less than 1 percent of all phone calls. It would appear that most telephone users not only can't be bothered with remembering and dialing the blocking code (which is all the more true for persons with rotary phones, who have to dial four digits), they aren't even aware that it exists (some are probably not even aware that Caller ID exists).

In addition, most telephone users are totally unaware of the fact that per-call or per-line blocking will not work if the number called is an 800, 888, or 900 number. (Skip tracers, you can be sure, are taking advantage of this.) Nor, for that matter, are most people with unlisted phone numbers aware that, if they call a person with deluxe caller ID service, their number and name will appear on that person's Caller ID screen unless they use the blocking code.

Even if a caller uses a pay phone, his or her privacy may be in jeopardy. Learning the location of the phone (along with the time the call was made) can often provide clues about the caller's identity. If the phone is located near suspected caller X's home (and the call was made during hours when X is usually at home), or near X's workplace (during X's known lunch hour or immediately before or after his or her shift), or on the route X usually travels between home and work (and during X's normal commuting hours), you have a strong possibility that X made the call. You can then call him or her at home, say "I know it was you," and see if he or she admits it.

An alternative to Caller ID is call return, which allows you to call back automatically the last number from which you received a call and which also tells you the number from which the call was made. As in the case of Caller ID, this method won't work if the caller has used the per-call blocking code or has an all-call block on his or her line.

For more information about caller ID, see section 4.34, "Caller ID."

12.

Checking Out Your Physician

This chapter is intended for medical consumers who want to check a doctor's credentials and competence. The information given here could be a life-and-death matter for those who must choose a surgeon and an anesthesiologist or who want to select a cardiologist or other specialist with the necessary skill to spot life-threatening illnesses at an early, treatable stage. The information can also be useful in choosing a primary healthcare provider for one's children or in preparing a malpractice suit.

12.1 Basic Background Information

The Physician Masterfile of the American Medical Association (AMA) is a database that tracks virtually all licensed medical doctors (MDs) and doctors of osteopathy (DOs) in the United States (over 650,000 individuals) from medical school through retirement. It provides each doctor's address, date and place of birth, where he or she attended medical school (and year of graduation), dates and places of internship and residency, fellowships and board certifications (if any), disciplinary sanctions (if any), states in which the doctor is licensed, and the year each license was granted. Although the masterfile itself is not available to the general public, the AMA has placed portions of the information online under the name "AMA Physician Select" at www.ama-assn.org. You can also use the AMA's hardcover *Directory of Physicians in the United States*, which is updated every two years and is available at many public libraries. Additional professional data on MDs and DOs can be found at the Web sites of state medical boards or state health departments or in print rosters such as the *Medical Directory of New York State*. For more information on DOs only, consult the annual *Yearbook and Directory of Osteopathic Physicians*.

For information on a physician's status as a specialist, consult *The Official ABMS Directory of Board Certified Medical Specialists*, a four-volume set (hereafter referred to as the *ABMS Directory*) published annually by Marquis Who's Who in cooperation with the American Board of Medical Specialties. This directory (also available on CD-ROM) is often found in public libraries. It includes biographical and professional data on most board-certified specialists in the United States and Canada (more than 535,000 doctors certified by the 24 member boards of the ABMS) and lists among other things the type and date of certification, postresidency fellowship training, and current academic and hospital appointments. Note that the *ABMS Directory* uses abbreviations and codes; study the instructions carefully, or you may misinterpret what you find or miss important information altogether.

Information on specialists certified only by osteopathic specialty boards can be found in the *Yearbook and Directory of Osteopathic Physicians* (some DOs, however, are also certified by the ABMS board in their specialty and hence are included in the *ABMS Directory*).

A physician's certification by a member board of the ABMS can be verified by calling the ABMS hotline at (800) 776-2378 or by accessing the ABMS's verification service at www.certifieddoctor.com. Certification by an osteopathic specialty board can be verified at (800) 621-1773 (ask for "Board Certification").

Biographical information of a more detailed nature than that provided by the AMA or the ABMS can sometimes be found in works such as the American Psychiatric Association's *Biographical Directory*.

The most detailed information on a physician will be in his or her curriculum vitae, which in many cases can be found at the Web site of the hospital or medical school with which he or she is affiliated or on his or her personal Web page. If you don't find your doctor's CV online, simply ask him or her for a copy.

12.2 Is Your Doctor a Menace to Your Health?

According to Dr. Robert Derbyshire, past president of the Federation of State Medical Boards, 10 percent of America's doctors are less than competent. These are the doctors who are the targets of a majority of malpractice suits and state disciplinary proceedings. How do you spot them?

Consumer Watchdog Lists

Ask at your public library for *16,638 Questionable Doctors*, a four-volume directory published by the Public Citizen Health Research Group. It includes physicians, dentists, chiropractors, and podiatrists nationwide who have been disciplined for providing substandard health care and for a variety of unethical and illegal activities. Covered are disciplinary actions by state medical boards, Medicare, and the Drug Enforcement Administration. If your public library doesn't have the full reference set, it may have the regional edition that includes your state. The regional editions, of which there are 18, can be purchased for $23.50 each at the Public Citizen Web site (www.citizen.org/hrg/majorpublications/qdform.htm). Each entry by state will cross-reference the given doctor's problems in other states; you can then call the state medical board in each of the states involved for further information. Note that the information in the regional listings and in the four-volume set will inevitably be somewhat out of date.

Also check with consumer groups in your locality to see whether they have published a guide to local doctors that includes information on disciplinary actions, malpractice awards, and so forth.

State Medical Boards

Each year, several thousand doctors nationwide are subjected to state medical board disciplinary action on such grounds as gross negligence, incompetence, sexual abuse, moral unfitness, fraud, professional misconduct, practicing while impaired with a psychiatric disorder, intoxication on the job, and failure to disclose a previous license revocation in another state. The most severe disciplinary action is license revocation. Lesser actions include license suspension, various license limitations (for instance, a temporary prohibition against prescribing addictive drugs), censure, or reprimand. In a few states, all records of completed investigations are open to the public, even if no disciplinary action was taken. But in the majority of states, the public gets access to disciplinary records only when a public sanction is imposed. Most complaints are never seriously pursued (because of lack of staff); of those that are seriously pursued, most never result in any public sanction (therefore, the records of most state medical boards are clearly of limited use to the medical consumer). Furthermore, even if disciplinary action is eventually taken, the administrative procedure may drag on for years, during which time the incompetent doctor continues to victimize unwitting consumers without hindrance.

If the physician you are checking out has no history of disciplinary action in the state(s) in which he or she is currently practicing medicine, don't assume that he or she is clean. Although safeguards are supposed to be in place to prevent a physician from skipping to a new state after losing his or her license, some state boards let dangerous doctors slip through the cracks. For instance, these boards will not tell the Federation of State Medical Boards about a license revocation if a doctor voluntarily surrenders his or her license. As a result of this administrative "plea bargaining," the physician can relocate to another state and establish a new practice.

A thorough background check on a doctor (as when you are contemplating a malpractice suit) should include requests for information regarding disciplinary actions from the state medical boards in every state in which you believe he or she might previously have been licensed as well as from the states in which he or she currently holds a license. If the doctor you are checking out is a DO, be aware that in several states you must check with a separate osteopathic board.

The AMA's Physician Masterfile includes an asterisk beside the name of each doctor against whom disciplinary action has been taken by a state medical board (*if* the board reported that action), but no asterisks or any other indications of disciplinary action are included in the AMA's online Physician Select. However, if a doctor is not listed at all in Physician Select, it may be because of a record of serious sanctions (the AMA's policy is to simply exclude such doctors from the online database). If your own doctor is not listed in Physician Select, call the AMA to find out why.

Check the Administrators in Medicine Web site (www.docboard.org), which is sponsored by the Association of State Medical Board Executive Directors and provides information about disciplinary actions against physicians in a dozen states. Information about sanctions in other states can be found at various state medical board or state health department Web sites. For instance, refer to the excellent Professional Misconduct and Physician Discipline Web page covering New York physicians (www.health.state.ny.us/nysdoh/opmc/main.htm).

If you are trying to conduct a thorough check of a physician's past record, always remember that the U.S. medical licensure system includes 54 licensing jurisdictions (the District of Columbia, Puerto Rico, Guam, and the Virgin Islands as well as the 50 states).

Commercial Search Services

Several companies have compiled databases that merge AMA data, malpractice data, and state and federal disciplinary records. For instance, Medi-Net at www.askmedi.com provides reports on physicians for $12.50 per report.

Malpractice Suits and Other Legal Actions

The defendant/plaintiff index at the state district court in any locality in which the subject has practiced may list malpractice suits against him or her. Depending on how the court indexes are organized (see Chapter 9, "Court Records"), it may be difficult to find all the cases involving a particular doctor. If the index lists only first-named defendants in multiple defendant cases, you may want to compile a list of cases in which certain physicians who share a group practice with the subject are the listed defendants—you could then check the docket sheet to see whether the subject's name is also included for any of these cases.

If you find any malpractice suits against the subject, check with the plaintiff's attorney. And if you don't find any suits but want to continue your search, check with local attorneys specializing in medical malpractice. They may know about horror stories that never reached the courts. They may also know about suits against your doctor that you didn't find in the court index or suits or disciplinary actions against him or her in other localities that you might not have located on your own.

Also check the court indexes for any suits filed by a certain physician against a patient who failed to pay his or her bills. Although many of these patients may be deadbeats, some may have withheld payment because of sincere indignation over the poor treatment they received. This is a way to uncover medical victims who never sued the doctor. (Only a small percentage of malpractice atrocities ever result in a suit because the patient is too intimidated or is unaware of his or her rights.)

An online search of the LEXIS Medical Malpractice Library, which includes malpractice case law from all 50 states as well as from the federal courts, might turn up a case involving your subject that was appealed to a higher court. However, over 90 percent of all malpractice cases never go to trial, much less to an appeals court, but are settled out of court.

The fact that a malpractice suit was filed against a physician may not have any relevance in determining whether you can trust him or her. A majority of malpractice suits are found to be without merit. Even if the doctor is found liable at trial, the incident may represent an isolated mistake on his or her part (it is impossible in the imperfect science/art of medicine for even the best doctors to avoid mistakes).

If you find that a case was settled before trial in the plaintiff's favor, this does not mean automatically that the defendant did anything wrong. It may just be that the doctor's malpractice insurance company pressed for settlement to avoid trial costs, even though the defendant would almost certainly have won such a trial.

County, State, and Specialist Medical Societies

Peer review committees of county, state, and specialist groups will sometimes investigate complaints against a doctor independently of the state board. However, their findings may not be publicly available.

Eyewitness Informants

Former nurses or receptionists of a doctor may have horror stories to tell and may remember the names of victimized patients. (Whenever you visit a doctor's office, jot down the names of staff members just in case you have to contact them later if you file a malpractice suit. Also, if you hear a patient in the waiting room complaining loudly about the results of a procedure, try to get his or her name.)

Indirect Evidence of Incompetence

If a doctor's entry in the latest edition of a directory no longer lists him or her as having privileges at a certain local hospital, and yet the doctor is still in private practice in the same locality without any other hospital affiliation, this may mean that his or her privileges at that hospital were revoked, and that other hospitals are avoiding him or her for some reason.

Note that your local hospitals all have access to the U.S. Department of Health and Human Services' National Practitioner Database, which tracks malpractice awards/settlements and disciplinary actions nationwide on a massive scale (but is not available to medical consumers because of pressure from the AMA). Your local hospitals may also check out doctors using expensive commercial tracking services to spot potential problem doctors. If a doctor in your community lacks any hospital affiliation whatsoever (or has ended up with admitting privileges at only a single third-rate hospital), the hospital review committees may be exercising a justifiable caution. Until you know more, avoid this doctor.

Your Doctor's Own Behavioral and Health Problems

Although the currently available databases on problem doctors do not include adequate information about any history of alcoholism, drug addiction, mental illness, or sexual misconduct, you can sometimes pick up vibes during your first visit or a subsequent visit to his or her office. Feel free to question this doctor bluntly about his or her questionable behavior. If you feel too nervous or intimidated to do this (or if the doctor responds evasively or angrily), choose another doctor.

Evidence of substance abuse can sometimes be found in the doctor's driving record, available from the Department of Motor Vehicles in some states. For evidence that he or she is a sexual harasser, look in civil court records for lawsuits filed against him or her by patients.

Any medical malpractice suit, if pursued to the point of interrogatories and depositions, will probably uncover evidence about a doctor's past behavioral and health problems if such evidence exists. If the discovery record is sealed pursuant to an out-of-court settlement, you can sometimes unearth this information from the plaintiff in the case, who may still be very angry with the doctor.

12.3 How Competent Is Your Doctor?

Following are some of the elements to consider in selecting a doctor. If the doctor in question is a board-certified specialist, much of what you need to know on each of these items is available in the *ABMS Directory*. If you belong to an HMO, you can get background information on any affiliated doctor from the member services department. However, you should *also* raise directly with any doctor you visit your questions and concerns about his or her professional background and status. If the doctor expresses exasperation or anger, get another doctor.

Hospital Affiliations

As well as being a warning flag regarding incompetent doctors, hospital affiliation can also be a pointer to the very best doctors. Look for a doctor who is affiliated with a prestigious hospital or medical center and who is on the attending staff rather than just having admitting privileges. Top hospitals seek top doctors for their attending staffs, and applicants undergo rigorous screening. In addition, doctors affiliated with such institutions undergo peer review from doctors who themselves are among the most highly qualified. Be aware, however, that the reputations of hospitals vary from specialty to specialty. The supposedly less-prestigious hospital with which your specialist is affiliated may actually have the best local reputation in that particular specialty.

If your doctor is affiliated with a small hospital with which you are unfamiliar or a larger hospital about which you have received conflicting opinions, you can obtain information on the hospital (including accreditation status) from the online Quality Check service offered to consumers by the AMA and AHA's Joint Commission on the Accreditation of Health Care Organizations (JCAHO) at www.jcaho.org/lwapps/directory/intro.htm. You might also check the American Hospital Directory (www.ahd.com), which provides summary federal data on hospitals that treat Medicare patients, and the Web site of your target hospital (a directory of hospital URLs can be found at neuro-www.mgh.harvard.edu/hospitalweb.shtml).

At the *U.S. News & World Report*'s Best Hospitals Finder Web site (www.usnews.com), you can examine nationwide, regional, state, or local rankings of hospitals as well as the annual "honor roll" of the very best nationally ranked hospitals and medical centers. Also, reprints of the magazine's annual special report, "Best Hospitals," can be ordered at this site.

Peer Review

At the minimum, your doctor should belong to at least one health-care organization that requires some kind of peer review. Generally, a doctor will be subject to peer review if he or she is on the organized medical staff of a hospital approved by the JCAHO (mentioned in the preceding section). In addition, peer review is often required by HMOs, physician networks, group practices, and so on. The reliability of peer review varies, of course, from organization to organization. Always check out the organization in question with the JCAHO or the National Committee on Quality Assurance.

Academic Appointments

An appointment to a medical school faculty is further evidence that a doctor's career is one that can withstand close scrutiny. But is he or she a clinical teacher involved on a daily basis in direct patient care? And is the medical school in the top tier? (See the following discussion of medical school rankings.)

Specialty Certification

The American Board of Medical Specialties (ABMS) is composed of 24 boards offering certification in 25 specialties (neurology and psychiatry share a single board). A board-certified doctor is referred to as a *diplomate* of the board. This title is evidence that he or she has undergone rigorous supervision and testing in that specialty. About 30 percent of the doctors who call themselves specialists in a given field are not certified by the specialty board, and their use of the specialty designation (for example, "dermatologist") is somewhat misleading although not illegal. For information on how to check the certification or lack thereof of an MD or DO, see section 12.1.

Your physician may have a certificate hanging on the wall from a self-designated medical specialty board or a society that is not recognized by the ABMS. Some of these groups do offer specialized training on their own. Others, however, exist chiefly to promote research in a particular field and do not offer any kind of training. It speaks well for your physician that he or she belongs to such societies (most ABMS board-certified specialists also belong to one or more), but his or her membership should not be confused with ABMS-approved certification.

To quickly check whether your doctor's certificate is from one of the 24 ABMS boards, go to www.abms.org, where you will find a list of the boards and of all the recognized specialty and subspecialty certificates. For information on osteopathic boards, go to www.aoa-net.org/AffiliatedOrgs/specialty.htm.

Note: Some unscrupulous physicians have been known to display on their walls specialty certificates from altogether phony mail-order "boards." The ABMS maintains a list of these fraudulent entities.

Some physicians refer to themselves as "board eligible." This simply means they have completed their residency and are qualified to sit for the board exams in the given specialty.

Board-certified physicians are organized into "colleges" such as the American College of Radiology. In each college, there are two levels of membership: that of Member and that of Fellow. The status of Fellow signifies a higher level of peer recognition and experience. Note that this term should not be confused with a "fellowship" in the sense of a post-residency training program in a subspecialty (see the following section).

Subspecialty Certification

Specialties in today's medicine cover a wide range of subspecialties. You will thus want to know whether the specialist you are consulting has adequate training and experience in the subspecialty category that includes your own medical condition. Subspecialty certificates (such as the American Board of Pediatrics' certificate in Pediatric Endocrinology) are usually granted by the specialty board only to physicians who have completed a board-approved fellowship in the given subspecialty. There are also unapproved fellowships that may provide training in the same subspecialty but without leading to a certificate. Sometimes the unapproved status of the fellowship reflects the inferior quality of the training offered by the program (although an unapproved fellowship is better than none).

Other times the unapproved status may mean simply that the subspecialty is a new one in which approval from the board has not yet been obtained. Note that in some new subspecialties that do not yet have an adequate number of approved fellowship programs, physicians who have gone through not-yet-approved programs are accepted as candidates for the sub-specialty certificate.

Recertification and Continuing Medical Education (CME) Credits

Board certification used to be a one-time thing: After you were certified, you remained so forever. Today, most boards require their specialists to undergo reexamination and recertification every 6 to 10 years. Even if a board does not have this requirement, a responsible doctor will under-go voluntary recertification every few years. Unfortunately, there is a grandfather provision in the rules of many boards, meaning that doc-tors who were certified before the adoption of the recertification re-quirements are exempt from those requirements and that only the newer doctors must comply.

As well as requiring recertification exams, some specialty boards require a doctor to earn a certain number of Continuing Medical Education (CME) credits to maintain certification. In addition, the state medical boards in some states require CME credits as a precondition for medical license re-newal, and the AMA encourages voluntary CME by presenting Physician Recognition Awards to doctors who complete 50 hours of CME each year (look for this award on your doctor's office wall).

Whether or not CME credits are required in a particular state or by a particular board, you should select a doctor who is on the cutting edge of his or her specialty and is well acquainted with any and all new findings or procedures that might save your life. This of course means CME and periodic recertification, even if it is not required. It also means reading the refereed medical journals in the particular specialty and attending medical seminars and conferences. It may, in some cases, mean participating in clinical trials or other clinical research and joining in the work of medical societies related to the specialty. (Note that membership in the AMA is not a significant factor in any of these systems; only 40 percent of MDs nationwide bother to keep up their membership in an organization widely regarded as bureaucratic and outdated.)

Before you visit a specialist for the first time, read over some of the lat-est important research articles concerning your condition. You can obtain these from the Web sites of research foundations and information clearing-houses that focus on your particular illness (such as the Lupus Foundation of America). A directory of such Web sites can be found at dir.yahoo.com/Health/Diseases_and_Conditions. Ask your new doctor about these recent research studies and see whether you get a knowledge-able and thoughtful response—or a blank stare.

The Subject's Published Articles

Another measure of a physician's competence is whether or not he or she has published articles or research studies in recent years pertaining to his or her specialty. This question can be checked in the National Library of Medicine's *Index Medicus* or its online version, MEDLINE, which is accessible for free at www.nlm.nih.gov. MEDLINE provides abstracts of over 9 million articles dating back to 1966 and currently covers almost 4,000 medical journals. In addition, MEDLINE provides the "Lonesome Doc" Document Delivery Service so that you can order the full text of any article from a medical library in your region. MEDLINE also provides links to publishers of about 250 leading journals so that you can order articles from these journals directly.

If you see an article by your doctor in his or her waiting room, don't be impressed unless it's from a *refereed journal* (a journal whose editors submit each article to a panel of leading researchers or clinicians before deciding to publish it). There are many "throwaway" medical journals that print substandard work and that are the medical equivalent of vanity publishers. (Note that the National Library of Medicine has a rigorous review process for determining which journals to index and which to exclude from *Index Medicus*/MEDLINE. If a journal is not included, it's likely to be a throwaway.)

Never judge a physician's competence by the fact that he or she has written books for laypersons on diet, plastic surgery, holistic medicine, and other trendy topics; has a column in a tabloid newspaper; or appears frequently on talk shows. Some of the worst quacks use these methods to attract victims.

Peer Ratings

Consult the latest edition for your region of Steven Naifeh's *The Best Doctors in America*, a collection of guidebooks covering the entire nation. In addition, see whether there is a guide for your state or metropolitan area—for example, *How to Find the Best Doctors: New York Metro Area*, a Castle Connolly guide by John J. Connolly that includes a roster of "Doctors of Excellence" based on peer ratings by nurses as well as doctors.

You can also conduct your own informal survey. When you need treatment in a given specialty or subspecialty, call several board-certified practitioners and ask whom they would recommend. Then make an appointment with the doctor whose name is mentioned most frequently (of course, you should get a second opinion no matter how good this doctor's peers say he or she is). Depending on the seriousness and complexity of your problem, you may want to search either for the best local specialist or for the best national one. In either case, the *ABMS Directory*, which provides listings geographically for specialists and subspecialists, can help you identify doctors for your survey.

Don't forget to poll your primary-care physician and any specialists you have been seeing for related ailments. They possess details about your medical condition that any doctor you merely contact by phone will not have. Such details may be extremely pertinent in choosing the "best" specialist.

The Subject's Medical School Training

All U.S. and Canadian medical schools are accredited, and the standards are generally high (this statement does not apply, of course, to mail-order diploma mills). Various guidebooks for applicants will give you a sense of which are better than others (although relative ranking may shift over the years). See especially *U.S. News & World Report*'s annual "Best Graduate Schools," which includes ratings of the top medical schools according to reputation ranking by medical school deans, senior faculty, and directors of intern and residency programs as well as by objective scores (the online version is accessible for free at www.usnews.com). Elements that various guidebooks use in ranking the medical schools include median scores of those admitted on the Medical College Admissions Test (MCAT), the median undergraduate Grade Point Average (GPA) of those admitted, and faculty-to-student ratios. When you first visit a doctor, you might ask, among other things, what his or her class standing was in medical school. If you think it's not tactful to ask this particular question (especially of a doctor who has been out of school for quite a few years), ask instead where he or she did his or her residency: The larger and more prestigious hospitals tend to get the top-of-the-class medical school graduates.

The U.S. system of medical education includes 19 colleges of osteopathic medicine, all of which are accredited. The majority are independent institutions, but several are affiliated with state universities such as Michigan State. For a list, go to the Web site of the American Association of Colleges of Osteopathic Medicine at www.aacom.org.

Students attending osteopathic schools must, like students at "allopathic" (mainstream) medical schools, be graduates of four-year colleges and must pass the MCAT. The education provided at an osteopathic school parallels that given at allopathic schools in most respects. About half of all osteopaths become primary care physicians, a larger percentage than among medical doctors. (Note that medical colleges are generally regarded as superior in producing top-flight specialists).

The Subject's Residency Training

In general, the best facilities for training residents are in major teaching hospitals (those closely linked to a medical school where there is a strong overlap between the hospital medical staff and the medical school teaching staff). However, a smaller or less well-known hospital may offer better and more varied practice in some fields.

Residencies last at least three years, but some states will grant a license to a doctor after his or her first year of residency. If a doctor did not thereafter complete his or her residency, you should want to know why.

If Dr. X attained the position of chief resident at the hospital where she did her residency, this is generally a good sign of her competence at the time in comparison to other residents in that particular residency program. But this does not necessarily mean that her performance was superior to that of someone who never became a chief resident but did successfully complete his or her residency at a major teaching hospital.

Most doctors obtained their residency training in programs approved by the Accreditation Council for Graduate Medical Education (ACGME). A list of the over 7,000 currently accredited programs is published by the AMA in its annual *Graduate Medical Education Directory*. You should consult the back-edition directories for the years in which your doctor did his or her residency—*not* the current edition. Note that there are various types of accreditation for residency programs: full accreditation, probationary accreditation, and so on. To understand ACGME's system and procedures, consult its Web site at www.acgme.org.

Foreign-Trained Doctors

According to the AMA, graduates of foreign medical schools comprise about 20 percent of all doctors practicing in the United States. (Note that Canadian medical schools are not regarded as foreign in these calculations.) For many years, any graduate of a foreign medical school who wanted to practice medicine in the United States had to pass the Foreign Medical Graduate Examination in the Medical Sciences (FMGEMS) before he or she could obtain a hospital residency and be licensed to practice medicine in a U.S. state. There were problems with FMGEMS, however. In 1984, 9,000 physicians who passed were ordered to retake it after officials discovered that almost half had obtained the questions in advance. Beginning in 1993, foreign doctors were required to take the United States Medical Licensing Exam (USMLE) along with U.S. medical school graduates. However, in the first year of this new exam, the failure rate on the clinical portion was 61 percent for foreign graduates as opposed to only 7 percent for U.S. graduates.

The problem of evaluating foreign medical schools (except Canadian ones) is quite complicated. If the degree is from an accredited medical college in a developed country such as Great Britain or Israel, it may represent an education as good as if not better than one obtained at a comparable U.S. school. But in some parts of the world, entrance to a medical school (and even the degree itself) can be purchased through bribes. And medical schools in some countries may, as a result of lack of financial resources, offer a substandard and outdated education even for the most sincere and hardworking students. However, residency training at a U.S. hospital and the rigorous study required to pass the USMLE do guarantee that most foreign medical graduates who obtain U.S. medical licenses have a reasonable level of competence.

A special problem concerns the many Americans who gain medical degrees overseas after failing to get into U.S. schools. Some foreign medical schools, especially in the Caribbean and Mexico, cater exclusively to Americans or have special programs for Americans. Less than 10 percent of American graduates of Caribbean and Mexican medical schools, however, end up qualifying to practice medicine in the United States. Several of these schools are so notorious that California and New York won't license their graduates even if they pass the licensing exam. The sole exception is the St. George's University medical school on the island of Grenada. Although its educational facilities are limited, its graduates do have good pass rates on the USMLE.

Whether you are looking at the diploma of an immigrant doctor or of an American who studied overseas, one measure of the diploma's worth is the annual passing rate of graduates of the given school on the USMLE. The rates range from nearly 100 percent for Israeli medical schools to below 20 percent for some of the Caribbean and Mexican schools. (To find out details on a particular foreign medical school, contact the Philadelphia-based Educational Commission for Foreign Medical Graduates. Its telephone number is (215) 386-5900; its Web address is www.ecfmg.org.)

Unlicensed Doctors

Thousands of medical school graduates are practicing in the United States without a license. They include many foreign doctors who have immigrated to this country but have been unable to get into residency programs and obtain licenses even though they have passed the USMLE. Some of these frustrated doctors enter the "medical underground" and practice in inner-city or rural clinics that can't attract anyone else. Although some of them may develop into competent general practitioners, the same cannot be said for individuals with degrees from substandard schools who have been unable to pass the USMLE or the many doctors with U.S. degrees who have been stripped of their licenses as a result of repeated malpractice. A doctor's medical license should be displayed on the wall of his or her office. If you don't see it or have doubts about its legitimacy, check with the state medical board.

If you have chosen a physician out of the phone book, without any referral, there is always the possibility that he or she is a totally untrained fraud. In 1980, the FBI's "Dipscam" probe found that bogus medical diplomas could be purchased through the mail for less than $50. In 1984, a congressional subcommittee estimated that upwards of 10,000 individuals—including many outright impostors—were practicing medicine in the United States with fraudulent credentials. Thus, if you *must* visit a new doctor without a referral, ask what medical school he or she graduated from or check the diploma on the wall. If you have any suspicions (if the office seems grungy, the doctor behaves strangely, or he or she suggests weird therapies), look up the school he or she claims to have graduated from in the list of all accredited U.S. and Canadian medical schools included in the *ABMS Directory*. Also check out his or her name with the state medical board. Note that many bogus doctors as well as those driven to the fringes of the profession through past malpractice may prey on minority immigrant communities (as in New York City's Chinatown, where a police crackdown on quack doctors occurred in 1996).

Doctors Offering Unorthodox Treatments and Quack Cures

Beware of any doctor, no matter how legitimate his or her medical license, who promises miracle cures through unorthodox methods for which there is no substantiation in research studies published in refereed journals. Such doctors frequently cite only their own haphazard clinical results (often reported in some throwaway medical journal or in an interview with a non-medical newspaper or magazine) with no real scientific backup. They often complain that they are being persecuted by a medical establishment that refuses to recognize their brilliance; or that their findings are being suppressed by a conspiracy involving the American Cancer Society, the National Institutes of Health, and even the CIA. Usually a search of the public record will turn up malpractice suits or medical board disciplinary actions against such a doctor.

A Word on Surgeons

If you are planning to have surgery, you will want to check out your surgeon and anesthesiologist—and the hospital—as thoroughly as possible. In the surgeon's case, you should not only gather information on his or her certification status, malpractice lawsuit record, and the like, you should also find out how many times he or she has performed the procedure in question. The theory behind this recommendation is that the more experience a surgeon has with a procedure, the greater the likelihood of a successful outcome. But what constitutes "adequate" experience varies from procedure to procedure. For a common procedure, one hundred times might be regarded as adequate. In the case of an uncommon procedure, it may be that no surgeon in your locality has performed it more than a dozen times.

Comparative surgery success rates and death rates are available for hospitals in many localities and even for the various surgeons within a given hospital. However, such score cards are often difficult to interpret; for instance, high death rates for a particular type of surgery at a given hospital may simply mean that the hospital takes on the most difficult life and death cases.

If the surgery you are contemplating is of a very risky or delicate nature, you should call up the relevant department chairperson at the nearest high-ranking medical school. This person may have information about the procedure or about possible alternative procedures that are more up to date than what your local doctors are aware of.

Always obtain a copy of any prospective surgeon's curriculum vitae (see section 12.1), which will be a comprehensive (and checkable!) guide to his or her professional training and experience. Comparing the CVs of two or more surgeons will help you make a fully informed decision about which surgeon to use.

For detailed information on the hospital where your surgery is to be performed, see "Hospital Affiliations," earlier in this chapter.

12.4 What About Your Doctor's Ethics?

Although *ethics* is not the same thing as *professional competence*, a physician with a history of ethical problems or criminal misconduct is more likely than the average MD to provide substandard medical care.

Medicare Sanctions and Other Public Records

The Inspector General's Office of the U.S. Department of Health and Human Services (HHS) maintains a list of physicians and other health-care professionals currently excluded from the Medicare program. This list can be searched online at www.hhs.gov/progorg/oig/cumsan/index.htm. If a doctor is reinstated to the Medicare program, his or her name is promptly taken off the exclusion list; however, his or her name will then appear on the monthly reinstatement roster, also available at the HHS Web site. In addition, his or her name will be on the HHS's long-range cumulative sanctions list. To check the latter, call (410) 786-9603. If you want details on a particular case (for example, the length of and reason for suspension), you must make an FOIA request.

The Drug Enforcement Administration (DEA) can tell you whether a physician's license to prescribe controlled substances has ever been revoked and whether or not there is an open case against the physician. For details, you must file an FOIA request or get the jurisdiction and file number of the case, if any, under which the physician was prosecuted (you can then order a copy of the case file, as described in section 9.8, "Criminal Court Records").

Information from the HHS and DEA files is also included in nongovernment databases and publications (see section 12.2) that track the disciplinary records of doctors. Other evidence of questionable behavior may be found in civil or criminal actions against the doctor (see Chapter 9, "Court Records"); look not just at cases involving alleged malpractice but also at those involving alleged fraudulent behavior by the subject in his or her dealings with former medical partners and other business associates.

Your Doctor's Financial Conflicts of Interest

Conflicts of interest can greatly affect the quality of your medical care. One such conflict arises when HMOs secretly give incentives to doctors to keep costs down by skimping on tests, referrals to specialists, and the like (see section 12.6). However, the opposite problem may occur when a physician, unchecked by managed care oversight, suggests unnecessary and potentially dangerous surgical procedures simply to collect the hefty fees. In such cases, the patient may not stop to think about just how much the doctor is going to earn from a routine surgical procedure for which the insurance company, not the patient, will have to pay. Indeed, the doctor will, in many cases, be grotesquely overpaid (a factor that increases his eagerness to perform the procedure) as a result of his or her arcane billing practices, especially what is known as "unbundling" (the billing codes are manipulated so as to break a single operation down into four or five suboperations, for each of which the insurance company is billed separately).

To find out whether your doctor routinely practices "unbundling," obtain copies of the bills he or she sends to your insurance company. You may find that, after your brief visit to his or her office last month, your insurance company was billed separately for such things as drawing blood, writing a prescription, and talking to you on the phone about your test results.

The Self-Referral Game

Your doctor might be practicing *self-referral*, defined as the process of sending patients for lab tests, MRI scans, diagnostic surgical procedures, and so on to a facility in which the doctor has a financial stake. A recent Florida survey estimated that 40 percent of the state's doctors had an interest in one or more clinical laboratories or other referral facilities. Often the doctor's relationship to such a facility will result in *churning*, the ordering of unnecessary tests and procedures for which the doctor gets what amounts to a kickback.

To check this out, ask the doctor whether he or she has any financial stake in or arrangement with the given facility. If you are not satisfied with his or her answer, look in the state corporation and partnership files. Self-referral joint ventures usually offer a doctor a limited partnership in which the key element is not the amount of money invested but the number of patients referred. Doctors sometimes try to hide such arrangements by investing under a corporate name (one medical lab in Florida was owned by 200 corporations, each of which was a front for a different doctor). *Note:* If a lab won't accept Medicare, this might be a tip-off because Medicare prohibits self-referral.

Other forms of self-referral include sending a patient to a private hospital in which the doctor is an investor, or sending the patient to a specialist across town with whom the referring doctor has a legal partnership (a sort of "group practice without walls"). In such cases, the treatment the patient receives may turn out to be markedly inferior to what he or she would have received as a result of a disinterested referral to a better hospital or a more experienced specialist.

Becoming a Guinea Pig

Your doctor may suggest that you try an experimental drug or medical device or undergo an experimental procedure. In the majority of cases, the suggestion is probably well-meaning, but your doctor may have a conflict of interest nonetheless. He or she may be getting consulting or research fees from the manufacturer developing the experimental product, or he or she may be an investor in the development company. In addition, he or she may hold a patent on the product or have some other proprietary interest in it.

Self-Defense Tactics

One way to insure yourself against being manipulated in any of the preceding situations is to insist from the beginning of your relationship with a doctor that he or she tell you about *any* conflicts of interest or hidden financial incentive that should arise at any time while you are under his or her care. If your doctor tries to dismiss the idea, remind him or her that an attorney who failed to disclose similar conflicts of interest to a client would probably be disbarred.

Of course, your doctor might lie to you regarding (or subtly misrepresent) a conflict of interest situation. Your next line of defense, therefore, should be to seek a second opinion on any important medical procedure your doctor suggests, and to do your own research and make your own decision about any hospital to which, or specialist to whom, your doctor refers you.

12.5 The American Medical Accreditation Program (AMAP)

The AMAP is a new program started by the AMA in 1997 and operative in only about 10 states as of early 1999. It is a voluntary program that provides health care organizations with comprehensive and reliable information on a physician's qualifications. When a physician applies for AMAP accreditation, AMAP will verify his or her credentials, check his or her record for ethical violations and disciplinary sanctions, and conduct an office site review. If the doctor passes this evaluation process, he or she will be accredited for two years. At the end of that period, he or she can apply for accreditation for an additional two years. To obtain this reaccreditation, the physician has to pass a fresh credentials check and site review.

To tell whether your doctor is accredited, look for the AMAP certificate on the office wall or check in the AMA's online Physician Select database (see section 12.1). Physician Select will tell you whether a particular doctor is currently accredited under AMAP, but it will *not* reveal whether or not a doctor was ever denied AMAP accreditation.

Because this program is still in its infant stage as of 1999, the lack of AMAP accreditation should not be a warning flag against a doctor. However, if you *do* see the certificate on your doctor's wall, it is an indication that he or she passed a rigorous evaluation (just how rigorous can be seen by examining the description of the evaluation process at www.ama-assn.org/med-sci/amapsite/standard/standard.html).

Note that some state medical boards have their own accreditation programs. If AMAP certification is not yet available in your state or is only in its beginning stages, check with your state board.

12.6 The HMO Problem

With the vast expansion of HMOs since the last edition of this book, the question of finding the best doctor can no longer be viewed in isolation from that of finding the best type of health insurance. A second-rate HMO may offer doctors who mostly are second rate. Even if your HMO is highly rated, you may be the stuck with less than the best treatment if you can't afford the point-of-service (POS) option. In addition, some HMOs have gag rules prohibiting a doctor from telling his or her HMO patients about costly treatment options or from revealing his or her financial stake in keeping health care costs down (as by failing to order certain expensive but necessary diagnostic tests). President Clinton issued an executive order in 1998 barring gag rules in the treatment of Medicare patients in HMOs, but Congress has not yet passed a federal law covering all HMO patients. Some states have outlawed such gag rules on their own, but the majority have not. In addition, HMOs are skilled at finding loopholes in any law or executive order.

Other problems with an HMO might include a lack of qualified specialists (many of its so-called specialists may actually lack board certification) and access to only second-rate hospitals.

In checking out an HMO, go first to the National Committee on Quality Assurance's Quality Compass database (www.ncqa.org) or call the NCQA at (800) 839-6487. Also check the evaluation of your HMO by the AMA and AHA's Joint Commission on the Accreditation of Healthcare Organization (JCAHO). You can search the JCAHO's online Quality Check service at www.jcaho.com, which covers about 18,000 health care facilities, or call the JCAHO at (630) 792-5800. Never rely on score cards of patient satisfaction issued by the HMO itself. And if an HMO supplies you with a list of its affiliated doctors, be aware that this list is probably out of date. A doctor whose reputation you know to be excellent may have quit the HMO in disgust or have been fired for refusing to skimp on necessary care.

Before joining an HMO (if the choice is up to you rather than your employer), or as part of evaluating your current HMO, you should get the answers to certain questions: Are the plan's doctors rewarded for keeping costs down? If so, how? Are they given incentives to keep down the rate of referrals to specialists or the number of diagnostic tests ordered? Are the doctors under a gag rule not to discuss expensive medical options with their HMO patients? How does the HMO select its doctors? Are its specialists all board certified? How does the HMO pick the hospitals to which it steers its patients? Under what circumstances will you be shuttled for treatment to a nurse practitioner rather than a physician? What is the turnover rate of the HMO's patients *and* of its primary-care doctors?

If the benefits coordinator or other plan representative you talk with is evasive or gives incomplete answers to these questions, your primary-care doctor under the plan (or the doctor you think you will choose *if* you join the plan) might be more forthcoming. You might attempt a frank discussion with him or her about such questions as these: How much time on average does the physician spend with each HMO patient? How does this compare with the amount of time he or she spent with patients before affiliating with the HMO or the amount of time he or she currently spends with non-HMO patients? Does he or she feel pressured to provide assembly-line care? Is he or she thinking seriously about quitting the HMO in question?

This discussion only scratches the surface of the HMO problem. For further information, see the managed care consumer guide at the American Association of Retired Persons Web site at www.aarp.org.

13 ·

Checking Out Your Date, Lover, or Spouse

Millions of American women are routinely beaten by their boyfriends or husbands. An estimated 1,400 of these victims are murdered each year; thousands more are disfigured or maimed. In many cases, their children also suffer direct physical and sexual abuse from the out-of-control husband or lover. And many other tragedies can result from getting involved with the wrong man: He may be (or become) HIV positive as a result of high-risk sexual behavior or needle sharing that he neglected to tell the woman about. He may be a compulsive philanderer who will sleep with all her friends and make her life miserable even if neither he nor she becomes infected with any disease as a result. Or he may turn out to be a con man or professional bigamist whose ultimate aim is to loot her bank account and abscond with the cash.

If you have entered or are about to enter into a new sexual or marital relationship, you need to check out your partner. Some of the tips that follow are applicable to any and all new relationships, but others relate only to situations in which you harbor the strongest of doubts. In the latter such cases, a thorough background check on your partner may be psychologically necessary for you to convince yourself to do what you already know deep down inside that you should do—split.

These techniques are presented in an order that reflects the dynamics of an average new relationship rife with conflicting emotions and ambiguous signals. We begin with simple things you can do to learn about your partner's background without actually snooping. We then examine various methods for learning about the things he may be attempting to hide from you. Naturally, certain of these methods involve a risk of embarrassment for you if he should find out. I personally believe that it's wiser to run that risk early on rather than to wait until after the emotional, physical, or other forms of abuse have already begun.

13.1 Your First Steps in Protecting Yourself

You lessen your chances of getting involved with the lover or spouse from Hell by being extremely choosy about how and where you meet potential partners. The best situation is one in which a certain amount of prescreening is involved: Friends or relatives invite you to dinner to meet a person they know fairly well. Some dating services claim to prescreen applicants, but any screening they might actually perform will be extremely superficial.

If you meet a person who is entirely unvetted (for example, through a classified ad or at a bar or museum), always get his phone number rather than simply leaving him yours. Insist on getting his home number as well as his business number. If he won't give you his home number and refuses to say why, you'll know you don't need him in your life. If, on the other hand, he explains that he's already married or living with someone and doesn't want you calling his home, at least you're forewarned.

If a man gives you his home number, take a few seconds to look in the telephone white pages, just to make sure that the name and number fit. If you don't find the man's name, check with Directory Assistance (the number may be a new one or unlisted). If that doesn't work, try one or more of the continuously updated Internet people-finder directories.

It's also a good idea to spend an hour or so chatting with him on the phone between the time of your initial contact with him and the first date; if you begin to pick up bad vibes, you can always cancel the date.

Listen to What He Tells You

In your early dates and phone conversations with the subject, you should find out certain basic and easily verifiable facts such as where he grew up, where he went to school, what type of work he does, who his current employer is, his marital status, whether or not he has any kids from a previous marriage, and so forth. These are things that usually come out spontaneously in conversation. If not, you can easily ask about them without seeming intrusive. (This means staggering the questions over the course of several conversations. If you ask them all at once, you'll sound like a cop.) If you're talking with him on the phone, write down any important names or other details on the spot. If he reveals a key name while you're on a date, jot it down as soon as you're alone (you might want to excuse yourself to the powder room to do so).

If the subject was a complete stranger to you (and to your close friends) when you first met him, you should without fail check out some of what he says about himself. For instance: Call his alleged previous job to verify whether he ever worked there. Call his alleged present job to verify whether there's an extension listed in his name. Call the registrar's office or the alumni association at the college he claims to have attended and verify that he's in their records. Check the Internet white pages to verify that his parents do, in fact, have a phone listing in his alleged home town. If he says his parents are dead, search for their names in the Social Security Death Index at www.ancestry.com.

One easy thing to find out is his date and place of birth. Simply steer the subject to astrology or offer to read his palm as a pretext for asking this. Also at some point find out his full name and his mother's maiden name. If a thorough background check should become necessary, these facts will be important (see Chapter 7, "Collecting the 'Identifiers'").

Take your time getting to know this man before making any commitment, and get him to talk about himself as much as possible. Fortunately, this is something most men love to do. With a little encouragement from you, he may tell you all about his past and present sexual conquests. If he has a narcissistic personality, he will be quite vain about this and will talk in great detail if he gets subtle cues that this turns you on (what you hear may be enough to decide you against pursuing this relationship).

Whether he's talking about former girlfriends or anything else, listen carefully and interject tactful little questions that can lay the basis for further investigation if necessary. When he talks about "this girl I was once involved with," ask when and where he met her and encourage him to elaborate with as much detail as possible (hopefully including her name). Be alert for improbable elements within any of his stories and also for contradictions between one story and another (as when the "Nancy" in one story becomes "Jane" in a later version of the same incident).

The telephone rather than a candle-lit dinner is the best medium for such conversations because you can take detailed notes as he talks. But if, for some reason, he rambles best over drinks at a bar, write down afterward as much as you can remember—the *who*s, *what*s, *when*s, and *where*s.

Above all, encourage him to talk about his childhood and family. Most men who abuse their wives or girlfriends come from dysfunctional families in which abuse was a way of life. If Joe comes from such a family, you have a strong possibility of trouble unless he's gone through intensive therapy. Of course, Joe will not open up about the traumas of his childhood during the first or second date (and why should he? he doesn't want you to think he's emotionally disturbed), but eventually you should steer him into this area. Make things easy for him by first revealing a few of your own childhood traumas (such as they may be).

If you jot down notes during each telephone conversation and after each date, you will soon have a considerable reservoir of information for potential checking. (*Warning:* Don't leave the notes where he can find them if he decides to snoop on *you*.)

Don't expect that what he tells you will be 100 percent truthful. Most people have very imperfect and selective memories; they exaggerate things to put themselves in a better light (or to heighten the humor in a story); they smooth over their failures; they concoct all kinds of rationalizations for things that went wrong. However, you should be alert for any claims or stories that appear to go beyond the normal kind of fibbing we all engage in. If Joe tells you he majored in psychology (because he knows you're interested in psychology) when he really majored in business but *wishes* he majored in psychology (and in fact took courses in psychology), that's one thing. When Joe tells you he has a degree from Harvard when he really only attended a local community college for a couple of semesters, that's more serious. When Joe tells you he spent three years traveling around the world in the late 1980s when he really spent those years (as you learn later from a mutual friend) in prison for burglary, that should be the final straw.

Is He Hiding Something from You?

You can never know for sure whether or not your new boyfriend is hiding any secrets from his past. If you're really suspicious, you might induce him to disclose his secrets by casually remarking that a girlfriend of yours has a brother who works as a PI and who once saved her from getting involved with the wrong guy by checking him out ahead of time. Or you might remark that you once dumped a guy after finding out he'd lied to you about his past. Your new boyfriend might then, after some reflection, start volunteering certain negative information about himself to put a spin on it and thus minimize the damage or even make himself look like a martyr (ex-cons are often geniuses at this). For instance, he may tell you that a girlfriend once filed assault charges against him but it was really just a misunderstanding, and besides she withdrew the charges. Although his story may sound plausible, you should remember that the woman in question isn't present to give her side of the story (nor are the cops who answered her 911 call or the emergency-room doctor who treated her bruises).

If Joe fails to talk about his past much on the first date or so, this might just be a natural reticence. But if he continues to be closemouthed about himself, try to discuss with him the reasons for his reticence. If he flatly refuses to recognize it as a problem, be aware that he'll probably take the same attitude to other problems in your relationship later on. This, as well as the possibility that he's hiding something, should be considered if you're trying to decide whether or not to continue seeing him.

Keep Your Eyes Open

If you decide to get romantically involved with Joe, don't let it become a relationship that revolves exclusively around your own house or apartment and your own family and friends. First, encourage him to introduce you to people in his own life. Insist on spending much of the time at his place—and while you're there, keep your eyes open. I'm not talking about overt snooping, just the kinds of things you might normally notice. For instance, are there any prescription medications in his bathroom medicine cabinet, on kitchen shelves, or in the refrigerator? Don't ask him about this (he will regard it as a highly intrusive question, and even if he doesn't display any anger, he'll hide future prescriptions that you might have an even greater interest in). If a medication arouses your suspicion, go to the public library and look in the *Physicians' Desk Reference*. This book, which is cross-indexed by brand name, generic name, and picture (color/shape of pill), will tell you exactly what a given medication is used for. (You can also find out about the medication at www.rxlist.com.) If it has multiple uses, you can sometimes figure out which condition your friend is taking it for by the dosage or the physician's name on the prescription label. The specialty of this physician (if he or she is board certified) can be learned in *The Official ABMS Directory of Board Certified Medical Specialists*. If the physician is not listed there, you can learn his or her claimed specialty through the guide to physicians (divided by type of practice) in the telephone yellow pages or by calling his or her office.

If you see a photo of a woman (or of a woman and children) prominently displayed in Joe's apartment, by all means inquire about it. If you want to be super-tactful, you might say "Oh, is that your *sister?*" But phrasing it this way may just encourage him to lie.

If you notice women's clothing in plain view in one of Joe's closets, or cosmetics on a dresser, this also is something you should ask him about. It may be that another girlfriend spends enough time with Joe to keep some of her belongings there, although this is a matter you and Joe should have already resolved (you should have asked about other women, and he should have answered frankly, before you ever set foot in his apartment). Of course, the presence of the clothing and makeup may simply mean that Joe engages from time to time in a harmless bit of cross-dressing.

You may later begin to notice things that are not quite as obvious; for instance, the sudden appearance of packages of herbal tea in his kitchen when you know he drinks only coffee and has zero interest in holistic medicine and health foods, or the remains of a Chinese take-out meal for two in his kitchen garbage. Whether to ask him about such things is a tricky question. On the one hand, you're dying to know. On the other hand, if you ask him, he may give you an extremely plausible (but totally dishonest) answer—and the only result will be that you've alerted him (as in the case of the prescription bottles) to the necessity of being more careful (that is, more systematically deceptive). In general, you should *not* ask him about something you observed unless it was something in plain view and that you could have plausibly spotted without overt snooping.

Keep an eye out for pornographic magazines or videotapes that indicate kinky sexual interests he has failed to tell you about (for you to look at any magazine that's lying around or to examine his collection of videotapes is not regarded as snooping, even if it is, kind of).

Also look for racing forms, turf magazines, and the like scattered around his apartment (potential trouble, if he's a gambling addict) or for any pamphlets and videos on strange religious or political topics (he may be under the influence of some religious cult or hate group, many of which are violent and almost all of which engage in criminal activity). You can easily check out a suspicious religious or political group by using the Internet. First, search for its Web site. Second, look for relevant information at the hundreds of sites listed at the Webgator directory of cults and hate groups (www.inil.com/users/dguss/wgator.htm). Third, contact experts for help (the American Family Foundation at www.csj.org for cults; the Southern Poverty Law Center at www.splcenter.org for hate groups).

Doing a Quick Search of His Apartment

If you really must do aggressive snooping, offer to cook dinner at his place—and then send him out with a list of things to purchase that should keep him occupied for an hour or more (include items that necessitate going to more than one store and that require him to pass by his favorite pub or video shop). Make sure that he's well down the street before you start your search. The main things you should look for are his address book or Rolodex, his appointment calendar, and his checkbook register. These will quickly give you a sense of the basic pattern of his life. Are there a large number of women's names in his address book? Does he have notations in his Rolodex about who's the best lay? (The latter information may be in a personal code of some kind.) What about doctor's appointments in his appointment book? And meetings with a lawyer or court appearance dates? Checkbook registers are not as important in this era of plastic credit, but you might find a record of child support payments or payments to a psychotherapist.

If you see a phone bill on his desk, you might look quickly at the toll records. If you see any 900 numbers or audiotex numbers listed, write them down. If you call one of these numbers later, you may find that it's a phone-sex line specializing in practices or proclivities that you weren't aware your partner had an interest in. (Certain of his sexual interests might also be revealed on his computer; see section 13.6.)

Your subject may also have scrapbooks or photo albums either in plain sight or in a closet; these may include pictures of a former wife and children he has not told you about or of former girlfriends. Scrapbooks may also have news clippings about his past that provide information very different from what he has been telling you. (See section 13.7 for more on his old photos.)

13.2 Observe Him in Action

You can often learn more from observing how he interacts with his ex-wife, children, parents, and siblings (both in person and on the phone) than you can by snooping. Does he see his kids frequently? Does he talk with them on the phone in a caring manner? Does he pay child support regularly? Before committing to this guy, you are well advised to spend some time with him and the kids and see how he interacts with them in person, not just on the phone. Does he lose his temper easily? Is he over-critical? Do the kids seem afraid of him or excessively withdrawn in his presence?

If possible, you should go with him to pick them up and observe how he interacts with his ex-wife. Does she seem afraid of him? Or do the two of them still seem to be pals? Some women get jealous if their new lover is still on friendly terms with an ex-wife or ex-girlfriend, but you should view this as a golden opportunity to observe his behavior in situations that offer vital insights into his personality and character.

Also note how he deals with his parents and siblings. We have already discussed how you should encourage him to talk about them. But talk is cheap: The man who says he has the world's greatest mom may demonstrate the most grotesque loathing for her when you go with him to visit her. Before committing to a long-term relationship, insist on meeting any of your partner's parents or siblings who live within practical traveling distance. (Among other things, this is a good way of checking that he's really who he says he is and not a con artist using false ID.)

When you have dinner with his family, it is important to observe not only his behavior toward the others (with you there, he may be artificially on his best behavior) but also their behavior toward one another. Do they appear to be warm and affectionate as a family group? Or is there tension in the air to an abnormal degree? The interaction at the dinner table may provide your first clue that he comes from a dysfunctional family (he himself may be blithely unaware of this on a conscious level and therefore may have given no indication of it when talking to you about his childhood). Of course, if you are not a mental health professional, you can't really make a final determination on family dysfunction (in some families, yelling and screaming serves a healthy purpose). But you do have two eyes and two ears: If Joe's father controls Joe's mother through verbal intimidation and put-downs, you have grounds for concern that Joe might try the same tactics on you at some point.

13.3 Cultivating Informants

Always try to make friends with your lover's best buddies' girlfriends or wives. At least one of these women may have learned many of your lover's secrets during pillow talk with her own partner. If she likes and trusts you, she will pass on much of the gossip (unless, of course, she's the one secretly involved with your lover on the side).

13.4 Checking Out His Paper Trail

How deeply you want to look into your lover's past depends on many circumstances: If he's someone from out of town who was unknown to any of your friends and acquaintances before you met him, if some of his stories don't quite add up, or if you just have an instinctive feeling that something's wrong, you would be well advised to do some checking in public records.

Criminal Records

To check criminal records, you must know where the subject has lived in past years, his date of birth, his SSN, and his full name. For tips on how to conduct such a search, see section 9.8, "Criminal Court Records." But be aware of the pitfalls: County and state court records often are inaccurate or less than current; a sloppy search can conjure up false links between an innocent person and crimes that in fact were committed by someone else with the same name; and records accessible to the public include only *convictions* (if Joe's ex-wife chose to drop the assault charges against him before trial, you will not learn about it through a routine public-records check, nor will you learn about his rape trial if he was found innocent on a technicality). In addition, a criminal records check will be worthless if Joe is living under a carefully crafted false identity and has not revealed to you his real identity. If you suspect that the latter is the case, you could look for Joe's face on one of the many Internet "wanted" sites maintained by police departments and citizens' anti-crime groups (a directory of such sites is at www.inil.com/users/dguss/wgator.htm).

If your suspicions about Joe's past just won't subside, you might consider paying a public records search firm to verify his identity and do a *thorough* criminal records check nationwide. This advice is not just for a new relationship but also for a situation in which the guy you've been with for a couple of years suddenly starts to act abusive or strangely secretive.

If you have kids, and the man was a stranger both to you and to your community when you first met him, you should *always* check to see whether he's listed as a sex offender, no matter how sweetly he behaves. A state-by-state directory of online sex offender registries can be found at www.inil.com/users/dguss/wgator.htm. At a minimum, check the state in which he was living when you first met him and the state or states in which he claims to have lived (or in which you have learned on your own that he lived) before meeting you.

If he has a child or children living with him who seem not to have any contact with the mother (or if he tells you the mother is dead), you should search the missing children's sites on the Internet (such as www.childquest.org), which often include age-enhanced pictures of missing children as well as pictures of their alleged abductor (usually a parent). Links to many of these sites are found at www.inil.com/users/dguss/wgator.htm (go to "Missing Persons").

Civil Records

If your lover is someone who's lived in your metropolitan area for a number of years, it's feasible for you to check out his financial stability on your own. You may already have questions on this score because of letters from credit collection agencies you've seen lying around in his apartment or because of dunning phone calls he's received while you were in the apartment. You can search at the county courthouse for tax liens, wage garnishments (the latter may be for child support), and listings in the judgment docket of money judgments obtained against him in court cases. You can search in the bankruptcy files at the federal courthouse to see whether he (or any business he owns or used to own) has ever filed for bankruptcy. You can search the UCC filings to see whether he has a heavy debt load. You can search at the register of deeds office for any foreclosure actions against his home. You can search at the parking violations bureau to see whether he has a pathologically excessive number of unpaid parking tickets. What you uncover may suggest a pattern of disordered behavior that will inevitably spill over into his relationship with you. (It also may suggest that he has, or has had, a gambling or cocaine problem.)

Also check the local court indexes and those for any jurisdictions in which he previously lived to find any cases in which he is listed as either plaintiff or defendant. (Chapter 9 explains how to search the local court indexes on your own and how to obtain searches elsewhere.) You may find that he's been sued for fraudulent activity or for harassing a former girl-friend (be sure to get the full court record on *any* case in which a woman is the plaintiff and he's the defendant).

This brings us to the question of his divorce. If you've listened carefully while he talked (and talked and talked) about it, you'll already know where it was obtained and the approximate date. If court records in divorce cases are open to the public in the given jurisdiction, check to see whether there's any allegations of spousal abuse (either physical or emotional) or of child abuse, any restraining order against your lover, and whether or not he has to pay child support or alimony under the terms of the divorce. If the court records are sealed, you can at least get the name of the ex-wife's attorney. It may not be wise to contact a volatile ex-wife directly while you're still involved with her former husband, but you might ask your best friend to call her on a pretext of concern for your well-being.

Just because there are no divorce records involving your lover does not mean he doesn't have an ex-common-law wife or has not otherwise fathered children. Indeed, a man who has never been legally married may still have a string of paternity suits, restraining orders, palimony judg-ments, and so on in his past. Always check for such cases in the relevant court indexes, and also check with the state office of child support to see whether Joe is wanted for failing to pay up. (Web links to deadbeat dad wanted lists from several states can be found at www.inil.com/users/dguss/wgator.htm.) If Joe has not told you about any children, you may still find pictures of them in his wallet or in his bedroom chest of drawers.

Selective Public-Records Searching

Although you might not have time to check the entire paper trail on your new lover, certain incidents might trigger a check of a specific record. Let's say you and he decide to rent a car to go away for the weekend. He may try to rent the car but is rejected, and the car has to be rented in your name. Because car rental agencies generally check with driving history databases nationwide before accepting a driver, this rejection may indicate that your lover has a conviction for driving while intoxicated or under the influence of a controlled substance. Depending on the policies of the given rental agency, the rejection might also indicate that he has been involved in one or more serious accidents or has been convicted for fleeing the scene of an accident or of being in possession of a stolen vehicle. You might call the car agency the following week (after being careful to do most of the driving over the weekend) to find out what its criteria for rejection of a customer are. And then you might conduct a search of the subject's driving record (see section 10.2, "Department of Motor Vehicles Records").

Note that your suspicions on his driving record should also be triggered if, before the trip, he comes up with some excuse for not renting the car himself and asks you to do it. A subsequent driving check may uncover information suggesting that he was aware his application would be rejected and that, in effect, he lied to you.

13.5 If You Think He's Not Who He Says He Is

Let's say he's never told you anything about his past life. You might search his wallet while he's in the shower (if you haven't already done so), or wait until he goes out to the convenience store and then search any drawers in which he's likely to keep additional ID cards. If you find ID under another name or multiple names, don't bother to confront him about it. He'd probably just tell you he's a government secret agent (the time-worn excuse of con men and other users of false ID). Simply walk out the door and never return.

If you don't find alternative ID, you may want to conduct a more systematic search over time for various other signs of deception. Most of the following items may, each by itself, be meaningless (or easily rationalized away). Taken severally, however, they may form a clear pattern:

- Possession of a Social Security Number that that was issued only very recently (see section 7.4, "Making Use of the SSN Code")

- Lack of a driver's license (this may be because the subject has recently concocted a new identity and hasn't had time to add a driver's license to his ID cocktail, or it simply may be because his license has been revoked—see section 13.4)

- A current learner's permit or a new driver's license that was preceded by a learner's permit, road test, or the like (this should be especially puzzling if the subject claims to have lived in places where you know a driver's license would be essential or if the subject is, to your own knowledge, a skilled and experienced driver)

- Lack of a voter registration card or of any evidence at the local Board of Elections (or in voter records from other localities where you believe he has lived) that he has ever been a voter

- Use of personal checks with low numbers such as 100–150 or 1000–1050 (these numbers indicate that the account is a brand new one)

- Occupancy at his present address for only a very short time

- Residence in your town or city for only a very short time

- No friends, or at least no friends that he knew before moving to your community

- No phone numbers of relatives or out-of-town friends in his address book

- No sign of any correspondence (or birthday or Christmas cards) from relatives or from out-of-town friends

- No high school or college yearbooks, family photos, or other personal memorabilia

- Possession of yearbooks that seem to fit the years the subject would have been in school but that don't include the subject's name (look through the photos, and you may find his face linked to another name)

- Photos of a woman signed "to Sam with Love" (or the like) when you know the subject as Joe, not Sam

- Personal letters of any type addressed to a male name other than the one the subject is now using

- Evidence that he purchased or rented his house or ordered the initial utility connects several months before he actually arrived in town (this might suggest a planned disappearance from a previous address in order to evade a reverse trace—see section 4.33, "Reverse Traces")

- Brand-new credit cards (you can tell this by the validation and expiration dates on the cards and especially by the "member since" date; be aware, however, that the reason for the new cards may be that he's simply transferred his balances to take advantage of interest rate variations)

- Secured credit cards with low credit limits

The last item may be the most revealing of all. If the subject's credit card bills show that his card is secured (that is, the card holder agrees to keep in a savings account with the issuing bank enough money to cover the credit limit), and if the limit itself is quite small, this may mean that the subject is in the beginning stages of building a new credit history under a new identity. (Even if his identity is for real, you might ask yourself why the subject would need a secured card if he appears to always have plenty of cash and if he boasts about his high salary at vaguely described former jobs. Does he perhaps have a disastrous credit history? It would be foolish to commit yourself to a long-term relationship with this man until you've learned a lot more about his current and past finances.)

13.6 Is There Another Woman?

Whether or not you're married to him, all bets are off in the age of AIDS if you have strong reason to believe that he's fooling around behind your back. You have the right to know for sure so that you can make your decision either to leave him or to give him one final chance.

In this war of the sexes, the advantage is all with you. Most men who cheat want to get caught subconsciously and will provide you with little clues. Those who are psychopaths (those who lack more than a rudimentary conscience) may not want to get caught but lack impulse control and thus also provide inadvertent clues. Likewise, men in both these categories have a certain contempt for women; they underrate their girlfriend's or wife's ability to detect their deceptions.

Paranoia?

Before you launch your investigation of your husband or lover, make sure that you're not on a paranoid jealousy trip. What seems strong evidence to you may not seem that way to an objective observer. Sure, Joe's taking showers twice as often, but maybe it's just because he's playing more racketball. Discuss things with your therapist or your mother (but not with your best friend—she may be the reason for those extra showers or his new brand of cologne). If your suspicions continue, look first for concrete evidence such as lipstick on his clothing, an earring on the floor of his car, and certain intimate physical details.

In Your Own Bedroom?

You may suspect, among other things, that he's smuggling women into the house when you're not home. This may especially be a problem if you're working and he's not (he entertains the woman from down the block while you're slaving away to pay the rent) or if the two of you work different hours. You can check for hairs on the bed that are neither yours nor his by wrapping scotch tape around your finger and then rubbing it over the pillows and sheets. Of course, other evidence may be available on the sheets and in the bathroom.

To Videotape or Not to Videotape

Although you may be tempted to hide a long-playing tape recorder under the bed before you leave for work, don't do it. Secret audiotaping of a person is a violation of federal law. However, secret *video*taping (providing that there is no audio component) is allowed under federal law and also under state law in all but a few states. Thus, if your lawyer assures you that there is no law against it in your own state, you might buy a new bedside lamp with a built-in video camera, as advertised in mail-order catalogs or in display ads for retail "spy shops." But the video camera must not under any circumstances be set to record audio sound. Otherwise, you can be prosecuted just as if you were using a tape recorder or a wiretap device. (It is probably best to use a video camera that *cannot* be set for sound; otherwise, your boyfriend and his other lover could set you up both for prosecution and for a civil suit.)

Telephone Warning Signs

If you and Joe still maintain separate residences, you may notice that he disconnects the phone or leaves it off the hook overnight when you're not there (or that he screens his calls and simply doesn't answer you on occasions when you know he's home). You may also notice that he disconnects the phone, leaves it off the hook, or simply ignores the ringing when you *are* there. (If you ask him about this, he may get visibly agitated or give you a story about how he doesn't want his boss calling him at home.)

You may also notice that he gets calls when you're at his home that seem to make him nervous and that he abruptly terminates.

Finally, you yourself may become the target of frequent hang-up calls at the residence you share with Joe, at your own separate residence, or even at your office. Possibly such hang-up calls are from Joe's other girlfriend, who is expressing her hostility toward you or her curiosity about you (or both).

Whenever you receive a hang-up call or Joe receives a call under any curious circumstances, you can press the call return code (*69) to find out the number from which the call was made. Whenever the call comes in at Joe's home rather than yours, wait until he's in the shower or taking out the trash before pressing call return.

If Joe has Caller ID (see section 11.7, "Making Use of Caller ID"), don't hesitate to check the incoming numbers when you're alone in his apartment.

Your Secret Ally

In your effort to collect evidence on Joe, you may find that the other woman is your ally of sorts: She *wants* you to know and will "accidentally" leave cosmetics, shampoo, bobby pins, or even more intimate traces of her presence in the bedroom or bathroom. Whether she's trying to drive you out of Joe's life or just being catty is immaterial. She's giving you the clues you need—use them!

His Cheating at Hotels and Motels

More often than not, Joe will be cheating at motels, hotels, or at his secret lover's apartment rather than at home. Start keeping a record by date and time of every evening when he claims he has to work late, every weekend when he cancels on you because of alleged work emergencies, or every night you call him late but he's not yet home. You may need these records to cross-check against his credit card charges at restaurants, motels, or the toll calls on his phone bill. Also look for such telltale signs as matchbooks from a hotel, motel, or candlelight-mood restaurant in his coat pocket.

Note that many shady establishments (such as motels frequented by prostitutes and their Johns, companion services that send call girls to a client's hotel, strip clubs that serve as fronts for prostitution, or high-class houses of prostitution located in private residences) take credit cards. However, such businesses are very sensitive to the privacy needs of their clientele. Thus, they usually adopt innocuous business aliases for credit card transactions (which is completely legal and never a problem with the credit card companies). If a transaction in Joe's credit card records strikes you as suspicious (for example, $500 spent at a "Church Street Health Club" that is not listed in the local yellow pages), you may be able to trace the real name using the business alias index or the corporate name index at the county courthouse.

If the credit card receipt happens to provide an address, go to the online street directory (both the yellow pages and the white pages) to get the telephone numbers and names of all telephone subscribers at the address in question or on the same block. If it turns out to be a residential block or apartment house, you can be sure that many residents will be willing to give you an earful about the illicit activities they have observed.

Clues in His Wallet and How to Follow Them Up

- **Business cards.** If you see a woman's business card in his wallet, don't jump to conclusions—she might just be the Xerox service rep and nothing else. However, if she has added her home number to the card, you will definitely want to check her out.

- **Names on scraps of paper.** Here you may find the woman's full name and phone number, her first name and phone number, initials and a phone number, or a phone number by itself. Observe the kind of paper the number is written on. Is it the inside of a restaurant matchbook cover? Is it from a paper napkin on which you can see also part of the Starbucks logo? Generally, business-only contact numbers are not transmitted on coffee-bar napkins.

- **Calling the numbers.** You may want to call the most suspicious numbers and see whether you get an answering machine that gives you a name and tells you whether it's a home or office number and whether it's a single person's line or a couple's. (To get the answering machine at a person's home, call during a weekday when the person would be at work.) Always use your Caller ID blocking code when making such calls. If you call a woman's number from Joe's wallet and a man's voice answers, it may be the woman's husband *or* it may be that the woman actually lives alone and the recording by a male voice is intended to ward off telephone sexual harassment. If you call a number designated by initials or with no name attached, and a man answers, it may be for one of the preceding reasons *or* it may be that Joe has a male lover *or* it may simply be the number for one of Joe's drinking buddies or Joe's shrink.

To get a better sense of just what kind of household you're dealing with, call back as a supposed pollster in the early evening. If a man answers, ask for the lady of the house. If a woman answers, ask for the man of the house.

- **Reversing the numbers.** Your next step should be to reverse the most suspicious numbers through an online people finder to get the names and addresses that correspond to each number. If a particular number is unlisted, it may not be reversible in the people finder directories; in such a case, you can get it reversed using an online information broker or you might simply make another pretext phone call to the household in question (tell them you're looking for a long-lost relative).

After you have a woman's full name and address, and you are reasonably certain she's the one Joe's involved with, try to gather some more background information on her. See whether any of your girlfriends know her. If feasible, get to know one of her close friends (or someone who dislikes her) to pick up some gossip.

Conducting a Thorough House Search

If you and Joe are living in the same household, you may decide to do a thorough search of the house. Arrange to stay home some day while he's at work or at a ball game. Systematically search his closet, his chest of drawers, his home office desk and filing cabinet, and especially the filing cabinet drawer (or the shoebox) in which he keeps his financial and other personal papers. Look at his credit card receipts and monthly statements and his bank statements and canceled checks. Especially look for receipts from bars, restaurants, hotels, or motels (as described earlier in this chapter). Look also for records of purchases that might be gifts for another woman (such as items from a florist or a jewelry or lingerie shop). Check especially the records of any periods when he was out of town on business—you may find that his trip last winter to a business conference in Denver was really more like a week for two at an Aspen ski resort. (Note that some of his credit card charges may be made on a corporate rather than a personal card. The only way you can know about these charges is by peeking at the receipt in his wallet before he turns it in.)

To search the apartment systematically if you're not living with Joe is a drastic invasion of his privacy. I don't advise doing this, but if you feel you must, do it only when you are on the premises with his express consent. *Never* enter the apartment without his invitation—you could face criminal charges. One approach is to arrange to stay in the apartment when he leaves for work some morning. Tell him the place is getting grungy and you want to clean it for him. If he accepts your offer, you will have gained the perfect cover for your search. You really *will* clean the apartment for him—until it's absolutely spotless. But in the process, you'll keep your eyes open and let your fingers do the walking through the kitchen garbage bag, the bedroom and bathroom trash baskets, the outdoor trash can, and the medicine cabinet.

You'll also peek at his bills and private papers (just as a wife or live-in lover would do), especially if these papers are cluttered all over his desk and need straightening. In looking through them, you may strike pay dirt—a love letter or "Love You Forever" birthday card from his other girlfriend. If not, you may find suspicious credit card receipts or telephone toll records showing that he has been making lengthy late-night long-distance calls to a single number in another city or suburb (by reversing this number through the online white pages, you may find the other woman at last).

Whether you are a live-in or live-out lover, you can use this systematic house cleaning as a means to satisfy your curiosity about a wide variety of things that Joe may or may not have been hiding from you and that you never had the time or motivation to search for thoroughly: his medical bills, the little black book he once joked about, the pornography hidden in the locked drawer of his desk (if you can find the key), and so forth.

Searching His Computer

Many PC users today have personal-organizer software programs to keep track of addresses, appointments, checking accounts, and other aspects of their personal and business lives. Such a program may provide direct or indirect evidence of your subject's liaisons.

You might also examine the chronological list of URLs he's visited to find any sexually oriented ones. A list of his most recent URL visits can be found simply by clicking the down-arrow button next to the Address box on the Web browser toolbar. For a longer list, click the History folder in the Go menu.

You may find far more revealing information by clicking the Favorites button on the browser toolbar to get his "hot list" (the list of URLs to which he has created shortcuts). Generally, these are sites he visits frequently or would like to visit frequently if he had the time. A sexually oriented site listed here (especially an alt.sex newsgroup) is usually more significant than one he casually visited while Web surfing.

Records of email he has sent and email he has received may be found in his Sent Items folder and Incoming Messages folder, respectively. However, he may choose to create special subject folders for certain types of messages. Usually, all such folders will be listed on the Filing Cabinet menu, which is accessed through the File button on the browser's menu bar.

His personal list of important email addresses (including possibly those of women with whom he has been chatting online) will be in his Address Book, also accessed from the menu bar's File button.

Also look in his word-processing files, where you might find drafts of letters he has sent to various women under obvious or not-so-obvious file names (such as "Barbara," "Barb," "Bar," "Ba," "Baba," or "XXX").

He may have deleted many embarrassing files in anticipation of your snooping. But unless he used shredder software, they weren't really destroyed. When he clicked the Delete button, he merely removed a file from the directory so that it could be automatically overwritten when and if more disk space is needed. In a computer with a large hard-disk drive, most recently deleted files will not yet have been overwritten and can be retrieved from the Recycle Bin. However, if Joe has "permanently" deleted them by emptying the Recycle Bin, you can still retrieve them by using Norton Utilities' UnErase Wizard.

Note: Searching your lover's computer is something that might be construed as illegal, especially if the two of you are not living together. You will be on safest legal grounds if you have already been using the computer with his consent and have files of your own on it. Do not remove any printouts or floppy disk copies of his files from his home or office without his permission.

Hint: If he has a new computer, you might get him to give you his old one. When it's yours, you can unerase his files at your leisure.

Another hint: If you own a computer and he doesn't, encourage him to use yours, even offer to train him a little. But don't tell him the secrets of file recovery.

Searching His Office
If you don't find evidence of his cheating anywhere in the house, it might be in his office desk at work. Here, if you're his wife, you have a definite advantage: You can show up unannounced a few minutes before he's to return from lunch and tell the secretary you'll wait for him in his inner office (with the door closed of course).

His Car and His Parking Tickets
Don't forget to search his car. Here again, the evidence might be cigarettes in the ash tray, matchbooks or receipts of various kinds in the glove compartment, a used condom under the seat, and the mileage on the speedometer—you may find he traveled a couple hundred miles last weekend even though he *claims* he spent the entire weekend locked away in his office finishing an audit report.

You can also go down to the municipal building and check the parking violations bureau index. Get the index number for each of his unpaid parking fines and then pull the original ticket to see the location of the violation. It may have been a residential block in a neighborhood where you've never known him to go. Get all the names and phone numbers on that block from an online or CD-ROM crisscross directory. Cross-check it against all the names and phone numbers of women in his address book or in his company's internal phone directory.

The Stake-Out
If you're pretty sure that he's seeing a certain woman and you have her street address, you can stake out her house during the hours when he's likely to visit her. (You should conduct this or any other form of surveillance

described here only if you are confident that you can stay cool and calm; if you are emotionally distraught, get your best friend to do it for you.) The traditional procedure is to borrow or rent a car he won't recognize, put on a wig and sunglasses, park down the street, and see whether he enters or leaves the house. If he enters or leaves along with the woman, snap their picture using a telephoto lens.

If you think he's bringing women home to his own house, you can adopt a method from Sherlock Holmes. The great fictional detective watched the comings and goings at the evil Professor Moriarty's residence by disguising himself as a tramp. Well, you can disguise yourself as a homeless woman, complete with wig and sunglasses, ragged old clothes, heavy makeup, and pillows to add the appearance of an extra forty pounds to your weight. (You can even change the shape of your face by stuffing your mouth with surgical cotton.) You can then ensconce yourself with a shopping bag full of old blankets (to conceal your camera, not a machine gun) down the block from your lover's house. If his new girlfriend arrives in her own car and you don't recognize her, jot down her license plate number (see section 11.5, "License Plate Surveillance of a Subject's Visitors"). If she later leaves the house alone and passes you on the way to her car or the bus stop, you can shout wild imprecations at her (if it makes you feel any better) without her having the slightest suspicion of who you really are.

Following Your Suspect

You also might try shadowing your wayward lover. Again with the borrowed or rented car and the sunglasses, stake out his place of work in the afternoon and follow him when he leaves (or park near his house in the morning and follow him on his sales route). If you have only the evenings available, park near his home and wait for him to come out after supper for his tomcat prowl. A camera is essential if you want to confront him with your evidence, but you should also take along a tape recorder with a microphone clipped to your blouse so that, without taking your hands off the wheel, you can dictate a record of the addresses he visits. Also essential are binoculars or a nightscope so that you can read off the license plate numbers of other people who arrive at those addresses (such as the woman who arrives in her own car and goes into the motel room with him) as well as the names on the mailboxes of any homes he visits.

In tailing your lover, stay a couple of cars behind him and don't do anything to draw attention to yourself (such as running a red light to keep up with him), even if it means losing the tail. You can always try again another day *unless* he realizes he's being followed.

If he goes into a bar, you can inquire later about this establishment to determine whether it's a gay bar, a pick-up spot for heterosexual singles, or simply a friendly neighborhood watering hole like the one in *Cheers*.

Note: If you have *any* reason to believe that your lover at this stage in your relationship could turn violent if he knew you were following him, or if you find that he's traveling into dangerous neighborhoods (after drugs or prostitutes, perhaps), do not attempt to tail him. Just get out of the relationship.

13.7 Finding the Women in His Past

In general, it's not a good idea to seek out the women from his past while you're still involved with him. But if you've made a decision to leave him (or are strongly considering doing so), a chat with one or two of these women might strengthen your resolve. Perhaps this might be the time finally to have that heart-to-heart chat with the ex-wife he's always raging against. If you don't know where she lives, you may be able to locate her through her divorce attorney (see section 4.12, "Tracking a Person Through His or Her Family, Friends, and Ex-Spouse(s)" for other methods of locating ex-spouses).

If you had the foresight early in your relationship to encourage Joe to talk about his ex-girlfriends, you will already have a string of names to contact. But if you didn't, or if you suspect that he withheld certain names, you can look in his little black book (if you can find it) and in any ordinary address books he has kept from years back. If you can't find any such book, you can look in the back-edition white pages, city directories, and crisscross directories (and the archives of out-of-date voter registration street listings) in your city—and in nearby cities where he previously lived—to find the names of persons with whom he once shared a household. Such a search might include the back-edition campus directories of colleges he once attended. Of course, some of the names you uncover may just be relatives, former landlords, or co-tenants rather than former girlfriends.

His filing cabinet or desk files (or the shoebox files stuffed away in his closet) may contain old letters or birthday or Christmas cards from ex-girlfriends. The books on his bookshelf may include a volume that was a gift from an ex-girlfriend and has her signature and expressions of undying love on the flyleaf. An old photo album or scrapbook he's squirreled away on the top shelf of a closet may contain pictures of some ex-girlfriends.

If there's no identifying information on the back of a photo (or written underneath it in the album), you may be able to match it against the picture and name of a girl in his college yearbook. You may also find clues in the photo itself and in other photos that appear to be from the same roll. *When* were the photos taken? Fashion and hairstyle cues may help you here, as may the year of manufacture of a car in the background (the latter will at least tell you the first *possible* year in which the photos could have been taken). *Where* were they taken? If it was during a vacation or honeymoon, you may recognize a familiar tourist attraction in the background. If not, study the vegetation, terrain, and architecture in the photos for clues to the approximate location; for instance, bare hills or mesas, cactuses, a house built in a pseudo-adobe style would suggest that the picture was taken somewhere in the American Southwest. Also look for street, highway, or store signs in the background (you might even find a license plate with enough detail displayed to reveal the state).

You may have enough knowledge of your subject's past that you will quickly recognize from such clues the probable location of the photos. If not, you can narrow down your search area by using the various people-finder, business-finder, and street-map locator services on the Internet (see section 4.2, "Important Search Tools").

As discussed earlier, an ex-girlfriend or common-law wife may have sued the subject and possibly obtained a judgment against him. Or he and she may have jointly owned real estate or a business—or a pet—at some point (look in real estate records at the register of deeds office and also examine the county's property tax rolls and pet license records). In general, the more carefully you have listened to your lover's ramblings about previous romances, the more pointed the questions you have asked, and the better the notes you have taken, the easier it will be for you to find his previous victims.

14 ·

Businesses and Nonprofit Organizations

By learning how to background an individual, you have picked up much of what you need to know to background businesses and nonprofit organizations. Many of the records that apply to individuals (such as UCC filings and tax liens) also apply to corporate entities. In researching a corporation—or in backgrounding its CEO or chief stockholder—an experienced researcher will jump back and forth from corporate filings to individual filings, using the clues found in one to search out information in the other.

14.1 Businesses, Legitimate and Otherwise

Finding a Business

At KnowX (www.search3.knowx.com), you can use the "Ultimate Business Finder" to search for any of over 11 million business names listed in corporate records, yellow pages, the federal employer ID number list, d/b/a records, and sales tax records. If you purchase a detail record (prices range from $0.95 to $6.95 for a single-state search), you will receive the company's address and telephone number, D-U-N-S number, federal employer ID number, and SIC code/Line of Business, as well as the name of the company's principal officer. (Of course if you just want to locate the phone number, you can go for free to the online yellow-page directories such as yellow-page.net and www.bigyellow.com.)

Another option is to consult Dun's Business Locator Disc, a CD-ROM available for free at many public libraries. This product (compiled from the same Dun & Bradstreet databases that KnowX accesses for much of its information) provides the addresses, phone numbers, Standard Industrial

Classification (SIC) codes, D-U-N-S numbers, and employee size ranges of over 10 million businesses nationwide.

Note that, through these electronic searches, you end up with the two most important identifiers for a business entity: the federal employer ID number (which is used in tax records) and the D-U-N-S number (which is used in credit checks). These two numbers are, for businesses, what the Social Security Number and date of birth are for individuals. A third identifier provided by the preceding searches, the SIC code/Line of Business, defines a business entity in terms of its product or service category (rather like naming the block a person lives on but not the street number). One or more of these identifiers may become important in an intensive search of online and offline business records.

Special Problems in Finding an Obscure Local Business
If you have an address for the business but cannot find a phone number listed in its name, look in the electronic crisscross directory to see what other businesses or individuals are listed at that address. You may discover that your target business is a subsidiary of, or a registered business alias or defunct former name of, another business with offices in the same suite. Or you may find that the address is a private residence, suggesting that the business is a small one that may be operated over a residential phone line of one of the household members. In other cases, the address may turn out to be that of a corporate registration service (described later in this section) or of a mail-receiving or mail-forwarding service (called a *mail drop*).

A foreign-language yellow-page directory or a foreign-language weekly newspaper will guide you to businesses that never advertise or attract customers outside their own ethnic community and that may not even be properly registered with the state or county because of language and cultural barriers. Local pornographic newspapers (and also alternative newsweeklies (such as the *Village Voice*) and many gay and lesbian newspapers that accept sex-industry display and classified advertisements) may help you find other small businesses that are not properly registered or that hide the nature of their services under an innocuous-sounding name.

Credit Reports
You can obtain a credit report on any of over 10 million U.S. businesses (and pay by credit card online) at the Dun & Bradstreet (D&B) Web site or at the Web sites of the various value-added gateway services that access the D&B databases. At the KnowX gateway (www.search3.knowx.com), select "D&B Business Records Plus," which offers a comprehensive background report including the business's credit rating, payment history, up to three years of financial summaries, and public filings such as UCCs, liens, judgments, lawsuits, and bankruptcies. (For information on obtaining business credit checks from Experian and directly from D&B, see section 8.2, "Alternatives to the Individual Credit Check.")

Post Office Box Renters

If a post office box is used for business purposes—for instance, the sale of printed material or the solicitation of funds—the postmaster of the station is required by postal regulations to give you the name and address of the person or business entity renting the box. This is how you can find the identity of, say, an advertiser of products for sale in your local newspaper's classified section if the ad provides no name but only the box number. If the ad does include a business name, the postal records may give you a more recent street address than can be found in the business name or corporate registration files at your county courthouse.

Postal Mailing Permits

Businesses can obtain several types of mailing permits. If the permit is identified by a number on the envelope (as in the franking of metered mail or the use of envelopes with postage-paid imprints), you can obtain the name and address of the permit holder simply by calling the nearest U.S. Post Office mail classification center (there are 37 throughout the United States). If you want a copy of the permit holder's permit application, you must make a request under the Freedom of Information (FOI) Act to the central post office of the city in which the business is located.

The types of permits include metered mail, precanceled stamp, imprint permit, first-class presort, and second-class mailing (the latter is used by newspapers and periodicals). Sometimes the different permit applications for a particular business will be filled out by different individuals; this information may give you the name of a silent partner whom you otherwise would not have learned about.

Business Name, Corporation, and Limited Partnership Indexes

Even the shadiest of businesses needs a bank account for depositing its checks. To open an account (and to comply with state registration laws), an entity might file as a partnership or limited partnership, a limited liability company (LLC) or limited liability partnership (LLP), a corporation incorporated within the state, a corporation doing business in the state but incorporated in another state, a not-for-profit corporation, an unincorporated association, or an individual, corporation, or partnership operating under an assumed business name (the assumed name is often called the d/b/a, which means *doing business as*).

Corporations generally file their registration papers with the corporation division of the state's department of state. You can usually obtain a search in person or by mail; in some states, you can order a search by phone or fax. The court indexes (although not the full files) are usually accessible online through public records information vendors or at a state or government Web site (see "Finding a Business" at the beginning of this chapter; also see section 8.27, "Corporate, Partnership, and D/B/A Files").

Partnership and business name (or d/b/a) filings may be found either on the state level or the county level (in the county where the entity has its mailing address), or there may be dual filing at both levels.

The indexes to the business name, partnership, and corporation registrations may be merged into a single alphabetical listing that is searchable at a computer terminal (or, for older records, in index books) in the file room. The business name file will usually contain a copy of the business name certificate telling who obtained it and providing an address for service of process. If the business was subsequently incorporated, the business name file may include a notation to that effect and the file number of the corporation file.

The corporation registration file will include the articles of incorporation (and amendments thereto) as well as certificates of incorporation, merger, or discontinuance and change-of-name certificates. If required, the incorporation papers will reveal the names and addresses of the corporation's principals; if not, you may find only the name and address of an agent authorized to receive legal papers (this may be either the company's attorney or a company specializing in corporate registrations). You should look on the jacket of the registration papers for the address, if any, of a law firm. (If you see the name *Julius Blumberg*, note that this is not the name of an attorney but simply the company that prints the legal forms most widely used in many states.) If you don't find an attorney's name anywhere, the owners may have done the filing without an attorney's help, and the person listed as the registering party is probably one of the principals.

Always take down the name and registration number of the notary public who witnessed the signature of the registering party: The notary may be the principals' attorney, a secretary for the attorney, or a secretary for the principals. A notary's address, and sometimes his or her license application, will be public record information that is filed with the county clerk and the state's department of state. (A nationwide directory of notaries can be found at www.notary-services.com; although this site currently lists only a fraction of the nation's notaries, it hopes to have listed more than 100,000 within a year or so.)

The limited partnership files are often more detailed than the corporate files, including names and addresses of general and limited partners, the percent ownership of each, agreements for how decisions will be made and profits shared, amendments to the rules, and all changes in the identities of limited and general partners and in the classes (for example, Class A or Class B) of limited partners.

In searching either electronic or hardcopy indexes, you should have the complete name of the business accurately spelled. The alphabetical listings in a large city or state will have many names containing the same key word (for example, "Princeton Associates, Inc.," "The Princeton Company," "Princeton Corporation," and "Princeton Enterprises"). Sometimes, if a name has already been registered, a new business that wants the name will simply use a different spelling; thus "Masada Real Estate" could become "Massada" or "Maseda" Real Estate.

Before you begin to search a hardcopy index book of older records, familiarize yourself with the alphabetizing system. For instance, are acronyms listed at the beginning of each letter listing, or are they listed throughout in strict alphabetical order? Are names that begin with numbers (for example, "301 West 13 Street Corporation") listed separately, or are they in alphabetical order as if spelled out?

Inexperienced researchers often waste time chasing down the names of apparent company officers who really are only employees of a corporate registration firm. One of the best known of these firms is CT Corporation System, which can register a business in all 50 states. Such firms are used by businesses that want to operate in many or all states without opening an office in each. A corporation incorporates in one state only—either its home state or in a state with minimal regulation, such as Delaware—and then acquires certificates to do business in other states. CT Corporation System maintains offices in all states and can guarantee that state and local law is being complied with in each case. It can also provide an address within the state for service of process on the corporation.

Sometimes the registration company's name will be on the registration papers; in other instances, individual employees of the registration company will be listed without the registration company's name appearing. In still other cases, the names of one or more of the actual principals will be listed as an incorporator or officer, but the registration company still will be designated as the agent for service of process. The registration company usually will not give you any information about a principal unless authorized to do so; however, they will forward your request to speak with one of the principals.

The corporation file will usually include any name-change certificates. However, you will not necessarily learn from the file whether the corporation previously existed as a d/b/a business or a limited partnership (LP). When you request the file, therefore, you should also request the files on previously registered d/b/a's or LPs with similar names. For instance, if the Markco Corporation, Inc., was registered in 1983, and you see that a Markco Associates was registered as a d/b/a the previous year, the latter may be the predecessor entity. If you search the file for this entity, you may uncover the name of a previous principal or previous attorney. And while you're at it, look for a Markco Foundation or Markco Fund set up for tax purposes.

If you are trying to chase down the various dummy names used in a sensitive real estate deal or a white-collar scam of some kind, the business registration indexes can be very useful. Often a complicated deal will involve a multiplicity of entities, each of which will be used only for a single transaction in a chain of transactions. You can sometimes spot the connection if all the registrations of these entities were filed during the same narrow time span by the same attorney. The key to this is the file numbers, which generally designate the order in which registrations were filed during each year. This order of registration can be easily checked online or at a computer terminal in the business registration office, provided that the database is searchable by file number or date. However, if you need to search older index books that have only a cumulative alphabetical listing without any reverse listing by file number, the order of filing may be difficult to trace. Your best shot will be to look in the supplementary monthly indexes for the file numbers closest to your target company's. If the company's file shows that it was incorporated in March 1985, you can ask the file room clerk whether the supplementary volume for that month is still available. Also, there may be a separate record of the filings in a daily ledger book that will reveal this information.

Corporations that fail to file their tax returns within a set period may lose their registration status. A notice to this effect will be placed in the corporate registration file, and the firm may also be listed on a roster of delinquent tax filers.

Annual State Corporate Filings

All states require domestic corporations (those incorporated in that particular state) to file an annual report with the secretary of state. These reports are more or less revealing, depending on the state's laws and regulations. Generally, if you study a corporation's annual reports going back to the first year of its incorporation, you can get some idea of its history: changes in address, changes in attorneys, and changes in officers and directors. If the corporation has changed its name, the name-change papers will usually be in the file. If the annual reports filed by the corporation under its old name before the change are not in the file, be sure to ask for them.

The paper trail of annual reports will sometimes turn up lively informants. A former officer may have quarreled with the principals and thus be willing to tell all. The office building manager at the corporation's former address may have information on its financial problems. In addition, the names of the firm's past and present attorneys may be a tip-off to secret corporate or organized crime links. If the business is controlled by a political or religious cult, the disappearance of a name from the list of officers and directors may indicate that the individual has defected.

Sales Brochures

A business may be extremely secretive around everyone *except* potential customers. In the late 1970s, a computer software company controlled by Lyndon LaRouche published a glossy sales brochure that listed dozens of its supposedly satisfied clients. A foray into the waiting area of the computer company's midtown Manhattan office produced a copy of the indiscreet brochure. Likewise, a trip to the office of another business—a Miami export/import firm—produced a copy of a brochure intended for distribution almost exclusively in the Middle East. The brochure included a mail drawer address in the Bahamas that turned out to be the same mail drawer used by a Mafia drug bank.

Signs on the Door; Lobby and Floor Directories

A friend of mine was trying to trace the business affairs of a Ku Klux Klan–linked toy distributor that for many years had been running several small businesses out of a suite of offices in a Manhattan office building. My friend went to the building and copied from the lobby directory all the business names for that suite. Then he went up to the floor the suite was on and copied the names from the floor directory. Then he went to the door of the suite and copied the names listed on the frosted glass. The listings were somewhat different in each case, and he ended up with nine names. He then headed for the business names index at the county courthouse.

This was admirable attention to detail: My friend recognized that each of the three sets of signs had been put up at a different time (it was an old building), and he was able to read them off like geological strata.

Clues in the Office or Waiting Area

If you visit the offices of a suspicious local business on some pretext or other, note any business permits or licenses, diplomas, or testimonials framed on the walls—this information will give you a fresh paper trail to follow. Note the receptionist's or secretary's name tag or the name plate on his or her desk—this person may become a source later. If there is a calendar on the wall, note the name of the company that gave it as a gift—this may be the business's printer or insurance underwriter. If there are magazines in the waiting area, note the names and addresses on the subscription labels—these may give you the home address of a company employee or they may be addressed to a company officer whose name you would not otherwise find. You may also discover in the waiting area various company promotional brochures, an annual report, a copy of the company's internal newsletter, and other useful materials. The company's in-house phone list or directory may be on the receptionist's desk or next to the waiting area phone provided for the convenience of visitors (or in the desk drawer underneath this phone). The waste basket next to the phone may contain a piece of paper revealing the name and address of an earlier visitor, perhaps a client or a supplier's customer representative. In some offices, a copy of the latest internal newsletter or phone list will be tacked to a bulletin board above a water fountain or next to the coffee machine or in the snack room; look here also for state and federal Labor Department notices and Occupational Safety and Health Administration (OSHA) injury and illness notices. Sometimes employees will tack up personal notices offering cars or condominiums for sale or announcing that they need a roommate or that their cat just gave birth to three kittens who need loving homes. Such notices (often found also in the company newsletter) will give you the names, the phone extensions, and sometimes the home phone numbers of potential sources.

Business Rip-offs

Business rip-offs fall into two basic categories: the fly-by-night business, which takes the customers' money fast and then disappears only to open under a new name and usually at a new location; and the year-in-year-out sleazy business that stays put at the same location and just brazens things out (for example, a dishonest auto repair shop). Businesses of both types leave behind irate consumers who often will lodge complaints with public and private agencies. Check first with your city and state consumer protection agencies, both of which may give you information regarding a company's (or a fly-by-night artist's) complaint file over the phone. Also check with your local Better Business Bureau, which provides information from its complaint files on various local companies.

If the business operates under either a city or state license (auto repair shops, for instance, are licensed by the Department of Motor Vehicles in some states) or is subject to a professional or trade licensing board or other oversight agency, see whether there have been any complaints or disciplinary actions. Also check whether summonses have been issued (for example, a summons for health violations in the case of a restaurant) and whether the business has ever been closed temporarily for violations.

Also check whether the business or its principals have been the target of a civil suit or criminal prosecution by the state attorney general's office, which in most states is the consumer's legal watchdog. And search the court indexes for suits filed against your target business by consumers themselves, including actions in small claims court (usually claims of up to $2,500) and civil court (usually claims from $2,500 to 20,000).

Web sites devoted to helping consumers should also be checked. The Better Business Bureau site (www.bbb.org) offers descriptions of a wide variety of scams and rip-offs, plus online access to reports on questionable businesses from 25 (the number is growing) out of the 150 local BBB offices throughout the U.S. and Canada. A Web directory to other consumer fraud sites can be found at www.excite.com/business.

Fraud on the Internet

Several services have emerged for certifying Internet businesses. These won't tell you who is operating fraudulently, but they will tell who probably isn't. The Better Business Bureau provides a reliability seal at the Web sites of many businesses; if you click it, it takes you to www.bbbonline.com for confirmation of the seal and summary information about the company. The Public Eye certification service (www.thepubliceye.com) provides a gold seal (signifying that the merchant has agreed to continuous online monitoring) or a silver seal (signifying that the merchant has agreed to allow customer complaints to be made available to the general public at the certification service site). Bizrate (www.bizrate.com) provides detailed ratings and a "Customer Certified Report Card." Note that all three services provide their certifications only for merchants who sign up voluntarily—it is unlikely that a hard-core scamster would submit to such monitoring.

The National Fraud Information Center (nfic.inter.net/nfic) provides information on a wide variety of Internet and telemarketing scams.

Securities Fraud

The crookedest operations in the securities business often are found on the NASDAQ Over-the-Counter Bulletin Board, which facilitates trading in the stocks of small companies with large ambitions. Often dummy companies are established, or marginal companies are bought up, in order to run "pump and dump" operations that leave thousands of investors with worthless shares. Scamsters of this type often work out of telephone boiler rooms. After completing a scam, they may move to another boiler room operating under a different name and often in another state.

In any case of telephone, mail, or Internet solicitation—and especially those involving the Over-the-Counter Bulletin Board, penny stocks, and the like—check out the brokerage firm and the individual brokers with NASDAQ (www.nasdr.com/2000.htm); also obtain a credit check at www.bnb.com on any company whose stock a suspicious broker wants you to purchase.

Deceptive Tactics: Fraudulent or Otherwise

A fraudulent intent should generally be suspected when a business uses a mail drop, even though many small businesses and individuals may do so for legitimate purposes. Mail drops and related services can be found in the yellow pages, but anyone investigating white-collar crimes should consult the listings in *How to Use Mail Drops for Profit, Privacy, and Self-Protection* (included in this book's bibliography). *How to Use Mail Drops* is sold by mail-order booksellers whose clientele includes many individuals with an unhealthy interest in criminal methods; thus, a scam artist might gravitate to one of the listings in this book.

Some companies that serve as mail drops also offer a full range of related services: mail forwarding, telephone answering (with the person answering the phone pretending to be the full-time receptionist for a bustling business), and the part-time or occasional use of a well-appointed office (or even a suite of offices) to impress a client. In New York City, such services can provide the "prestige" of a Park Avenue or Madison Avenue address, thereby giving an entirely false impression of a company's financial solidity.

A fly-by-night firm planning a major scam may actually sign the lease on a full-time office at a seemingly fancy business address. But you should inquire whether they really have a long-term lease (which is a sign of financial solidity: the landlord would not rent to them otherwise) or whether it's just a short-term lease in a building with a high vacancy rate (usually in a less-desirable range of blocks on the street in question), a temporary sublease, or a room in an office suite rented by the hour but with mail and telephone service included at all hours. In the latter case, you may check further and find that the real office for most purposes is either the proprietor's home or simply a local bar from where he or she makes calls on a cellular phone.

The listing of a fancy address can be bolstered by a variety of other trappings, including an 800 number, a Web page, an online office suite (which may suggest to naïve customers that the business has its own in-house computer network), a big ad in the yellow pages, fancy stationery providing a list of nonexistent branch offices, and a glossy brochure that includes stock photos showing a large room filled with dozens of brokers busy at their desks and computer terminals, an office building that is the supposed corporate headquarters, and so on.

Note: If you call the office of such a business, what you hear may also be a trick. One software product currently on the market directs calls to numerous supposed voice mail boxes, even though only a single scamster will receive the messages. Another software product will imitate a background soundscape of intercom announcements and ringing phones, which can make the caller believe that he or she has indeed reached a bustling office. A third product imitates the voice of a live secretary, with a repertoire including "Will she know what this is about?" and "Please hold." (For evening calls, when a secretary would not be on duty, the scamster—if operating out of his or her own home—might answer the phone in a gravelly voice, identify himself or herself as "Security," and tell the caller to try again during regular business hours.)

In bolstering the illusion of branch offices, the business can also have RCF (Remote Call Forwarding) numbers. This service from your local phone company enables a business to give the impression of having a branch office in a city when it really doesn't—the calls are forwarded without the caller's knowledge to an office in another city. A firm can meanwhile list as its local address the office of a mail drop or mail forwarding service that has instructions not to give out the real location. (This trick could be arranged in a number of different cities, thus bolstering the illusion created by the list of phony branches on the firm's stationery.)

Another trick, used especially by dubious stockbrokers, is to adopt a name that sounds similar to that of a long-established and prestigious firm (for example, one that includes "Morgan" or "Rothschild" in its title), a famous university or university town (for example, "Princeton" or "Cambridge"), or a founding father ("Franklin," "Hamilton," and the like).

A scamster operating alone might register a business name that ends with "Associates" or "Group" and put on his or her business cards the title "Chief Executive Officer." And although the address on this individual's stationery or business cards might simply be his or her address or a mail drop, he or she might disguise the apartment or private mail box number as a "Suite" number.

Many of these tricks are used not just by scamsters but by legitimate small businesses. A freelance consulting business trying to attract new clients might use a few of the less objectionable tricks simply because all its competitors are doing so. A business that operates by telecommuting (with each employee or partner operating out of his or her own home to avoid overhead costs) may feel that it needs to bolster its image with old-fashioned customers who are not yet comfortable with telecommuting. But if the officers of a business use the more elaborate of these tricks with apparent glee, you might ask what they are going to do next.

The preceding deceptions can all be fairly easily unmasked through a business credit check, online or CD-ROM business and residential criss-cross directories and street maps, calls to neighboring businesses or residents, pretext phone calls to the business itself, or a visit to the premises.

14.2 Publicly Held Companies and Other Large Established Businesses

For established businesses in the United States, there is a vast wealth of research sources. What follows is a capsule description at best; for full treatment of the subject, the most up-to-date book as of early 1999 is *The Prentice Hall Directory of Online Business Information*. Two classic works covering both online and offline sources are Lorna M. Daniell's *Business Information Sources* and Leonard M. Fuld's *The New Competitor Intelligence*. Still authoritative for offline research, these two books should also be consulted for online searching as soon as new editions come out. The massive *How to Find Information About Companies*, if you can find it in a research library in your locality, is also highly recommended, even if the library has only a non-current edition. You should also consult the DIALOG and LEXIS-NEXIS online catalogs, which describe hundreds of business-oriented databases. Finally, check out the various Web directories of business sites; one of the best of these directories is located at www.nytimes.com/ library/cyber/reference/busconn.html.

Note that, for any sizable corporation in our tightly interrelated economy, all good research work includes parallel, indirect, and operative back-grounding (see sections 1.3, 1.4, and 1.5). At the outset, you should define a company's relationship to the company that controls it or the company or companies that are controlled by it or are under common control with it.

Business Directories and Databases

Sketches of the financial status and types of activities conducted by publicly held and relatively large privately held businesses, as well as the names of directors and officers and other information, are easy to find online and in various published directories. Check as many of these sources as possible. If you are using the print directories, do not neglect the weekly, monthly, or quarterly supplements that keep them up to date. Note also that there are variations in how often CD-ROMs or online databases are updated.

The following list includes print and electronic (CD-ROM and online) business reference works produced by the best-known publishers of information about individual corporations. In most cases, the print and CD-ROM versions are easy to find at public libraries.

- **D&B—Dun's Financial Records Plus (DIALOG file 519).** This database from Dun & Bradstreet contains information on about two million public and private companies. For 700,000 of these companies, the database provides detailed financial information including balance sheet, income statement, and various business ratios for determining profitability, solvency, and efficiency. History and operations information only is provided for over one million privately held companies.

- **D&B "Million Dollar" products.** The six-volume *D&B Million Dollar Directory Series* covers 160,000 leading public and private companies. The CD-ROM versions, "D&B Million Dollar Disc" and "D&B Million Dollar Disc Plus," cover 240,000 companies and 400,000 companies respectively. An online version is available to subscribers only at www.dnbmdd.com.

- *Thomas Register of American Manufacturers.* This giant print, CD-ROM, and online work is described under "Competitors, Suppliers, and Industrial Customers," later in this chapter.

- *Ward's Business Directory of U.S. Private and Public Companies.* This venerable reference work covers firms with gross annual sales of over $500,000.

- *Standard & Poor's Register of Corporations, Directors, and Executives.* This three-volume work provides information on over 55,000 public and private companies and brief biographies of their executives and directors. It is especially useful in tracing the overlapping boards of directors of various firms. A CD-ROM version is available in some libraries. DIALOG offers an online version (files 526 and 527).

- **Moody's Manuals.** These volumes evaluate in detail the public filings of thousands of firms. Industrial, banking/finance, and transportation companies as well as public utilities are each covered in a separate volume. There are also two volumes covering firms traded over the counter. (To know which to consult, see the index volume.) An online version is available from DIALOG (file 555). DIALOG also offers additional information from Moody's dating back to 1983 (file 556).

- **Reed Elsevier's Corporate Affiliations set.** This three-volume work includes *Directory of Corporate Affiliations/U.S. Public, Directory of Corporate Affiliations/U.S. Private,* and *Directory of Corporate Affiliations/International.* This is where to go if you want to find the subsidiaries of a parent company or the parent of a subsidiary. About 115,000 companies are covered. For the online version, see DIALOG's file 513.

Securities and Exchange Commission Filings

If the business you are investigating is a publicly held corporation registered with the Securities and Exchange Commission (SEC), detailed information is available on the public record. Filings required by the SEC include stock offering prospectuses, proxy statements, the annual 10-K and quarterly 10-Q reports to the SEC, copies of annual reports to shareholders, and many other documents. In these, you will find out who the major stockholders are, who the officers and directors are (with biographical data on each), who the attorneys and outside accountants are, as well as information on the firm's lines of credit. You will also find audit reports detailing the firm's current financial status and capital structure, brief assessments of legal suits in which the firm is involved, and information on the firm's subsidiaries, both domestic and international. The 10-Ks and annual reports to shareholders may include valuable information about the firm's major clients and the government contracts it has received. The proxy statements will reveal the holdings of officers and directors, institutional investors, and beneficial owners of 5 percent or more of the company's stock; these statements may also contain details of any in-house loans or other financial transactions between the firm and any of its officers or directors. Always examine Form S-1, the registration statement filed by a company when it first comes under SEC jurisdiction. This form contains details about the firm's finances and about the personal and business backgrounds of its officers that may not be repeated in subsequent filings.

By tracing SEC filings by a company over the years, you can gather the names of officers, directors, and beneficial owners who are no longer associated with the company—these may be potential sources. You can also find out about investors who have made unsuccessful bids for control and those who have been squeezed out by hostile takeovers; see Schedule 13-D (Report of Securities Purchase), Schedule 14-D1 (Tender Offer Statement), and Schedule 14-D9 (Solicitation Recommendation).

The annual *Directory of Companies Required to File Annual Reports with the Securities and Exchange Commission* (now online at www.sec.gov/asec/cfnew.htm) will tell you whether your target company is required to file. If so, the company's SEC filings since at least May 1996 will be searchable for free at www.edgar-online.com. For filings since the late 1980s and up to the advent of the EDGAR system, see DIALOG and LEXIS-NEXIS. For the microfiche of earlier filings back to the beginning of the company's filing history, go to the SEC's Public Reference Rooms in Washington, D.C., New York, or Chicago; a university business school library or the business divisions of any major public library.

Summary information on past and current SEC filings of thousands of companies can be obtained from Standard & Poor's and Moody's databases described in the preceding section.

For help in interpreting SEC filings, see the works listed under "Business Research" in the bibliography of this book.

State Securities Filings

Note that corporations selling securities within a given state must file a variety of disclosure statements with the state securities regulator. These disclosures can be almost as revealing as SEC filings and should always be checked when backgrounding a local corporation.

Newspaper and Periodical Business News

If you want to search the business press, start with LEXIS-NEXIS. It offers full-text searches for key words (for example, the names of your target business, its subsidiaries or parent, and its officers and directors) in hundreds of city, state, regional, and national business newspapers and periodicals, newswires and newsletters, and the business and general news sections of hundreds of metropolitan dailies and popular magazines. Is your target firm in the Seattle area? The LEXIS-NEXIS News and Business Library includes several locally and regionally oriented business periodicals such as the *Puget Sound Business Journal* (from 1985) and the *Pacific Northwest Executive* (from 1986), and also the daily newspapers: the *Seattle Times* (from 1988) and the *Seattle Post-Intelligencer* (from 1992). Does the company manufacture aircraft components? You can search *Aerospace Daily* and *Aviation Daily* (from 1989), *Aerospace America* (from 1984), and *Aviation Week & Space Technology* (from 1975). Is the firm designing high-tech components for Navy jets? You can consult *Defense Electronics* (from 1983) and *Defense and Aerospace Electronics* (from 1990).

If you don't have access to NEXIS, try DIALOG's IAC Trade & Industry database (file 148), which provides the complete text of over 200 trade journals and industry-related periodicals as well as selective coverage of over 1,000 others (many records date back to 1981).

Rather than searching databases, you can check the published indexes in your local library. Most important are the *Business Periodicals Index*, which covers 344 business magazines and has retrospective volumes dating back to 1959; the F&S domestic and international indexes; the *Wall Street Journal Index*; and the *New York Times Index*. Although all of these are available online, a relatively efficient search can be done in the print volumes because the latter include indexing by company name. Even obscure local businesses can be found if they were ever the subject of a news item relating to the development of a new product, Chapter 11 reorganization, a liability suit, and so on.

There are thousands of trade journals covering every type of business, most of which are not indexed in the *Business Periodicals Index* or the annual F&S indexes. Some you will find on LEXIS, but often for the most recent years only. To find the names of relatively obscure publications, look in *Standard Periodical Directory*. If the periodical you want is not in a local business library, check the local branch of the trade association in question; they may have it on file. Or you can contact the editors of the publication directly; they may agree to search their own files and send you clippings in return for access to your findings. They might also provide you with a bit of unpublished gossip about your target company.

Trade journals can also be found through a Web directory of trade association Web sites. One place to start is at dir.yahoo.com/ Business_and_Economy/Organizations/Trade_Associations. When you go to a given trade association site, it may include the latest issue of the association's publication. Indeed, it may even include a short-term archive going back a year or two, although this archive will probably not cover the full text of the print version. If an association does not offer its publication online, it may have subscription information (or even order information for back issues).

Brokerage House Reports

Brokerage house reports are based on interviews with corporate officials and the individual judgment of the analyst preparing the report. They contain facts and analysis focusing on a firm's clients, management difficulties, government contracts, and future plans. These reports are available in business libraries or online through the LEXIS Company Library, which includes reports from over 110 international, national, and regional brokerage firms. For further information on a given company, call the analyst who wrote the report.

LEXIS Law Libraries

Specialized LEXIS law libraries enable you to search online a vast wealth of court decisions, administrative rulings, regulatory commission decisions, and government filings (as well as newsletters and bulletins reporting thereon) in over 30 subject areas. You can either do a global search of an entire library or look through various special file combinations. Some of the libraries are specific to a particular group of industries, such as the Communications Library and the Transportation Library. Others deal with specific problems that face industries across the board; for instance, the Federal Tax Library, the State Tax Library (files for each state), the Labor Library, and the Bankruptcy Library. In studying any company that does business with the government, you will want to consult the Federal Public Contracts Library. Note that the LEXIS law libraries offer broad coverage beyond the law itself; for example, the Patent Law Library includes full-text coverage, dating back more than a decade, of scores of business and technology journals in such fields as telecommunications, computers, and aerospace.

Government Regulation: Audits, Inspection Reports, and So On

As you gather government data on a corporation, keep asking yourself what other government departments or regulatory agencies might require it to file or might be investigating it. Information may be available from dozens of government sources. Is your target business a limited partnership constructing federally subsidized housing? There will be reports and audits available from the Department of Housing and Urban Development (HUD). Is an office supply firm doing extensive business with civilian federal agencies? General Accounting Office (GAO) reports may be available. Is a computer hardware company gaining an increasing number of contracts with the military? The public affairs office of the Department of Defense (DOD) can provide you with a printout—unless the data is classified—of all the firm's current and past military contracts, broken down by general purpose, location, and amount of money involved. You can then request the DOD's reports on how well the firm has fulfilled its contracts. (*Note:* Always check whether a firm has been listed in the government's monthly *Lists of Parties Excluded from Federal Procurement or Nonprocurement Programs*, which is now online at www.arnet.gov/epls.)

Environmental, Consumer, and Social Policy
The Environmental Protection Agency (EPA) provides access at www.epa.gov (select "Envirofacts") to seven major EPA databases covering Superfund data, hazardous waste, biennial reporting, toxic releases, water discharge permits, and air releases. For example, if you go to the toxic releases database (the EPA's annual Toxics Release Inventory), you will find a summary of the data that every manufacturer with 10 or more employees is required to report to the EPA and state agencies regarding the total amount of each of about 330 toxic chemicals it has released into the environment.

Much of the Envirofacts data can also be accessed through the RTK Net Web site (www.rtk.net), which also includes the Comprehensive Environmental Response Compensation Liability Information System (CERCLIS) list and the EPA's Civil Docket database (DOCKET). RTK Net's version of DOCKET contains not just the online record of all civil cases filed on behalf of EPA by the Justice Department but also a partial record of EPA administrative actions and penalties.

The Environmental Defense Fund skewers polluters at www.scorecard. org. You enter your zip code at the home page to find out what pollutants are being released into your community and which companies are directly responsible.

Information on a company's environment record will also be available through the company's SEC filings at www.edgar-online.com. Since 1989, the SEC has required companies to disclose on their 10-Ks any potential liabilities they might face under the federal environmental cleanup laws.

Broader information can be accessed through the LEXIS Environmental Law Library, which includes not only environment-related court decisions and administrative rulings but also the full text of newsletters that carefully monitor the public record, such as *Pesticide & Toxic Chemical News*.

Both federal and state levels of government are a gold mine of information about consumer complaints and product safety. An excellent guide to these sources is *Lesko's Info-Power III*, which describes, for instance, the various databases maintained by the Consumer Product Safety Commission. (For a Web directory of government consumer sites, go to www.consumer.gov.) Many state consumer affairs departments or local consumer protection offices will give you information about a company's complaint record over the phone (a list of the offices for each state and their disclosure policies is in *Lesko's Info-Power III*).

Corporate misdeeds in general are monitored by various public-interest groups. The Manhattan-based Council on Economic Priorities collects data regarding such issues as corporate support for charities, job equality for women, and animal testing; check out its ratings of hundreds of top companies at www.cepnyc.org. The various state Public Interest Research Groups at www.pirg.org and Ralph Nader's Center for Study of Responsive Law at www.csrl.org are strong on consumer issues. Many other nonprofit agencies that monitor the corporate world can be found in the *Encyclopedia of Associations*—and don't forget state and national trade and industry associations, which sometimes keep files on the most egregious offenders in their ranks.

Kinder, Lydenberg, Domini & Co., an investment advisory firm, researches 3,500 companies a year for its *Domini 400 Social Index*. Its list of 400 benchmark companies for socially responsible investing can be accessed at www.kld.com.

If a corporation is going to donate to charities, it will generally do so through a corporate foundation. You can check its generosity in the *National Directory of Corporate Giving* and *Corporate Foundation Profiles*, both published by the Foundation Center. Also see the Taft Group's *Corporate Giving Directory* and its two CD-ROM products, Prospector's Choice and Grants on Disc.

Bankruptcy Files

Whether a business is large or small, it may at some point have applied for Chapter 11 reorganization, under either its present name or a previous one. The bankruptcy files will contain a wealth of information about customers and clients, vendors and suppliers, claims by or against the firm, pending litigation in any jurisdiction, mismanagement, and possible fraudulent practices. The Chapter 11 status may continue for several years, during which period the firm must file extremely detailed reports on its business affairs.

Bankruptcy files in active and recently closed cases are found at the federal bankruptcy courts (which generally cover the same jurisdictions as the U.S. district courts). The court indexes and, to varying degrees, the docket sheets of all bankruptcy courts are now searchable online using the Public Access to Court Electronic Records (PACER) system. In addition, you can now use the PACER-based U.S. Party/Case Index to see whether a given business has filed for bankruptcy at any bankruptcy court in the nation. Old, closed cases, however, are not searchable online; you must search for these in the microfiche or card-file indexes at the court in question. Note that the files of closed cases are held at the bankruptcy court for a number of years and are then sent to a Regional Records Services Facility. (For more on bankruptcy filings, see section 8.10, "Bankruptcy Court Records.")

Licenses and Permits

All legitimate businesses are subject to city, state, or federal licensing and permit provisions. Consult your local government handbook or call the city and state licensing agencies to find out which requirements apply to your target business.

Miscellaneous Public Records

Check the state and federal court indexes (both civil and criminal), the federal tax lien files, and the county judgment docket. Also check a company's UCC filings to get a better picture of its liabilities. For details on how to access each of these records systems online, see Chapter 8, "Credit and Financial Information."

Official Company Sources

Even relatively small companies now have Web sites, which often provide a comprehensive view of the company's products, the activities of its subsidiaries, and the like. Industry-specific directories of such Web sites can be found at www.nypl.org/ research/sibl/trade/industry2.html#pub.

You may find at your target company's Web site a wealth of promotional information, a shortened version of the company's catalog, an archive of the company's press releases, and the names of and contact information for certain key employees. Meanwhile, the full print version of the company's sales catalog, recent press releases (if not on the Web site), copies of public speeches by the CEO, a copy of the latest issue of the company's house organ, and a copy of its annual report may be obtained from its public affairs office.

Note that the slickly printed annual report a firm circulates to stockholders and the general public should not be confused with the 10-K annual report sent to the SEC by publicly held corporations. The printed report generally will be more limited in the amount of information it discloses and will contain some flagrant hype. Nevertheless, it will include a financial statement, a list of directors and officers, information about major new contracts, and so forth. (Annual reports on over 3,600 public companies can be ordered for free at www.prars.com.)

A firm's older pre-Web press releases and those for firms that do not put their press releases on their own Web sites (or do not archive them online) may be available from Business Wire (since 1983 on LEXIS-NEXIS and since 1986 on DIALOG). If the information in a press release was of much significance at the time, an article based on it (perhaps evaluating it critically) can probably be found in various business or trade publication archives available on LEXIS-NEXIS.

Another good information source is the firm's house organ. A list of such publications can be found at your public library in the *Magazines and Internal Publications Directory* (volume II of *Working Press of the Nation*). Whether or not your target firm is listed there, call the firm's public affairs office to see whether such a publication exists. In the context of a later interview with the public affairs director (if you are, say, a business graduate student or freelance business writer), you might ask for access to the company library to look at various company publications, including the house organ backfiles.

Another possible route is through the firm's outside public relations consultants; under some circumstances, these entities might be more cooperative than the in-house public affairs office.

Former Officers, Directors, or Managers

Former officers or directors who resigned or were sacked may be willing to discuss the firm's past. To get their names, look in old SEC or state securities filings, old editions of *Standard & Poor's Register of Corporations, Directors and Executives*, or the firm's annual filings with the state department of state. If a person's name has disappeared from the list of a firm's top executives, it is almost certain that he or she has left the firm rather than accept a demotion. (Note, however, that in some cases, the disappearance of a name from the list may mean that the person was transferred to the firm's parent company or to another subsidiary of the parent company—as described later in this section.)

Former top officers or directors are generally easy to find. If such a person is not in the current edition of *Standard & Poor's Register*, look in the relevant national or local professional or trade directory ordirectories.

Former mid-level or lower-level managers of a firm may be more difficult to identify or locate. You might try the following approaches:

- Look in back editions of the local city directory for people once listed as employees who are no longer listed. If the old directory does not give their job title, you can estimate from the income level of their neighborhood whether or not they were likely to be on the management level.

- Get both an old edition and the latest edition of the firm's in-house phone directory (from your source in the mail room or at a local headhunting agency), and compare them to see who's left the firm. If you have only an old edition obtained from the firm's trash, call the extensions of people with management titles to find out which of them no longer work there.

- Search the Federal Election Commission's online records at www.tray.com to find campaign contributions by your target firm's employees during all election cycles back to 1980. Look for persons listed as having made a campaign contribution in, say, 1994 while working for the target firm but who are listed in contribution records for a subsequent year as working for another firm. For more on this technique for finding former employees, see section 10.10, "Federal Election Commission Records."

Before calling a former employee of a given firm, always check that his or her new employer is not affiliated as a parent, subsidiary, or co-subsidiary with the old firm, or that the supposed new firm is not simply a new name for the old one (companies that become the target of media attacks or legislative hearings will frequently change their names shortly thereafter for marketing reasons). The affiliations of a firm can be determined for over 114,000 companies by looking in the Corporate Affiliations database on DIALOG or in the print version of same: the six-volume *Directory of Corporate Affiliations Library*. Name changes can be determined by looking in the corporation files for the state in which the company was incorporated. Information on affiliations or name changes can also easily be determined by a pretext phone call to the supposed former employee's new place of business.

Labor Union and Shop Floor Sources

In its preparations for contract negotiations, a union must keep well informed about the company's profit margins—to know what the traffic will bear. If the union is locked in a bitter dispute with management, it may be willing to help you in the hopes that you will turn up something useful for its own purposes. The situation varies, however, from union to union and from local to local: Sometimes the workers are represented by a union whose leaders are so corrupt that it might as well be an old-fashioned company union. Sometimes the union will not want to rock the boat by cooperating with a journalistic probe (for example, an article on the environmental effects of a certain company's logging operations) because the result might be a loss of jobs. In many unions, however, there are national or local rank-and-file groups at odds with the official leadership. Often it is best either to work exclusively with such a group or to work with both it and the official leadership simultaneously. For instance, if I were backgrounding a Midwest trucking firm, I might or might not approach the official leadership of the Teamster local (depending on the recent history of reform efforts in that local), but I would surely talk to the Teamsters for a Democratic Union, a rank-and-file group that is not only untainted by mob connections but happens also to be very well informed about the business woes of various trucking companies.

Even if a local business is not unionized, it is useful to contact workers to find out about whether orders or sales are up or down in recent months, whether management is covering up shoddy production standards (in the case of a retail establishment) or forcing sales clerks to push shoddy or unsanitary items, and whether environmental laws are being secretly violated, as by dumping at unauthorized sites.

Contacting workers if the firm is nonunion or if the union leadership is uncooperative can be tricky. Obviously you can't just walk up to employees on the factory or sales floor and start interviewing them. One way to find the names and home addresses of workers is through a city directory that lists each householder's occupation and place of work. Another method is to copy down license plate numbers of cars in the company parking lot and then get the owners' names and addresses from the Department of Motor Vehicles (if such information is still available in your state).

Of course, with these approaches, you might inadvertently contact a supervisor who will inform his or her superiors. Dashiell Hammett's Continental Op in the classic detective novel *Red Harvest* had a way around this: When he arrived in town, the first person he looked up was the local leader of the IWW (Industrial Workers of the World, or "Wobblies"). Today there are almost no Wobblies left, but there will often be a scattering of workers who have engaged in unsuccessful unionization drives or, if the plant is unionized, who belong to the national rank-and-file caucus.

If you're doing an investigative journalism piece on, say, occupational hazards at a local plant (to illustrate, among other things, the greed of the corporate raiders who recently took over the parent company), you might contact local community activists who don't work in the plant—and thus don't have to look over their shoulders constantly—and get them to act as your go-betweens to workers at the plant whom they know personally.

Look for former shop-level employees with a reason to be angry at management: those who were fired on trumped-up charges after attempting to unionize, those who lost their jobs during the latest cutbacks, those who were forced into early retirement and now find their pensions almost worthless in the wake of that corporate takeover. Such people may be more willing to talk than workers still clinging to their jobs, although many will have left town for greener pastures.

Also try to find individual workers whose disputes with management are a matter of public record. The most obvious place to look is in the local court indexes—for lawsuits by employees or former employees against the company (sexual harassment suits and discrimination suits are a booming business all over the country). You might also search for the company's name in the LEXIS Labor Library, which includes labor-related case law and also National Labor Relations Board, Equal Employment Opportunity Commission, and Occupational Safety and Health Review Commission decisions dating back to the early 1970s.

Competitors, Suppliers, and Industrial Customers

To find companies that provide a particular product or service, look in the *Thomas Register of American Manufacturers*. This 34-volume work, available at most large public libraries, can now be searched online for free at www.thomasregister.com and also at many libraries on CD-ROM.

In the Products and Services section of this massive work, you will find 155,000 producers and suppliers in over 58,000 industrial and service categories listed by state and city within each category. This will give you an idea of who your target company's competitors are. To figure out who its suppliers are (or the companies that it is supplying), you will have to learn something about the particular processes of the industry and then study carefully the relevant product or service listings and consult the supplier catalog file (over 2,000 company catalogs in the print version, over 5,000 in the electronic versions). In some cases, the supplier nearest your target company may be the most likely one if transportation cost is a significant factor. For some services, a nearby location will be likely because of the need for personal visits. (In figuring out who the smaller suppliers or customers might be, you may have to consult state manufacturing directories as well as the *Thomas Register*.)

Other useful free Thomas databases include the Thomas Food Industry Register (www.tfir.com), which covers 30,000 companies and 6,000 product categories; the Thomas Regional Directory (www.thomasregional.com), which covers 480,000 distributors, manufacturers, and service companies in 19 industrial markets; and the Product News Network (productnews.com), which covers over 50,000 industrial products searchable by product attribute.

As you gather lists of probable suppliers, competitors, or customers, look in court indexes and business news databases for any litigation between any of these firms and your target company. Also look in courthouse judgment books or judgment databases for any judgments obtained by your target company against a customer or supplier (or vice versa).

14.3 Investigating a Nonprofit Entity

Nonprofit corporations become plaintiffs or defendants in lawsuits, purchase real estate, experience cash flow problems, and engage in disputes with their unionized employees. Thus, in researching a nonprofit corporation, you should proceed pretty much as if you were backgrounding any other type of corporation.

Not-for-Profit Corporate Registration Papers

Nonprofit entities must file their certificates of incorporation, amendments, changes of name, or dissolutions with the state's department of state. Copies may also be found at the county clerk's office. The indexes to these files are searchable through any online vendor such as KnowX (www.search3.knowx.com) or Dun & Bradstreet (www.dnb.com). The indexes for many states can also be searched for free at state government Web sites; for a directory of such sites, go to www.inil.com/users/dguss/gator.htm (select, "Companies, Corporations, and UCC Listings"). For further descriptions of these records and how to access them, see section 14.1, "Businesses, Legitimate and Otherwise," and section 8.27, "Corporate, Partnership, and D/B/A Files."

State Charity Filings

Nonprofit organizations must file annual reports with the state division of charities under certain circumstances (in New York, for example, if they solicit more than $10,000 in the given year).

State Attorney's Office

In most states, the state attorney general's office is responsible for investigating violations of the laws governing nonprofit organizations. If complaints have been lodged against a nonprofit organization, the charities bureau at the state attorney general's office may have an extensive file on it.

Federal 990 Forms

Tax-exempt nonprofit organizations must file an annual 990 form (or, in the case of smaller charities, an annual 990-EZ) with the Internal Revenue Service (IRS). To see whether your target organization qualifies as tax exempt, check the IRS's *Cumulative List of Organizations* at the public library or the online version at the Internet Nonprofit Center's Web site (www.nonprofits.org). All 990 filers must make their three most recent 990s available for inspection by the general public at their principal office during regular business hours and must send a copy to a requester within 30 days of receipt of a request in writing. (The rules are somewhat different for the 990-PF filed by private foundations, as described a little later in this section.) Disclosure applies to all parts of the form except for contributor lists.

Note: Nonprofits are being encouraged by the Multi-State Filer Project to file their 990s electronically and to make them available online at www.form990.org. This project, however, is still in an experimental stage as of early 1999.

If you experience difficulty obtaining an organization's 990s from the organization itself, you can get them from the IRS. The IRS will take its time, however, and occasionally will tell you it can't find the records. Fortunately, copies are often filed with the state division of charities along with the state-required annual report. In requests to various states, I have usually received the 990s within a week or so. In addition, the state attorney's office, if it has a complaint file on the organization in question, will also have copies of the 990s and might be willing to let a journalist look at them.

Note that if you request a nonprofit organization's 990s from the IRS, always make your request under IRS Code section 6104 rather than the Freedom of Information Act and be sure to include the organization's Employer Identification Number.

A guide to interpreting IRS Form 990 and its attachments can be downloaded at www.guidestar.org/phil/easy0005.html.

Note: Charities frequently conceal certain aspects of their finances by shifting costs and income between the charity itself and various for-profit subsidiaries. This tactic is used not only as a tax dodge for the for-profit subsidiary but also to disguise the high fundraising overhead of the charity itself (so that donors will continue to give generously). In addition, a for-profit subsidiary might be set up to provide an additional salary check for a top executive of the charity or a job for his or her spouse or lover.

Directories and Listings of Tax-Exempt Organizations and Other Nonprofits

- **Online.** The Internet Nonprofit Center (www.nonprofits.org) provides access, as noted earlier in this chapter, to the IRS's list of over one million federally tax-exempt organizations. For directory-style information on these and other nonprofits, go to the Guidestar Web site (www.guidestar.org), which covers more than 650,000 nonprofits.

- **Online, CD-ROM, and print.** The *Encyclopedia of Associations* (available in print, on CD-ROM, and online from GaleNet) includes information on 23,000 nonprofits of national scope and 113,000 of regional, state, or local scope. The CD-ROM and online versions include IRS data on about 300,000 tax-exempt 501(c) organizations.

- **Print only.** The *National Directory of Nonprofit Organizations* covers over 260,000 organizations—foundations, endowment funds, scholarship funds, religious organizations, and many other types—with annual revenues of $25,000 or more.

Web Sites of Nonprofit Organizations
A vast number of nonprofits now have Web sites. Directories of these sites can be found at www.guidestar.org, www.ipl.org/ref/AON, dir.yahoo.com/Society_and_Culture/Organizations, and dir.yahoo.com/Society_and_Culture/Issues_and_Causes.

Contributor Lists
Although they are not required by law to reveal their contributor lists, many nonprofits will publish donors' names to enhance giving as well as to satisfy the vanity of the donors. These lists are found in everything from promotional brochures to annual reports and even in program publications of the local symphony orchestra.

You can find out about foundation grants to a particular nonprofit organization in the *Foundation Grants Index* (see "Records on Private Foundations" later in this chapter).

Court Cases

The LEXIS Corporate Law Library includes case law regarding nonprofit corporations from all 50 states. In addition, you should check the court indexes for the locality in which the nonprofit corporation has its headquarters (and other localities if appropriate). Look especially for any lawsuit filed by the state attorney general's office against the organization.

Records on Private Foundations

A tax-exempt private foundation has a somewhat different legal status than does a public charity or a nonprofit institution such as a church or university. To qualify as a tax-exempt private foundation, an entity must receive contributions from only a very limited number of contributors (a single family, for instance) and must make grants only to nonprofit organizations, not to individuals. If it chooses, it may also operate its own charitable or public-service programs. There are currently over 40,000 private foundations in the United States.

All private foundations must annually file Form 990-PF with the IRS. This form provides a detailed picture of the finances of a foundation and how it spent its income during the previous year. The form also includes a list of officers and directors, the salaries of top officers, and information on any political activities or changes in control of the foundation.

The IRS requires private foundations to make their most recent 990-PFs available to the public for 180 days each year; during that period, they must provide free copies on request. If you want to examine previous forms or the current form after the 180-day period has passed, many foundations will gladly send you a copy. If not, you should check with the regional office of the Foundation Center, a private organization that collects past and current 990-PF forms as well as printed annual reports of many private foundations. If the center doesn't have the reports you need, you can obtain them from the state division of charities or from the IRS.

Directories of Foundations

Brief descriptions of most U.S. private foundations are given in the Foundation Center's *Guide to U.S. Foundations, Their Trustees, Officers, and Donors*, which covers over 40,000 foundations. The center also publishes *The Foundation 1000*, which gives detailed profiles of the 1,000 largest foundations. The center's classic guide, *The Foundation Directory*, provides key facts on over 8,600 of the larger foundations; it has two companion volumes, *The Foundation Directory Part 2* (which covers about 5,000 mid-sized foundations) and *The Foundation Directory Supplement* (which updates entries from the other two volumes). You should also check *The Foundation Grants Index* (over 86,000 grant descriptions from over

1,000 foundations) to find out which nonprofit is being funded by which foundation, and for which purposes.

These directories (with the exception of *The Foundation 1000*) can be searched all at once using FC Search, the Foundation Center's CD-ROM product. The Foundation Center's database can also be searched through DIALOG; see file 26 for information on grantmakers and file 27 for the grants they distributed. File 27 is of special interest because it provides cumulative records on grants from 1973 to the present.

The Foundation Center also publishes regional and subject directories (in print only) that may help you narrow your search.

Other directories in this field are published by Gale Research, Inc., and its subsidiary, The Taft Group. These include *Foundation Reporter*, with information on the history and priorities of the top 1,000 private foundations in the United States (and valuable biographical information on top foundation officers and directors), and *America's New Foundations*, with profiles of nearly 3,000 foundations established since 1988. For coverage of a broader range of foundations, see The Taft Group's two CD-ROM products, Prospector's Choice and Grants on Disc. For information on corporate foundations, see section 14.2.

Foundation Center Libraries

The Foundation Center (www.fdncenter.org) operates five regional libraries in New York City, Washington, D.C., San Francisco, Atlanta, and Cleveland. Affiliates of the center maintain smaller collections at about 175 public libraries and other locations around the country, focusing on the records of foundations in the given locality. The center's libraries are open to the public, but before visiting the nearest one, you should search the center's Web site where much information is now available to the general public including a foundation name index, a donor/officer/trustee index, links to grantmaker Web sites, and summary financial information on top foundations. In addition, the Web site has an electronic reference desk with links to various nonprofit resources and an "online librarian" service that accepts email queries from the public.

The Foundation Center does not maintain systematic records on public charities, fund-raising organizations, or nonprofit institutions such as churches and private universities.

Watchdog Organizations

The National Charities Information Bureau (www.give.org) monitors national charities with annual budgets of over $500,000. It has information on conflicts of interest, fund-raising tactics, budgets, and boards of directors. The NCIB's Web site includes a quick reference guide by which you can search a list of almost 500 charities to see whether they meet the NCIB's Standards in Philanthropy; you can then order a copy of the NCIB's report on a given charity using the site's order form.

The Council of Better Business Bureaus' Philanthropic Advisory Service monitors mostly 501(c)(3) organizations that operate nationally. You can access hundreds of its reports on these organizations at www.bbb.org/about/pas.html.

Organizational Publications

Nonprofit organizations often publish in-house newsletters for their staffs and volunteers, as well as public newsletters for their members, donors, and the general public. These are easily obtained from the nonprofit's public affairs office or (for back issues) by visiting the organization's library. Also inquire about the annual report sent out to members and donors; most nonprofits will send a copy to anyone making a telephone or email request. Back issues of the annual reports of a foundation, if they are no longer available from the foundation itself, can usually be found at a Foundation Center library. Note that if you delve into back issues of a non-profit publication, you will find the names of people no longer employed at or no longer on the board of directors of the organization in question. Some of these people may be disillusioned with the organization and be willing to discuss their experiences.

15.

Indirect Backgrounding

15.1 Finding the "Experts"

In looking into a topic on any but the most superficial level, you will develop questions that can't be answered easily by books. These questions are often very detailed and subtle and require a chat with an expert. Indeed, you may need the expert to steer you to the books. An expert can rattle off the names of articles and books on the phone that you might find only by luck during your library research.

To locate experts and eventually to find *the* expert with the most relevant information, you can draw on a wide variety of sources:

- Public-interest advocacy groups, trade and professional associations, and other nonprofit organizations are almost always willing to help you. To find the most relevant groups, look in the subject and location guides of the *Encyclopedia of Associations* and the *National Trade and Professional Associations of the U.S.* You can also search online through Associations Unlimited at GaleNet or through the organization subdirectories (by topic) at www.yahoo.com. If a group's research director or newsletter editor doesn't have the information you need, he or she can at least steer you to a staff member in another department, an outside expert, or another nonprofit group.

- Directories published specifically to help reporters and others in the media find experts are often the best place to start, especially if you're in a hurry. Among the most widely used are these:

  - The Heritage Foundation's *The Guide to Public Policy Experts*. This book is your key to finding conservative-minded experts who tend to be quite generous with their time in telephone interviews. The guide is available for free in print form and can also be searched online or downloaded for free (go to www.policyexperts.com).

- *The Reporter's Source Book.* This work, published by the Center for National Independence in Politics, covers a broader ideological range of experts than does the Heritage Foundation guide. The online version can be accessed at www.vote-smart.org/about/services/reporters.html.

- The *Yearbook of Experts, Authorities & Spokespersons.* This is the publication used by radio and TV talk-show hosts to find guests for their shows. (The online version is at www.YearbookNews.com.) It contains a number of offbeat specialties (such as UFO research) not easily found in other directories. Because appearing on talk shows usually doesn't pay any money, the presence of a person's name in this list suggests that he or she is not stingy with his or her time. However, people in this directory who lack strong academic or professional credentials should be used with caution: Some have hidden agendas or personality disturbances that render much of their information dubious.

- *Newsletters in Print* (in print, on DIALOG, and on GaleNet) provides detailed descriptions of 11,000 specialty newsletters. Although the editors of nonprofit newsletters are usually helpful to journalists, some editors of commercially published newsletters (that sell for high prices to very small subscriber lists) are reluctant to share information. Nevertheless, the high quality of their information and files makes them worth a try. If a newsletter editor knows that you intend to quote him or her and mention the newsletter in an article likely to be read by potential subscribers, you will get better cooperation.

- *American Men and Women of Science* (on LEXIS-NEXIS, DIALOG, and CompuServe, and in print) and the *Directory of American Scholars* provide listings by specialty along with brief educational and career data. The latter directory ceased publication in 1982 but is still useful in identifying experts.

- The *Research Centers Directory* and its supplement, *New Research Centers*, can help you track down many of the best university-affiliated research experts. The public affairs office of a research center or of the larger institution with which it is affiliated can help you find the right scholar or scientist to interview.

- *The Wilson Guide to Experts Series* is a new 1,800-page reference set; it includes *The Wilson Guide to Internet Experts*, *The Wilson Guide to Experts in the Arts and Humanities*, and *The Wilson Guide to Experts in Science and Technology*. Consult these volumes at your public library.

- The Expert Marketplace Web site (http://expert-market.com) provides free access to a database of 214,000 consulting and technical service firms, with performance appraisal information on many. Experts at such firms could provide excellent background information on industry or on technological questions, but don't expect them to gossip about past or present clients or would-be future clients. Many consulting or technical service firms are eager for publicity regarding their expertise and thus would allow a knowledgeable staffer to give an interview to a science or business reporter.

- Faculty directories and course guides from local universities (often available online at the school's Web site as well as in print versions) will help you find teachers in every field in which courses are being offered. Here you can find experts in some very practical fields, such as real estate finance and hotel administration, as well as in the liberal arts and sciences. To find out what the specialties of each department member are (if the course guide or the Web site faculty biographies don't tell you), you might check the *Faculty Directory of Higher Education*. Although this directory has ceased publication, copies in the public library will inform you of the courses taught by individual professors nationwide up through the late 1980s. Note that universities love to see their faculty members quoted in the media, and therefore most university news and information officers maintain lists of quotable faculty experts on a variety of topics and also participate in ProfNet (described in the next entry).

  Professors at your local college will rarely be the ranking experts in their specialty, but they will be more likely to spare time for you than will a national academic celebrity. In addition, you can talk face to face with them and perhaps get access to their personal research files without having to invest in an airplane ticket. Be aware that local professors often toil away, unappreciated, in a narrow but important field. They are often overjoyed to be contacted by a journalist.

- ProfNet (at www.profnet.com) enables you to search for experts at a wide range of universities, colleges, corporations, think tanks, national labs, medical centers, and PR agencies. Billed as the "shortest distance between a journalist and a source," ProfNet will help you search for experts nationwide or locally on any topic, no matter how narrow. The ProfNet Web site has an online directory of over 2,000 experts, but if you want ProfNet's help in conducting a broader search or in finding someone in a detailed subspecialty, you must send an email query (the form for such queries is available at the site). ProfNet will then route your query to the appropriate persons among 5,100 news and information officers at affiliated entities.

- Local alternative education centers and college continuing education programs list in their catalogs many teachers with unusual specialties.

Although you may not need an expert on Hot-Air Ballooning or How to Flirt in Art Museums, such centers and programs also offer courses in very hard-nosed practical subjects. The teachers are often freelance writers, consultants, or editors of specialty newsletters. As avid self-promoters, they will often cooperate with a journalist.

- Textbooks in the field covering your specific topic will guide you to a wide range of experts, as will books of investigative journalism, biography, contemporary history, and the like. Look for the bibliography (which may be at the end of the book or at the end of each chapter) and also note the authorities cited in the text and in the footnotes, chapter notes, or endnotes. In addition, look for the author's list of the individuals whom he or she interviewed, which may be in an appendix at the back of the book or in the acknowledgments section at the front.

  Extensive bibliographies can also be found in articles published in academic and scientific journals (see the following entry).

  To take your search for scholars and other writers on your topic to the highest level, consult the print or online version of the *Bibliographic Index* at your public library. (For more on bibliographies and library catalog searches, see section 15.2.)

- Indexes and abstracts of dissertations and theses (see section 11.1, "Backgrounding a Subject's Educational Past") and of scholarly, scientific, and professional journals (see section 11.3, "The Subject's Published Writings") can help you narrow your search for a learned expert to the most minute subspecialties. After you locate a dissertation or article that deals directly with your topic, you can find the author's address through the *National Faculty Directory* or an online people-finder service. When you contact Professor X, he or she may be so flattered that someone (other than his or her dissertation adviser) has actually read the turgid tome that he or she will cooperate eagerly and even give you the names of experts whose knowledge is more up to date than his or her own.

- Investigative Reporters and Editors (IRE) (at www.ire.org) can aid you in finding journalists who specialize in the topic you are researching. IRE maintains a membership directory including the name, address, phone number, and subject specialties of over 6,000 members. It is searchable online by IRE members, who also receive a print version. Non-members must contact the IRE office for information from the membership directory but can search directly the IRE's Directory of Investigative Journalists, which includes about 2,000 U.S. and foreign journalists, many of them IRE members.

  IRE's Resource Center offers the online IRE Story Library, which includes a subject index/abstract of almost 12,000 investigative articles and series published over the past 25 years. You can obtain photocopies of any article included in the index, as well as contact information on the reporters who worked on it, from the IRE office.

▪ In many communities, at least one private citizen collects and files away all the dirt and scandal involving local politicians, business-people, and so on. Some of these amateur muckrakers are like pack rats, collecting everything they can get on everyone around them. Others are "selective" muckrakers, concerned with a particular topic. For instance, a corrupt trade union local may have at least one rank-and-filer who occupies his or her spare time by collecting evidence of the union leadership's misdeeds.

Unlike newspaper reporters, who must flit from assignment to assignment, amateur muckrakers have the leisure to concentrate on their pet target(s) year after year, gathering every scrap of documentation they can find. Frequently, their files overflow the basement or attic. Almost invariably, they are eager to cooperate with anyone who shows an interest in their findings.

Let's say that you need an expert on Sun Myung Moon's Unification Church. National newspapers will have one or more reporters who cover religious cults, although not too closely. Get their names from IRE and call them and ask for a referral to someone with special knowledge of the Moonies. They may give you the name of their favorite amateur muckraker as a favor to the muckraker rather than as a favor to you. After all, by providing the muckraker with a new potential collaborator (you), they are placing the muckraker in their debt.

After you find an amateur muckraker, he or she may refer you to other muckrakers, including those who like to keep their identities secret.

▪ Federal government bureaucrats are often remarkably conscientious in helping journalists, corporate researchers, high school science project students, and any other member of the public in need of information. Here's an example: I was backgrounding a businessman who was involved in offshore banking schemes in several small Third World countries. By looking in various directories, I obtained the names and telephone numbers of the State Department and Commerce Department country officers for these nations as well as other relevant officials. None had ever heard of Businessman X, nor would it have been appropriate for them to discuss him if they had. They did, however, share with me their intimate knowledge of the countries in question, citing various government and private reports, and they sent me clippings from newspapers in these countries. In addition, they referred me to experts in other government agencies and the private sector. One official referred me to a white-collar criminal in a federal penitentiary whom he described as the best expert on certain aspects of offshore banking. A second official referred me to an investment promoter long active in one of the countries involved; he, in turn, was willing to make a few inquiries for me.

To find government experts, look first in *Lesko's Info-Power III*. If this book doesn't have what you need, you can begin an online search at www.yahoo.com/Government/U_S__Government/Web_Directories.

When you find the right agency or department, its public affairs staff can help steer you to the most knowledgeable person.

- Congressional committee and subcommittee research staffers are among the most valuable contacts in government for an investigative reporter. The committees for which they work frequently investigate areas such as white-collar crime, government waste and inefficiency, labor racketeering, offshore banking, and corporate pollution of the environment. Quite often, these investigations will shed light on the activities of an individual, corporation, or trade union in which you are interested.

   To find the right committee for your purposes, look in the *Congressional Directory* and consult the Congressional Information Service's cumulative index and abstracts, which cover congressional hearings and reports since 1970. This research tool is available online at LEXIS-NEXIS's GENFED Library. CIS's Congressional Masterfile 1, also on LEXIS-NEXIS, covers hearings and reports from the 1960s and earlier decades.

   You may find that a committee investigated and held hearings on your topic of interest several years ago, but that the committee staffers who did the research have moved to new jobs. Track them down!

- Your local congressperson may not be an expert on much of anything except raising money from special interests, but he or she has a personal legislative staff at his or her disposal as well as the research staffs of the House committees to which he or she belongs. In addition, your congressperson has the entire resources of the Library of Congress to draw on (through the Congressional Research Service) and can make the congressional liaison staffs of every department and agency of the federal government jump to his or her tune. You are a constituent; if you are also an investigative journalist, Congressperson Jones will have a very strong incentive to keep you happy. Put him or her to work!

- Look in your state and local government handbooks to figure out who's most likely to be useful, both in the various departments and agencies and in the legislative bodies. Remember that state legislative committees, like congressional committees, hold hearings, publish reports, and employ staff researchers.

- Tap the energies of retired experts. Throughout the United States, there are vast numbers of retired college professors, scientists, politicians, corporate executives, and the like (as well as the even vaster numbers of retirees who worked in ordinary civil service or private sector jobs but learned those jobs thoroughly and became *de facto* experts). Viewed as a whole, these retirees represent a vast wealth of knowledge and experience in thousands of fields. Many of them are tired of playing golf or shuffleboard and would be delighted to help with a journalism project that relates to their former specialty or job. Note that your retired expert or retired ordinary person with special knowledge will often talk more frankly about the Way Things Really Work than might his or her former colleague or co-worker who still has to worry about getting fired. Thus, if you are looking into industrial pollution, you might seek out retired chemical engineers (who spent many of their working years reluctantly doctoring reports for the polluters) or retired members of blue-collar cleanup crews (who spent years putting a cosmetic face on the polluters' dump sites).

▪ Go on the Internet and advertise for help through the vast number of email lists concerned with hobbies and popular fads as well as serious scholarly, scientific, or political topics. If you join an email list, you will receive the messages sent out by all the members, and you can send your own messages to the entire list or to selected members. If you're investigating whether or not Elvis is still alive, you can send a message to members of your Elvis list, soliciting any hard facts they may have (if it's a large list, you might receive dozens of responses almost immediately).

In addition to email lists, there are thousands of Usenet newsgroups and scholarly/professional electronic conference (or "e-conference") sites; what was said about advertising for help through email lists applies equally here.

Email lists and newsgroups are often the best way of finding the information you need because they rope in not just the people we normally think of as the "real experts" (such as professionals, academics, and think-tankers) but also people from all walks of life who have special knowledge or experience on practical questions that may be more important to your story than any statistical analysis or scholarly theory. A good example might be the guy who knows every group of bikers on the West Coast, where they usually hang out, and how to safely approach them for information.

Note that if you join newsgroups or e-conferences on scholarly or scientific topics, you will be able to find not just the top names in a given specialty but also the many independent scholars, self-styled generalists, and amateur enthusiasts who sometimes have insights as valuable as those of the recognized authorities. You may also find one or more experts with impeccable credentials whose ideas go against the grain (and hence who are never recommended to journalists by those who adhere to the dominant paradigm) but who may represent the wave of the future.

To find searchable directories of email lists (including an updated version of the original "List of Lists" directory), go to www.dir.yahoo.com/Computers_and_Internet/Internet/Mailing_Lists/Web_Directories. To find Usenet newsgroups, try www.dejanews.com and alabanza.com/kabacoff/Inter-Links/cgi/news.cgi. To find e-conferences, go to the Directory of Scholarly and Professional E-Conferences at www.n2h2.com/KOVACS.

15.2 Finding the Books You Need

If there is a thorough, up-to-date book on the topic you are researching, you should spare no effort to find it—no matter how obscure the publisher. This lesson was brought home to me in 1979 while researching Lyndon LaRouche's ties to the Teamsters Union. I had been making phone calls for weeks with only modest results. Then I happened to mention to a Teamster dissident the name of an obscure (I thought) Midwest Teamster official who had been cooperating with LaRouche. "Oh, that s.o.b.," said the dissident, "you can read all about him in *The Hoffa Wars*." He then told me about a book that, if I had begun my research at the public library, I would have found long before. I rushed out and bought the book (Dan Moldea's classic account of Teamster strife) and looked in the index. There I found dozens of references to the thuggery of this "obscure" Teamster official and his underlings.

In searching for the right book, you can always just look in the catalog at your local public library as well as in R.R. Bowker's *Books in Print* series. But if you're dealing with a complicated or obscure topic, you might begin by searching the Library of Congress databases at lcweb.loc.gov.

If a certain book is unavailable at your local library or bookstore, you can easily purchase it online. The online bookstores, such as Amazon (www.amazon.com), Barnes and Noble (www.barnesandnoble.com), Borders (www.borders.com), and Book Stacks Unlimited (www.books.com) together offer just about every book in print, including obscure self-published works. (A directory including hundreds of other online dealers can be found at the American Booksellers Association site at www.bookweb.com.) For out-of-print and used books, go to the Web sites that provide centralized access to million of titles listed by thousands of big and small out-of-print/used dealers (including amateur dealers with just a few titles they want to unload from their own personal libraries).The largest of these out-of-print/used book marts can be found at www.bibliofind.com, www.alibris.com, and www.abebooks.com. You can search all three simultaneously at www.emailman.com/books/ metasearch.html.

If the preceding sites don't list the out-of-print title you are searching for, you should send email queries to dealers who specialize in the given category. (Note that most out-of-print/used bookstores do not list their entire stock online.) Email links to thousands of such dealers can be found at the out-of-print/used book Web sites listed in the preceding paragraph. You might also check *Book Dealers in North America* and *Directory of Specialized American Bookdealers* or the various online yellow pages.

If you find a certain out-of-print book but the price is too high, you should ask the research librarian at your public library to search the RLIN and OCLC databases (which detail the holdings of member libraries nationwide) to find out which conveniently located public libraries, university libraries, or special libraries own the title in question. If the book is available at, say, a local university library, you can arrange through your public library to get a one-day pass to examine the book and photocopy the pages you need. If the book is not available locally, RLIN or OCLC will identify libraries elsewhere that have a copy and then obtain it for you through the interlibrary loan system.

An alternative to searching RLIN and OCLC is searching the hundreds of online library catalogs nationwide or worldwide from the Internet. One place to begin is at http://dir.yahoo.com/Reference/Libraries.

The reach of the Internet extends to library catalogs in every state and metropolitan area. In many cases, the catalog will not only give you bibliographic information but will also tell you whether a given book is currently checked out, whether it's a noncirculating copy, and whether it can be borrowed through interlibrary loan.

A search of catalogs by subject, title, key words, and the names of authors whom you know specialize in the given field may guide you to the books you need. When you find even one good book on a topic, its bibliography will lead you to others. For a more thorough search, check in the relevant specialized bibliographies (see H.W. Wilson's *Bibliographic Index*, a cumulative subject guide available in print from 1937 and online from 1984). A thorough search might also include a trip to the library stacks. I have often found relevant books—books I had not identified through my catalog search—by browsing on either side of where the catalog had informed me that a relevant book (usually missing!) was located.

It would be wonderful if library catalogs contained abstracts of each cataloged book to help you decide whether a given book is worth obtaining for your purposes. In the absence of this, you can find detailed information online or on CD-ROM about hundreds of thousands of books:

- Full-text book reviews can be accessed through the full-text databases covering newspapers, popular periodicals, and scholarly, scientific, and professional journals. Abstracts of many such book reviews can found through online and CD-ROM index/abstract databases (see sections 6.4, "Newspaper Databases," and 6.5, "Periodicals Databases.")

- H.W. Wilson's *Book Review Digest* is available online and on CD-ROM dating back to 1983; it covers over 6,500 English-language books each year with brief critical evaluations culled from reviews in over 90 periodicals.

- Summaries of reviews and other descriptive material about an author's books are contained in the nearly 100,000 biographical/bibliographical entries in the online and CD-ROM versions of Gale's *Contemporary Authors*.

- Dissertation Abstracts Online provides the abstracts of a vast number of scholarly works that were published as books after being accepted as dissertations.

- Descriptive information on new books is usually found at the publisher's Web site and at the author's home page; this information may include excerpts from or the table of contents of the book. In addition, you may find at the same site information about some of the author's previous titles.

- At www.amazon.com, many publishers and authors post information about their books (including the table of contents and quotes from book reviews), and readers often post their own opinions and grumblings about a given title.

- A massive number of reviews can be found at Usenet newsgroups and at email lists. To find those related to a particular book's topic, see the directories listed in section 15.1. For miscellaneous book reviews, see news:alt.books.reviews. Note that important books on a given topic will often produce multiple reviews from newsgroups and email lists devoted to that topic or to the broader subject that includes it.

- Electronic journals often include multiple reviews along with a summary or précis by the book's author; see, for instance, the archives of the journal *Psycoloquy* at www.princeton.edu.

- Excerpts, summaries, and the tables of contents of recently published technical books may be found at relevant Web sites; for instance, see the information on mathematics books at www.siam.org.

- Tables of contents (but not excerpts) of books that have multiple contributors but a single editor are often included in research library catalogs, as are the tables of contents of some short-story collections and business texts.

15.3 Finding the Right Library

Don't judge a library only by the size of its total collection. Instead, look at the strength of its collection in the field in which you are interested. If I were researching the history of a left-wing party, for instance, I would not go to the giant New York Public Library (NYPL); I would go to the Tamiment Institute Library at New York University. Tamiment is tiny compared to the NYPL, but radical labor history happens to be one of its specialties.

To find the strongest collection for your purposes both locally and nationally, look in *Subject Collections*, the *Directory of Special Libraries and Information Centers*, and the *Directory of Archives and Manuscript Repositories in the United States*. If the collection you most need turns out to be in another part of the country, its catalog will probably be searchable online. And if the collection's librarians are not too overworked, and you can interest them in your research task, they may be willing to look up names in book indexes for you, photocopy material for you, and speed up the interlibrary loan process.

The Library of Congress (LOC), with its 100-million-item collection, is the largest library in the world (its nearest competitor in the United States, the New York Public Library, has only about half as many items). As well as its famous scholarly holdings and periodicals collections, the LOC has all kinds of miscellany, such as pamphlets and brochures, current and back-issue telephone books, and city directories for localities throughout the country. The LOC's National Reference Service will help you over the phone or by email with relatively simple questions. If you need complicated research done at the LOC, its Reading Room maintains a list of private researchers who will help you for a reasonable hourly fee (call 202-707-5522). Washington journalists on tight deadlines sometimes call the LOC's public affairs office for research on urgent specialized questions.

For your everyday needs, investigate the various libraries in your locality. You may find one library best for a particular topic or use, and another library for other topics. But to determine which library is best overall for your needs, use the following checklist:

- Does the library allow public access to its stacks for serious scholars? If not, does it have a large enough collection of shelved books in the public areas (especially reference copies that can't be checked out) so that you can do extensive hands-on searching by topic?

- Does the library have state-of-the-art photocopying machines in good working condition? Does it have enough machines so that you don't always have to stand in line? Do the machines use bills or prepaid cards so that you don't have to bring rolls of quarters each time you visit the library?

- Does the library have basic reference works used in the investigator's trade (for example, the local city or crisscross directories, *BGMI*, *Directories in Print*, and, on CD-ROM, such products as Select Phone and The Complete Marquis Who's Who)?

- Does the library provide free patron access to the online services of major reference book publishers and to online vendors such as DIALOG?

- How much access does the library provide (by a combination of CD-ROM, library automated system, and online vendors) to newspaper and periodical full-text, abstract, and index databases?

- Is the library open seven days a week and in the evenings?

- Are the seats wired for notebook computers and portable scanners? Are fax facilities available? Are there enough computer workstations so that you can access the library's in-house databases and online subscription databases without making a reservation days in advance?

- Is the library a member of the Federal Depository Library Program (FDLP)? Is it one of the regional FDLP libraries that receive *all* government materials distributed through the program?

- Does the library offer high-speed lines for the most efficient Internet searching and downloading?

- Is the library within reasonable travel distance from your home or office, relative to other libraries in your locality?

If your local public library can't meet your needs on the majority of these counts, consider using a large university library in your area at least part of the time. Many universities offer semester passes, for a fee, to serious scholars or to family members of university employees. Others offer day passes that can be renewed for several days in a row. If you find a university library's policies too onerous, note that archival collections at this library may be open to the general public, even if access to the rest of library is sharply restricted. The archival department may, as a matter of library policy, offer serious researchers access to certain of the library's other facilities, such as the photocopy machines and interlibrary loan. You may even be able to order books from the library's general stacks (for use on the archive's premises only) if the books are relevant to your archival research.

As well as seeking access to large institutional libraries, think small: There may exist scores of specialized libraries/archives in your metro area maintained by genealogical or local history societies, corporations, religious institutions, and municipal, county, or state governments. Such libraries often offer many of the checklist features just listed in addition to in-depth coverage of their specialized subject areas. To find such libraries, consult the yellow pages, the library reference directories listed earlier in this chapter, and local guides to genealogical research. Also ask a research librarian at your local public library for further tips, because some of the smaller specialized library/archival facilities may not be listed in any directory you consult.

15.4 The World of Research Filing Cabinets

Nonprofit organizations often maintain clippings files on subjects of interest to their members or sponsors. These files may range from a single filing cabinet to vast clippings libraries (such as the one maintained by the Anti-Defamation League of B'nai B'rith in New York), which rival those of the great daily newspapers. In some cases, these files can be a researcher's dream. They can shortcut the process of searching print indexes and microfilm and the expense of downloading articles from LEXIS-NEXIS and other online vendors. In addition, an organization's clippings files may include articles from obscure periodicals that you probably would never come across on your own.

Often, these clippings files have been developed as an adjunct of the organization's library, which may be listed in the *Directory of Special Libraries and Information Centers*. Many of the file collections themselves are listed in *Prospect Researcher's Guide to Biographical Research Collections*. But many small in-house organizational libraries are not listed in any directory, and even when they are, the directory may not specify the existence of clippings files.

The easiest way to find such files is to ask the experts in the field you are researching. Failing this, check the *Encyclopedia of Associations* and *National Trade and Professional Associations of the U.S.* or go to the directories of nonprofit organizations (listed by category) at www.yahoo.com. Many trade and professional organizations and other non-profits regard the dissemination of information to the general public as one of their major functions. Often, they will search their files for you and send you photocopies. If you visit their headquarters, they may help you find what you need and provide photocopying on the spot.

If an organization has extensive files relating to your topic and is within convenient distance, you should visit it to search the files yourself. After you meet the staff in person and explain your purpose in some detail, they may let you look through files not ordinarily available to the public.

Here's an example: When I was researching Lyndon LaRouche's ties to the former apartheid government of South Africa, I went to an anti-apartheid research organization in New York, which was glad to help me. Within minutes, I was looking through thick folders of clippings from South African daily and weekly newspapers, South African government reports, and reports by various anti-apartheid groups. When the office closed that afternoon, I left with my briefcase stuffed full of photocopies of materials directly pertinent to my investigation, such as an article from a South African newspaper praising LaRouche's economic theories, an article from another South African newspaper quoting a government commission as charging that the first newspaper was funded by BOSS (the South African secret police), and reports suggesting that BOSS propagandists had worked directly with LaRouche's group. I don't think I could have done much better with help from the CIA—and this is only one of many such experiences I have had with the clippings files of nonprofit organizations.

Bibliography and Resources ·

I. Books

Business Research

Daniells, Lorna M. *Business Information Sources.* 3d ed. Berkeley: University of California Press, 1993.

Engholm, Christopher. *The Prentice Hall Directory of Online Business Information.* 2d ed. Paramus, NJ: Prentice Hall, 1998.

Fuld, Leonard, M. *The New Competitor Intelligence.* 2d ed. New York: John Wiley & Sons, 1994.

Tracy, John A. *How to Read a Financial Report: Wringing Vital Signs Out of the Numbers.* 5th ed. New York: John Wiley & Sons, 1999.

Credentials and Identity Documents

Bear, John, and Mariah Bear. *College Degrees by Mail and Modem 1999.* Annual. Berkeley, CA: Ten Speed Press, 1998.

Charrett, Sheldon. *The Modern Identity Changer: How to Create a New Identity for Privacy and Personal Freedom.* Boulder, CO: Paladin Press, 1997.

Martin, James S. *Scram: Relocating Under a New Identity.* Port Townsend, WA: Loompanics Unlimited, 1997.

Newman, John Q. *The Heavy Duty New Identity.* 2d ed. Port Townsend, WA: Loompanics Unlimited, 1998.

———. *Understanding U.S. Identity Documents.* Port Townsend, WA: Loompanics Unlimited, 1991.

Finding People

Askin, Jayne. *Search: A Handbook for Adoptees and Birthparents*. 3d ed. Phoenix: Oryx Press, 1998.

Johnson, Richard S., and Debra Johnson Knox. *How to Locate Anyone Who Is or Has Been in the Military: Armed Forces Locator Guide*. 8th ed. Spartanburg, SC: MIE Publishing, 1999.

Tillman, Norma Mott. *How to Find Almost Anyone, Anywhere*. Rev. ed. Nashville, TN: Rutledge Hill Press, 1998.

Interviewing

Brady, John J. *The Craft of Interviewing*. New York: Random House, 1977.

Metzler, Ken. *Creative Interviewing: The Writer's Guide to Gathering Information by Asking Questions*. 3d ed. Needham Heights, MA: Allyn & Bacon, 1997.

Investigative Journalism and Public-Interest Research

Benjaminson, Peter, and David Anderson. *Investigative Reporting*. 2d ed. Ames: Iowa State University Press, 1990.

Denniston, Lyle W. *The Reporter and the Law: Techniques of Covering the Courts*. New York: Columbia University Press, 1992.

Harry, M. *The Muckraker's Manual: How to Do Your Own Investigative Reporting*. Port Townsend, WA: Loompanics Unlimited, 1984.

Houston, Brant. *Computer-Assisted Reporting: A Practical Guide*. 2d ed. Boston/New York: Bedford/St. Martin's, 1999.

Rose, Louis J. *How to Investigate Your Friends and Enemies*. Rev. ed. St. Louis: Albion Press, 1992. (Especially valuable are Chapter IV, "Investigating Real Estate," and Chapter V, "Finding the Hidden Owners.")

Weberman, A.J. *My Life in Garbology*. New York: Stonehill Publishing Company, 1980. (Full text online at www.weberman.com.)

Weinberg, Steve. *The Reporter's Handbook: An Investigator's Guide to Documents and Techniques*. 3d ed. New York: St. Martin's Press, 1995. (Indispensable for every journalist and investigator.)

————. *Telling the Untold Story: How Investigative Reporters Are Changing the Craft of Biography*. Columbia: University of Missouri Press, 1992.

Library and General Research

Barzun, Jacques, and Henry F. Graff. *The Modern Researcher*. 5th ed. New York: Harcourt Brace College Pubs., 1992. (Although written for historians, there is something in almost every chapter for both investigative journalists and private investigators. See especially the chapters on "Verification" and "Truth and Causation.")

Berkman, Robert I. *Find It Fast: How to Uncover Expert Information on Any Subject.* 4th ed. New York: HarperCollins, 1997.

Lesko, Matthew. *Lesko's Info-Power III.* Kensington, MD: Information USA, 1996.

Luebking, Sandra Hargreaves et al. *Family History Made Easy: A Step-By-Step Guide to Discovering Your Heritage.* Salt Lake City: Ancestry Incorporated, 1998.

Mann, Thomas. *A Guide to Library Research Methods.* New York: Oxford University Press, 1990.

Prucha, Francis Paul. *Handbook for Research in American History.* 2d ed. Lincoln: University of Nebraska Press, 1994.

Online Databases and the Internet

Basch, Reva. *Secrets of the Super Net Searchers.* Medford, NJ: CyberAge Books, 1996.

Maxwell, Bruce. *How to Access the Federal Government on the Internet.* Rev. ed. Washington, D.C.: Congressional Quarterly Books, 1998.

Notess, Greg R. *Government Information on the Internet.* 2d ed. Washington, D.C.: Bernan Press, 1998.

Paul, Nora, and Margot Williams. *Great Scouts!: Cyberguides for Subject Searching on the Web.* Medford, NJ: CyberAge Books, 1999.

Rugge, Sue and Alfred Glossbrenner. *The Information Broker's Handbook.* 3d ed. New York: McGraw-Hill, 1997.

Schlein, Alan. *Find It Online.* Tempe, AZ: Facts on Demand Press, 1999.

Privacy

Cate, Fred H. *Privacy in the Information Age.* Washington, D.C.: Brookings Institution Press, 1997.

Lyon, David et al. *Computers, Surveillance, and Privacy.* Minneapolis: University of Minnesota Press, 1996.

Smith, Robert Ellis. *Compilation of State and Federal Privacy Laws.* 8th ed. Providence, RI: Privacy Journal, 1997.

———. *The Law of Privacy Explained.* Providence, RI: Privacy Journal, 1995.

———. *War Stories: Accounts of Persons Victimized by Invasions of Privacy.* 2d ed. Providence, RI: Privacy Journal, 1997.

Private Investigators' and Legal Investigators' Methods

ACM IV Security Services. *Secrets of Surveillance: A Professional's Guide to Tailing Subjects by Vehicle, Foot, Airplane, and Public Transportation.* Boulder, CO: Paladin Press, 1993.

Binder, David A., and Paul Bergman. *Fact Investigation: From Hypothesis to Proof.* St. Paul, MN: West Publishing Co., 1984.

Culligan, Joseph J. *When in Doubt Check Him Out: A Woman's Survival Guide for the '90s.* Rev. ed. Miami: Hallmark Press, 1997.

De Mey, Dennis L., and James R. Flowers. *Don't Hire a Crook!: How to Avoid Common Hiring (and Firing) Mistakes.* Tempe, AZ: Facts on Demand Press, 1999.

Golec, Anthony M. *Techniques of Legal Investigation.* 3d ed. Springfield, IL: Charles C. Thomas, 1995.

Hauser, Greg. *Greg Hauser's Pretext Manual.* Austin, TX: Thomas Investigative Publications, 1998.

Probe, Inc. *Private Investigators Pretext Manual.* Beverly Hills, CA: Probe, 1989. (Can be ordered at www.spytechagency.com.)

Rapp, Burt. *Shadowing and Surveillance: A Complete Guidebook.* Port Townsend, WA: Loompanics Unlimited, 1986.

Sample, John. *Methods of Disguise.* 2d ed. Port Townsend, WA: Loompanics Unlimited, 1993.

Scott, Robert. *The Investigator's Little Black Book 2.* Beverly Hills, CA: Crime Time Publishing, 1998.

Slade, E. Roy, and James R. Gutzs. *The Pretext Book.* Austin, TX: Thomas Investigative Publications, 1991.

Thomas, Ralph D. *How to Investigate by Computer.* Rev. ed. Austin, TX: Thomas Investigative Publications, 1999. (Includes interactive computer disk.)

Public Records

An * means that the contents of this book are also included in The Public Record Research System.

Levine, Stephen, and Barbara T. Newcombe. *Paper Trails: A Guide to Public Records in California.* 2d ed. San Francisco: Center for Investigative Reporting, 1996.

Morehead, Joe. *Introduction to United State Government Information Sources.* 5th ed. Englewood, CO: Libraries Unlimited, 1996.

Murray, Thomson C. *The Official License Plate Book: How to Read and Decode Current United States and Canadian License Plates.* Rev. ed. Jericho, NY: Interstate Directory Publishing Company, 1998.

Sankey, Michael L., and Carl R. Ernst (eds.). *The County Locator: The Guide to Locating Places and Finding the Right County for Public Record Searching.* Rev. ed. Tempe, AZ: BRB Publications, 1998.*

———. *Find Public Records Fast: The Complete State, County, and Courthouse Locator.* Rev. ed. Tempe, AZ: Facts on Demand Press, 1998.

———. *The MVR Book.* Tempe, AZ: BRB Publications, annual. (State-by-state analysis of privacy laws and DPPA compliance; covers both driver history records and motor vehicle records.)

———. *The MVR Decoder Digest.* Tempe, AZ: BRB Publications, annual. (Translates the codes and abbreviations of violations and licensing categories in MVR records of all states.)

———. *The Public Record Research System.* Tempe, AZ: BRB Publications, semi-annual. (Includes federal, state, and county court records plus county asset/lien records, college and university records, and county/zip code locator. Available in print and on CD-ROM.)

———. *Public Records Online: The National Guide to Private and Government Online Sources of Public Records*. 2d ed. Tempe, AZ: Facts on Demand Press, 1999.

———. *The Sourcebook of County Court Records*. Rev. ed. Tempe, AZ: BRB Publications, 1998.*

———. *The Sourcebook of Federal Courts—U.S. District and Bankruptcy*. 2d ed. The Public Record Research Library, Tempe, AZ: BRB Publications, 1996.*

———. *The Sourcebook of State Public Records*. Rev. ed. Tempe, AZ: BRB Publications, 1998.*

T.I.S.I. *Guide to Background Investigations*. 8th ed. Tulsa, OK: T.I.S.I., 1998. (One-stop state-by-state guide to public records; available in print and on CD-ROM.)

White-Collar Crime

Bologna, Jack. *Handbook on Corporate Fraud: Prevention, Detection, and Investigation*. Stoneham, MA: Butterworth-Heinemann, 1993.

Dickinson, Peter S. *Civil RICO: A Research Guide to Civil Liability for Business Crimes*. Buffalo, NY: William S. Hein, 1989.

Luger, Jack. *How to Use Mail Drops for Profit, Privacy, and Self-Protection*. 2d ed. Port Townsend, WA: Loompanics Unlimited, 1996.

Nossen, Richard A., and Joan W. Norvelle. *The Detection, Investigation, and Prosecution of Financial Crimes*. 2d ed. Tucson, AZ: Thoth Books, 1993.

Schilit, Howard M. *Financial Shenanigans: How to Detect Accounting Gimmicks and Fraud in Financial Reports*. New York: McGraw-Hill, 1993.

II. Reference/Business/Legal Publishers (Includes Producers and Vendors of Databases)

Burrelle's Information Services. . . . . .www.burrelles.com
Commerce Clearing House (CCH). . . . . .www.cch.com
DeLorme Mapping. . . . . .www.delorme.com
Dialog Corporation, The. . . . . .www.dialog.com
Dow Jones. . . . . .www.dowjones.com
Dun & Bradstreet Corporation. . . . . .www.dnb.com
Experian. . . . . .www.experian.com
First American Real Estate Solutions. . . . . .www.firstam.com
Gale Group, The. . . . . .www.gale.com
H.W. Wilson. . . . . .www.hwwilson.com
Information Access Company. . . . . .www.informationaccess.com
Information Today. . . . . .www.infotoday.com
Journal Graphics. . . . . .www.tv-radio.com

LEXIS-NEXIS. . . . . .www.lexis-nexis.com
Marquis Who's Who. . . . . .www.marquiswhoswho.com
Martindale-Hubbell. . . . . .www.martindale.com
Metromail. . . . . .www.cyberdirect.com/metromail
Moody's Investors Service. . . . . .www.moodys.com
NewsBank. . . . . .www.newsbank.com
Ovid Technologies. . . . . .www.ovid.com
PR Newswire. . . . . .www.prnewswire.com
Reed Elsevier. . . . . .www.r-e.com
R.R. Bowker. . . . . .www.bowker.com
Standard & Poor's. . . . . .www.standardpoor.com
Thomas Register of American Manufacturers. www.thomasregister.com
UMI. . . . . .www.umi.com
West Group (legal publishing, Westlaw). . . . . . . .www.westgroup.com

III. Publishers of Investigative Manuals

BRB Publications. . . . . .www.brbpub.com
Investigative Reporters and Editors. . . . . .www.ire.com
Loompanics Unlimited. . . . . .www.loompanics.com
Paladin Press. .www.paladin-press.com
Thomas Investigative Publications. . . . . .www.pimall.com

IV. Web Sites for Finding People

Big Foot. www.bigfoot.com (The Internet's largest, most accurate collection of email addresses and white-page listings.)

ClassMates. www.classmates.com (Locate high school alumni friends in the United States, Canada, and their territories.)

Cyndi's List of Genealogy Sites on the Internet. www.cydislist.com (Includes more than 40,150 links; begin by selecting your ancestors' homeland.)

Electronic Activist. www.berkshire.net (Contact your state's U.S. senators and representatives; also provides instructions on how to organize grassroots activities.)

Email Search. www.dir.yahoo.com/Computers_and_Internet/Internet/Mailing_Lists/Web_Directories (Searchable directories of email lists; also contains a search button for over 50,000 free email lists.)

Four11: The Internet White Pages by Yahoo! www.four11.com (Find a phone number if you have a first name, last name, street address, city, or state.)

InfoUSA. adp.infousa.com (Search for people by first name, last name, city, and state; you can also run a reverse phone number search.)

Missing You. www.netsalesuk.co.uk (Find a person in the United Kingdom, or look for someone in the Armed Forces. To contact the person, you post a message on this site.)

Net Address Book of Transportation Professionals. dragon.princeton.edu (Look for someone in the transportation industry; also offers a direct link to the Truckers 411 Directory.)

PeopleFinder. www.peoplesite.com (Look for birth parents, adopted or missing children, and lost loves; create a profile of the person you're searching for, submit the profile, and wait for that person to contact you.)

WhoWhere?! www.whowhere.lycos.com (Search by first or last name to retrieve an email address or a phone number and street address.)

World Wide Profile Registry www.wizard.com. (A central database for personal profiles of Internet users from all over the globe.)

Yahoo! People Search. people.yahoo.com (Conduct an email or telephone search by first name, last name, or domain; you can aslo search for someone by areas of interest.)

V. Investigative Database Vendors

ARISTOTLE, 205 Pennsylvania Avenue S.W., Washington, D.C. 20003
(800) 296-2747
Nationwide database of registered voters.

CDB Infotek, 6 Hutton Centre Drive, #600, Santa Ana, CA 92707
(800) 427-3747
The Wal-Mart of information brokers; provides access to over 1,600 databases.

Commercial Information Systems (CIS), 4747 S.W. Kelly #110, Portland, OR 97201
(800) 454-6575

CourtLink, 400 112th Avenue N.E., #250, Bellevue, WA 98004
(800) 774-7317
Front-end access and a complete index to federal PACER system; also provides access to many state court indexes.

Database Technologies, 4530 Blue Lake Drive, Boca Raton, FL 33431
(800) 279-7710

Informus Corporation, 2001 Airport Road, #201, Jackson, MS 39208
(800) 364-8380

KnowX, 245 Peachtree Center Avenue, #1400, Atlanta, GA 30303
support@knowx.com

Merlin's Data Research, 1031 Loch Vail Drive, #25, Apopka, FL 32712
(888) 434-6337

Superior Information Services, P.O. Box 8787, Trenton, NJ 08650
(800) 848-0489

TML Information Services, 116-55 Queens Boulevard, Forest Hills, NY 11375
(800) 743-7891
Specializes in DMV (motor vehicle and driver) records.

NOTES

NOTES

NOTES

NOTES

NOTES

NOTES

NOTES

NOTES

NOTES

NOTES

NOTES

NOTES

NOTES

NOTES